London's
East End Survivors

East End children keep their gas masks handy as they leave for their evacuation
destinations on 2 September 1939.

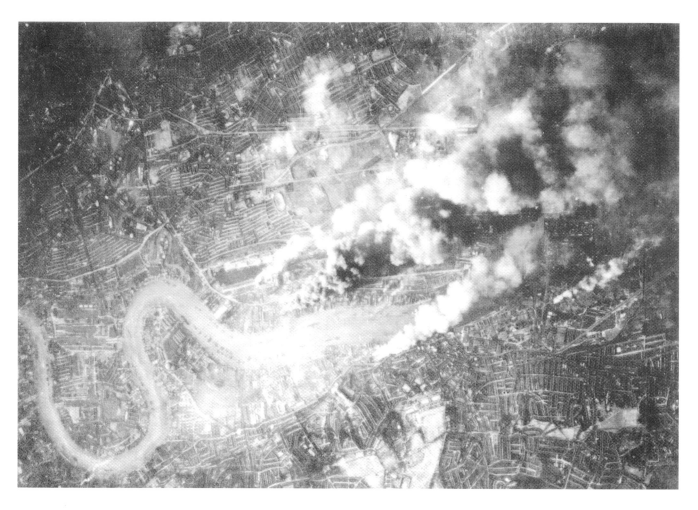

Great plumes of smoke billow from the Royal Docks during the early evening of 'Black Saturday', 7 September 1940.

London's East End Survivors

Voices of the Blitz generation

Andrew Bissell

A Centenar Book

Published by Centenar in 2010

Editorial office
70 Broughton Avenue
Bournemouth
Dorset
BH10 6JA

www.centenar.co.uk

ISBN: 978-1-907680-00-7

A CIP record for this book is available from the British Library

Set in Adobe Garamond Pro

Printed and bound in the United Kingdom by
the MPG Books Group

Contents

East End Map
including locations of Second World War incidents

1. Abbey Road School, West Ham.
2. Abney Park Cemetery, Stoke Newington.
3. Arundel Road, Leyton.
4. Barnby Street, off West Ham Lane.
5. Beckton Gas Works.
6. Beckton Road, Canning Town.
7. Bethnal Green Underground Station.
8. Cable Street.
9. Canary Wharf Estate.
10. Columbia Market, Bethnal Green.
11. Crownfield Road, Leyton.
12. Dames Road, Forest Gate.
13. Duckett Street, Stepney.
14. Edinburgh Castle.
15. ExCeL Exhibition and Conference Centre.
16. Fieldgate Street, Whitechapel.
17. Gardiner's Corner.
18. Glasshouse Street, Stepney (which became John Fisher Street in 1937/8).
19. Great Assembly Hall, Mile End Road.
20. Grove Road, Bethnal Green.
21. Harrow Green ARP depot, Leytonstone.
22. Hermitage Riverside Memorial Garden, Wapping.
23. Hope Place, Stepney.
24. Hughes Mansions, Bethnal Green.
25. Jamme Masjid Mosque.
26. Old Palace School, Bromley-by-Bow.
27. People's Palace, Mile End Road.
28. Petticoat Lane (Middlesex Street).
29. Plaistow Road, Newham.
30. Princelet Street, off Brick Lane.
31. Prospect of Whitby pub, Wapping.
32. Royal London Hospital, Whitechapel.
33. St Dunstan's and All Saints Church in Stepney.
34. St Mary and Holy Trinity, Bow. (St Mary's Church, Bow)
35. St Mary-le-Bow, Cheapside.
36. Smithfield Market.
37. South Hallsville School, Canning Town.
38. Thames Barrier Park containing Newham's Pavilion of Remembrance.
39. Tilbury Arches.
40. Toynbee Hall, 28 Commercial Street.
41. Upper North Street School, Poplar.
42. Victoria Park.
43. Wanstead Flats.
44. Watson's Wharf, Wapping.
45. Whitechapel Foundry in Plumbers Row off Whitechapel Road.

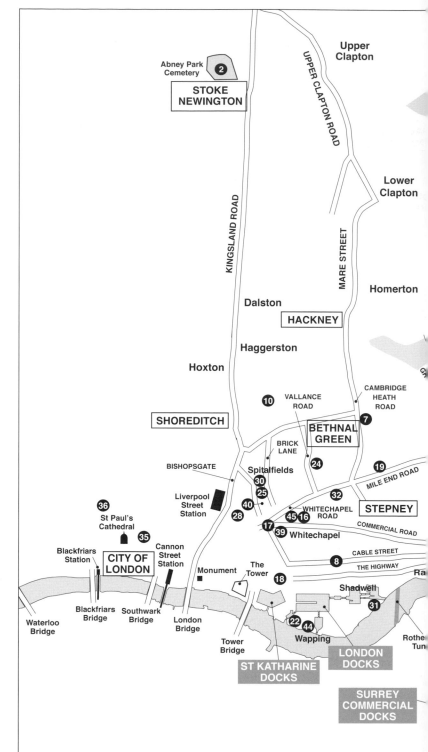

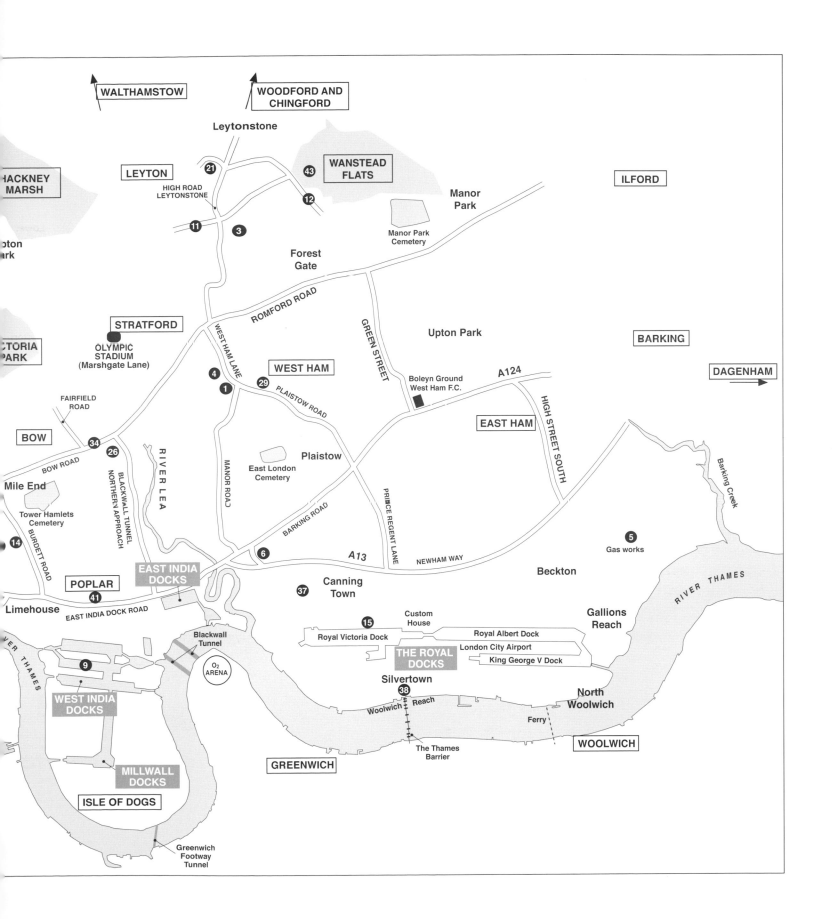

Conversion table

Length

1 inch = 25.4 millimetres = 2.54 centimetres

1 foot = 0.3048 metres = 30 centimetres

1 yard = 0.9144 metres = 91 centimetres

1 mile = 1.609 kilometres

Weight

1 ounce = 28.35 g

1 pound = 16 ounces = 454 g

1 stone = 14 pounds – 6.35 kg

1 hundredweight = 8 stones = 50.80 kg

1 ton = 2240 pounds = 20 hundredweight = 1.016 tonnes

1 ton = 1016kg

Capacity

1 pint = 0.568 litres

1 gallon = 4.546 litres

Money

£1.00 = 20 shillings (s) = 240 pennies (d)

1s = 12d = 5p

10s = 120d = 50p

6d = 2.5p

Steel-helmeted members of the London Fire Brigade confront warehouse fires at the Surrey Commercial Docks.

Author's preface

A BOOK OF THIS MAGNITUDE would have proved impossible without the generous help of several hundred people. They chose to respond to a newspaper appeal and ensured that a deluge of East End memories poured through my letterbox. Their collective input vividly stirred my imagination and ignited the creative process, thus providing the prerequisites for this addition to London's history. This is essentially their book, a tribute to each and every one of them and a 'thank you' for their unique contributions.

Memories that they submitted – whether in oral or written form – have been faithfully recorded and reproduced in this book. Wherever possible, I have checked for historical accuracy but these are personal accounts and reminiscences, not cold facts. Recalling experiences 60 or 70 years after an event can lead to occasional inaccuracies, but what cannot be taken away is the intensity of feelings, which I have tried to capture. It has indeed been a rare privilege to listen to these men and women and bring their experiences to life again.

In particular, I am deeply indebted to the late Eddie Siggins, who courageously chose to tell his family's moving story, which lies at the heart of this work. His verbal and written descriptions of Stepney life were truly inspirational and I thank him, his wife Pam, sister Irene and Dr Paul Siggins for their generous support, kindness and hospitality.

I also sincerely thank the following key contributors for their valued help, advice and encouragement: my father – Eric Bissell, George Mooney, Ellen Ackred, Maisie Canterford, Rose Gowler, Charles Young, Charlie Smith, Bob Humphreys, Peggy Chusonis, Frank Rose, Mary Kavanagh, Marianne Fredericks, Maureen Davies, Edward Tilbury, Alf Morris, Ken Snow, Doris Bailey, James White, the late Bill Peet, Joe Marks, Peter Herrington, Sandra Scotting and Johnny Ringwood.

In addition, I offer special thanks to Professor Bill Fishman, the late Cyril Demarne OBE, Christopher Lloyd and Lieutenant-Colonel Bill Woodhouse, who so willingly shared their specialist knowledge and generally pointed me in the right direction.

My gratitude similarly extends to the staff of numerous archives and libraries, who provided excellent help and guidance: Librarian Christopher Lloyd and Archivist Malcolm Barr-Hamilton at Tower Hamlets Local History Library and Archives; Bob Aspinall, Librarian at the Museum in Docklands; Ben Richardson at Canary Wharf Group plc; Beverley Boyle at Barnardo's; Nikki Braunton at the Museum of London Picture Library; Sarah Harding at the Newham Archives; Colin Grainger and Pat Coughtrey at the Newham Recorder; Hugh Robertson and Robert Excell at the London Transport Museum; John Hughes and Alex von der Becke at the Salvation Army International Heritage Centre; Janice Mullin, Yvonne Oliver and Emma Crocker at the Imperial War Museum, London; Carrie Goeringer at the United States National Archives, College Park, Maryland; and Mike Rodgers at the United States Signals Corps Museum, Fort Gordon, Georgia.

The aforementioned helped considerably with picture research and photographs are published courtesy of the following: the Imperial War Museum; Museum of London/PLA Collection; Canary Wharf Group plc; Transport for London/from the London Transport Museum Collection; Salvation Army International Heritage Centre; Barnardo's photo archive; Newham Archives; Newham Recorder; Tower Hamlets Local History Library and Archives; London Metropolitan Archives; London Development Agency; Deutsche Dienststelle (Wehrmacht Information Office) in Berlin; US National Archives; US Signal Corps Archives; Ullstein Bild, Berlin; The Daily Mail; AP/ Press Association Images and the Humphrey Spender Archive. All other photographs have been kindly donated by members of the public.

Maps were provided by graphic designer and friend Andy Puntis, who again displayed patience and produced artwork of customary excellence.

Background information has been drawn from a plethora of fine published works and the bibliography lists those that I would recommend for either casual enjoyment or scholarly research. It includes: Professor Bill Fishman's definitive study, *East End 1888*; Gilda O'Neill's colourful classic *My East End*; Frank Lewey's *Cockney Campaign*; and the encyclopaedic *The East End, Then and Now*, edited by Winston G. Ramsey.

In addition, Ramsey's unrivalled trilogy, *The Blitz Then and Now*, deserves special mention. The second volume contains Ken Wakefield's masterly analysis of Luftwaffe operations over Britain, with the statistics of each individual raid carefully pieced together from British records (held in the Public Records Office and the Air Historical Branch of the Ministry of Defence) and German records made available by the Bundesarchiv at Freiburg. The result is a comprehensive and unparalleled study of the Blitz. Nonetheless, it is important to stress that casualty figures cannot be 100 per cent reliable, a point made in *The Blitz Then and Now*. Different sources may give different figures, making discrepancies difficult to reconcile. On a final statistical note, figures relating to the First World War have been largely drawn from Sir John Hammerton's *World War 1914–1918: A Pictured History*, a colossal work that also draws attention to the accuracy problems posed by both official and unofficial records.

My thanks among the professional ranks must also extend to my publisher, Crispin Goodall, for his friendship, patience and humour, and to my editor, Maggie O'Hanlon, for her valued and constructive suggestions.

Finally, this book represents a huge family effort. I therefore thank my parents, Molly and Eric, for their love and words of wisdom; my brother Geoff for his encouragement; and Rhona, Steve, Gregory and Bobby for their help and kindness. Above all, I thank my wife Jill for her loving support and our children, James and David, who inspire me to put pen to paper and write about history.

Andrew Bissell
2010

Introduction

SILENCE HAS crept up and stolen the hustle and bustle of Wapping's riverside. Only the faint hum of traffic crossing Tower Bridge, the creaking rigging of moored sailing barges and the soft, rhythmic plodding of lunchtime joggers can be heard today. A perfect stillness has descended, particularly upon a small oasis of greenery at the end of the High Street – the Hermitage Riverside Memorial Garden.

Long ago, this was the hub of London's Empire trade, a scene of perpetual commotion at the St Katharine and London Docks, and home to the enormous Hermitage Wharf and huge, heavily laden vessels. Today, the hushed little park is ringed by expensive, bow-fronted apartments with wrap-around balconies and green sparkling glass that reflects the brooding, churning Thames beyond.

Yet here, alongside the restless river, the past stubbornly refuses to leave the present. A path meanders around the planted borders to a memorial, a vertical slab of black stone from which a soaring dove has been cut out. As a small information stand states, the dove represents the loss of loved ones, while a photograph shows plumes of smoke rising from this area on one day many years ago.

That day was 'Black Saturday', 7 September 1940, when the Dockmaster at Wapping could be seen trying to count the number of bombers that had suddenly filled the London sky. On that day, 600 tons of explosives fell, carpeting the narrow streets of Wapping and beyond. They fell on the tailors of Whitechapel; the factories, warehouses and gasworks of Poplar; the wood-working firms of Shoreditch; the docks of West Ham; and the homes, pubs, shops and markets that were wedged into every impoverished crevice in between.

This was a place where people knew little of the world beyond their immediate neighbourhood. They spent their lives in the streets where they were born, sharing their pleasures and their sorrows, and marrying close to home, so that two or three generations of the same family often lived next door to each other. It was also a place that worried the wartime Establishment. Ten

The Hermitage Riverside Memorial Garden in Wapping. The memorial with cut-out dove, designed by Wendy Taylor, is on the right.

The Hermitage Entrance into London Docks in 1937, with the massive Hermitage Steam Wharf on the right.

A photograph taken from London Bridge during the early evening of Black Saturday, the first day of the Blitz. A vast pall of smoke rises up from the burning docks and warehouses east of the Tower after hundreds of tons of explosive rained down on the capital.

The author's paternal grandfather, Edward Bissell, a private in the Essex Regiment in the First World War.

days after Black Saturday, parliamentarian and war diarist Harold Nicolson revealed his concerns over the effect of the relentless Blitz:

Everybody is worried about the feeling in the East End… there is much bitterness. It is said the King and Queen were booed the other day when they visited the destroyed areas.

If these people lost heart, it was feared that the chain reaction would cripple London's morale. Yet they didn't lose heart; instead London folklore was further enriched and its fabled East End became synonymous with civilian courage and defiance.

Two men who inhabited this mythical world inspired me to write this book. Their evocative musings painted a picture as heart-warming as it was horrific and as humorous as it was tragic. Both of them felt privileged to have belonged to a special place yet lucky to have survived. This world, with its curiously contrasting features of hunger, deprivation, warmth, camaraderie and neighbourliness, was the East End of the 1920s, 1930s and 1940s. These men maintain that the East End they once knew now exists in name only and that their old community has simply passed away, leaving its restless spirit to hover over an alien cityscape that they no longer recognise. They recall a community where conversing in the street was not a sign of being neighbourly but simply politeness; true neighbours in those days had open access to your house, they sat in your chairs and shared their feelings, their fears and their lives. That era, they insist, vanished long ago, together with horse-drawn carts, music halls, and the camaraderie of wartime.

My father, Eric Bissell, is the first of these two men. Born in Plaistow's Falcon Street in 1927, his childhood was one of markets, the 'tuppenny

rush' cinema and roaming the streets while his invalid father, a casualty of the First World War, attempted to find work. Times were proverbially hard but life had quality, fun, purpose and community 'togetherness'. Then came the Second World War. After a severe bombing raid, 13-year-old Eric had pedalled up Liddon Road and stopped his bike outside No. 26 where his grandparents lived. There, before his young eyes, was Grandma sitting on top of a huge pile of brick and rubble in the back garden. The smoke and choking brick dust cleared to reveal Grandad sitting beside her. The old couple were huddled together beneath a blanket, framed by the remaining walls of the house. Grandparents and grandson stared at each other in utter hopelessness. Grandma and Grandad, homeless, disorientated and traumatised, never got over it and died soon afterwards.

The second man was Eddie Siggins. Three miles away, in Stepney, 10-year-old Eddie's life of poverty was tempered by the loving embrace of an extended family and enriched by community characters and closeness. The Second World War similarly blighted his precious childhood. Some of his memories were so traumatic that he buried them deep in the secure recesses of his mind and never discussed them, not even with his sister Irene, who had shared the same experiences.

These two parallel life stories slowly came together to produce this book. My father's childhood experiences provided the initial spark and then, some years before his death in 2005, Eddie Siggins chose to share his family's history with me. While Eddie's wonderful pre-war descriptions overloaded and excited my senses, his vivid recollections of wartime had a cold, raw and disturbing clarity

I then began to seek for other East End memories of the Blitz generation and was soon swamped with hundreds of letters, diaries, photographs and

Eddie Siggins and his sister Irene:
(right) in the early 1930s. and **(above)** in later years.

(left) The author's father, Eric Bissell, pictured in 1938 and today.

assorted memorabilia. It was an exceptionally rich archive of hitherto unseen material. Amid the stories of tragedy, heroism and stoicism were further glimpses of the pre-war era and, collectively, these contributors provided me with the opportunity to briefly explore life before the Blitz.

I chose to cast the family of Eddie Siggins as the main players and assigned the lead role to his matriarchal grandmother, Mary Ann Bowyer (née Marshall). Likewise, her home in Duckett Street, Stepney, assumes a prominent position on the main stage, while the memories and testimonies of the large supporting cast are chronologically dovetailed into the drama. The fortunes of some of these families are also threaded through the text as mini-biographies.

Writers invariably confront a number of interpretative issues when they stray into this part of London. Most importantly, what is this place that these contributors call the 'East End' – this swathe of London with its ghostly traces of past times?

At this point, it is appropriate, fleetingly, to explore how the 'east' of London became physically, spiritually and emotionally detached from the 'west', and to introduce key names and locations in the story about to unfold.

By AD 100, *Londinium* had replaced Colchester as the capital of *Britannia*, the Roman Empire's most northerly province, and by AD 225 a protective wall stretched around the landward side of the city, to the north of the Thames. It was accessed by six gates, including Aldgate and Bishopsgate on the eastern side, where farms and hamlets provided food and services. The River Walbrook flowed through the centre of the city, effectively dividing it into two halves: east and west. When the Saxons occupied the abandoned Roman city in the late sixth century, they chose to live to the west of the River Walbrook, while the native Romano-British settled on the east bank.

This settlement in the east – covering what is now Stepney, Poplar and Bethnal Green – became increasingly populous and was named 'Stybba's Island', probably after the Saxon leader. Their seventh-century descendants built a small wooden church north of the 'island' (a well-drained gravel bank between the Thames and a tributary), which became the forerunner of the East End mother church, St Dunstan's and All Saints. The Manor of Stepney, owned by the Bishop of London, became the largest estate in the area and the manor house was in Bethnal Green, on the site now occupied by part of the London Chest Hospital.

After William the Conqueror's invasion in 1066, Stepney, including what is now Hackney, became the most important of the manors held by the Bishop of London. This office was of national significance and the people living in and around the 21 hamlets beyond the walls of the White Tower, the basis of the future Tower of London, found themselves the feudal tenants of their new lord (an obligation that was imposed on the population of Tower Hamlets until the nineteenth century).

However, the Manor of Stepney had a population of only 900, according to the Domesday Book of 1086. This also shows Stepney village as having a small port, 'Stibenhede' (Stybba's landing place), which later (in 1232) became known as 'Stybeney' and then (in 1466) as 'Stepney'.

Closer to the city, another well-known area derives its name from a chapel that stood outside Aldgate in 1282. By the 1320s, this chapel had its own parish, St Mary Matfelon, and its white stone walls gave rise to the name 'Whitechapel'.

Medieval East London slowly emerged as the focus for burgeoning international trade and, by the mid-sixteenth century, river trade had led to the emergence of Ratcliff, Limehouse, Wapping (named after the Anglo-

(left) St. Dunstan's: according to tradition, Dunstan, Bishop of London in 959, rebuilt the wooden church in stone. It was dedicated to him after his canonisation in 1029. This engraving is by artist James Basire in 1746.

(above) A 1753 paper engraving of the London Hospital in Whitechapel Road, from the south. Whitechapel Mount (right) was believed to have been built of earth dug from Civil War trenches and Great Fire of London debris.

Saxon chieftain Waeppa) and Blackwall as ship-building centres. Yet, by 1500, the East End was still essentially no more than green fields, through which the old Roman road from Colchester to the City of London passed. At this time, the landscape was dominated by the old Roman city wall and the Norman St Paul's Cathedral, which would have towered over the present-day version.

In the 1530s, Henry VIII's dissolution of the monasteries and nunneries, and the confiscation and consequent selling of church lands, opened up new development opportunities. Houses and streets began to spread eastwards and this portion of the Thames developed a notorious stink as industrialization gradually took hold of riverside communities. Limehouse, Wapping and Shadwell were now building bigger ships to feed the growing trade with the Far East and Middle East, and a slum town

was steadily developing in Whitechapel to house the Thames workers. The narrow streets of Spitalfields, some just 15 feet wide, earned a disturbing reputation for overcrowding and squalor. The die had been cast.

By 1700, the population of the suburbs to the east had grown, in just over 100 years, from less than 100,000 to 250,000. The residents of Stepney parish – a vast area that now included Mile End Old and New Towns, Spitalfields, Poplar, Bethnal Green, Bow, Limehouse and Ratcliff – numbered 50,000 and they were living in 9,000 homes.

By 1801, when the first Census was taken, the population of London had swelled to 958,863 and slums blighted the east side, where the overspill from Spitalfields transformed Bethnal Green. Here the population swelled from 15,000 in 1746 to 45,678 in 1821. Old Stepney was swallowed in the urban sprawl as the mother church, St Dunstan's, gave rise to 67 daughter parishes. As the East End groaned at its poverty-stricken seams, three-quarters of all British overseas trade now passed through the Port of London, which was the busiest in the world. A dock, belonging to the East India Company at Blackwall, was joined by the West India Import Dock in 1802, the London Docks three years later and St Katharine Docks in 1828. These were followed by the Royal Docks complex – Victoria, Royal Albert and King George V – in 1855–1921.

While London's western boundary, defined by the City of London, remained fixed, the eastern area of the capital continued to sprawl

uncontrollably outwards as the foul living and working conditions centred on the industrial hub of the River Lea slowly intensified and new districts were spawned at Canning Town, Silvertown and Beckton. By the 1870s, the area was packed with engineering works, jute mills, and factories making soap, matches, ink, dyes and paraffin. The putrid, sickening stench of boiling bones filled the air as Britain enjoyed the financial privileges bestowed upon the world's only workshop, the only massive importer and exporter, the only imperialist and the principle investor.

It was at this time that 'East End', as a specific term meriting the use of initial capital letters, first appeared. The phrase was coined by the London press at a time of declining newspaper sales during the 1880s. Determined to increase sales, they were keen to publicise – and sometimes exaggerate – the cries of the poor living within walking distance of Fleet Street. Walter Besant's best-selling, socially instructive novel, *All Sorts and Conditions of Men*, set the trend for the first generalised geographical picture of the area in

(above) St Mary Matfelon, the famous 'White Chapel' landmark: The old church was subsequently rebuilt in the seventeenth century and this watercolour was executed in 1811 by John Coney. The church was rebuilt in 1876/77 but destroyed by fire in 1880. A new St Mary's opened in 1882, dominating the eastern end of Whitechapel High Street. Bombed in 1940, it was demolished in 1952.

(below) London, Westminster and Southwark, as they appeared in 1543 in a drawing by Anty Van Den Wyngrerde. The sketch shows rural East London four years before the death of Henry VIII. Stepney, just visible on the horizon beyond the Tower of London, is one of the few places of significance to the east. The complex in the foreground on the south side of the Thames is the 'Monastery of Bermondsey'.

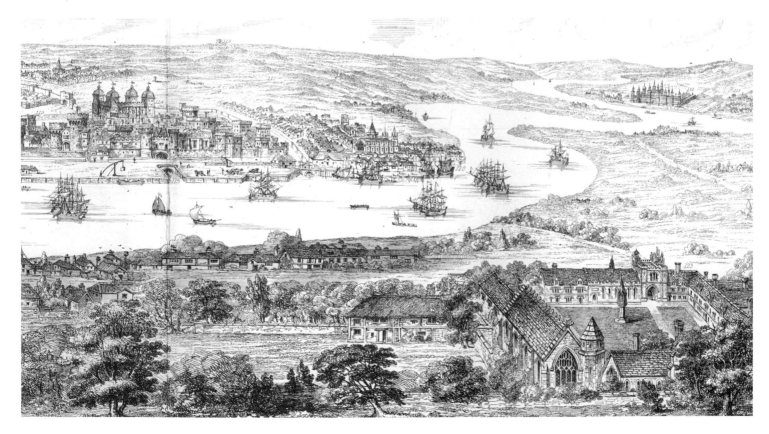

Home industries in late nineteenth-century Bethnal Green:

(left) A late nineteenth-century Bethnal Green home: a flower-worker makes bunches of violets at a halfpenny per dozen.

(below left) Mother and child rest after matchbox making. The scene was captured in late nineteenth-century Bethnal Green.

(below) Brush-making in Bethnal Green during the 1890s.

(right) Rag and mop-making in Bethnal Green in the late nineteenth-century.

(below) Children queue for a 'farthing breakfast' in Hanbury Street, Whitechapel, circa 1905-1910.

1882. The following year, George Sims, whose compassionate investigative reporting made a striking impression on the public, penned a series of articles in *Pictorial World*. As a result, he was commissioned by the *Daily News* to write another series exposing 'Horrible London'. Sims described this part of the capital as 'a dark continent' and as 'interesting as any of those newly explored lands which engage the attention of the Royal Geographical Society'. He described coming 'face to face' with the 'dark side of life' in a place where the 'vilest outcasts bide from the light of day'.

Fast-forward 127 years and today's media warmly embrace an East End of vast geographical dimensions. Plaistow, for example, would once have been deemed too upmarket to be considered part of the gritty East End.

Indeed, here, on the very fringes of London, it is still possible to detect traces of a rural atmosphere, reflecting the open countryside to which Plaistow, East Ham and West Ham belonged until they were absorbed by the Borough of Newham in 1965. Similarly, Hackney would once have been judged part of North London. Yet today's newsmakers welcome Hackney, as they do Ilford, Barking and other great chunks of Essex where post-war East Enders in Southend-on-Sea proudly proclaim their origins.

The only geographical consensus seems to be the position of the traditional entrance to the East End: Gardiner's Corner, at the junction of the two great highways: Whitechapel Road and Commercial Road. This was once the site of the grand Gardiner's clothing store, the 'Harrods of the East'.

(left) East End street scene in the 1890s: children queue outside a pie shop.

(right) Gardiner's Corner, the entry point to the East End, with Whitechapel Road straight ahead and Commercial Road to the right of the landmark Gardiner's building.

(below) Today's view is almost unrecognisable from the scene photographed in July 1934. Most notably, the Gardiner's clothing store has been replaced by a branch of Lloyds TSB.

With its distinctive clock tower, the store gave its name to the road junction and traded on the site for nearly 200 years before closing in 1971. The six-storey building was gutted by fire in 1972 and the 130-foot tower crashed into the streets below. Today, the site is occupied by the uninspired façade of the Lloyds TSB building. Only a Tubby Isaacs stall selling jellied eels, the traditional East End delicacy, outside the Thorley Tavern, reminds visitors that they have left the City well and truly behind them.

Taking advantage of the vagaries of geographical interpretation, I have flung my net widely and arbitrarily. The area that I have covered is shown on the map of the East End (see page 6), which shows the locations of many of the main places mentioned in this book. From the East End entrance at Gardiner's Corner, I have accepted stories from Whitechapel to Barking via Wapping, Poplar and Canning Town; from Eddie Siggins's Stepney to Ilford via West Ham, Forest Gate and Manor Park; from Bethnal Green north to Stoke Newington via Shoreditch and Hackney; and from Bow north to Leyton and Leytonstone.

Ultimately, the 'East End' is whatever individuals want it to be and the same appears to be true of the word 'Cockney', used to describe its inhabitants. This word may well have been derived from the medieval word 'cokenay', meaning 'cock's egg', and, by inference, 'an unnatural object' or 'a freak of nature'. This word was also used by Geoffrey Chaucer, in his fourteenth-century *Canterbury Tales* to refer to a 'mother's darling', or 'milksop'. By the early sixteenth century, the term was being used by country folk to describe people who had been brought up in cities and were ignorant of real life. An alternative and no less complimentary explanation is the story of a naïve Londoner, on his first visit to the country, who innocently asked: 'Does a cock neigh too?' Another explanation is the likeness of the undernourished Cockney, being small in stature and of characteristic boldness, to the determined cock sparrow scratching out a cheerful existence. There are other, more generous theories, such as the Latin word *coquina*, meaning 'cookery'. Indeed, London was once regarded as a world centre for excellent food, reflected in the fact that the Great Fire of 1666 began in

(top) A view of ship-building at Limehouse, Stepney. This lithograph, on paper, was completed by artist William Parrott in 1840.

(above) In 1842, the world's first underwater tunnel, The Thames Tunnel, was completed, linking Wapping and Rotherhithe. It was converted to a railway tunnel for the East London Railway Company.

(left) London Docks in 1898: unloading cargo at the North Quay, Western Dock. Customs officials, merchants and dockers pose for the camera.

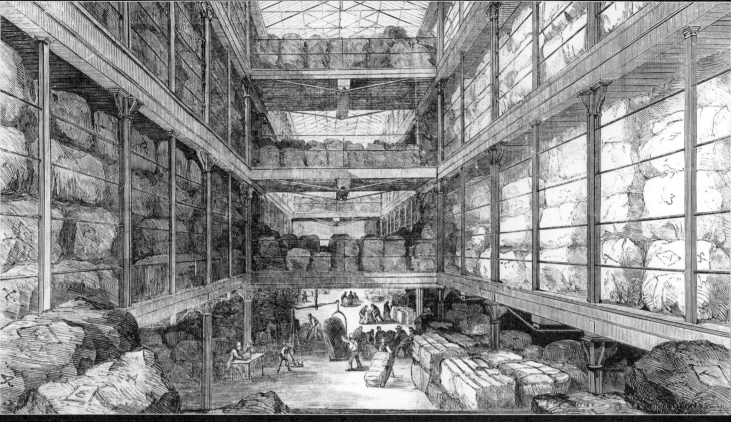

(above) The Wool Floor at London Docks in 1850, showing bales of wool being weighed and tallied.

(right) The 'Call On', 1902: at least twice a day, hundreds of casual workers would line up at a chain slung between the wool warehouses just inside the main entrance to the London Dock, hoping to be called on for work. The bowler-hatted hiring foremen, known as 'gangers', are taking the names of the lucky men who will be put to work. A dock constable keeps a watchful eye. The majority of the men not selected for work would move off to try again at one of the nearby riverside wharves,

The changing East End: **(left)** the junction of Grove Road and Mile End Road in April 1934. **(above)** and the same scene today.

Cause for confusion: **(right)** St Mary's Church in Bow and **(centre right)** St Mary-le-Bow in Cheapside.

(far right) Classic East End continuity: the Great Mosque, Jamme Masjid, on the corner of Fournier Street and Brick Lane in Spitalfields.

Pudding Lane and ended at Pie Corner. Another related term is 'Cockaigne', 'a place of milk and honey', which stems from a Celtic myth of a London where Cockneys were the true inhabitants.

As far as the Cockney language is concerned, there have been no fundamental changes for over 500 years and, by the eighteenth century, it was dismissed as the language of crime and poverty. Its only usefulness was as comic relief in the less distinguished dramas of the London stage. In 1791, John Walker, in his *Critical Pronouncing Dictionary and Expositor of the English Language*, proclaimed: 'Most [barbarous] is the Cockney speech of London'. He was appalled that Cockneys had not learned from their betters. Indeed, they had made so little of their proximity to privilege that he considered the Cockney tongue to be 'a thousand times more offensive and disgusting' than that heard in Cornwall, Lancashire and Yorkshire. A shocked Walker despaired at the catalogue of verbal crimes committed by the Cockney. These included the unforgivable dropping of the 'h' (so that 'heart' became 'art' and 'harm' became 'arm') and the use of 'f' instead of 'th' (so that 'thirsty' became 'firsty'). The charges mounted up when Walker's delicate ears heard 'There a'int nuffink to see', and 'ain't it' (which evolved into the equally unacceptable 'innit').

There was also a peculiar, puzzling dimension to the language. Cockney 'rabbit', or 'rhyming slang', was a colourful secret language used by the 'costermongers', who derived their name from the selling of Costard

apples, a variety known since the thirteenth century and one of the first fruits sold by London street-traders. Some 30,000 men, women and children were working as costermongers in the mid-nineteenth century, roaming the cobbled streets and alleyways of Victorian London with their laden barrows until 11 o'clock at night. Without them, the London poor would not have been fed because shops were usually too expensive and frankly unwelcoming of the great unwashed.

Much of the slang used by these workers has now become part of common speech, and classic phrases such as 'apples and pears' (stairs) and 'trouble and strife' (wife) made their historic debut in the first decades of the nineteenth century. At the same time came 'back-slang', in which the letters in words were reversed. Thus, 'yob' became back-slang for 'boy' while 'Fagin', as in *Oliver Twist,* became back-slang for *ganef*, the Yiddish word for 'thief'. Coster back-slang completely threw the police, as well as their rival Irish costers. 'On' meant 'no', 'say' meant 'yes' and, for the well-initiated, 'cool the esclop' meant 'look, the police'. The addition of proverbs, slogans and street catchphrases – often with vulgar or violent overtones – enriched the language further. By the 1930s, slang had almost died out but it was given a new lease of life by Cockney comedians on stage and radio. It was then adopted by all classes and today's older-generation Cockneys remain somewhat astonished by the fuss made over rhyming slang, which was once spoken naturally, and never purely for amusement. The same applies to swearing, now apparently

a prerequisite for every Cockney film character. Yet the children of the 1930s would invariably get a clip around the ear if they swore. Bad language was used only by hooligans.

Cockney language continues to go from strength to strength. While 'Flare Up' dominated the London streets in the 1830s, the radio and television age heralded such catch-phrases as 'There's a lot of it about', 'Can I do you now, Sir' and 'See you later alligator'. Popular music – notably rap and hip-hop – today provides the present generation with expressions relevant to a new time in an old place while 'Mars bar' (scar), 'Hong Kong' (pong) and 'Becks and Posh' (nosh) preserve the traditions of rhyming slang. Research in 2005 revealed that young white men in Tower Hamlets have begun to use Bangladeshi words acquired from their friends, such as 'nang' (good), 'creps' (trainers) and 'skets' (slippers). West Indian and West African influences have also contributed to the creation of a new composite language, a 'multicultural English', with a mixture of new accents and dialects.

True Cockneys have traditionally lived within the sound of Bow Bells – and there lies a longstanding misconception. The Bow Bells in question, cast at the Whitechapel Foundry, are not those of St Mary's Church in Bow, although this would appear to make geographical sense. In fact, they ring from St Mary-le-Bow in Cheapside, just behind St Paul's Cathedral. St Mary-le-Bow is one of a coronet of churches , all designed by Wren, whose prized gem, St Paul's Cathedral, stands at the centre; regrettably, it is difficult to appreciate Wren's original breathtaking vision amid the towering glass and concrete of the modern-day metropolis. It was Fynes Moryson who, in 1617, famously declared that 'Londiners, and all within the sound of Bow-bell, are in reproach called Cocknies, and eaters of buttered toasties'. However, the identification of the true Cockney church presents another obvious problem. In April 1994, the Meteorological Office conducted an experiment which concluded the St Mary-le-Bow bells would have been heard all over London in the days before cars, effectively making all Londoners 'Cockneys'.

When touring the East End today, it is difficult to comprehend the 'atmosphere', of the pre-war years so emotionally described in the pages that follow. Equally, the defiant, close-knit East End that confronted the Blitz is impossible to detect. Instead, the first impression is of frenetic business, constant din and colliding micro-worlds. Traffic roars past as groups of students huddle around shouting lecturers, who invite them to imagine the sights and sounds of Victorian life or the experience of Blitz life in shelters. The students gaze blankly at the surrounding graffiti, bleak estates and jagged skyscrapers before moving on to the next grime-encased factory wall.

The past world is becoming increasingly hard to either visualize or understand. An older generation has left, taking its memories – my father, Eric Bissell, lives in Dorset and Eddie Siggins lived in Essex – and new people have arrived in an East End where the past may be noteworthy but, to them at least, not particularly relevant.

The brash, confident East End of today is suited and booted. Parts of the East End have become gentrified and a trendy café society has made itself very much at home with its associated paraphernalia of smart restaurants, art galleries, museums, lavish restorations and plush apartments. Visit parts of Hackney and you could be in Georgian Islington or Hampstead, while riverside Wapping, home of the Blitz memorial, is now a young executive's playground. New luxury apartments have erupted from the yawning fissures left by the Blitz and new highways dissect the former bombed wasteland. Space-age glass towers shimmer over Docklands, where the tallest of them all – the embodiment of wealth and success – is One Canada Square at Canary Wharf. The past has disappeared in a swirl of power lunches and firm handshakes.

Canary Wharf in 2007, viewed from Greenwich Park.

However, do not be deceived. The East End today has a split personality and a complex Jekyll and Hyde patient lies upon the psychiatrist's couch. Beyond the iconic monuments to Docklands renaissance, hollow-eyed youngsters cower in doorways, the desperate prowl decaying streets and dire poverty drains life from some neighbourhoods. While the torch of the 30th Olympiad glows over regenerated Stratford, the Victorian East End is apparently still with us, mocking our inability to discard shameful old baggage.

While the East End today is a place of unnerving contrasts, change also happily co-exists with continuity. Indeed, while no other area of Britain has experienced the same degree of changing population as the East End of London, each successive wave has trodden familiar steps and confronted similar survival challenges.

Today's close-knit Muslim-Bengali community is akin to that of the Irish, Jews and French Huguenot weavers who came before them. Germans, Scandinavians, Malays, Chinese and West Indians have also been part of the historic and continuous exodus to the East End. One group merely followed another, a continuum epitomised by the current Jamme Masjid Mosque at the corner of Fournier Street and Brick Lane in Spitalfields. Built as a Huguenot chapel in 1742, it was transformed into a Methodist chapel in 1809 and then, in 1897, it was bought by the Jewish ultra-Orthodox immigrant Machzikei Hadath Society and named Spitalfields Great Synagogue.

The hauntingly beautiful Grade II listed building at 19 Princelet Street in Spitalfields, an unrestored Huguenot silk-weaver's home built in 1719, is another example. The Protestant Ogier family, escaping persecution at the hands of Louis XIV's militia, lived there amid the streets known as 'Liberty', which resounded with French voices. In 1869, in the garden where the Ogier children once played, Polish Jews built a Victorian synagogue (the oldest surviving Ashkenazi synagogue in London) which, in the century that followed, became a refuge for those fleeing Nazi persecution. Dubbed as the nation's answer to the Anne Frank House in Amsterdam, it is currently a museum to all East End immigrants, including Sikhs, Bengalis and Somalis. The building, in need of £3 million of urgent repairs, is so fragile that it can only be visited by prior arrangement. Like a chronic invalid, one of Britain's most important buildings spends much of its time in dusty slumber.

Elsewhere East End synagogues that were once packed for Yom Kippur are now mosques full for Ramadan. The rich legacy of the clothing trade, of faith and of family epitomised by the Jews, is today continued by the plethora of Indian and Bangladeshi tailors and export outlets in the old Jewish haunts of Brick Lane, Fournier Street and Whitechapel Road. Corner shops vacated by the Jews are now in Asian hands, Yiddish cinema has succumbed to the charms of 'Bollywood', halal butchers have replaced kosher ones, and Brick Lane is today crossed by the 'Banglatown' arch, inaugurated in 1997, in recognition of Spitalfields' Bangladeshi heart.

Meanwhile, the East End continues to offer a rich confection of popular imagery and folklore. Inevitably, it will always be associated with 'Blitz spirit', pie and mash, jellied eels, Jack the Ripper, Victorian ragamuffins, West Ham United's terrace serenade 'I'm Forever Blowing Bubbles', and street-wise chirpy Cockneys enjoying 'Knees-Up Muvvah Brahn' in cosy boozers. All are part of the veritable popular feast, along with the Old Vic pub in the soap world of *EastEnders*, amiable fair cop George 'Evening all' Dixon, and cinema portrayals of Cockney gangsters with a penchant for excessive violence.

Fact and fiction, fantasy and reality have seamlessly merged to create a durable and much loved cultural icon, the Cockney, inhabiting one of the most readily identifiable and romanticised parts of Britain: the East End.

This book now invites you, the reader, to enter the East End drama. Turn the page, step back in time and join young Eddie Siggins in Duckett Street, Stepney, where he reminisces about his grandmother's life and presents an evocative snapshot of the pre-Blitz community with the aid of fellow East Enders. Hear their voices, share their joy and feel their pain as the skies over London begin to darken.

Chapter one

'Walk down the street like you own it'

NANA'S OLD HOUSE at 63 Duckett Street gave her young grandson Eddie Siggins the creeps. He was sure it was haunted. How else could Eddie explain the strange rapping noises he sometimes heard coming from within the walls at night?

Nana's eldest son, Alfred, had also claimed to have seen a ghost warming its hands before the dying embers of a fire in the backyard, while the experiences of two daughters, Gladys and Jess, were no less disturbing. They had once inspected the unoccupied upstairs bedroom and found the bed vibrating and music playing to no one. Something was odd about the place and young Eddie had a theory: the unexplained occurrences were something to do with the old East London Cemetery that was once just up the road.

Nana – Mary Ann Bowyer – had brought up her 13 children at No. 63, including Eddie's mother, Sarah. Eddie often gazed up at the slender

three-storey Stepney abode – effectively three tiny rooms on top of each other – and wondered how on earth she had managed it. Yet somehow she had, despite losing her beloved husband, Alfred, in 1917 during the First World War. They never found the body of Private No. 17699 in the sludge at Cambrai after the world's first tank battle. Instead, his grieving widow was insulted to discover his name had been left off a memorial plaque unveiled

Five of Mary Ann Bowyer's 13 children in 1921 (from left to right): John, Ada, Fred, Gladys and Winnie, standing outside the ground floor window of 63 Duckett Street.

Mary Ann Bowyer, Eddie's 'Nana' (far left, with white hat), with Eddie's mother Sarah (far right) and local Stepney ladies during a pub outing to Southend.

The Edinburgh Castle.

Alfred Henry Bowyer who served in 13 Battalion, the Essex Regiment.

Children from the Mission Sunday School waving their invitation cards to the 1909 Christmas party at the Edinburgh Castle.

The People's Palace opening ceremony, as featured in *The Graphic* on 21 May 1887.

outside St Faith's Church in Shandy Street where, 21 years earlier, Mary Ann Marshall had married the local lad from nearby Bale Street. Alfred's name was missing because Mary Ann could not afford a donation towards the cost of the Roll of Honour. There had been too many hungry mouths to feed and no money to spare, so her husband's sacrifice was lost from public memory.

This was just one of many family stories which had tumbled down through the branches of the family tree and been caught by Eddie's fertile imagination. Equally intriguing were Mary Ann's anecdotes of her own childhood in Victorian Duckett Street. Born in 1877, young Mary Ann, her three siblings and her parents had occupied just the small middle room of No. 63 while a rickety, creaking staircase gave Mr and Mrs Brown, a young couple in their twenties, access to the single room above and the Richmonds lived below. An identical three-tiered house further down the terraced street accommodated 24 people. Duckett Street, Eddie had learned, was originally part of a dreary new housing estate that had devoured several fields north of Stepney village in the early part of the nineteenth century. At least it had

been given a grand name – the 'Beaumont Estate' –courtesy of its founder, the financier and philanthropist Barber Beaumont.

The origins of the street name and the surrounding landmarks also fascinated Nana's young grandson. The street itself had been named after a canal-builder, Sir George Duckett, who had shovelled out the Hertford Union Canal to link the River Lea to the Regent's Canal. His new road linked St Dunstan's Church, the East End's mother church, in the south, to the People's Palace in the north. The Palace, incorporating a concert hall, technical school, library, gymnasium and swimming pool, was a cultural beacon in an area which had no bookshops, hotels or restaurants. It had opened along the Mile End Road in 1887 and owed its existence, once again, to the generosity of Barber Beaumont. Also nearby was the Edinburgh Castle gin-palace, which plied a raucous trade in Rhodeswell Road. A kindly man known as Dr Barnardo had branded the establishment a 'Citadel of Satan' and had promptly taken it over and converted the building into a Working Men's Club and People's Mission Hall. When Nana was 11, poor

Dr Thomas John Barnardo: when Barnardo died in 1905, tributes poured in from across the globe. He was buried in Barkingside, Essex, where, in 1876, he opened the first purpose-built 'Garden City' for girls. Here 1,500 resided in cottages built around a green.

Hope Place: Barnardo's shelter, rumoured to be a former donkey stable.

local children had been treated to a great winter party there and some 2,000 of them, many without headwear or boots, had enjoyed a slap-up supper. Many of the youngsters had not used soap or water for a long time and had been starving in the market places, by the riverside, in common lodging houses or in the casual wards of workhouses. Nana also recalled another Barnardo's building: two converted cottages in Hope Place, not far from the Edinburgh Castle and to the south of Duckett Street. It was said to be a former donkey stable where the good Doctor had opened an 'East End Juvenile Mission'.

Yet it was another of Nana's memories that particularly intrigued grandson Eddie. Just two weeks before Mary Ann's 11th birthday in 1888, The *Star* newspaper's Late Final screamed details of the 'latest horrible murder in Whitechapel'. That morning a prostitute called Annie Chapman had been found disembowelled in a backyard in Hanbury Street. Three other women had already met a gruesome death and Mary's Ann's father banned his daughter from leaving the house after dark while 'Jack the Ripper' was on the loose. The East End of Nana's childhood was stewed in poverty and into this desperate mire – variously described by contemporary writers as the 'abyss', the 'netherworld' and a 'city of the damned'– stepped hundreds of social reformers, missionaries, wandering philanthropists and wealthy humanitarians, clutching Bibles, bread and lamps.

By the time Nana and Alfred were joined together in matrimony inside St Faith's Church in September 1896, the very worst housing conditions were being alleviated and the disadvantaged were fighting back in the workplace, where over 240 unions had been formed. The poor were at last finding their voice in a rapidly changing London, where a population of under 1 million in 1801 had expanded to 6.5 million in 1902. Ringed by rapidly growing suburbs, Greater London measured 18 miles across (it had been 4 miles in 1720) and contained the equivalent of the combined populations of Europe's four greatest cities – Paris, Berlin, Vienna and St Petersburg. In 1901, Queen Victoria's Empire covered more than one fifth of the land surface of the globe – containing some 400 million people – while half of the ships on the seas were registered in Britain, which controlled a third of the world's trade.

Newly-weds Mary Ann and Alfred Bowyer lived in a country that was undisputedly the most powerful and richest on earth, and at the very centre

Walthamstow in 1905.

Plashet Lane, Upton Park, at the turn of the century. It is today called Plashet Grove.

The High Street, East Ham, 1907.

was London, which now became fashioned as an Imperial Capital, with vast offices, hotels, landmark buildings such as The Old Bailey and Whitehall, new bridges over the Thames and new railway termini. The Bowyers' address changed too. The administration of the great city was overhauled to tackle inefficiency and corruption and, in 1900, all the East End parish vestries, hamlet vestries, precincts and district boards were swept away. They were replaced with three new Metropolitan Boroughs – Stepney, Poplar and Bethnal Green – which were to last until 1965, when they, in turn, were amalgamated to form the London Borough of Tower Hamlets.

As the new century dawned over Duckett Street, Queen Victoria's subjects enjoyed rising incomes, cheaper imports and shorter hours, which provided Londoners with more opportunity for leisure. A distinct working-class culture had emerged around the music halls, churches, chapels and pubs. Meanwhile, the spread of the Saturday holiday among clerks and working men, coupled with the provision of parks and playing fields, encouraged the Victorian hobbies of walking and cycling and facilitated the evolution of football and rugby.

However, the First World War changed everything for the Bowyers. Mary Ann had begged Alfred not to leave for the Western Front but off he went, a 39-year-old who had never handled a gun in his life. He returned unexpectedly one day, terribly tired, muddy and lousy from the trenches, and went straight to bed while the girls pressed his coat and his boys polished his buttons and badge. When it was time to leave once more, he suddenly turned to his wife and said: 'After what I've seen, I'll get at least one German before I die'.

His family never saw him again and Eddie's mother, Sarah, then just a girl of 12, helped her mother, Mary Ann, raise the Bowyer brood in a post-war Britain in serious economic trouble.

After a short boom, the Victorian economy had suddenly and catastrophically crashed into ruins after the First World War, and both the extent and the pace of decline paralysed the Establishment. A flabby, out-of-shape Britain was forced to feed off the carcass of Empire like never before. Like an out-of-condition heavyweight boxing champion, hanging onto the ropes seemed a better option than trading punches with competitors. Britain became a 'fixer', a financial facilitator and broker, as cotton exports nose-dived and figures for coal exports and ship-building made increasingly uncomfortable reading. Britain also turned inwards to provide goods for its own people and the country gradually split to reveal a nation of contrasting fortunes. London, the Midlands and the southeast generally flourished with their home-market industries, while the demise of traditional British export industries in the north and west ruined millions of lives through mass unemployment.

London in 1914: Whitechapel High Street looking east, with a helmeted policeman in the foreground allowing an omnibus to cross from Middlesex Street to Mansell Street.

Whitechapel High Street, July 1912: Gardiner's Corner is out of shot to the right; the road opposite is Commercial Street.

Whitechapel High Street today: Commercial Street is opposite.

(above left) Hundreds of barrels of wines and spirits are laid out for gauging by HM Customs at London Docks in 1920.

(above) West Ham Corporation tram at Stratford Broadway at the turn of the nineteenth century.

(left) Whitechapel High Street: tram-track reconstruction viewed from Gardiner's Corner and looking back towards the City, August 1929. The Old Red Lion pub on the left, on the corner of Leman Street, is today the southern exit of Aldgate East Underground station.

HM King George V is cheered by dock workers during his visit to the Royal Docks in November 1917.

Limehouse Causeway around 1920. This is a typical East End street scene close to the docks. People were free to wander in the middle of the street since motor traffic was very rare in these parts.

Neither was this solely a British disease. For the first time since industrialization began, growth of production of all the industrial powers slumped in a frightful malaise. By 1932, the worst year of the slump, Britain's official unemployment figure had soared to just under 3 million (23 per cent of the workforce), more than double that of a few years earlier. Those not included – agricultural workers, servants and the self-employed – probably pushed the real unemployment figure close to 3.75 million. Though unemployment never rose above 15 per cent in the Tower Hamlets as a whole (compared with 66 per cent in Jarrow), it was nonetheless grim in the East End black spots of Poplar and Stepney, and especially West Ham, where unemployment in 1931/32 was about 27 per cent.

Groups of jobless men stood on street corners, airing their grievances and cursing the hated Relieving Officers, whose means tests established eligibility for dole money. The amount usually given in benefit in the early 1930s ensured basic survival but not family health. Indeed, although a family of five in 1934 could expect £1 9s 3d (£1.46) a week, rent, insurance, fuel and food devoured most of this, leaving a surplus of just 2½d. Those who did not qualify for relief had to rely on the dreaded Poor Law for help; there were still 41,000 adults in London Poor Law institutions in 1929. People therefore sold everything except the bare essentials so that they could claim relief, while the desperate embarked upon regular scavenging trips to Spitalfields Market for discarded vegetables. These were almost covert operations because the proud East End poor were ashamed of their poverty. Then came the Relieving Officers' humiliating Friday visits to the Cockneys' threadbare homes to monitor their means and assess how the relief was being spent. Saucepan lids were lifted and cupboards inspected for any telltale signs of hidden luxuries. Shame invariably turned to anger and the officer would frequently leave with a bruise or two.

Depression and poverty were matched by dramatic social change in inter-war Britain. A Ministry of Health had been established in 1919 and the life expectancy of a newborn boy rose from 45 years in 1900 to 59 years in 1930. However, there were still 3,000–4,000 deaths each year from diphtheria, 2,000 from whooping cough and 30,000–40,000 from tuberculosis. Poorer areas were also redeveloped and former slum-dwellers were rehoused in new 'model' communities.

The 1909 Housing and Town Planning Act had paved the way by empowering authorities to plan the development of unbuilt areas. Along the High Street in Poplar, and in the centre of Wapping, jerry-built courts of housing and the wretched remains of seventeenth-and eighteenth-century tenements were swept away for new streamlined blocks of flats. The post-1918 era then witnessed a large-scale initiative to build houses in a bid to minimise the awkward political repercussions of battle-weary subjects returning home to slums, rather than decent homes. Government money was put into public housing for the first time and 60 per cent of all houses built between 1919 and 1921 were council homes, a 10-fold increase on pre-war figures. An East End exodus to suburbia was also given the green light when London County Council began building a new town at Dagenham in April 1920, which included a vast 3,000-acre estate called Becontree, costing £14 million. The estate was completed in 1935, with homes boasting front and back gardens, two or three bedrooms, a living room, scullery, bathroom and indoor toilet.

Yet there was a price to pay, as George Blake in Poplar recalled:

We were eventually successful in our application and were allocated a two-bed-roomed cottage at Dagenham. When we moved it meant the breaking of all our ties with both our families and the neighbours of many years and we could only hope that it would be for the best in surroundings that were so very different to what we had always been brought up in. I had to leave home very early in the morning and travel to my work on the railway at Poplar from the little country station at Dagenham and was away from home all day. When I got home, the wife was miserable. She was not used to the new surroundings and strange people, and so we had to admit that, notwithstanding the comfort of the new cottage and general atmosphere, it somehow didn't suit us. And so, after a few months, I managed to get a flat in Grosvenor Buildings at Poplar and we moved back.

Meanwhile, social mobility saw hundreds of Jews and Irish leave the slums and head for the provinces and newly built estates. The Jews headed east to middle-class Redbridge and, for the wealthier, Golders Green beckoned to the northwest. They poured out in the 1920s and perhaps one third of East End Jewry had gone by 1929. The Irish headed east to Dagenham and its Ford motor factory, opened in 1931, where they gratefully accepted work. In the former slum wasteland vacated by East Enders, huge five-storey blocks of affordable flats sprang up in the late 1920s as the old close-knit communities were slowly replaced with 'boxes in the sky'.

The world of leisure was changing too. In addition to the music hall, radio and cinema flourished after 1918. Radio was revolutionary and brought round-the-clock entertainment into people's homes for the first time in history, while cinema eclipsed the gin-palace and music hall as the poor man's opportunity for escapism and fantasy. The inter-war era ushered in the gigantic and baroque Trocaderos, Granadas and Odeons, with their plush seats, organs and glamorous coloured lights. An evening at the cinema cost 6d (2.5p), the same as a cheap music hall and a quarter of the cost of the theatre. People went twice a week and many local cinemas changed their programme every three days. By the 1920s, most of the major music halls had abandoned traditional audience participation and embraced more sophisticated musicals and revues in a bid to compete. However, by 1935, there were over 50 cinemas in the East End, forcing several of the best-known music halls to close.

Football had now become a working-class obsession and West Ham played Bolton Wanderers in the first Wembley FA Cup Final in 1923. An estimated crowd of 200,000 – the majority from the East End – shoved its way in, spilling over the hallowed turf and delaying kick-off. The occasion became immortalised as the 'White Horse Final' after a mounted policeman, PC Storey, and his trusty steed 'Billie', helped to clear the pitch. The fuming Mayor of East Ham could not even get into the stadium, despite buying a guinea ticket, and thousands sat or stood around the touchline when play commenced 44 minutes late. The record crowd saw Bolton's defence shackle Hammer's reliable goal-scorer Vic Watson, and Wanderers went on to win 2–0 in a match that dispensed with a half-time break. Nonetheless, countless thousands lined Barking Road to greet the gallant Hammers when the team returned to the East End aboard a brilliantly illuminated tram. West Ham would have to wait another 41 years before winning one of the most famous trophies in world sport for the first time. North London rivals Arsenal would dominate football in the 1930s, while more football pitches sprang up on Hackney Marshes than on any other playing field in Britain, giving Cockney lads a chance of future stardom.

The East End's love of boxing was similarly deep and long-standing. Town halls, skating rinks and swimming baths were all booked by promoters but a favourite venue was Premierland in Back Church Lane, Whitechapel, which had nurtured champions like Ted 'Kid' Lewis and Jack 'Kid' Berg. Lewis had added the European Featherweight Championship to his British title in 1914, and became the first English boxer to win a world title in America by beating Jack Britton in 1915 to secure the welterweight crown. Lewis, 'the Crashing Dashing Kid', won nine titles in his 20-year career and remains the most popular British fighter ever to have boxed in America. Meanwhile Berg, a fighter born in Cable Street in 1909, had begun his career at Premierland as a 14-year-old. The 'Whitechapel Whirlwind' became World Junior Welterweight Champion in 1930 and British Lightweight Champion in 1934.

The glamour and excitement of sport and the silver screen were also increasingly affordable. Although many of Britain's northern workers were engulfed in a tidal wave of depression and unemployment, workers in the booming home-market industries, aimed at mass consumption, were enjoying a rise in their standard of living. In fact, those in full-time employment in 1933 had a purchasing power that had increased by over 10

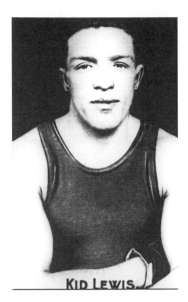

Ted 'Kid' Lewis (1894–1970). Born Gershon Mendeloff, he was known as the 'Aldgate Sphinx'.

KID LEWIS.

(below) 'White Horse Final': amazing scenes as PC Storey and 'Billie' help to push back the crowd.

East Enders arrive for the big day, including a fan (right) with a large hammer!

per cent since 1930, because prices had fallen more than their wages. Radio and cinema served to raise new hopes, aspirations and expectations in the late 1920s and early 1930s and, despite abundant hardship, these were also years that, today, prompt fond memories of East End community life, as the following extracts reveal.

Rose Gowler (née Wiggins) recalls:

My grandparents originally came over from Ireland and our family consisted of Mum, Dad and three children. We rented two rooms in a small terraced house in Myrdle Street in Whitechapel for 8 and 4 pence [42p] a week. Three other families were crammed inside the property and we shared the lavatory in the yard and the scullery for washday.

It was the street musicians who we adored in the late 1920s. The sad, plaintive sound of 'Hushabye' would drift down Myrdle Street and people like Whistling Rufus would appear to entertain us. Every Sunday, without fail, two men dressed in blazers, white plimsolls and yachting caps would come and play their banjos and their repertoire would always start with a song that went: 'I'm an airman and I fly, fly, fly, way up in the sky'. They were followed by a Jewish man who pushed a pram containing an ancient gramophone with a horn which played Yiddish records. There was also a group of six miners, a dour bunch, on the dole since the 1926 General Strike, who sang beautifully in harmony. However the highlight was seeing the famous Nancy Boys in Myrdle Street. They were a group with a barrel organ who dressed up in women's clothes and danced like chorus girls with high kicks and cries of 'whoopee'. We sat on the kerb mesmerized and thought they were very daring. They called everyone 'dearie' or 'ducks' and even smoked cigarettes, which we thought was very naughty. I don't think we even realised they were men. Another favourite was Johnny Fields, who had a smashing voice and used to enter the talent contests at the Mile End Empire and the Foresters in Cambridge Heath Road, which he always won.

Exploring beyond the close-knit streets became a real adventure for the Wiggins youngsters too. Mrs Gowler remembers:

We would go to Shadwell Park, which always seemed to smell of cut grass and biscuits thanks to the Wrights biscuit factory behind it. We used to go there every Saturday in the 1920s and being the eldest – I was 10 in 1928– I was always in charge and I would push a pram with my baby brother and sister inside. A big group of us went loaded up with sandwiches, a bottle of liquorice water and a penny to buy a 'pennorth' of broken biscuits from Wrights. They had a hatch door where you could buy the fragments and it was a lucky dip really. You were thrilled if you found a custard cream. The Park was about

(far left from top to bottom) Rose Gowler's father, Charles Wiggins, with work colleagues on a trip to Southend or Margate. He is third from the left, looking from the bus. Most of the revellers have drinks in their hands and an accordion-player, Patsy Mahoney, the son of one of the workers, is on hand to assist with sing-songs. In the white coat, is the driver.

26 Myrdle Street in 1921. Rose Gowler (née Wiggins) is pictured aged three in the front row with her mother standing on her left. Mrs Abbott (seated) also lived at the property with her sons Freddy (behind), Charlie (on her right) and Johnny (on her left). A total of four families lived at the house – and they shared one outside toilet.

Rose Gowler's father, Charles Wiggins (second from left), with friends on a charabanc outing in the 1930s. The trip was organised by the firm they worked for, haulage contractors Henry Vile. The charabanc was invariably piled high with drink.

Hughes Mansions, pictured on 7 August 1929.

a mile from Myrdle Street and we always headed for the pool. Our parents told us not to go to the pool but we went there first so our clothes had time to dry out and no one would be the wiser. Then we would make a house in the sandpit before tucking into the food.

At the end of the day I'd put everything back in the pram – including the children – and we'd go and watch the boats on the Thames. If we felt daring, we would go and investigate Rotherhithe Tunnel and once we walked all the way through to the other side. When it was four o'clock we made our way home, tired and filthy but filled with memories of the Park to keep us going until the following week.

I went even further afield too, thanks to a wonderful woman called Nurse Whitby, our district nurse who often called at our place when Mum was taken bad. She was tall and straight, with a crisp starched uniform with stiff white cuffs. The cuffs fascinated me because she would take them off as soon as she got in, put one inside the other and place them on the mantelpiece. Then she would have a scrub before starting her duties. She would scrub again at the end and put the cuffs back on. When she wasn't on duty, Nurse Whitby worked tirelessly for the poor. Every summer she would take children away. In July she took the girls, followed by the boys in August. We would all pile into a lorry and sing all the way to a destination that seemed hundreds of miles away. In fact, the place was Copthall Farm in Upshire, near Epping Forest, where we were met by the owner, Mrs Crawford-Brown, and given a palliasse and pillowcase to use in the hayloft. In the loft we would stuff the palliasse with straw before tucking in to a luxury tea of thin bread, real butter, scones, scotch pancakes and home-made jam. It was like being in heaven for 12 days.

Nurse Whitby took us on nature walks and to places like Waltham

Abbey, and by the end of it I viewed her as some sort of angel, especially when we said prayers with her in the morning and at night. She was a dear, kind lady and on certain days, when the sun is setting in a certain way, I can still see the circle of poor children standing in the meadow listening to her soft voice reciting her own special evening prayer.

'Abide with us O Lord, for it is toward evening
and the day is far spent,
May our evening prayers ascend up to Thee O Lord
and thy mercy descend upon us,
Keep us, O Lord, as the apple of thine eye,
Hide us under the shadow of thy wing.'

Once back home we wrote thank-you letters to the Earl of Winterton, who financed the trip, and the best one received a prize. The winner was announced at Nurse Whitby's house in Lower Chapman Street [now Bigland Street], where she held Christmas parties. I won one year and was given a watch – an absolutely amazing thing to have in those days. When I was 14 in 1932, my family moved from Myrdle Street to Hughes Mansions, a council block in Vallance Road, Bethnal Green. That was a different world. There were electric lights, a proper bathroom, a sink in the kitchen and a couple of rooms.

The Hughes Mansions flats, completed in 1929, were named in honour of Stepney Quaker, philanthropist, councillor and JP, Mary Hughes, who was the youngest daughter of the author of *Tom Brown's Schooldays*. Opposite the flats was the Dewdrop Inn, formerly the notorious Earl Grey pub, which

Doris Bailey (back row) pictured in 1932 with children from the Victoria Park Baptist Church Sunday School in Grove Road, Bethnal Green, on a day outing.

Doris Bailey (née Carr): (above) pictured in 1916 and below, aged nine (seated), with sister Gwen, aged seven, in 1926.

Doris Bailey (centre, in the second row with hands on knees) pictured in 1925 with class pals from Olga Street School in Bethnal Green.

the saintly Hughes had bought three years earlier and converted into a rest place for the homeless as part of her dedicated crusade to help the poor. The Mansions that bore her name would become synonymous with appalling tragedy in the East End – and heartbreaking loss for Rose Gowler.

On the other side of Bethnal Green, Doris Bailey (née Carr) was living in Hamilton Road (now Haverfield Road) off Grove Road. She recalls:

An Englishman's home may be his castle but the Cockney fellow's street was his kingdom and not lightly trampled on by outsiders. Even we small girls felt this bristling pride of belonging.

It was, she recalls, a community with a 'village air', where most of the neighbours, and probably most of the lodgers, were related. It was a world where dairy cows were let out into the street while their stalls were scrubbed and local women would emerge from their homes to collect the fresh dung for the garden. It was a place where young Doris was sent to Hackney Marshes by her father with a small case to fill with sheep droppings, which she picked up with a hairpin to earn a penny.

Meandering through this community, a succession of colourful characters made their way: the cheery milkman, hanging his cans of milk on the doorknockers; the slow, ponderous horse pulling the water cart; the hearthstone man, selling green hearthstone and whitening for gleaming doorsteps; and the carbolic man, with his white fluid that scoured drains and toilets and cracked your hands.

There was also the eagerly awaited shrimp-and-whelk man; the winter muffin man with his cloth-covered tray upon his head, ringing his hand-bell; and the characters in Green Street Market and in the more expensive Roman Market, whose stalls and clients were less scruffy.

Brick Lane Market: photographed in January 1932 from Hare Street and Sclater Street, looking towards Bethnal Green Road.

Characters were indeed plentiful recalls Mrs Bailey, and included men like the old Jew in Green Street who provided her father's favourite delicacy – Dutch herring.

At length, the old Jew, in his greasy coat and cap, would grab the plate, roll up his sleeve and dive his arm into the vinegar-filled barrel near the door and come up with a slimy, slithery herring, slap it on the slate and cover it with a scrap of plain paper.

Then there was the unforgettable 'cat's-meat man', who, with basket on arm, toured the streets yelling 'Meeeat! Meeeat!' Mrs Bailey recalls:

A veritable pied piper was he, with all the cats of the neighbourhood running at his heels. The pieces of meat were threaded neatly onto wooden skewers and he would throw down a skewerful to the customers' cats as he reached their doorway, collecting his penny on the way back… they were rowdy roughs, these cats'-meat people, and had a bad name in the whole area.

The barrow boys, selling peas, cherries and strawberries; the rag-and-bone man who would give a penny or china in return for rags; the old-iron man on the lookout for leaking kettles; and an assorted mélange of street singers and buskers – all added to the intoxicating mix.

Male entertainers wearing high heels and given a womanly shape with the help of balloons guaranteed a laugh in Bethnal Green too. Mrs Bailey recalls.

The women, especially the rowdy ones, would join them and have a good laugh, shrieking as the dancing men showed their bloomers, all lace-trimmed and hanging down over their knees. And maybe one of the women would go up to give them a penny and stick a hat pin in the huge bosom so that it exploded with a loud bang.

However, this was also a world where violence was part and parcel of home life – as it had been for generations of East Enders. Mrs Bailey remembers:

Love and punishment were meted out on the same lavish scale, especially the wallopings. But they were quick hard smacks which she (Mum) gave, and soon over, whereas Dad would prolong the agony, taking off his trouser belt, or taking the thin hooked cane from the wall and feeling it almost lovingly, prior to giving us a mighty swipe across the legs or the backside.

She recalls, too, how the demon drink brought out the worst in the man of the house, as it had for generations:

(from left to right): Sarah and James Siggins's eldest daughter, Irene, in 1932. She was born two years before the Siggins's first son, Eddie.

James Siggins.

Mary Ann's daughter Sarah, aged 16. Sarah married James Siggins in 1927 and their first son was born in 1930. He was named Edward Siggins and would be known as 'Eddie'.

Sometimes Mum came running up the stairs and came in and sat quietly crying on the end of our bed. We would pretend to be asleep and he would come belting up after her. He would open the bedroom door and point down the stairs. 'Come down and take your medicine,' he would say in a queer and level voice, and she would go sobbing down the stairs and the thumping began again.

The Band of Hope urged the devotees of alcohol to see the light. Meetings were held at the Methodist Church in Mile End Road, where children packed in to sing hymns advocating the consumption of pure water rather than the Devil's tipple. The lights were then lowered and a story illustrated by magic lantern slides typically told a tale of children in squalor thanks to an alcoholic father. However, the show's finale would witness the appearance of a vicar and the casting of light into darkness, which guaranteed both the family's salvation as well as beaming young smiles in the audience. Mrs Bailey recalls:

Then the lights went up and we sang another hymn and made for the door, taking a ticket and signing the pledge, week after week: 'I promise to abstain from all intoxicating drinks as beverages'. I didn't understand the last bit, but this one thing I knew. That ticket was my all-important pass to the Lycett Christmas party. After the party, the children sat in rows to receive a present and those with most attendance tickets sat in the front. There on display was the most wonderful collection of toys. Dolls by the dozen, dressed in every hue, books and games, and cars and wooden horses. We came out in turn to choose one thing from the array. There was no time for sympathetic pondering though. Your mind had to be made up before you got to the front. If you hesitated you'd get handed anything the helper thought fit. I always got a doll.

Back in Duckett Street, Stepney, Mary Ann Bowyer, widowed by the Great War, had faced enormous hardship in feeding and clothing her children in the desperate 1920s. Yet they had survived so far and now her 22-year-old daughter Sarah was about to fly the nest. Sarah was courting a lad living on the other side of Duckett Street at No. 58. He was 23-year-old James Siggins, a happy-go-lucky labourer. Sarah and James tied the knot at St Dunstan's Church in September 1927 and the following year the couple were blessed with a daughter, Irene – a grandchild for Mary Ann.

A grandson, Edward David, was born two years later in the East End Maternity Hospital in Commercial Road. He became known as 'Eddie' and, within four years, the young lad would have two brothers for company when Ronald was born in 1932 and Leslie in 1934.

The family settled at 33 Ocean Street (which ran parallel to Mary Ann's home in Duckett Street) and young father James Siggins struggled to pay the rent with an income from lorry driving and painting. His son, Eddie Siggins, wrote this account of his childhood in the early 1930s.

The front door of No. 33 was shabby, had once been painted green and had a dirty brass plate inscribed 'Dr Lewis', whoever he was. The exterior of the property was very dark, black really and grimy with years of accumulated soot and filth. The back end of it also butted onto the flank end wall of a fairly new block of flats called Frances Gray House [opened by the Duchess of York in March 1933], which towered over us. No. 33 was on the corner of Ocean Street and Mum, Dad and us kids occupied just the upstairs floor, which was illuminated by gas light and had two large living-room windows overlooking the street.

Our home consisted of two small bedrooms on a split-level, a living room cum kitchen, and a separate toilet, which boasted genuine Victoriana

Eddie Siggins's father, James, standing behind his brother Fred (on his left) and friend Charlie Rost (on his right). The photograph was taken in the 1920s.

Mary Ann Bowyer's family: taken in the garden of 63 Duckett Street at the wedding of one of Mary Ann's daughters, Jess, to Charles Self on 22 March 1926. Mary Ann's daughter Sarah (Eddie Siggins's mother) is behind the groom's right shoulder; Mary Ann, Eddie's 'Nana' and head of the family, is on the bride's left. Eddie knew Charles Self as Uncle Wag.

with a fixed mahogany wooden seat. Even the pan itself was beautifully decorated inside and out with flowers and garlands of leaves in a blue Chinese willow pattern. The living room was a reasonable size with a large wooden dresser and cast-iron cooking range. At the side of the chimneybreast was a grey enamelled cast-iron gas stove on a stone plinth, the property of the Gas Light and Coke Company, who supplied most of the equipment in the area. Next to this, and in the corner of the room, was a shallow kitchen sink – once white inside – and our pet guinea pig lived below, behind a short curtain.

We had a wireless set (which was battery operated and was recharged for a small fee in Shandy Street) and Mum, a tiny woman with glasses who possessed a terrific sense of humour, would always be listening to the dance bands and singers like Al Bowlly [who died in the London Blitz in 1941]. I remember the radio was plonked on the kitchen table, which was covered in baize cloth. I had seen some poorer homes where they simply used old newspaper as a covering and they could read the news as they ate.

In the bedroom, used by sister Irene and myself, the bed bugs were very active. Most of the houses were infested and you couldn't get rid of them. I think they lived beneath the wallpaper and they seemed to get in the bedsprings. Dad, thankfully a very relaxed man considering the circumstances, would regularly paint the springs with paraffin but it didn't work. Irene and I would have contests in the morning to see how high up the wall we could jump to squash the bugs with our little fingers.

The ground floor of No. 33 was divided into a couple of flats; one elderly woman lived in one room and a lady and her young daughter lived in a couple of rooms opposite. We became very friendly with the little girl, who became like a sister to us. Since her mum was known as Hetty, she was called Little Hetty. Little Hetty's grandfather ran the corner shop opposite and everyone called him 'Grandfather'. The shop had a covered yard at the back

and a side door from which loose coal and coke was sold in small quantities. It was possible to buy 14 pounds at a time, which was weighed in a large scuttle on scales. People would go over and collect this in small homemade carts, which were a bit rickety. Others used sacks or shopping bags. They could afford just enough to keep the fire going, so a shopping bag would usually do the trick.

I remember fixed to the black flank wall over the shop were some large enamelled metal posters for 'Sunlight Soap', 'Coleman's Mustard', 'Hudson's Powder', 'Lyon's Tea', 'Zebra Grate Polish' and 'Cherry Blossom' shoe polish. 'Grandfather' was a slim, bearded man, usually dressed in a peaked naval cap and roll-necked jersey. It was a general store – I particularly remember the stale jelly babies – and Dad would send me over to get him a packet of five Woodbines with the promise to pay the twopence [less than 1p] at the end of the week. Little Hetty helped out 'Grandfather' after school and often slept on the empty coal sacks at the back of the sheds all night, even though she was only eight. She became one of the family and when she moved away it was almost like a bereavement.

There were also some small stables in Ocean Street, owned by Mickey Shaw, and one of his buildings abutted No. 33. He would sometimes leave a horse and cart standing outside our front door and I would crawl underneath its belly and back. Oh, the smell in summer! The aroma was pungent in hot weather and filled the house with thick odour.

Beyond our street were a large number of shops, many of them Jewish, and I would often notice strange smells coming from them. Overall, the world outside our house was very scruffy and very run down. At least our relatives were very close. In Duckett Street lived my grandma at No. 63 – Mary Ann – who I called 'Nana Bowyer' and whose maiden name was Marshall. She had lost her husband in the First World War and was the head of the whole family.

(left) The Duchess of York opens Frances Gray House in Ocean Street, Stepney, on 23 March 1933, with Brownies in attendance.

(below) The Duchess of York inspects the balcony of Frances Gray House. The crowd below is congregated at the junction of Ocean Street and Master Street.

Eddie and Irene Siggins in the garden of 63 Duckett Street in the early 1930s.

Nana often wondered what had become of her little sister Alice, who was sent to Canada in the 1880s because the family couldn't afford to keep her. The children's father had announced Alice was going on a holiday but she never returned after he led her down to the docks where a young couple were waiting to collect her. Nana would quickly wipe away a tear when the subject cropped up. She became very upset about it and never came to terms with it.

My Dad's parents, the Sigginses, also lived in Duckett Street, at No. 58, which was almost opposite Nana's. Grandad and Grannie Siggins lived in a wonderful place. Grannie kept her best ornaments and other things she treasured locked in the small front room, and sometimes I was allowed a peek in. It was an Aladdin's cave, dark and musty, with porcelain and china figures on top of furniture and stuffed birds beneath domes. The fireplace, with its carefully black-leaded stove, had a wooden mantle shelf to which was fixed a dark velvet, scalloped mantle cloth with tassels on the front. Upon this shelf were polished brass shell cases and pride of place went to a German steel helmet, also blackened to match the fender. A hand grenade was placed either side and leaning against the grate was a bayonet used as a poker. All this had come from Uncle Bill, the eldest son of the family, who was gassed during the Great War.

Grannie Siggins was a jolly old soul and always keen to give a cuddle. She usually wore her hair in a little bun tied to the back of her head and sometimes wore a cloth cap with a hat pin passed through the cap and the bun to keep it in place. I recall seeing her go to the snug bar of the Anchor and Hope pub in Duckett Street, where you could get take-away beer. She took a china jug covered over with her long black apron and believed that looked more respectable when she went to get Grandad's pint of porter, which was similar to Guinness. Grandad meanwhile, with one leg missing, often sat out on the pavement on a bentwood kitchen chair, watching the world go

Nana was a lovely woman but quite capable of giving you a clump if you stepped out of line or became too cheeky. Her house, where my Mum Sarah had been brought up with 12 other children, was very dark and gloomy. It was where Nana had herself grown up during the time of Jack the Ripper but she now had all three floors and not just the middle room she had lived in as a child.

In Nana's backyard was a detached brick toilet with a wooden door, which had a gap at the top and bottom for ventilation purposes. Once, as a wind-up, I stayed in there when I knew Nana wanted to use it. Then a deluge of cold water suddenly came in through the gap at the top. That got me out pretty quick, but not before Nana clipped my ear as I passed her. It was not wise to upset her but she always gave us kids a penny on Sunday – known as the 'Sunday Penny' – if we had behaved that week.

(right) Eddie's Grandma Siggins, Grace.

(far right) Eddie's 'Uncle Bill' (second from the left, with hand on hip), pictured in France with World War One comrades.

(below) Thomas George Siggins, who was badly deformed and suffered from osteoporosis. He is seen here sitting with his sister Maud, who cared for him during his life.

by, as did many East Enders. He didn't smile a great deal and was not very approachable.

Another family character who would sit out on the street was my Dad's younger brother Thomas. He had been born quite normal but then suddenly began losing the calcium in his bones and became badly deformed. He suffered from osteoporosis and his case was featured in The Lancet *in 1927. He was cared for by his sister Maud and lived at the Sigginses' place at 58 Duckett Street. He used to pull himself around on his hands and then sit on a chair in the street and chat to anyone who would stop. He also used to push himself along in his wheelchair and earned a few pennies by taking bets to the bookmakers.*

The Anchor and Hope pub was the centre of life, situated as it was between Ocean Street and Duckett Street. An old charabanc used to turn up outside the pub to take local families to Southend once or twice a year. As we left, a cry would go up: 'Throw out your mouldies [spare change]!' and pennies would rain down from windows. There was also a lot of gambling outside the pub on Sundays — which was illegal. The men would gather in rings in the road and play 'Pitch and Toss', which involved betting on which side of a flicked coin would land first. Suddenly a great cry of 'Coppers!' would go up and everyone scarpered into anyone's house. Kids would naturally shout warnings too, just for fun, which added to the drama.

During this time my brother Ronald, who was frail, went to stay with my Auntie Jess and Uncle Wag in Leytonstone for a short while, so he could be fed up. He never came back. They brought him up as their own child and the arrangement suited everyone, since they were childless and we were poverty stricken.

I frankly don't know how my parents coped. If any neighbours had grapes in the house when nobody was ill, they were thought to be well off. We

Images of the 1930s

Humphrey Spender, who became a leading exponent of documentary photography, began to film living conditions in London in 1934 while studying to become an architect. At the time, he was influenced by the idea that many of the social problems in poor urban areas were due to substandard housing and believed that sound architectural principles might go some way towards alleviating them. A probation officer gained him access to homes in Stepney and his resulting portfolio included these evocative images entitled: 'Children playing in street' **(left)**, 'Woman with mangle' **(below)** and 'Teatime' **(right).**

(above) Two additional 1930s images from an unknown photographer entitled: 'A little Brady Street mother weighed down by the weight and care of a little sister' and **(below)** 'The slum child in bed, Bethanal Green home'.

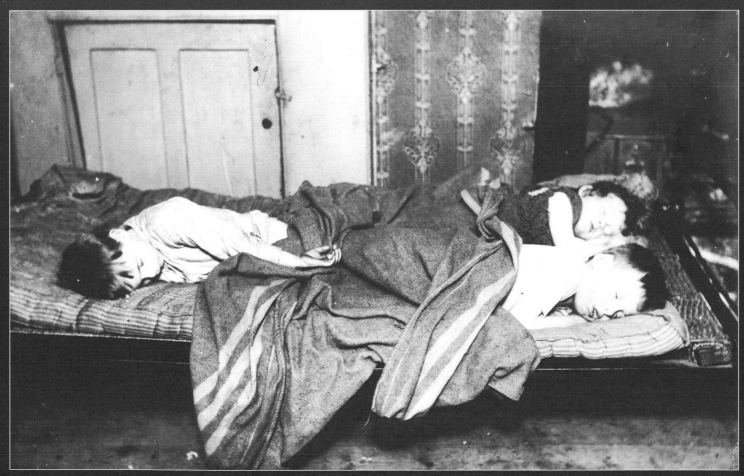

ate a lot of porridge, bread and jam and if any of us complained about the hard, stale bread Mum would reply: 'It's harder when there is none'. We also had snacks of bread and sugar or condensed milk on bread. Sausage stew was a regular too, and thick pea soup with a pig's knuckle thrown in was nice if you got any of the meat on it. On Sundays, we sometimes had a treat such as seedy cake [with caraway seeds], winkles, celery, watercress or jelly and custard.

They were certainly hard times but the old Stepney also had wonderful warmth about it and genuine community support. I recall how the poor Roman Catholic families would be visited by 'Guardian Angels', a Miss Slattery and Miss Pickett, who would leave a signed promissory note worth 1s 6d [7.5p] which could be redeemed at local shops. People did look out for each other and tried to do what they could for their neighbours.

Further east, young Charlie Smith was living in South Molton Road, Canning Town. He recalls:

I was born just within wedlock and 36 hours after my cousin Joyce Galvin, who was born in the very next bed in Plaistow's Howard's Road Hospital. East End childhood in the Thirties was a curious blend of naivety and craft. An environment where one was expected to be seen but not heard and to speak only when spoken to and, all too often, being reminded: 'You're only a kid'. In the harsh practical way of the poorer working class, one was a child yet not a child; loved yet feeling unloved. Another home rule was always to respect one's elders, which included being nice to all such persons, particularly visitors, even if you hated them. I painfully and embarrassingly remember being literally swept up by large aunts. After an age I would be dropped down breathless and feeling how a tube of toothpaste must feel while waiting for the inevitable comment: 'Doesn't he look like his father?' to which grandfather would retort: 'Yes, you can tell his mother didn't take in lodgers!'

I lived with my Mum at the small terraced home of the Mosses, who were an elderly couple with a son called Ernie, who was in his thirties. My Grandma and Grandad lived in the same road as us and would help look after me when Mum worked as a waitress. Mum and I had the front room for a shilling [5p] a week and we also had use of another room when old man Moss died, which was handy when Dad was on leave from the Gloucester Castle passenger ship.

Ernie became the man of the house when his dad died. He had weird decorating ideas like fixing several papier-mâché egg trays around the fireplace and painting them black and white. He also sawed the kitchen door in half to make a gate for his chicken run before hanging a Christmas chicken by its legs from the backdoor frame and beating the living daylights out of it with a broom handle. Mind you, his dad used to chop chickens' heads off and watch them career round the backyard until they dropped, so it wasn't that odd.

Ernie used to take me to school for Mum and serve up his speciality when I got home – cold custard in a brown glazed dish, which fell out in a solid lump. He was kind, however, and taught me draughts and other games, and he would cheat so that I could win. Nonetheless, I recall one occasion when my Dad came home. I was upstairs and Ernie said: 'Come on Smiffy, it's time for your bath'. Dad stormed up and said: 'Clear off – he's my kid not yours.'

Ernie died when I was seven and my Mum took over the tenancy. The house was a typical Canning Town property, the prized fixtures inside being the black-leaded grate, a butler sink, and the pièce de résistance – and what set us apart from the neighbours – an upright piano which no one could play. I remember how the closeness of the houses and a large blank factory wall seemed permanently to prevent sunlight from entering our living room window. Yet there were times when a ray would filter through the gap between the houses and factory and shatter into a million coloured lights against the wall as it passed through the coveted epergne, the ornamental glass centrepiece on the dresser consisting of crinkly-edged trumpets tinged in blue, green and red which rose majestically from a heavy base. It was used for flowers or sweets.

The focal point was the fireplace, topped with the traditional mantelshelf draped with fancy-edged lace or tasselled chenille runner. Poorer homes would cover the shelf with a poorer 'Empire Cloth' of the type usually seen on kitchen tables. Around every mantelpiece I saw were reminders of the Great War, like sepia photos, brass artillery shell cases in the hearth and odds and sods – like buttons – and pins for the Sunday night winkles. On top sat ornamental vases at each end and a centrepiece like a marble clock. One-upmanship was achieved by owning a pair of bronze statuettes on ebony bases. The houses of merchant seamen, I recall, were also adorned with wonderful curios from their travels. I remember seeing an elephant's foot, complete with toenails, hollowed out into a sort of dish, and stuffed tortoises made into ashtrays.

Outside was the toilet of course, the 'carsey'. Toilet rolls were for the rich and so we made do with newspaper from which the print readily transferred to the flesh. Grandma used to give me two jobs on a Sunday morning: rubbing triangular blocks of rock salt into granules for cooking and tearing the newspaper into 8-inch squares for the toilet. The loo seat was scrubbed white and to dispense with this chore Mum once painted it mauve. I wasn't told and came home from school and sat on it. I was stuck firm and only gained 'lift off' by using my little arms as lever props. Then my palms were stuck fast. But the pain of getting off was nothing compared to getting the paint off my buttocks with margarine and paraffin.

Family bath times were restricted to a Friday or sometimes a Saturday

(from left to right):
Charlie Smith (right) with cousin Joyce Galvin, 1929.

Charlie Smith, aged 27 months, in November 1931.

Charlie Smith, the cowboy in 1935, with Uncle Frank behind him and Uncle Stan alongside. Also pictured is Charlie's cousin, Joyce

night soak. *The bath itself was hung on the fence out the back during the week and brought in for the bathing ritual. Its dimensions – 3 feet by 2 feet – dictated a knees-up position for anyone over 4 feet tall and adults usually stood or risked large hips becoming stuck. The pecking order was youngest first and dads last, in mostly the same water, which was constantly ladled out and topped [up] by a kettle or saucepan. I was always warned not to pee in the water and, since perfumed soap was for cissies, we had carbolic or coal-tar brands like 'Family Health', 'Lifebuoy' and 'Wright's', which smelt so strong Mum said the germs were killed. If the Nit Nurse was due to visit school, our hair would be washed with 'Derbac' soap, an evil-smelling, eye-stinging black bar to control head lice. This was followed by torture dreamed up in Hell – a small–toothed comb used vigorously for lice and scurf removal, leaving me pleading with Mum to stop.*

The other main routine was Monday washday. The 'whites' were the priority and all of them seemed to be boiled for hours with 'Sylvan' soap flakes and soda. Many didn't have a gas boiler and had to rely on the old-fashioned copper. The bowl of the copper was a large cast-iron cupola about 2 feet in diameter. The grate below it, with its small opening, made it almost impossible to throw coal in so firewood was relied on instead. To get the boil started it had to be lit around 6.00 a.m. with wood. To earn a ha'penny, I would cut up the wood into regulation 9-inch by 1-inch strips to fit the copper's grate. I was always looking for wood and Bradley's, the corner grocer, always had old boxes. I was a gullible lad and once Uncle Alf suggested I ask Woodcock's, the undertakers in Freemasons Road, if he had any empty boxes to spare. George Woodcock said he'd put me in a polished box with brass handles if I came back again.

To bring the whites up to the correct pre-boil state, the linen was scrubbed with blocks of washing soap against a ribbed glass washboard and dunked in the sink or a bowl of warm water. Once in the copper for the boil,

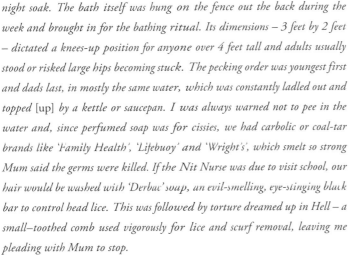

the clothes were pushed down with a copper stick. The mangle then awaited the boiled clothes, and ours stood in the backyard. Then the clothes would be hung out in the yard before being starched and ironed. Those without coppers bagged their washing in a hessian sack and took it to the 'Diploma', the bag-wash shop where the sack was ticketed and thrown into a large boiling tank with everyone else's dirty washing.

I hated coming home from school on Monday to find our place running with condensation and washing everywhere. But I loved watching Grandma ironing with two flat irons straight from the hob onto a tatty scorched piece of blanket laid on the kitchen table. Grandma would remove the iron, spit on it, and if it sizzled and danced across the smooth surface, it was right for ironing.

Hygiene was minimal in homes and council fumigation men were often called to deal with bed bugs, fleas, black beetles (Uncle Alf kept bike clips on his legs in their kitchen because he was so frightened of them), mice and rats. In the absence of fridges, food was kept in cupboards or food safes protected by perforated metal sides from fly invasion. Flypaper hung from lights and was changed regularly, the mass of struggling or dead flies being cremated on the range. With the family dining table situated in the centre of the kitchen, directly under the light fitting, the sight of close-packed fly paper did little to improve one's appetite as it dangled close to clusters of jars, packets and dishes directly beneath.

The children I mixed with seemed to come from homes containing at least six to eight people. They arrived at school looking tired and dishevelled. One of my best schoolboy pals had to share a 3-foot bed with three of his brothers and sisters, sleeping head to toe. There was always a problem if one was a bed-wetter and children would ask their mother if they could sleep 'in the shallow end'. Mother terrified me into keeping my bed dry by threatening me with 'a baked mouse for breakfast'. Most women in the area seemed to be instilled with the same toughness because of the harsh environment. They

(From left to right):

Ellen Ackred (née Neport), aged nine (top left), beside her brother James; in front, are sisters Renie (left) and Joycie (right).

Ellen Ackred's grandfather, Sam Neport.

Ellen Ackred's Nan, Mary, who lived in Falkirk Street, Hoxton.

had no alternative if they wanted their families to survive. Their ruddy faces and gnarled and chapped hands were testament to their inherited slavery over the washing and scrubbing board. They seemed old before they were 40, ravaged by poor health, poor diet and exhausted from giving birth to large families. To us children, all female neighbours were known as 'Auntie' and due respect shown.

The streets of Canning Town were as colourful as elsewhere. There were street photographers taking pictures for a penny and developing them on the spot; turbaned Indians selling from boxes around their necks; and horse-towed roundabouts, mounted on roller skates, which seated six children and were pushed around by the huffing and puffing owner. Bonfire Night was the most eagerly awaited occasion, apart from Royal processions. We'd collect wood for weeks and bonfires were built in the middle of the roads. However, there were few fireworks so they were ignited together. I came home once to see the best Guy ever, with bangers in its mouth, rockets in its hat and others in its hands. When I got close, the Guy came alive. My Uncle Alf had given me the fright of my life. Children used this ruse to get money until a boy, dressed as a Guy, was stabbed to death in the Thirties by a man testing to see if the dummy was real or stuffed. School assemblies gave out warnings after that.

Another memory was watching the bigger girls organise a mock May Queen procession. The unfortunate young Queen was dressed in a variety of old lace curtains and chenille tablecloths filched from the rag-and-bone man or 'borrowed' when Mum wasn't watching. The Queen's crown was fashioned from a battered old enamel colander with street weeds like dandelions and daisies poked in the holes and the Royal coach was a boy's barrow.

Returning to Bethnal Green once more, Ellen Ackred (née Neport)

remembers a 1930s' world where working hard and playing hard wove together to define a tough life on the very margins. She recalls:

I used to travel from my home in Hassard Street in Bethnal Green to see my Nan in Hoxton's Falkirk Street. It was a pretty lively area and places like Essex Street were simply no-go areas, where shady men played cards in the street and outsiders ventured at their peril. One place nearby even became known as 'Kill Copper Court'.

Nan lived in a big tenement block and was a clothes dealer who would pawn her jewellery in Hoxton for cash to buy stock. Then, with all her clothes to sell wrapped in a white sheet and slung over her back, she'd take them to Hoxton Market where she had a stall. Grandad had his own stall there selling menswear. This business of buying and selling clothes was called 'wardrobe dealing' and Nan and Grandad would also travel to Stamford Hill to see regular customers, or Southgate to buy more stock. I helped out at their Hoxton stalls in the Thirties and our family always had nice clothes thanks to Nan. My aunt, Caroline Cox, also had her own stall and she was a tough lady too. Aunt would shout at the punters and used to pretend to buy the goods herself if punters were hesitating and mucking her about. She would end up covered in hats and it was great market showmanship.

After trading, Nan and Grandad would gather their earnings and go on the booze for weeks at a time. They would meet up in the Rose and Crown and basically stay there for several weeks until they spent their money and returned to work. Then Nan would pawn her jewellery for stock and the whole process started again. There was a lot of fun in those days. Nan had great parties where my Aunt Caroline would play the piano and tell hilarious

Hopping in the 1930s: Ellen's Nan, Mary, is wearing a headscarf and Ellen's Mum, also called Ellen, is to Nan's left.

(below left) George Mooney, aged 17.

George Mooney's father, James, who served in the Royal Navy during the Second World War.

stories. I remember once her house being packed with a spellbound crowd as she recalled a chap called Old Paddy Riley who had died but suddenly came to life in his coffin.

Nan would also take us hopping.[1] *We all stayed in a hut at a Whitbread farm and were paid a shilling [5p] for each bushel we collected. It was a big occasion and Nan always had a new hat and arranged for a Daimler car to take us down there in style. At night we would all sit around a big table in our hut and pretend we were 'The Knights of the Round Table'.*

Violence, great pride and strict discipline meanwhile continued to underpin family life in the Thirties, as Ken Snow, living in Haverfield Road, Bethnal Green, and George Mooney, living in Exmouth Street, Stepney, recall. Mr Snow recalls the curious husband-wife loyalty which had existed for generations:

Grandad was a different man with drink in him and on Saturday night would storm upstairs to 'sort the old lady out'. Grandma often had black eyes and bad bruising and once someone said to her: 'Your husband's a bastard for doing that.' She snapped back: 'Don't call him that – he's my husband and I love him.' The women simply had to rely on the men for money so they

could bring their children up. My Mum and her two sisters had 29 children between them and it was desperate. And then even poorer kids would drop in and Mum would give them bread and dripping for tea too.

All the kids had holes in their shoes, hand-me-down clothes and shared beds. The smallest would even sleep in a chest of drawers. Yet still there was discipline all right. It needed only a look from Mum and Dad and we knew. When a woman relative came to visit, Dad just had to glare at the youngest and he would immediately get up and give up his chair. No questions. He did it or got a bad hiding.

---

[1] Hop-picking in Kent was a tradition that lasted from the late nineteenth century until the 1950s. Every September, families packed the railway stations, pushing rickety handcarts containing their belongings for the annual pilgrimage. It was a way of earning enough money for winter boots or a decent Christmas dinner and, despite the tiring work, it was the family's annual holiday. Many say these excursions were the happiest days of their childhood.

George Mooney recalls:

Despite the terrible poverty, I recall my grandfather, Charles Rockell, taking great pride in smelling his cigar, making a tiny hole in the end and constantly rolling it in his hands in a lengthy sort of ritual that one could almost mistake for good breeding. My Mum's brothers would also walk proudly down the street in their plus fours and Uncle Joe loved buying classy misfit suits – ones with buttons missing or which were not quite right – from Savile Row. They strolled about as though they were kings. Indeed, Grandad passed on his East End philosophy to me. He said: 'You walk down the street like you own it. You treat everyone down it with respect. And if you do neither, you'll get a clip round the ear'ole from me.' Discipline was at the heart of the family. Everyone was kept in line so all could survive. Discipline started with Grandma or Grandad and when your own Mum said 'no' you knew she meant it.

My Mum was tiny but her hands were hard and rough from years of cleaning at the Admiralty in Whitehall. She once confronted a man who had been beating my friend on the back with a belt, causing horrible weals. He was about to take off his belt again and have a go at his own son and me. Then Mum picked up some horse dung from the street and shoved it straight in his face. The man, a strapping docker, said: 'I'll get the old woman to sort you out.' Mum simply shoved another load in his face and replied: 'That can be for her then!' How could you not have respect for a woman like that?

She had had a tough upbringing herself. She was the oldest of 12 and once asked her Mum for a doll. Her Mum replied: 'I had 12 of you kids so what do you want a doll for? Your brothers and sisters can talk – play with them.' They were the last of the Victorian era where Grandfather was boss. I recall having to knock on his bedroom door before entering. It wasn't fear, just respect. In some homes, there were beatings to instil discipline but in the majority of cases the kids still cried their eyes out when Mum or Dad died. Discipline was reinforced in school too and I remember our sports master at Blakesley Street School flicking offenders with a cricket bat. The birch was also used, albeit rarely, if you fell foul of the courts.

A sense of community was the other binding influence, and all those streets crammed in between Commercial Road and Cable Street – Tarling Street, Cornwall Street and Martha Street – had their own sense of identity. If we were playing football in Blakesley Street (with a ball made from tied-up bundles of newspaper) and kids from another road appeared, they would be told to 'Op it'. It was a friendly rivalry but it preserved the closeness of the street and the feeling of village life in a town.

Meanwhile, Watney Street Market beat at the heart of Stepney's 'village' life. George Mooney recalls:

It was the place to meet people and catch up with news as well as do business. Stepney will never forget its characters. There was the stall run by the mum of boxer Harry Mizler, the Lightweight Champion of Britain, which sold fish at the top end of Blakesley Street. I can still picture Jewish grandmothers inspecting the gills of fish for freshness – even though they were still wriggling in a galvanised bath. Then there was the second-hand stall of Mr Bowles, who sat on an orange box with a straw hat looking like W. C. Fields. Outside Christ Church in Watney Street was 'Jackie Banana', who would auction hands of bananas for 1s 6d [7.5p] and a bag of old ones for 6d [2.5p]. There was also Apple's and Donner's general store, run by Jews, where toys were pinched and passed back through the legs of boys to a 'runner' who would scarper with it while those in the shop denied all knowledge.

Yet my favourite was Norman's Oil Shop in Watney Street. There was a wonderful smell in there, an accumulation of years of smells ingrained in the wooden floors. It was a mixture of vinegar, cabbage, onions, paraffin, firewood, mustard pickles, soda and soap. Nearby was Waller's the butchers in Watney Street, where Uncle Bill Rockell worked. He was always late and being told off and the parrot inside picked up on it. The bird could often be heard in the shop screeching: 'Rockell, you bastard – you're late!'

Further along was Payne's fish stall, where Gran sent me to buy bloaters [smoked herring] with the order: 'Make sure the roe are soft'. I stood there and squeezed it once and the owner threatened to squeeze me if I carried on doing it. I informed him my gran was Margaret Rockell, and he quickly said: 'That's all right then!' Such was Gran's reputation for no nonsense.

There was also Anderson's the bakers in the Market, where you could buy four cakes for the price of three. Gran gave me the money if I did my errands and went to church – and she would check with Rev. Groser at Christ Church that I had been there. Incidentally, Rev. Groser was a much-loved local man who would go to the Masons Arms in Watney Street in his cassock and challenge the dockers to darts over a pint. They loved him.[2]

Finally there was the sweet stall near Shadwell Station, where we stood mesmerized as a man worked his Bunsen burner beneath a copper dish to heat the sugar. The chap would then pull the soft toffee over a hook and pull it and pull it until he had enough to cut into sweets before it hardened. The smell was almost as good as that wafting from Anderson's the bakers or the wonderful Oil Shop.

---

[2] Australian-born Rev. St. John Groser was invited to be a priest at Christ Church in 1928, at a time when it was going to be pulled down. He built up such a thriving congregation that the building was reprieved. A great champion of the poor, he also played the part of Thomas à Becket in the 1951 film of T. S. Eliot's play *Murder in the Cathedral*.

High Street, Aldgate, March 1936.

High Street, Aldgate, north side,
March 1936.

Weighing ivory at London Docks in the 1930s. London was the centre of the world's ivory trade, handling over 90 per cent of total imports and exports.

(above) Aerial view of part of the Royal Docks in 1924 with King George V Dock in the foreground and Royal Albert Dock beyond. The large three-funnelled ship is the *Belgenland*.

(below) Aerial view of London and St Katharine Docks around 1930, looking east. The massive warehouses in these docks stored thousands of tons of cargo from all over the world.

Bob Humphreys with his father Joe and the family's racing greyhound 'Ribby'.

Bob Humphreys and parents, Joe and Lily, outside the family business on the corner of Francis Road and St Mary's Road, Leyton. Joe worked three nights a week on the *Hackney Gazette*.

The cramped streets also provided the Thirties children with both a playground and opportunities for enterprise. George Mooney recalls:

We would dig up lumps from the road, known as 'tarry blocks', which were then sold as fuel. Alternatively, we would break up old wet-fish boxes for firewood and surround it with scraps of dry wood and try and sell that for the same purpose. Anything, in fact, to earn the threepence [about 1.5p] to take down to Harding's Pie and Mash shop in Commercial Road. The threepence would get you a big dollop of mincemeat pie and mash, and the gravy there – we called it the 'liquor' – was fantastic and made from fish stock, cornflower and ground parsley. Other favourites were pease pudding with a savaloy stuck in it or 'skate eyeballs' – round fleshy lumps of fish which cost one penny [about 0.5p] for five. The Waste Market along Whitechapel High Street was another popular haunt. We'd take our earnings up there to buy ball-bearing wheels and then find planks of wood and tarry blocks to make scooters. Roller-skates were the toy to have but it could take a year to earn the 7s 6d [37.5p] they cost. It was well worth it, though. Blakesley and Watney Streets had asphalt surfaces and it was like skating on a ballroom floor.

Bob Humphreys grew up in Francis Road, Leyton, in the early Thirties, where his father opened up J. G. Humphreys & Son, a cycle and radio shop on the corner of St Mary's Road. He also remembers a life of street enterprise:

Horses were a source of money for us kids. When we wanted to earn a halfpenny for sweets, we would borrow a bucket and shovel from Mum and collect the horse droppings. Then we'd take the manure around the gardens and try and sell it for ½d [less than 0.5p] a bucket. Alternatively, the other good source of income was bottle collecting. We would get hold of as many as possible and return them to the various shops, who would then give back half a penny on each one. There was also the coalman. While he was delivering the coal bags in the back of houses, we would swiftly nick one or two lumps from his cart and then make ourselves scarce. When we had enough, a full bag could be sold for a few pence. Of course, there was a lot of fun to be had, too. Most of the street traffic was horse and carts and the carts would have a couple of hooks on the back to hold the oats bags. We would hold onto the hooks and swing along for a ride until a kid called out 'Whip behind, Guv'nor!' to warn the owner. Then he'd crack his whip in warning.

Spending half a penny or a penny on sweets was always a serious business. With our noses pressed against the window, we would debate the merits of the various goodies. There were Chicago Bars, Alphabet Cachous, Love Hearts, Sherbet Dabs, Tangerine Bouncers, Locust Beans, Lemon

Squirts, Fairy Whispers, Uncle Joe's Mint Balls, Trebor's Clickety Click 66, Cough Candy and Ogo Pogo Eyes, to name just a few.

Then it would be off to play football, which had to be seen to be believed. We played with a rubber ball and there could be 25 on each side, playing from one end of the street to the other. We played through front gardens, off house walls and even occasionally off the roofs. Games would go on for hours and have incredibly high scores. Other games included tops, marbles, and 'Tin Can Copper'. The tin was placed on a manhole cover and was then kicked or thrown as far as possible. Everyone then sprinted to hide. The seeker had to run and get the tin and on his return try and spot as many hiders as possible. If he saw someone, he'd run back to the tin, put his foot on it and shout 'Tin Can Copper 123' and the person's name. They then came out and stood by the tin. If a wrong name was called the prisoners were released, so children swapped jumpers to confuse the seeker.

There were lots of tag games too and 'Releaser' involved a lot of fighting as two sides battled to free team mates held captive in doorways.[3] 'Hi Jimmy Knacker' was another one. It involved one side bending over in a line and the other side jumping on top of the bent backs and attempting to 'break' them while shouting 'Hi Jimmy Knacker 123'. Then there were all the things to collect. Conkers would be all the rage one week, then marbles and then something else. Fads came and went just like they do with children today.

Lily Towner (née Barclay), who was born in 1931, recalls her childhood in Dora Street, Limehouse:

The girls would skip and play hopscotch and, when we were naughty, tie string between the door knockers of two houses, bang on one door and then run away (a game known as 'Knock Down Ginger'). Rounders was popular too, or we would just sit in the gutter and play cards for buttons we had nicked from a shop. We were always poking around the markets too, like Chisp Street, Watney Street or Salmon Lane, looking for ribbons, which were all the craze in the Thirties. We also had our very own live entertainment. Every Saturday night we used to wait for 'The Fight' across the road. The husband over there would come back from the Vulcan pub in Rhodeswell Road steaming drunk and, within minutes, the shouting could be heard inside their house. My Gran would say: 'They are at it again' and then, true to form, the man and wife would appear in the street for a scrap. It was a real spectacle. There were lots of hard people about and I used to hate going into Carr Street to get Grandad's radio battery recharged because the kids there were vicious. The coppers were

always there too because the kids' parents often joined in the fights as well.

On a lighter note, we loved the annual Catholic Procession. It was a must to see it and all denominations packed the pavements while the roads were made spotlessly clean. The sash windows in Catholic homes were pushed up and lovely altars created with statues of the Virgin Mary and blazing candles placed upon satin-covered boxes. We then used to tour around Locksley Street, Turner's Road, Dixon Street and Rhodeswell Road, looking at the displays and waiting for the Procession which would go down Burdett Road, where all the trolley buses had stopped, and on to the Guardian Angels Church in Mile End Road. The Procession was stunning, with all the women and little girls in their beautiful white dresses and the parish priest following at the rear. Nuns would also make wreaths of flowers for the girls' hair and garlands were strung across streets and hung from windows. However, my Mum didn't go in the Procession because she couldn't afford to put money in the priest's collection box or pay for a dress. Later in the evening, the priest would return to bless every altar and there would be a party. My Mum had a piano and her sash window was taken out so it could be lowered onto the street, where everyone could gather round for a sing-song.

Seven miles away, just off the Barking Road, Eric Bissell recalls a colourful street childhood in 1930s' Plaistow:

I lived in Falcon Street in a typical small two-up, two-down house. My school was Grange Road in Plaistow and one of my teachers, Mr Bailey, was a strict disciplinarian who bore an uncanny resemblance to Neville Chamberlain. He taught maths and kept three canes in a jar of water (some said it was vinegar) which was placed in a prominent position. Everyone hated arithmetic and he would stand with his back to the class and write sums on the blackboard. Suddenly he would bark someone's name and demand the answer to the sum. If you got it wrong he would spin round and hurl the chalk at you. He expected you then to take the chalk up to the blackboard and work it out while he continued with the lesson. If you still got it wrong, he'd whack you on the hand with his cane and tell you to pay attention in future. All the children disliked him and in the playground the old music hall song 'Won't You Come Home Bill Bailey?' was amended to 'Won't You Go Home Bill Bailey?', and sung by everyone.

School ended at 4.15 p.m. and I couldn't get home quick enough. There was a great stampede to the gates and children sang and danced up the road and played games. Every boy seemed to collect cigarette picture cards and some even waited outside shops to plead with customers coming out with a packet of cigarettes. Boys were expert at flicking them as close as possible to walls in competitions to win them from each other.

---

[3] Contributors recall residents of flats being driven mad by gangs of children chasing each other up stairwells and along landings in a bid to evade capture.

The Humphreys' shop on the corner of Francis Road and St Mary's Road, Leyton, was almost wrecked one day in 1936 when a car drove too fast down Richmond Road opposite and turned over after attempting a right turn. The driver was slightly hurt. Young Bob Humphreys can just be seen among the on-lookers. He is the boy standing on the pavement and nearest to the roof of the vehicle.

At weekends, you could always go to the local markets for a bit of a laugh. We had two quite close, Rathbone Street off Barking Road and Green Street, about a mile further on, where The Hammers played at Boleyn Upton Park. Saturday evening was a good time to visit and Green Street would be quite crowded by then. It was the ingenious methods the stallholders used to sell their goods to the most gullible which intrigued me.

One couple, who turned up occasionally, flogged second-hand suits. Unlike their competitors, they did not display any prices but a young lad in his teens would be at the front. He had a hearing aid from which a cord disappeared into an inside pocket. He would sit reading a comic until a potential customer would ask him how much a certain suit cost. He would then call to his father who was at the back and the reply would be shouted through: 'Thirty shillings [£1.50]'. The boy would cup his hand to his ear and shout back: 'How much did you say?' The price was repeated and then the boy would turn to the customer and say: 'Thirteen shillings, sir.' Taken aback, the customer couldn't believe his luck and would hastily hand over the money before the 'mistake' was discovered. Of course, they intended to sell it for 13 shillings [£0.65] all along.

Another stall sold jackets only and there was a full-length mirror on wheels so the customers could admire themselves before making a purchase. When a customer tried on a jacket, the salesman's left hand would deftly fasten the buttons while his right hand wandered unobtrusively to the rear,

taking up the slack should the coat be a little on the large side. 'Fits like a glove', he would beam. 'Straight out of Savile Row, Sir!'

There was also a shabbily dressed man called Charlie whose only concession to fashion was a bowler hat. He stood with a doleful expression on his face reminiscent of Stan Laurel. His companion, Dr Braithwaite, would explain he had been given a magic hair-restorer formula from an Indian tribe, while travelling by donkey in the foothills of the Andes in Peru. Pointing to a bald man in the crowd he would say: 'You Sir, yes you Sir, would benefit from this ointment'. The Doctor then explained his glum companion was actually going to sue him for money owed to his hairdresser because he now had to visit twice a week. With that Charlie took off his bowler hat and down fell beautiful golden tresses onto his shoulders, partially covering his face. The Doctor shrugged and said: 'Can I help it if he uses too much?' After the laughter subsided, someone would shout it was all a load of rubbish. The Doctor would reply: 'You'll be telling me next that hard work never killed anybody but why take the risk my friend?' Then Charlie would offer his bowler hat to collect the cash from those interested.

There were all sorts of other characters about. Joe was a busker who entertained the cinema queues while we waited to get into the Odeon at the Boleyn in Barking Road. He had a bent and battered trumpet, which he said had got trapped in the Boleyn pub door when he was once ejected. Red-faced and with inflated cheeks, he would try and force a tune from the wretched

Street markets have been part of the East End since the 1880s. A market in Green Street, bisecting West and East Ham, once sprawled along the road, but the advent of trams in 1904 forced a move to nearby Queen's Road, pictured here in 1925.

instrument and there was no escape from the din. Another cinema busker was a violinist, reminiscent of the American comedian Jack Benny in the way he interspersed his patter with his playing. With a doleful expression he would commence playing for a few minutes and then abruptly stop and say:

'My wife is very dear to me,
This fact I must concede,
With shopping trips and hair-dos,
Yes, she's very dear indeed.'

Then there would be more 'music' – it sounded awful – before he'd stop again and say: 'We were very poor when I was young… The mice would leave cheese out for us.' Then there would be another dose of atrocious playing before he'd say: 'I have a dog that doesn't eat meat… (pause)… I don't give him any.' And so the nonsense continued until he finished by proving he really could play the old fiddle pretty well. Sometimes it was better entertainment than the cinema show!

The advent of cinema was a great boon. We had several local ones – the Odeon Upton Park, Granada East Ham and the Broadway at Stratford. Their very opulence was something we had never seen, with wall-to-wall

carpets, plush seating, great central chandeliers, grand entrances and sweeping staircases. The programmes were long too, and the Granada had a one-hour variety show on occasions between two full-length films, plus Pathé newsreel. When there was no variety show, the great Wurlitzer organ came up from the bowels of the earth to entertain us. All this meant a three-and-a-half-hour show and, as the programmes were continuous, you could stay until the end if you had the stamina. In the winter the cinema was somewhere to go and keep warm, which was a real bonus.

At the other end of the scale was the 'tuppenny rush', which was a Saturday morning show for children only. Our local was the Greengate Cinema in Barking Road, which had seen better days, and the floor would be littered with peanut shells and orange peel by the time we left. Every Saturday we would pack in to see Tom Mix, Buck Jones and Hopalong Cassidy. They were usually Western serials which continued for many months. Our heroes would be left in irretrievable situations each week, only to be predictably rescued at the next visit. It was not uncommon for the film to break down or the sound to be lost. The management then had to try and keep us happy while it was fixed but it was not long before orange peel and the Smith's blue salt bags from crisp packets were being thrown at the screen. When the film resumed, it was not unusual to see Tom Mix chasing the Indians across the *desert while the silhouette of the cinema manager could be seen with a long-handled broom frantically trying to brush off a missile stuck to the screen.*

While youngsters flocked to the new cinemas, the Cockney exodus continued apace during the 1930s, with increasingly affordable homes springing up in Woodford, Ilford, Chingford and Barking. A three-bedroomed house with living room, scullery and bathroom could be bought for £600 in 1932, compared with over £1,000 in 1920. Though beyond the reach of the lowest paid, the lure of suburbia proved irresistible to the lower middle classes, whose worries about commuting were eased by expansion of Underground lines and improvement to roads. In fact, almost 2 million migrants (a third from Inner London) took advantage of the new arterial roads, bus and Underground services and moved to pastures new outside the capital between the two World Wars.

The better-paid manual workers also clambered aboard the bandwagon and, by the late 1930s, over 30 per cent of those taking out mortgages were wage-earners as opposed to salaried workers. Tens of thousands of seven-roomed semis were built to meet demand and, between 1921 and 1937, the population of outer London rose by 1.4 million, while that of central London fell by 400,000. The physical impact was dramatic: while Charing Cross was only 8 miles from the countryside (north or south) in 1900, this distance had almost doubled to 15 miles in 1939 as new buildings crept ever outwards from the capital.

The Late Victorian and Edwardian suburbs had consisted of neat rows of terraces and one extended East End family could occupy a large portion of an entire street. However, as detached and semi-detached construction came to dominate the inter-war years, a new lifestyle came with it. Front and back gardens appeared, signalling a discernible shift away from a tenement lifestyle hallmarked by families packed together in close proximity. Suburban space now gave the opportunity for isolated living and more privacy. Life in suburbia was curiously quieter and conducted with more discretion. The new Becontree council estate at Dagenham was rapidly filling up, leaving those left behind to joke that Bethnal Greeners were keeping coal in their posh new bathrooms because they did not know what they were for. By 1939, Becontree had 116,000 tenants. It was the world's biggest municipal estate, with 25,000 homes, 400 shops, 30 schools, 27 churches, 9 pubs and 4 cinemas.

Britain was emerging from the great depression by the mid-1930s and those in regular work enjoyed rapidly rising incomes in a brave new world. It was a world of petrol stations and bungalows with garages, a world of semi-detached houses equipped with electric power points, gas cookers and vacuum cleaners. 1935 also saw Britain's first flyover, Silvertown Way, carving its way through Canning Town.

London had largely side-stepped the economic stagnation which had so crippled other areas, thanks to its heavy involvement in serving the domestic market. Indeed, suburbia required wallpaper, irons and electric lamps, not to mention furniture, which the small workshop industries in Bethnal Green and Shoreditch gladly supplied. London also expanded its office workforce to meet the demands of banks, trading houses and government departments, while retail workers flocked to serve at new department stores and chain stores, like Boots, W. H. Smith, Lipton and Woolworth. The other Britain, encompassing Scotland and the north and west of England, was stuck in a Depression time-warp and 'hunger marchers' descended on the capital.

It was not all rosy in London's garden either; the docks and casual labour everywhere had been badly hit and the harshness of life permeated the East End as the following extracts reveal. Arthur McCartney lived in Silvertown, a tiny sliver of land sandwiched between the Royal Docks and the Thames:

We lived in a tiny terraced house in Clyde Road with two rooms upstairs and two downstairs. My father's brother and his family were upstairs – nine of them in all and they slept three to a bed. Downstairs was our family of five. There was a shared kitchen – in fact a tiny scullery – and the front door was used by all of us so the key was just left on a piece of string and left in the letter box. My Dad worked at the large Tate and Lyle sugar factory but it was casual work and he would just hope to be picked outside the gates by the foreman. I can't ever remember having a toy or present at Christmas or birthdays. I got a piece of fruit if I was lucky. I did find a penknife, however, and then began carving my own toys from bits of scrap wood. We were always so hungry and the best food was reserved for Dad because he needed his strength in the factory. I remember watching him eat lovely eggs and bacon while the rest of us made do with bread and jam.

For others, like Charles Young, living in Britannia Gardens, in Shoreditch, life was similarly hard:

Dad was a casual labourer so our family of six used to get our dinner from a Mission in Hoxton Square. We used to go down the markets too and pick up the rotten fruit and cut out the bad bits. At Christmas, there were no toys of course. We just used to get an orange or a bag of nuts. Needless to say, our family used the pawnshops all the time and there was one opposite our house. You could take anything in there and be given money for it. The catch was you had to pay a little more to get the item back and, if three months elapsed, the pawnbroker would simply keep the goods and sell them himself in his shop next door. We were so poor my Mum even took our sheets to the pawn on

Monday in order to get two bob [10p] and then she would pick them up again on Friday. I once had a little suit which we had to pawn and I never saw it again for three months. Then I had it back for one day and it went off again.

Harsh conditions bred a spirit of self-preservation and self-sufficiency, as the following two accounts reveal. Mrs Rosie Somers (née Ferman), living in The Buildings in Romford Street, Whitechapel, recalls:

Dad was a presser in the tailoring trade and often out of work. He borrowed £10 and became a barrow boy, and sold Covent Garden fruit in the East End. Mum also got a barrow when she was 40 and put it in Romford Street to sell fruit to The Buildings. There were four flats in all and they contained Jews. Once, Dad came home with three big barrels of apples. He took them into a playground and told us kids to 'cut away all the bad'. Then Mum sold them and we were given a few coppers for our help. Dad eventually went to work for a man in the West End as a presser, which was a big disappointment to my Mum because she wanted to set up a fruit and vegetable business. They were certainly hard times. My parents would borrow a pound from Mrs Lazarus upstairs to see us through and then lend the same to her when she needed it. We joked it was like the pound going up and down on the markets.

When my Mum died aged 47, I basically took charge of the household, even though I was only 14½. My Dad just sat there weeping and there were six of us kids to sort out. I had to buy all the food and I recall going to see a barrow boy once for vegetables. I collapsed in tears and the next day he came up with a load of vegetables as a present. A lady downstairs also helped me with the chores, and I looked after the younger children and prepared the food for Dad and the elder children to eat when they returned from work. I did all the washing in the sink, which was very hard, and if the sheets were not too bad I just left them. I remember the washing was strung out all around the kitchen so that the cooking would help it dry. We survived because we had to and, despite it all, I had a great sense of belonging to a community. The memory of Mum kept me going with the work I had to do. To this day, I can still see Mum sitting down for a chat and saying to me: 'I love talking to you'.

Ronald Wiltshire, living as a child in Old Bethnal Green Road, recalls:

The keeping of some sort of livestock was also a basic act of survival. My Dad was a milkman who worked for London Co-op and he used to take me down to Brick Lane Market to buy chicks. We reared them indoors with artificial light and had about 20 at one time. Then they went into the backyard where we fed them on boiled potato peelings. They gave us eggs through the year and at Christmas Dad would cut their throats and drain the blood from them in the larder. They were given as Christmas presents. We also grew as many vegetables as possible in the tiny garden, while next door my aunt and Grandad kept rabbits.

Back in Stepney, Eddie Siggins remembers sitting in class at Ocean Street School while his teacher was in full flow. Flushed and wide-eyed, she told them:

Boys, you are very lucky to be living in the greatest nation on earth. Privileged too. We have the biggest Empire. We rule the world. Lots of children would gladly change places with you lot.

Behind the teacher, a map of the world displayed the extensive splodges of red which identified an Empire 'where the sun never set'. A surge of pride swept through the classroom that day in 1936. It stopped at Eddie's desk. Eddie had heard the tales of his Nana Bowyer – Mary Ann – who had brought the mean streets of the Ripper era alive. He had heard Nana talk about her beloved Alfred, the grandad he had never known, who was lost in the Great War. Nana had endured a desperate struggle to bring up her 13 children at 63 Duckett Street. One of those children was Eddie's own mother, Sarah, who in turn had spoken of the hard, impoverished 1920s and the depressed Thirties in Stepney.

So was Britain so great? Why did some schoolmates have a dollop of malt ladled into their mouths while others received a bottle of milk to feed them up? Why did children try on tatty second-hand shoes from charity shops when they were brought into the classroom? Why did everyone have cardboard inside their shoes to cover the holes and why did the kids in Knott Street run in bare feet?

There were other stirrings too which young Eddie, at his tender age, would not have understood. The adult world was discussing Germany again, the building of a new Empire and something called Fascism. Both Germany and Italy were now ruled by Fascist regimes and civil war had broken out in Spain. In the pubs, people grumbled about troubled days ahead. Outside, a heavy, oppressive atmosphere suffocated Duckett Street. The heavens seemed peculiarly highly charged, as if Stepney was on the brink of an electrical storm. The new tension was accompanied by menacing, contorted faces, which snarled through the streets.

One night, young Eddie Siggins encountered them.

Chapter two

Men in black

A SINISTER SIGHT confronted Eddie Siggins. There, outside his Dad's favourite watering hole in Duckett Street, a hushed crowd were gathered around a small open-backed lorry parked in front of the pub. Standing on the back was a man dressed in dark clothes, speaking into a loudhailer. He was flanked by two intimidating individuals dressed in dark boiler suits. This pair wore khaki gas masks of Great War vintage from which short corrugated hoses coiled down to metal containers on their chests. They stood motionless and in silence. The whole shadowy scene outside 'Butterfill's' (as the Bull's Head was known) was lit by a couple of Tilley lamps positioned on the roof of the driver's cab. Young Eddie didn't like it one bit. He tugged at his Dad and asked to go home. The men in black were 'Blackshirts' and members of the right-wing British Union of Fascists (BUF), led by Sir Oswald Mosley, a Winchester-educated son of wealthy aristocrats. Eddie had seen them before when they marched down Duckett Street. He had watched them from Nana's window at No. 63 and remembered the strange silence that had enveloped the road. There was no noise, no shouting. Just an odd quiet until they were gone. Then a switch seemed to be clicked and life resumed its normal bustle.

The Fascists seemed to like meeting at this end of Duckett Street and perhaps, pondered Eddie, it was something to do with Sam's, the Jewish barber opposite Butterfill's. They also used the Mission Room in nearby Dongola Street (a venue above some stables known as 'Gudges', or 'The Hall'), where impressionable youngsters were handed treats and badges while the unemployed were told: 'It's the Jews who have your jobs and homes!'

At one such meeting, two Fascist youths had called out to the crowd: 'Who killed Christ?' A woman dared to reply: 'You did, you are doing it now!' The brave voice belonged to Edith Ramsay, head of Stepney Women's Evening Institute, who combined her adult learning classes with legendary and unofficial social work among the local poor. Edith had once received a letter from the Fascists demanding that Jews be turned out of the afternoon

Eliza Butterfill, licensee of the Bull's Head from 1881, pictured on the roof of the pub. Known as 'Auntie Butterfill' in the community, she would throw odd change down to the street from the roof to enable proud but jobless locals to enjoy a drink.

Inside the Bull's Head (known as Butterfill's) before the First World War, with landlady Eliza Butterfill, pictured on the right, holding a child.

classes that she held in Smithy Street, Stepney. She refused. However, a laundry class in Raleigh School in Ocean Street, which Jewish girls attended, was abandoned after Blackshirts stoned the building. The girls fled through a side gate but Edith walked calmly through the hate mob. Nonetheless, she would later blame herself for giving way when the class was re-formed at Trafalgar Square School and run by the Stepney Jewish Club instead.

Duckett Street was a Fascist stronghold and witness to scenes of violent raw hatred. Edith recalled a Jewish boy being tied up on an improvised cross in nearby White Horse Lane, and was shocked to hear how the only Jewish family living in Duckett Street returned home as late as possible so they could creep in unharmed by Fascists.

Rising tension radiated from Oswald Mosley himself. Tall, dark and debonair, Mosley had been Conservative MP for Harrow in 1918 but then converted to Socialism and won Smethwick for Labour in 1926. He was a rising star, even tipped as a future Prime Minister, and had succeeded to the family baronetcy in 1928. However, he became disillusioned with Labour and his public criticism of the Party led to his expulsion. Instead, Mosley became leader of the BUF, which he formed in 1932 after visiting Italy and securing an offer from Mussolini to secretly fund a British Fascist recruitment drive. It was a year before Hitler came to power in Germany, as Chancellor at the age of 43, and a year before the German Third Reich was born. Mosley's first priority was to deliver the BUF message that 'it was the intention of British Fascism to break for ever the power of Jews in Britain'. The British Jew must be 'excluded' from the host community urged Mosley, in an appeal to the basest sentiments of the East End working class.

The Jews had long gravitated towards East London and, from 1870 to 1914, this segment of the capital experienced its greatest influx of immigrants until the Commonwealth immigration after 1945. While the Thames waterside continued to attract Irish labourers, the Jews arrived to escape the pogroms and persecution in Alexander III's Czarist Russia. Building upon a long tradition of Jewish settlement, by 1887 the Spitalfields Jewish community stretched south to St George's, east to Mile End and across to Bethnal Green. It numbered around 45,000 and, in 1888, Whitechapel boasted over 1,000 tailoring workshops alone, as home-based sweatshops sprang up in tenements which, in an earlier era, had been stately homes built by the Huguenot merchants. The first Jewish youth club in Britain, 'The Brady Street Club for Working Lads', opened in Durward Street while the narrow streets filled up with close-knit *landsmanschaft* – families from the same town or village *shtetl* in Russia or Poland. They held a strong, emotional attachment to the *heim* (homeland) and unity was fed and nurtured via their *shtieblach* – small home-based synagogues.

By the mid-1930s, there were around 350,000 Jews in Britain and nearly half lived in the East End. Some 60,000 alone lived in Stepney, which housed more foreign-born residents than anywhere else in Britain. Further, Stepney and Shoreditch were the most overcrowded places in Britain in the mid-Thirties.

The East End therefore presented rich, fertile ground for Mosley to sow his seeds of prejudice, and he wasted no time. The BUF took to the road in a fleet of vehicles that became mobile speaking platforms for Mosley. His skilful oratory could fill the largest halls and membership of the BUF reached 20,000 at its peak. By 1934, the BUF had 42 London branches, and young men from the middle classes and white-collar workers formed the bulk of Mosley's membership and leadership. The young, the unskilled unemployed, dissatisfied municipal workers, unorganised workers in small workshops, costermongers, smallholders and shopkeepers also gravitated towards the organisation, yet only a minority were genuine activists, who swallowed the Fascist philosophy and followed Mosley on his grand tours.

It was in Stepney, Shoreditch and Bethnal Green that Mosley attracted his first mass following, at a time (1936–1938) when Britain's political landscape was subjected to major upheavals. The Labour Party had split between those who supported the National Government (effectively a Conservative administration) and those who did not. At the same time, the small but influential Communist Party had increased its membership from 7,700 in 1935 to 17,756 in 1937 and there was enormous mass support for the 'hunger marches' and Britain's northern unemployed, whose lives were still blighted by the Depression.

Then developments abroad sent new shockwaves rolling towards Britain. In 1936, bloody civil war erupted in Spain when Franco's right-wing Nationalists threatened the left-wing Republicans, who had been in power since 1931. Britain officially remained neutral, fearing a Republican victory might result in a Communist state on the western fringe of the Mediterranean. However, the British public was suddenly galvanised into an anti-Fascist movement in support of the Republicans and many left to fight in the International Brigades.

Violence had erupted closer to home too. During the autumn of 1932, there were battles between several thousand unemployed workers and mounted police when the Communist-led National Unemployed Workers Movement marched from depressed industrial areas to London. Two years later, there were appalling scenes of Blackshirt thuggery when hecklers at a BUF rally at London's Olympia were brutally beaten. Festering political turmoil came to a head in 1936. First, Mosley's Fascist activity and propaganda aimed against the East End Jews had reached a peak. The Jews were accused of clannishness and filthy habits; of swindling the innocent Gentiles and depriving them of jobs; of being both capitalists on the make and Communist agitators. Second, there was an outburst of British patriotism following King George V's death on 20 January, and 'Britons First' became a favourite Fascist rallying cry. Third, on 7 March, Fascist aggression demonstrated its global potential. Adolf Hitler, in the process of 'Nazifying' the German state, fortified his popularity and power in Germany by sending troops to re-occupy the Rhineland (a part of former Germany

Sir Oswald Mosley inspects his Blackshirts in Royal Mint Street, October 1936.

taken away by the Versailles Treaty, imposed after the First World War in order to straitjacket and humiliate the defeated nation). Britain complained but took no action against Hitler, whose foreign policy remained on a pre-set course: war.

Back in the East End, Fascist full-time workers had been installed in Bethnal Green, Hoxton and Poplar, and attacks on people and property escalated. As Mosley's Fascists effectively imposed a reign of terror in East London, the walls of Stepney became daubed with 'Get rid of the Yids' and 'PJ – Perish Judah'. The Labour Party, champion of the unemployed, tended to ignore the BUF, advising its own followers to stay away from Mosley's

meetings and to leave Labour MPs to make protests in Parliament. This left the Communist Party to fill the vacuum, together with minority groups such as the Jewish People's Council Against Fascism and Anti-Semitism, the Jewish Ex-Servicemen's Association and the Labour Party League of Youth. Tradesmen also signed petitions opposing the Fascists, and the Communist *Daily Worker* ceaselessly stressed the link between events in Nazi Germany and in Britain. Meanwhile violence on the streets escalated. Blackshirts made vicious nocturnal forays into the Jewish heartland and a huge anti-Fascist march to Victoria Park, led by Whitechapel MP J. H. Hall and veteran Suffragette Sylvia Pankhurst, was brutally ambushed by Mosley's thugs.

Then, in late September 1936, Mosley's BUF announced its intention to hold a Fascist march, terminating in Stepney – the heart of the Jewish East End. The marchers were to meet at 2.30 p.m. on 4 October 1936 in Royal

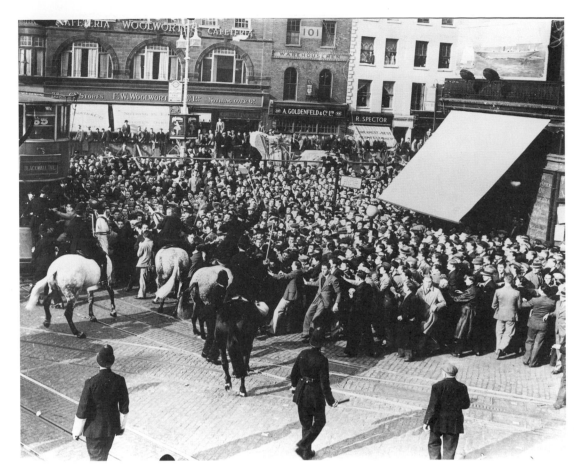

Police attempt to contain the huge crowd gathered at Gardiner's Corner, Whitechapel High Street, 4 October 1936.

Mint Street, where Mosley, 'The Leader', would inspect his troops. They would then march north up Leman Street to Gardiner's Corner and enter the East End via its two main arteries: Whitechapel Road and Commercial Road. The marchers would then disperse into support meetings at Aske Street in Shoreditch, Salmon Lane in Limehouse, and Stafford Road in Bow. The event would conclude with a triumphant finale at Victoria Park Square at 6.00 p.m., where Mosley would address his followers opposite their favourite pub, the Salmon and Ball. The date of the march, 4 October 1936, was significant because it was the fourth birthday of the BUF. It was to be an act of deliberate provocation against both Jews and Communists, but the East End had other plans. The slogan 'They Shall Not Pass' – borrowed from the Spanish Republicans – was on East End lips and being whitewashed onto walls and pavements, and action was to accompany the words.

The Young Communist League had already planned to hold a demonstration on 4 October in Trafalgar Square, against the Nazi-backed Spanish Nationalists, who threatened the Spanish Republic. Instead, the Trafalgar Square demonstration was called off and all branches of the Communist Party were ordered to Aldgate at 2.00 p.m. to confront Mosley's Fascists. Others sought to avert potential trouble. The Jewish People's

Council delivered a 100,000-name petition to the Home Office, protesting at Mosley's march being permitted, while George Lansbury, MP for Bow and Bromley, and the mayors of four East London boroughs appealed directly to the Home Secretary, Sir John Simon, to ban Mosley's inflammatory stunt. He refused, believing it would be undemocratic to do so. The anti-Fascist alliance now undertook a massive campaign of propaganda and mobilization, unseen since the days of the 1926 General Strike. Battle HQ was set up in Manningtree Street, a matter of yards from the front line at Gardiner's Corner, where Mosley's massed ranks would be approaching from the south. First-aid posts were also set up at Whitechapel Library, Cable Street and Toynbee Hall (perhaps the East End's best-known settlement for the poor, where Rev. Samuel Barnett had established an education centre in 1884).

As Mosley had already helpfully announced the route of his march (see the map, right), maximum opposition was arranged at Leman Street and Gardiner's Corner, which, if strong enough, would force the march down the one remaining East End access point – Cable Street.

It was a beautiful autumn day on 4 October 1936 and an amazing scene was taking place in the East End. From the alleys, courtyards and slums poured thousands upon thousands of Jews, Gentiles and tenement-dwellers

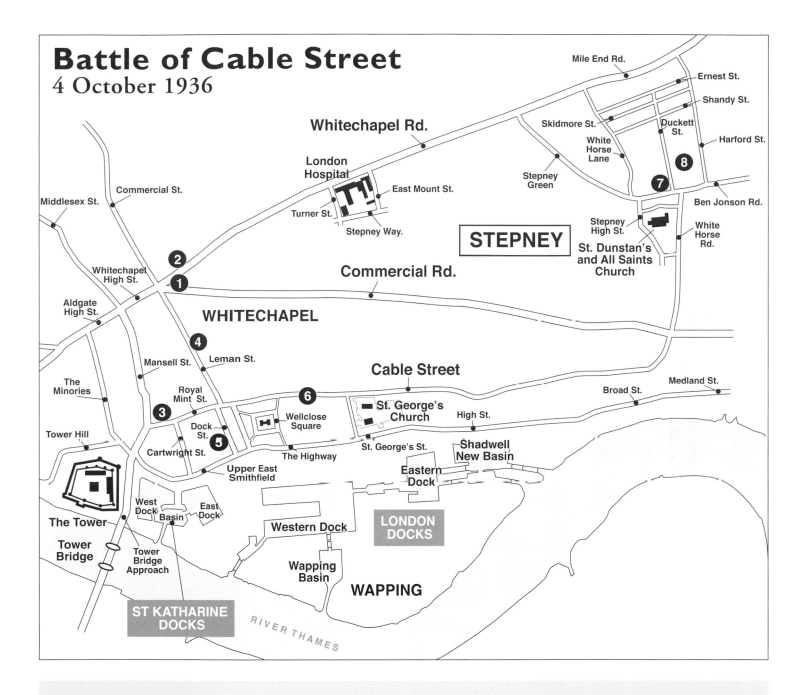

Battle of Cable Street
4 October 1936

1. At noon, a huge crowd of anti-Fascist protesters barred entry to the East End at Gardiner's Corner, at the junction of Whitechapel Road and Commercial Road.

2. At Whitechapel Library, contributor Bill Fishman watched the amazing gathering.

3. From 1.25 p.m., uniformed Mosley Blackshirts began to arrive in Royal Mint Street for their East End march.

4. Mosley's Blackshirts planned to march north from Royal Mint Street to Gardiner's Corner via Leman Street.

5. Crowds held back in Dock Street as Mosley arrives.

6. Mosley's march from Royal Mint Street had not even begun but, by 2.15 p.m., Blackshirt access to the East End at Gardiner's Corner was impossible due to the size of the anti-Fascist crowd. The police decided to divert Mosley's supporters east from Royal Mint Street into Cable Street but anti-Fascists also blocked Cable Street and the battle with police erupted.

7. Duckett Street was a Blackshirt stronghold and contributor Eddie Siggins witnessed a classic rally outside Butterfill's pub.

8. The Mission Room in Dongola Street, a meeting place used by 'The Leader', Oswald Mosley.

Man being arrested in
Royal Mint Street.

to oppose Mosley. A forest of banners arose, bearing the slogans 'THEY SHALL NOT PASS' and 'BAR THE ROAD TO FASCISM' emblazoned in a variety of colours, with red predominating. Red flags also fluttered from office windows, beneath which a vast sea of East Enders formed into huge columns, with chanting youngsters joining at the rear. Loudspeaker vans manned by Communist Party members and Jews toured the streets, urging the massed battalions to rally to the defence lines at Cable Street and Gardiner's Corner. Walls were chalked with slogans and shops were either closed or boarded up.

By noon, a huge, impassable crowd had collected at Gardiner's Corner – at the junction of Whitechapel and Commercial Roads – with overspills south into Leman Street and through to Cable Street. Two hours later, some 15,000 people had packed the Aldgate area and formed a solid, heaving mass at Gardiner's Corner across Commercial Road, their fists clenched in the Communist salute. The chant 'They shall not pass' boomed from the East End hordes. The whole junction – the main entry into the East End – was completely jammed, thanks to one of the most spectacular mass mobilizations in modern British political history. Meanwhile, 6,000-foot police and the whole of the mounted division were on duty between Tower

Hill and Whitechapel, and their Commissioner, Sir Philip Game, established a field HQ on the corner of Mansell Street and Royal Mint Street. A spotter aircraft, an autogyro, flew overhead. There were also 500 St John Ambulance men on standby.

From 1.25 p.m., uniformed Fascist Blackshirts began arriving by coach from all over Britain for Mosley's march. They congregated at their starting point, Royal Mint Street, ready to head north up Leman Street to Gardiner's Corner. Scuffles broke out as soon as the Blackshirts attempted to get off their coaches, and vehicle windows were smashed. Four people lay unconscious in the road as the fighting escalated and police with batons charged into the warring factions. Three of the unconscious men were Fascists, who had been clubbed with chair legs wrapped in barbed wire. The fourth was a bystander, struck by a milk bottle. Meanwhile, the harassed police, armed with long, weighted clubs, charged repeatedly into the massed ranks of anti-Fascists in the Leman Street and Gardiner's Corner area, in a bid to clear a path for the march to begin. Fighting broke out everywhere, a firework went off and shop windows were broken. At Messrs Kirtz, the clothiers, dazed and lacerated people were hauled from the smashed shop front, while women and children fell beneath the hooves of police horses.

Bill Fishman, born in 1921, is pictured on the right, aged 16, with his brothers, Albert (centre) and Morris (left).

Back in time: Bill Fishman returns to Whitechapel Library in Whitechapel Road where, in 1936, he was confronted by the huge swarm of demonstrators marching towards Gardiner's Corner.

The situation was already out of control and the Fascists, still encamped south in Royal Mint Street, had not even begun their provocative march.

Bill Fishman, a 15-year-old member of the Hackney Labour Party League of Youth, recalls:

I arrived on the tram from Clapton and was standing at Whitechapel Library in Whitechapel Road, looking towards Gardiner's Corner. It was an amazing sight.

There were masses of people trooping past – there must have been 100,000 gathered by now. [The estimated turnout for the whole East End ranged from 250,000 to 500,000.] *They sang: 'We'll hang Oswald Mosley on a sour apple tree when the Red Revolution comes'. Up above there were lots of unfurled banners hanging from windows in Whitechapel Road proclaiming 'They shall not pass'. There was a massive black one with the equivalent phrase in Spanish, which Spanish Anarchists had put up. I joined the march at Gardiner's Corner and it really was like being part of an army. There was such a buzz, such an atmosphere among the crowd. There was scuffling at the front and marbles were thrown, which tripped up police horses. Next a tram was just left at the junction of Leman Street and Commercial Road to act as a barrier.*

Then a Communist Party member who had infiltrated the Fascist ranks heard details of new police plans. The police now wanted to forget attempting access to Gardiner's Corner via Leman Street, and instead take the march straight down Royal Mint Street and into Cable Street as a way round to Commercial Road. The new re-routing plan was quickly relayed to Communist Party headquarters and people with megaphones in the Gardiner's Corner area then urged everyone to head south to Cable Street. I was at the rear of a massive mob of Jews and dockers when I arrived in Cable Street.

In the meantime, a blockade had been erected in Cable Street, where a lorry had been pushed onto its side and reinforced by Jews and Anglo-Irish with bits of furniture and mattresses. Irish dockers with grappling irons, silk-coated Orthodox Jews, Communists, local toughs from billiard halls armed with cues, and old ladies in aprons, all emerged and waited for action. Then planks of wood were taken from a builder's yard to reinforce the road barrier, bricks were stacked behind it to be thrown at police, and glass was scattered in front of it. Paving stones were torn up and added to the barricade, and marbles were thrown to impede the police horses. Fireworks were also set off.

The police repeatedly charged the blockade, while housewives and pensioners appeared from the roofs and windows of Cable Street, from where they hurled milk bottles, rubbish, cabbage leaves – and plenty of verbal abuse. There were many sickening scenes. As mounted, baton-wielding police tried to weather a barrage of stones and bricks, one officer was struck in the face and his eye was seen hanging out. Two of his colleagues were taken captive and held hostage, and it is rumoured that their helmets and batons are still in the possession of local families today.

George Mooney, then aged 13, was in Cable Street with a friend, Freddie Mears, and his younger brother, Joe:

All hell was breaking loose. Bits of chimney pots, bricks and stones were being hurled down from the roofs. When the horses charged, one came straight in our direction. The officer had his truncheon drawn and he brought it down heavily on Freddie's shoulder, smashing it and his collarbone. He was in agony. We had only been curious bystanders and naively thought the Mosley march would be something like the wonderful Catholic processions we enjoyed going to see. This was not fun, however, and the police were not mucking about. They hit anyone in their path. It was a frightening place to be.

Cable Street during that historic day **(left)** compared with the quiet scene today **(above)**.

(right) Mosley arrives in his Bentley from Leman Street. Police attempt to keep the crowd at bay at the entrance to Dock Street as the car sweeps round into Royal Mint Street, where his followers were gathered. A red plaque commemorating the battle can today be seen above an estate agent's office in Dock Street, formerly the Minories Machine Bakery premises.

At 3.30 p.m., Mosley himself arrived in an open Bentley with a motorcycle escort. Some 2,000 Fascists, including women, Fascist cadets and four bands, had now mobilized in Royal Mint Street and, as his car slowly drove between them, they shouted out, letter by letter, 'M O S L E Y. We want Mosley!' He was wearing a new uniform for the occasion in place of the plain black shirt and trousers he normally sported. Now a peaked cap adorned his head and a black military-cut jacket, grey riding breeches and jackboots completed the attire. Twice he drove the length of the street, which was bedecked in the swirling Union and Fascist flags of his followers, returning their Fascist salutes. Jeers resounded from the Cable Street direction, where the bloodied anti-Fascist demonstrators hurled insults.

Commissioner Philip Game realised it was futile to attempt to clear Cable Street, just as it had been to clear a route to Gardiner's Corner. The Blackshirts were still in Royal Mint Street, waiting to leave, and Game approached Mosley and told him he had to call off the proposed march. 'Is that an order?' Mosley asked. 'Yes,' replied Game, and Mosley complied. At 4.00 p.m., the Fascists lined up in columns, turned about and marched away west, led by a fife and drum band. They meandered through the quiet streets of West London to the Embankment where Mosley dismissed them, the majority disappearing into Temple Underground station, leaving a hard core to engage in minor clashes in Trafalgar Square and the Strand.

In all, 83 anti-Fascists were arrested and 100 police and protesters injured. The streets were strewn with iron bars, chair legs wrapped in barbed wire and broken bottles. Bill Fishman adds:

I think the actual fighting against the police was worse at Gardiner's Corner than in Cable Street. People were actually being thrown through windows in Leman Street. The whole event could more accurately have been called the Battle of Cable Street and Gardiner's Corner.

In any case, it was a humiliating outcome for Mosley, and the jubilant East Enders were left to converge on Victoria Park Square and celebrate on the spot where the Fascist 'Leader' had planned his own finale.

Some 3,000 police remained on duty, while the East End had one of its greatest ever 'knees-ups'. Bill Fishman recalls:

People were dancing in all the streets and I went to Dubosky's pub off Cannon Street Road where many Jews and many Communist Party leaders were. The

whole place was singing 'The Red Flag'. It was a marvellous victory for the Jews and Irish, who respected each other so much.[1] It was a unique bond between them. On the Sabbath, I remember being with my grandad, a Rabbi called Berl Orloff, who walked the streets wearing the traditional silk top hat, long frock coat and old pin-striped trousers which smelled of mothballs. The Irish dockers would doff their caps to him because he was always helping the poor. He had a simple philosophy based on the Judaic-Christian principle of tzedakah – a duty to give to those in need. If any beggar in the street was in need and asked for money, he would give and then say to them in Yiddish: 'Thank you for asking me'. The dockers loved him for his compassion.

There was always a lot of friendly banter between the two groups too. They would taunt us with: 'Take a bit of pork, stick it on a fork, give it to

the Jew babies' while we would respond with Yok Schmock *(Gentile idiot). In truth, we were brothers – true brothers. There was a strong camaraderie based on the poor helping the poor. Both groups suffered the same degradations and it united us.*

The 'Battle of Cable Street' began its journey from event into legend unhindered by the fact that it was actually fought between anti-Fascists and the police rather than between anti-Fascists and Mosley's Blackshirts. One consequence of the battle was the Public Order Bill, which quickly became law on 1 January 1937, giving police new powers to ban processions for up to three months, subject to the Home Secretary's consent. It also banned the wearing of political uniforms.

However, the Fascists did not simply melt away after Cable Street and neither did the intimidation of Jews. There were further marches that descended into savagery, and journalists noticed a siege mentality developing

---

[1] The strong friendship between the Jews and the Irish had been forged during bitter industrial disputes in 1889 and 1912.

among Jews living near the borders of Bethnal Green. Indeed, fireworks were pushed through letterboxes and ferocious beatings occurred on the streets. The Jews, scared and angry, stayed in behind bolted doors. Fascist orator William Joyce also appeared in Stepney where he ran a candidate against Frank Lewey in the local borough elections. Mr Lewey, who was Mayor of Stepney from November 1939 to November 1940, later recalled:

I remember how amused we were at the theatricality of the Blackshirts – the way they used to converge in loudspeaker vans on a chosen spot in darkness bawling: 'ACTION! JOYCE WILL SPEAK! JOYCE WILL SPEAK!' And then they would suddenly switch on half a dozen spotlights, and, standing on a van roof, there would be this funny little man in black trousers so tight that I think they must have hurt him; the mountain had laboured and brought forth a louse… Blacktrousers was bottom of the poll. But, bless you, it didn't touch their vanity one bit. Then, at subsequent London County Council elections, Joyce came again and swaggered about at the count. 'When I'm in charge here I'll show you Jewish bastards where you belong!' he announced viciously.

Joyce would never hold the reins of power but the East End had certainly not heard the last of him.

The tension of the late Thirties is revealed in the following testimonies. Joe Barr, then a young boy, recalls:

At the bottom of Burnside Street in Stepney, I saw the Blackshirts shouting abuse during a big march past. They were also throwing stones through the windows of the little Jewish shops. They hated the Jews – you could see the boiling rage in their faces. Even at the age of five, I could tell something very nasty indeed was going on, something very violent and unpleasant. It was chilling really to watch it then and think about it now.

Young Basil Shoop, living in Newark Street, Whitechapel, recalls:

We were a Jewish family and Dad was a master tailor, making clothes for City and West End outlets. They were frightening times, since Mosley was operating in the Bethnal Green area. A friend of the family was slashed across the face and I also remember getting cries in the street like: 'The Yids, the Yids, we've got to get rid of the Yids!' and 'Go back to Palestine!' Even at the age of three, both I and brother Stanley had been chased in Bow, and thankfully a kindly lady let us take refuge in her house.

Twelve-year-old Dorothy Brown (née Moss) remembers:

I was once in my bedroom on the sixth floor of Grosvenor Buildings in Poplar and had a bird's-eye view of the area. Suddenly there was a real din down below and the Blackshirts were marching from Poplar High Street to Cotton Street. There were lots of police on horseback and it was an amazing sight. It was incredibly unruly too, and people were trying to get at them. There was fighting everywhere and to this day I remember wondering: 'Why are those men in black shirts so angry? Why are they filled with so much hatred? What is going on inside their heads?' Their faces were red, their eyes were bulging. I had never seen such raw hatred before and I never forgot it.

There was excitement too for the young. Dorothy Crofts recalls:

I remember Dad warning me that the Blackshirts had set up under the guise of a social movement for young people and had offered them physical training and a chance to better themselves. As a young man, he had found this appealing and joined, but soon left after finding out its covert nature and sick philosophy, involving basic hatred of Jews and foreigners. One day in Hackney, in 1938, my brother Bill and I joined the rear of an anti-Fascist march to Stamford Hill. I was 11 and Bill 15. No one seemed to mind us trailing behind. A very hostile crowd of Blackshirts met us, scowling, shouting abuse and giving Fascist salutes. I should have been terrified but I wasn't. It was electric. We just felt part of a crowd that wasn't going to be bullied by people like the Blackshirts. Everyone stood absolutely firm and eventually the police moved us off.

(far left) Joe Barr, aged nine.

(left) Basil Shoop (right) with brother Stanley.

The Siggins children (front row) pictured in 1938 at 63 Duckett Street. Back row: Mary Ann, or 'Nana' (centre) with daughter Jess (left) and Jess's husband, Charles Self (right). Front row (from left to right): Leslie, Ronnie, Eddie and Irene.

(below) The clinic queue outside Dame Colet Cottage in Duckett Street.

The East End of the mid-Thirties was not just standing up to Fascism either. Stepney's women also confronted exploitative landlords, and the highly effective Stepney Tenant's Defence League demanded an end to payment of high rents and bad housing. Rent strikes began, barricades and barbed wire kept bailiffs at bay and mothers stood with their children outside landlords' homes, demanding an end to rent overcharging. Agreement was reached and the 6,000 members and supporters of the League held a victory parade from Brady Street to Philpot Street. The rally was told £25,000 had been refunded to tenants for rent overcharging and £60,000 worth of repairs carried out.

When the tenants of Lydia Street and Duckett Street won a three-week rent strike, a grand children's party was held in celebration. However, young Eddie Siggins was more interested in watching the workmen gradually demolish the houses between his home in Ocean Street and Duckett Street where his Nana, Mary Ann Bowyer, lived. Slowly but surely, Duckett Street appeared through the huge man-made gash, hazy at first amid swirling brick dust. As each property tumbled, children, packed onto the balconies of Frances Gray House, roared their approval.

They would, however, miss the shop on the corner of Duckett Street and Master Street, which sold wonderful toffee apples in summer. The property two doors along – an oil shop belonging to kindly Albert Knight – was also just a heap of bricks, as was a small pub called Cooksley's, Steven's sweetshop, and Bruce's greengrocery. Then the labourers moved in and a new building slowly filled the void. The new four-storey block in Duckett Street was called Searle House, an impressive U-shaped development, constructed in yellow bricks and embracing an inner courtyard where a clinic was built.

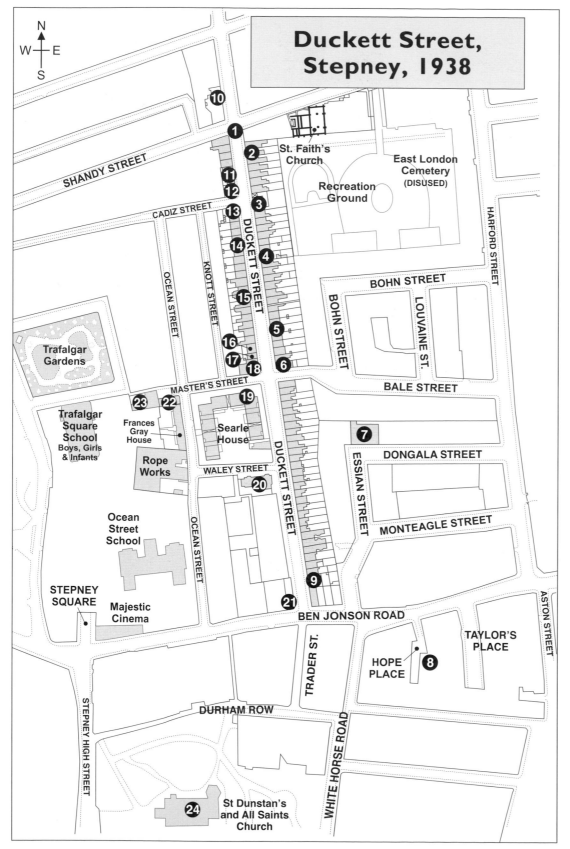

Duckett Street, Stepney, 1938

KEY:

1. The crossroads of the early nineteenth century Beaumont Estate, founded by philanthropist J. T. Barber Beaumont.
2. Hudson's hardware shop.
3. Dame Colet Settlement.
4. Scottish Sanitary Laundry (East London) Ltd.
5. 63 Duckett Street, home of Mary Ann Bowyer – Eddie Siggins's 'Nana' – between 1877 and September, 1940.
6. W. Betts (W. Busmer), Baker.
7. The Mission Room, a meeting place used by Oswald Mosley and the Blackshirts.
8. Hope Place, where Dr Barnardo opened his first children's shelter in 1867, the East End Juvenile Mission.
9. Edward Blackwell, confectioner.
10. Miss Esther Saunders' hardware shop.
11. Mrs Molly Cobb's sweet shop.
12. Lunn's beer retailer.
13. Albert Whitney, greengrocer.
14. 58 Duckett Street, home of Eddie Siggins's 'Grannie and Grandad Siggins'.
15. Mrs Emma Goody's general store.
16. Charles Perryman's general store.
17. Jane Norris's cats'-meat store.
18. Anchor and Hope public house.
19. 28 Searle House, home of Eddie Siggins between 1938 and 1940.
20. Prince of Wales public house (known as 'Kate Hodder's).
21. Bull's Head public house (known as 'Butterfill's).
22. 33 Ocean Street, home of Eddie Siggins between 1933 and 1938.
23. Mickey Shaw's stables.
24. St Dunstan's and All Saints Church, the East End's mother church.

Hardship in Duckett Street: a pre-war Stepney Housing Trust booklet featured the plight of Mr and Mrs Holmden and their three boys, who lived three doors away from Eddie Siggins's 'Nana.' The Holmdens and their parents had rented the property for 75 years and had never owed rent. In October 1936, rainwater began to leak through the roof into the boys' bedroom but the landlord did nothing, despite repeated pleas. Part of the ceiling and wall then collapsed while the boys slept and the rear of the house was eventually pulled down to make it safer. The family had to struggle on in the remains of the property and the back was not replaced until the following year. However, the roof still leaked. The booklet adds: *It is now April (1937), the rain is still coming in and another notice has been served on the landlord. All three boys have bad coughs; it is remarkable they are not really ill.*

The new block was named after Miss Searle, a warden at Dame Colet House, which was a settlement of crucial importance to the welfare of the Stepney poor. It provided a children's health and dental clinic and offered many clubs and activities for the young. Initially, Dame Colet House had been based in Mile End Road near the People's Palace, but Miss Searle wanted to get closer to poverty to carry out her work. Indeed, as one mother put it: 'I haven't got clothes for the Mile End Road'. Duckett Street was a perfect venue and a derelict pub was converted into Dame Colet Cottage in 1923, until a disused kipper factory in the street was rebuilt and became a new base in 1927. Here a great Stepney centre of care and community support evolved. 'Boot clubs' helped provide footwear for the barefooted, young heads were deloused at a cleansing station and a clinic tended to countless children suffering from sore eyes, running ears and impetigo.

On 13 March 1937, the new Searle House opened its doors and there was a good reason for Eddie Siggins to take such a keen interest in its construction. His family was going to rent one of the plush new homes,

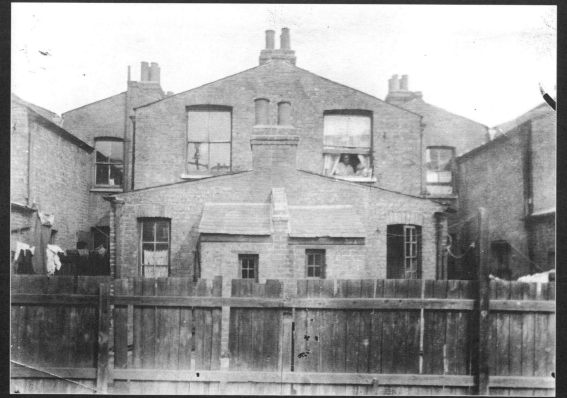

Duckett Street characters: (left) Jane Norris, the cats'-meat woman; **(right)** Albert Knight, owner of the Oil Shop. Contributor Albert Rush, nephew of Jane Norris, recalls:

I lived at No. 96 Duckett Street above Albert Knight's Oil Shop which made way for Searle House to be built in 1937. Mr Knight was a great character and used to take loads of us kids on outings to coffee shops and places like Greenwich Park. He is pictured with my brother John. My auntie, Mrs Norris, had a large wicker basket full of various weights of cats' meat all wrapped in newspaper. How she knew which parcel was which was a mystery. I used to do a cats'-meat round during my school dinner break for pocket money.

Rear view of typical homes in Duckett Street, Stepney.

The junction of Duckett Street with Bale Street in 1939; Bale Street is today Bohn Road.

Local children from the Duckett Street area, pictured at the Ben Jonson School in 1933. Mr Albert Rush, who provided the picture, is in the second row from the front, third from left.

and their furniture had already been fumigated to ensure the bugs of Ocean Street stayed behind. The big day finally came in 1938, and his Mum's beaming face was a picture when she excitedly ventured across the threshold of ground-floor flat No. 28, on the corner of Duckett Street and Master Street. A welcoming fire was lit and, remarkably, the smoke actually went up the chimney instead of back down into the room, as it had in Ocean Street. Their modern, green and cream flat boasted three bedrooms, brown cork lino flooring and, of course, an indoor bathroom, which soon attracted a weekly pilgrimage of relatives each Saturday.

The difference that the new development made to the grim Stepney of the Thirties cannot be overestimated. A Stepney Housing Trust report was suitably entitled 'A Study in Contrasts' included is this first-hand experience:

The scene was a drab back street behind a busy thoroughfare. A dilapidated building in the last stages of decay abutted onto a narrow pavement strewn with garbage. A diminutive boy, with a sharp Cockney face, stood at a dark entry. There was nothing to indicate the name or number of the building. 'Ooja want, Miss?' I inquired the whereabouts of an address I was trying to find. Without a word, the boy dived into the dark entry, and I followed warily. The walls crumbled and oozed black filth. Light and air were strangers in that land. He pushed open a door and, in semi-darkness, a woman peered out. The small boy disappeared. It was his 'home'. The rooms were narrow and angular and nearly dark. I was unaware of a young girl crouched over a fire until she spoke. The faded paper had been stripped from the walls because of bugs, the woodwork was paintless, the floor rotten and riddled with rat holes. I inquired the names and ages of the children. The woman put her hand to her head wearily. 'I shall have to write them all down, Miss', she said, and then smiled. 'I can't remember them all without.'

The second scene is a few weeks later at Searle House – fresh and new, green-painted railings, grass plots, window boxes gay with daffodils, lofty rooms flooded with light and air, and bright attractive walls. Searle House tenants have a violently developed taste in window curtains; each favours a different hue. The result is brilliant! Each flat has its own balcony, a choice of electricity or gas for heating and cooking, and a geyser to supply bath and sink with hot water. The contrast has been summed up in two words: 'It's 'Eaven!' Searle House might aptly be called a 'Youth Hostel'. We have 82 children under 16 years old in the 18 flats. It has been our aim to rehouse large families and, with such a big proportion of four and five-roomed flats, we have achieved it. We are able to apply a rebate system to this block on a rather more generous scale, and rents vary from 10s 6d to 14s 2d [52.5p to 71p] for three rooms, 14s 2d to 17s 6d [71p to 87.5p] for four rooms, and 15s 6d to £1 0s 5d [77.5p to £1.02p] for five rooms.

The Sigginses were indeed in 'Eaven,' as Eddie recalled:

Whenever I hear two of the most popular songs of that time – 'Bei Mir Bistu Schein' sung by the Andrews Sisters, and 'South of the Border, Down Mexico Way' – I go straight back to those days and can see the street vendors that worked Duckett Street on a fairly regular basis. One was a woman we knew as 'Old Liz' who was a bit eccentric. She would wheel an old pram along the pavement, calling out 'Bagels, bagels – they're lovely!' She would wear a big Victorian hat with artificial red and white roses sewn around the rim and an old tight-fitting coat, also of similar vintage. The kids sometimes called after her and tormented her and she would get quite angry.

Another street trader was 'Curly', who had a mop of dark curly hair and was the rag-and-bone man. He drove around the streets with a small pony and cart, collecting old rags and bones in exchange for a goldfish and you had to provide your own jam jar to take it away. Or he would give you a few coppers or a piece of cheap china tableware in exchange. Piemen wandered around too, with their shallow baker's trays on their heads, while a Walls ice-cream man, sporting a white jacket, a leather money satchel slung across his chest and peaked military-style cap, rode a tricycle with a painted wooden box between the wheels. His contraption was emblazoned with the words: 'Stop Me and Buy One!' and he advertised his goods by constantly ringing his bike bell. The winkle man, yelling 'Yem prime winkles!', also came on a Sunday and his cart carried a couple of open-topped barrels crammed with pickled herrings and other salted fish, which he measured out in a half or pint pot.

Barrel organs were a common sight too and usually played by disabled ex-soldiers of the First World War. I remember the medals pinned to their jackets, and missing limbs, and they stood and turned a handle fixed to the side of the machine in a circular motion. These machines were not really barrels but small, portable pianola-type organs, which were mounted on two wheels and pulled along by two shafts. They were hired from the 'Barrel Organ King', Mr Albert Faccini, for half a crown [12.5p]. He had a small shed in Ernest Street at the top end of Duckett Street.[2] On the opposite corner of a side street, and facing our flat, was the Anchor and Hope pub with its small snug bar where you could buy takeaway beer. There were a couple of wooden bench seats on either side of the wall and it was not unusual on a Sunday to see two or three old dears sitting there shelling peas and preparing various vegetables for the Sunday lunch. They would have a glass of beer on the shelf behind them, and also a couple of pots standing on the floor or bench ready for the vegetables. The baker's shop opposite the pub was called Betts. The baker

[2] Faccini had 50 pianos and his regulars included the Nancy Boys remembered by contributor Rose Gowler (see page 34).

would keep the ovens hot after the early morning bake and the ladies would bring in their prepared Sunday lunches in baking tins covered over with a tea towel, ready for him to cook for them. He would give them half of a raffle ticket, placing the other half on the dish in exchange for 3 or 4 pence [about 1.5p], which was the going charge to cook the dinner. The ladies would then go to the pub with their men and pick up the cooked food on the way home.

It was also customary for the baker to give the children a small slice of bread pudding or Tottenham cake topped with pink icing and coconut when they went in for a loaf for their mum. This was to make up the weight of the bread.

Although the centrally located Anchor and Hope pub was the hub of Duckett Street life, Eddie Siggins retained fond childhood memories of other business premises in the road, notably among the small parade of shops opposite his Nana's house at No. 63. Emma Goody's was at No. 72, where you could take your own dish and buy just a spoonful or pennyworth of mustard pickles from a jar, or individual dollops of jam if that was all you could afford. Further along was Charles Perryman's general store at No. 86 and Mrs Norris's at No. 88. Known as 'Queenie Cats' Meat', Mrs Norris in her shop was surrounded by cuts of raw horseflesh hanging down from wooden skewers. If you bought two pennyworth for the cat, you would receive a handful of unshelled peanuts. Eddie had tasted the meat once – and vowed never to try it again.

The residents of Duckett Street particularly fascinated young Eddie Siggins. Gazing from a window of the new flat in Searle House, he often saw Mr and Mrs Morris go by. They were Nana's neighbours and also greengrocers, with a stall at the local Old Road Market. The beetroots they sold were boiled in their back garden in a large old copper, which they also used to do their washing. They also owned a small pony and, after a day's work at the market, the animal was led through the front door and straight out to the back, where he was kept in a shed. One of their daughters died at the age of five and she was laid in state in the small front parlour, as was traditional in the East End. Eddie had been taken to see little Violet, lying so white, cold and still, with her Cleopatra haircut. Mrs Morris had kept saying: 'Doesn't she look lovely, we laid her out well didn't we?' She had seemed oddly pleased with herself.

On the other side of the Morrises lived the Butlers, who were in the fish trade and had installed a fish-fryer in their front room. They sold fish and chips, wrapped in newspaper, through the ground-floor slide-up window to customers waiting on the pavement. In fact, fish-curing was an important local industry in the area. At some houses, Billingsgate fish was smoked over oak sawdust in backyard smoke-holes for West End shops.

The brand-new Sigginses' residence housed Eddie, Mum and Dad,

brother Leslie, aged 4, and sister Irene, aged 10. His younger brother, Ronald, now six, was still living with Auntie Jess in Leytonstone. During the summer of 1938, they were all hit hard by the death of Grannie Siggins, who lived at No. 58, opposite Nana Bowyer. Grandad then passed away in the following autumn, leaving his son Tom, the man terribly deformed by osteoporosis, and his sister Maud at the house. They would later move out to Richmond.

Later in 1938, the front pages of all the newspapers detailed dramatic developments far removed from the micro-world of Duckett Street. Britain's Prime Minister, Neville Chamberlain, had just returned from Germany after a meeting with Adolf Hitler and large crowds had gathered to meet him in Downing Street. Chamberlain was treated to a rousing rendition of 'For He's a Jolly Good Fellow' before he spoke to the masses from a second-storey window at No. 10. On that day in September 1938, he told them that peace would prevail in the world and *The Times* declared: 'No conqueror returning from a victory on the battlefield has come adorned with nobler laurels'. Hitler and Chamberlain had signed the Munich Agreement, granting the Sudetenland portion of Czechoslovakia, which contained a German population, to Germany. Hitler had already invaded Austria six months earlier, thereby adding 7 million further subjects to the Third Reich. However, Chamberlain's Munich trip and the euphoria of 'peace for our time' had apparently put an end to future German empire building. By 15 March 1939, Hitler's troops had expanded from the Sudetenland and devoured the rest of Czechoslovakia as well. Chamberlain realised that he had been deceived and his eventual successor, Winston Churchill, who had branded the Munich Agreement a 'total, unmitigated defeat', was vindicated.

Poland was next. On 31 March 1939, 16 days after Hitler entered the Czech capital of Prague, Chamberlain told the House of Commons that Britain would support Poland should she be attacked. The ultimatum was in place and the French backed Britain's stance. Londoners held their breath. Frank Rose, then a young Jewish boy living within the complex of the Great Synagogue in Duke's Place, where his father was an official, recalls the growing fear of war:

As a boy in the Thirties, I was regularly taken to visit my grandmother, who lived a short distance from Whitechapel Road. We had to pass by the house of a colourful local character, Mary Hughes, the daughter of the author of Tom Brown's Schooldays. *Her home was the Dewdrop Inn in Vallance Road, opposite a flat complex named after her (see page 35). Mary Hughes, a striking old lady who walked about wearing a bright red cloak, made it her business to alert people to the horrors of a Second World War by plastering her window with frightening pictures of skulls wearing steel helmets and similar material. I used to find the display in her window so disturbing that I averted my*

The world on a knife-edge: children begin to leave the capital.

Frank Rose, aged nine.

gaze whenever I passed.[3] The Nazi menace was by now inducing deep fears within us. I had been brought up to view Hitler as a demon. All Jews in particular were well aware of the Fascist threat at home and abroad, and it was impossible to feel relaxed.

A blanket of fear and trepidation settled upon the nation but some precautions had already been taken. A booklet circulated in 1938 had suggested that 'children, invalids, elderly members of the household and pets should be sent to relatives or friends in the country if this is possible'. In May that year, London County Council also agreed that it had a duty to evacuate at least the City's children, while mothers should accompany youngsters too young to travel with a school party. Arrangements were made for the evacuation of 637,000 children and, on 28 September 1938, the first batch of 1,200 children from nursery schools and 3,100 physically impaired children left London. Three evacuation zones were defined: target areas, which people had to leave, such as the East End and ports like Southampton; reception areas where the children would be sent; and neutral areas where the children could remain in relative safety. Yet, up to August 1939, a general 'wait-and-see' policy had limited the scheme's success.

The world was on a knife-edge and the stakes could not have been higher. It was a world where Britain, despite the regrettable demise of its traditional industries, conducted half the world's business within its capital's 'Square Mile'. London, the hub of the greatest Empire the world had ever seen, was the world's most populous city (with 8.6 million inhabitants) and its vast conurbation was now twice the size it had been in 1914 and six times the size of the 1880 capital. London was also the world's greatest port, its finance king and was, quite simply, the most famous place on earth.

By 1939, Adolf Hitler had destroyed those opposed to him, unified and Nazified the state, regimented Germany's institutions and culture, suppressed individual freedom and invigorated industry. The nation that had given the world Bach, Wagner and Beethoven now offered men of a different calibre. They included Heinrich Himmler, Joseph Goebbels and Hitler's chosen successor, his future Reich Marshal, Hermann Goering. As early as 1933, the year Hitler became Chancellor, Britain's Ambassador to Germany, Walter Rumbold, had perceptively remarked: 'Many of us have a feeling that we are living in a country where fantastic hooligans and eccentrics have got the upper hand.'

As darkness settled over Europe on the evening of 31 August 1939, 1.5 million German troops moved up to the Polish border and, at daybreak, the Nazi legions poured across it. As the German forces advanced towards Warsaw, Cockneys awoke in an East End that would soon change forever. On 1 September, the blackout began, television went off air (apparently

---

[3] Other contributors remember the gruesome Pacifist shop in Buxton Street, featuring photographs of mutilated soldiers.

A newspaper-seller on the Embankment in London on 3 September 1939.

because its signal could aid incoming bombers) and the BBC announced that broadcasts would be restricted to a single radio channel, the Home Service. A 6.00 p.m. curfew was also imposed on all traders except newsagents, tobacconists and confectioners. Germany's invasion of Poland also heralded the official evacuation of 3.5 million schoolchildren, mothers with toddlers under five, expectant women and the disabled.

Evacuation was ultimately the parents' choice, yet they had no say in where their children would go. Indeed, when the youngsters duly arrived at the designated railway stations on 1 September, they were put into whatever trains happened to be waiting. Parties of children from the same area, the same school, and even the same family, were split up and sent to different destinations.

Arrangements for receiving them at the other end ranged from excellent and organised to chaotic and shambolic. At best, the volunteer billeting officers had worked out in advance which families could take evacuees; at worst, local families simply turned up and chose children as the trains and buses arrived, which meant the healthiest and fittest were picked first while the rest were ignored. In addition, little or no attempt was made to match the social backgrounds of evacuees and host families. While women's magazines tried to ease tensions by urging all concerned to 'pull together', and 'have a bit of give and take', inevitably nightmares were in store for many young East Enders.

At 11.15 a.m. on 3 September 1939, the voice of Neville Chamberlain broadcast from the Cabinet Room at No. 10 to inform the country that

Britain was at war with Germany. The West family, who lived in Sewardstone Road, Hackney, were staying with friends in Woodford, Essex, when the broadcast was made. Julia West, who was 19, recalls:

Our hostess, Elizabeth Dudley, a natural drama queen, threw herself into her doting husband's arms – much to my mother's disgust – and my mother, father and I just stared disconsolately at each other. Len Dudley, their only son, held me in his arms for a moment or two, which was more important at the time than the news. I felt relieved that the previous tension over an unknown outcome had at last been resolved, and I felt strangely excited at the challenge ahead.

Meanwhile, young June Lewzey (née Guiver) remembers:

I was living with my family at 21 Abingdon Buildings in Old Nichol Street, Bethnal Green, when war was declared. We suddenly heard a thud outside and Dad joked: 'The man upstairs has finally done his wife in then!' In fact, an old Jewish lady thought the Germans were coming and had thrown herself from the top of the building. She was impaled on the railings below and sand was hastily laid to cover up all the blood which seeped onto a playground.

So, Britain was at war. What now? Memories came flooding back of

June Lewzey (née Guiver) pictured on the left, with her sister Joan and their mother Ellen.

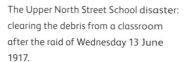

The Upper North Street School disaster: clearing the debris from a classroom after the raid of Wednesday 13 June 1917.

The tragedy at Upper North Street School, as seen by *The Sphere* artist, D. Macpherson. Firemen and men on leave from the Front are seen helping to remove the young casualties.

The funeral of the 18 children killed at Upper North Street School: the cortège passes along East India Dock Road.

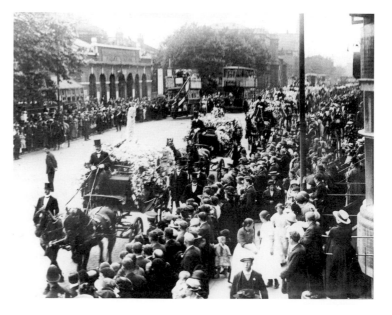

the First World War air raids, 25 years earlier, when Britain was attacked 111 times in total (52 by Zeppelin airships and 59 by aircraft) and 1,413 citizens lost their lives. London was raided 31 times. Some 9,000 bombs fell on Britain and 670 Londoners perished – almost half the nation's total death toll. In one appalling incident on 13 June 1917, 18 Gotha bombers arrived over the city in perfect formation. A total of 72 bombs were dropped on London and 160 people were killed at Liverpool Street Station and the Royal Albert Dock. One bomb also smashed through three floors of a school in Upper North Street in Poplar, exploding on the ground floor and killing 18 youngsters. Many remembered the children's funeral, wreaths smothering the eight horse-drawn hearses that took their bodies from Poplar Mortuary to East London Cemetery via the packed East India Dock Road. Others recalled sheltering in the Underground stations (as did some 100,000 on one September night in 1917) and the shocking sight of the limbless veterans in the streets.

Based on past experience, it was predicted that the new air raids would cost up to 3,000 lives and result in 12,000 wounded per attack. Philosopher Bertrand Russell gravely proclaimed that London would become 'one vast raving bedlam' and witness scenes of pandemonium. Many had seen the 1936 film *Things to Come*, starring Raymond Massey and Margaretta Scott. It now seemed chillingly prophetic, with its story of a 1940 London destroyed by war and consumed by plague and rebellion.

Just eight minutes after Chamberlain's five-minute BBC broadcast to the nation, the air-raid sirens in London sounded when a lone French aircraft strayed into British airspace and triggered a false alarm. Reactions to that first alarm varied and, disconcertingly, a sprint to the nearest shelter was not first priority. Ron Warner recalls:

Ron Warner and his younger brother George pictured just after the outbreak of war in the garden of the Powell House flats in Lower Clapton Road, Hackney.

Peggy Spencer (née Hathaway) pictured in 1939, aged 14.

I was lying in bed reading comics in Powell House, Lower Clapton Road, Hackney, and suddenly you could hear the Air Raid Precautions wardens outside in a real flap. There was meant to be a whistle to prompt people to take shelter and a rattle to warn of a gas attack. But on that occasion they were blowing and rattling in total disarray. There were two reactions. Some like me just shrugged and stayed put. Others were panic stricken. Mind you, after that scare everyone looked at each other every time there was a noise outside.

Ten-year-old Iris Pledger (née Atkins) had just got out of the bath at her home in Dunelm Street, Stepney.

A warden was outside shouting pompously: 'Please keep calm, keep calm!' We were dumbstruck and just stood on the doorstep and stared across to our neighbours, who were all there staring back or looking up. We all just watched the sky for something to happen. It was my 11th birthday in three weeks so I turned to Mum and said: 'Will I still have a birthday now?'

Meanwhile, back at the Dudley home in Woodford, Essex, guest Julia West recalls:

Our host, Elizabeth, now captured the moment of the first alarm by flopping out on a settee with everyone in attendance with water, fans and brandy. I went into the garden and looked for a German plane over Woodford.

The drama had a tragic twist for 14-year-old Peggy Spencer (née Hathaway), who recalls:

I had been listening to Les Miserables *on the radio at home in Athelstane Grove, Bow, when Chamberlain came on and told us we were at war. Mum wept and we went across the road to discuss it with the neighbours. Then, when the false air-raid alarm went, my paternal grandma in Cornwall Avenue, Bethnal Green, had a drop of whisky and went down to her Anderson shelter and died inside. It was my first experience of death in the family and very upsetting.*

The false alarm merely served to intensify general unease. East End eyes scanned the heavens as the rumours escalated. Thousands of tons of bombs would pour onto the East End said some; each ton would harm 50 residents; and didn't the Nazis have secret weapons too? The situation wasn't helped in September 1939 when, following a Foreign Office mistranslation of a Hitler speech, the press unhelpfully informed the British public that Germany had a weapon which the Allies did not possess. The East End pubs were full of alarmist speculation but life-saving tips abounded too. Some recommended plugging the ears with rubber during bombing to protect the hearing or biting on a cork to prevent cracked teeth or bitten tongues. Others had their own ideas. Betty Redwood (née Smith), living in Kingsland Road, Plaistow, recalls:

Mum suddenly came downstairs with a soaked blanket, which she hung across the front door. She said it would protect us from gas. Then we religiously went under the stairs every night and simply waited and waited and waited.

There were other signs symptomatic of a city with increasingly frayed nerves. Hundreds of couples married, police leave was cancelled, hospitals began to clear out their wards, and businesses considered moving out from the hub of Empire. The impending bombing disaster also saw a banning of football matches, the closure of cinemas and theatres (branded 'unimaginative stupidity' by playwright Bernard Shaw) and the lights went out at sports grounds, speedway venues and dog-racing tracks. On Guy Fawkes Night on 5 November 1939 there was not a single rocket, let alone a bonfire.

When the eerie, velvet blanket of the blackout descended over the capital, the cry of 'put that light out' echoed the length and breadth of London. Street lights went out and neon lights disappeared. No light could shine from any building after dark for fear it would aid enemy bombers locate their targets. The blackout was annoyingly inconvenient. It could take 10 to 15 minutes each day to black out a house, which housewives resented. Moreover, blackout curtain material soon became difficult to find and extremely expensive. Pat Patmore, (née Moore) living in Chalgrove Road, Hackney, recalls:

'Turn the bleedin' light out' from Grandma was a familiar cry in our house. She also warned me to leave my Jewish friend's house during a raid in case the Germans came down our street and found me there. Our windows not only had brown paper and heavy blackout curtains but shutters outside too. Going out was bizarre and even my torch glass was papered over with just a little slit cross in it to let light out. It was almost pointless using it.

Women's magazines recommended various products to help during the hours of darkness, including the 'Lumic' armband which emited:

… such a strong luminous glow that it illuminates adjacent objects two or three inches away from it… it is clearly visible at 25 feet and is an essential safeguard that everyone will immediately appreciate the wisdom of wearing.

Householders were also warned of the dangers of approaching their homes in the blacked out streets. 'It is therefore a wise precaution', advised *Woman's Magazine*, 'to whiten front door steps, kerbs, path edgings, garage runs etc. with White Cardinal Polish, which gives an intense whiteness to all stonework… .' Lamp-posts and letterboxes were soon adorned with white stripes, and one Essex farmer painted his dark cows to make them more visible. Going out was a precarious business. Leslie Norman, a 23-year-old nurse probationer, remembers once attempting the short walk from his rented digs to Hackney Hospital where he worked.

I was going along and suddenly walked straight into a lamppost. I smashed my glasses and bruised my face. Some nights it was very black and bumping into people was commonplace.

Many simply stayed in and magazine articles helpfully featured 'Books to Brighten Blackout Evenings'. Two recommendations included *Mrs Miniver* by Jan Struther and *The Blackout Book,* publishied by George Harrap, the latter containing 'problems for father, quiet corners for mother, puzzles and things to make for the children… and humorous odds and ends to suit the mood of everyone'.

It was getting dangerous outside, where car headlamps had been covered to give only a narrow strip of light. In December 1939, there were 37 fatal accidents every day – double the number recorded in pre-war Britain. Road accidents trebled in East and West Ham during the first month of restrictions and even three months later there were 10 fatalities. There was a relaxation of the rules in the New Year so that a mother could no longer be fined for turning on a light in an uncurtained room to attend a baby. In fact, the visibility of lights on the ground when viewed from 5,000 feet or more was wildly exaggerated and reports of people being asked to stub out cigars tried the city's patience. The Government introduced Summer Time in February 1940, supplemented by double Summer Time in the summer months, to assist movement in the standstill capital.

Londoners themselves were changing. Normal topics of conversation seemed trivial or irrelevant in the light of the anticipated apocalypse. Many detected a new collective bonding, an unspoken coming together. People spoke differently to each other and seemed to have more time for each other. There was an almost innate human demand for closeness. Perhaps a united city, a united East End, could somehow deflect, absorb or repel the coming ordeal.

Slowly the East End mobilised. The Home Office urged London's boroughs to turn the zigzag open shelters previously dug in parks into permanent shelters, lined and roofed with steel or concrete and covered with 3 feet of earth. There was also an appeal for Air Raid Precautions (ARP) (left) Two typical blackout posters.

Nurse probationer Leslie Norman.

(far right) Typical ARP recruitment
poster used in 1939.

AIR RAID WARDENS WANTED

A RESPONSIBLE JOB FOR RESPONSIBLE MEN

ARP

APPLY TO YOUR LOCAL COUNCIL NOW

NATIONAL SERVICE

wardens. In 1937, the Air Raid Precautions Act had made it compulsory for the 250 local authorities to set up Civil Defence organisations. These were divided into specialist sections, including Rescue, First Aid, Ambulance, Communications and Decontamination (poison gas). In a flurry of Home Office circulars sent after Munich, local authorities were also urged to proceed with recruiting an Auxiliary Fire Service (AFS), which would boost the strength of the regular fire service 15-fold. Joan Breeze (née Noakes) was one of thousands who came forward. She recalls:

I volunteered to join the AFS in 1939 as a 19-year-old and was trained at the fire station in Glamis Road, Shadwell. Then, when the war was imminent, I was allocated to a school in Senrab Street off Commercial Road. I was a trainee telephonist and life was not easy. There was a fair amount of bullying by the men, who looked down on us because we were women. Ten of us used to sleep in dorms and once a Station Officer, an ex-Navy man and a bully, came in and shouted: 'You should be up!' One little Jewish girl said something and he ordered: 'Stand up when you speak to the Station Officer!' She got out of bed and stood before him looking very embarrassed in just her camiknickers.

It was tough outside too. The East End people spoke their mind and during this period the AFS was not popular. People would say we were evading the war and shout: 'Do something useful!' or 'Join the troops!' But once the bombing started, they did everything they could for you.

The full-time ARP workers were also criticized for having cushy jobs and being prying busybodies, yet their knowledge of the local area and residents would prove invaluable when the raids came. The ARP was a personal blessing for some too, as Ivor Morgan, living in Sutherland Road, Walthamstow, recalls:

My Dad, a former Great War soldier, had been the victim of a very bad fire at his business premises in 1936. He used to buy old films from cinemas and strip the films with acid so he could sell them back to Kodak. During the fire, Dad received 80 per cent burns, was bandaged head to foot and was terribly disfigured. He spent two years in hospital and I wasn't allowed to see him. He actually received sterilized sheepskin grafts and poor Dad's skin was incredibly clear and waxen afterwards. Children made his life a misery when he went out and so he rarely did. When the war began, he joined the ARP and suddenly he was a proud man again. It gave him a new lease of life, a real purpose and focus after years of pain and upset. He also joined the Home Guard and was doing the two in tandem before he was asked to choose. He chose the Home Guard.

The Stoke Newington ARP proudly pose for the camera. The photograph was donated by Mrs Sheila Raznick, (née Schwalb), whose father Sam is standing between the second and third rows from the front, on the far right.

Wardens gather around their post at Lebon's Corner in Dalston Lane, Hackney, in 1940. The post was known as 'The Mustard Pot' because of its colour and shape and a steep set of steps led to the HQ beneath the pavement.

The Women's Voluntary Service (WVS) was also to play a key role. Founded in 1938 by Lady Reading, the WVS, or 'women in green', had half a million members by early 1940 and was to provide meals and drinks for the victims of the bombing attacks as well as clothes for 'bombed out' citizens.

Yet, as the weeks passed and raids failed to materialise, the once-feared secret weapons became something of a joke and were dismissed as Nazi bluff. Nonetheless, gas attacks had made their battlefield debut in the First World War and no chances could be taken. Pillar boxes were given a lick of gas-sensitive yellow paint to give warning of toxic air levels and loudspeaker vans toured the streets, urging everyone to be fitted with gas masks at designated points. The nation's adults, children, babies, carthorses and pet dogs were given a range of gas masks and, by the time of the Munich crisis in September 1938, most Londoners possessed one. Lily Towner (née Barclay), aged nine and living in Dora Street, Limehouse, recalls:

The masks were absolutely revolting. They suffocated you and the rubber would stick to your face and make you very sweaty. But if a copper found out you didn't have it with you, he'd tell you to go home and get it.

Audrey True (née Marshall), living in Glamis Place, Shadwell, adds:

I was five and really furious when I got mine. It was a black adult model and I wanted one like my younger brother John's – a coloured Mickey Mouse mask with ears. But I was too old. My mask was uncomfortable and the smell of the

rubber was horrid. I couldn't actually breathe in mine and my breath would steam it up so I couldn't see anything either. Some girls decorated their gas mask boxes and you could even buy covers for them if you were that fashion conscious. I think I just scribbled on mine to make it stand out.

For Charlie Smith, gas-mask training ended in hilarity:

We were given gas-mask tuition in a shelter building at Russell Road School in Custom House. It was ludicrous. We eventually learned to talk to each other in sign language because the condensation steamed them up so badly and our noses just wouldn't stop running.

Cartoon poster urging people to volunteer as firefighters.

(right) gas-mask advice poster.

A mother and her child venture forth with their new gas masks.

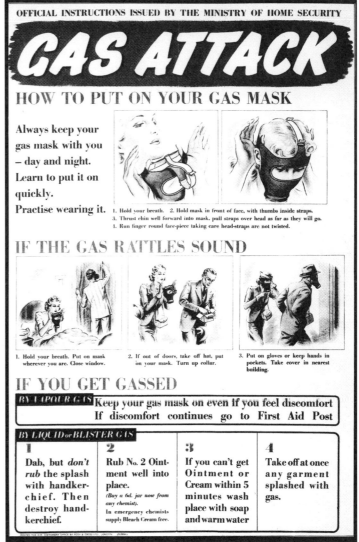

Also in Custom House, young Johnny Ringwood was given some stern parental advice:

> My parents warned me to take the mask everywhere and take the matter seriously or I'd suffer death by gassing. Dad simply said: 'You see, son, those bleedin' German pilots will be dropping the stuff soon.' I recall that well-off kids had tailor-made carriers for their masks while everyone else had a cardboard box. I was also really jealous of my brother's grand affair. Being a baby, he was able to fit right inside and air was pumped in by hand, using little bellows.

The wait for the bombers continued and the East End became a shelter community. The Underground was closed to would-be shelterers at this time because of the acute official fear that the deep tunnels would create a 'shelter mentality' and people would refuse to come out. Therefore, most Londoners were expected to rig up their own defences. One option was the Anderson shelter, which was both simple to manufacture and erect, and consisted of two curved sections of corrugated steel bolted together to form

a semi-circular hut. It was sunk 3 feet into the ground and its entrance was often covered by a solid steel shield or earth embankment to protect it from blast. The roof was covered with at least 18 inches of soil and the resulting garden home could protect four to six people against anything except a direct hit. It was to prove effective too. The Anderson had been tested to withstand the weight of a house collapsing on top of it and was later shown to be capable of withstanding the blast of a 250-kilogram (550-pound) bomb falling 50 feet away. There were terrible drainage problems, however, and the inhabitants would never forget the insects, mud and dirt, which oozed through the curved roof joints when they vibrated during raids.

Anderson shelters were free to those on an income of less than £250 a year and hundreds of thousands of Londoners had one. Experience and improvisation could pay dividends. Doreen Dennis (née Cook) recalls:

Charles Cook, the father of Doreen Dennis (née Cook), poses by the family Anderson shelter. The containers on the ground were kept full of water and sand as part of his air-raid preparations.

The 'square' Anderson shelter: 12-year-old Stanley Bartels sitting in front of the shelter. Behind are brothers Len (left, with finger to chin) and Arthur (centre, in his Royal Engineers uniform), and a fellow Royal Engineer (right).

Dad was a Great War veteran from the Somme. He brought a certain calmness to the proceedings and built our Anderson, in Oswald Street, Clapton Park, with a sandbag porch. He also made sure there was a whistle hanging on a string inside so we could attract attention if we were ever buried. It was a clever and potentially life-saving addition.

Stanley Bartels' father, also a First World War veteran, had another idea:

Dad worked in a Stratford food factory, Standardised Food Products in Chatsworth Road, and he came home with lots of tins. These were placed around our shelter in Harcourt Road, Plaistow, to make another 1-foot layer and held in place with a smothering of concrete on top. The rounded Anderson in fact became a solid square pillbox and we had 12 people in there once. It was useful having a flat roof too – Mum could stand on there to hang out her washing.

Edward Tilbury's father also sprang into action while the family became accustomed to the pitfalls of Anderson life. Mr Tilbury recalls:

I was nearly 11 and there was an average of six sleeping in our Anderson in Appleby Street off Kingsland Road in Shoreditch. To stop the condensation, Dad had the idea of painting the internal walls cream and then applying sawdust on the wet surface to make it more absorbent. I remember once the dust started trickling onto my brother-in-law's face and he awoke thinking he was choking. In fact, my brother-in-law Bill – a big, likeable man who was in the ARP – was often the cause of frayed tempers in the shelter. Forced to lie on his back due to the cramped conditions, he would snore loudly – and make weird noises quite different from your average snorer. His were a series of snorts

and grunts, blood-curdling in their intensity. The bombs would have been better than that. My mother would control her irritation but her huffing and puffing were very expressive.

I particularly hated the spiders and I would sit up on the bunk with my jacket over my head. I once even said: 'I wish the bombs would fall on this shelter' and Mum whacked me sharpish because she thought it was a bad omen.

I used to make balsa-wood models to while away the hours and everyone moaned about the cellulose smell. I once made a Westland Lysander spotter plane which I stuck at the end of my bed to admire. In the morning I found it had fallen down and was now a crumpled mess.

I also recall we left our parakeet, Polly, indoors while we were in the Anderson and you could hear her shouting 'Mother, Mother! Have a cup of tea!' I was in school one day – Randall Cremer School in Shap Street – and the class could hear the bird from there. The master, Mr Sledge ('Sledgehammer') said: 'Who is making that terrible noise?' A boy replied: 'It's Tilbury's parrot, Sir' and I had to stand up and give a talk to the class about it.

In Hackney, Dorothy Crofts was also trying to adjust to the metal hut:

Our Anderson in the garden at Woodland Street, Hackney, was planted up by my Dad to supplement the potatoes, runner beans, cabbages and lettuces in the garden. He grew rhubarb on top of the shelter and it sprouted between the sandbags covering the sides too. We called the shelter the 'dugout' and I remember my first horrendous night in there. The smell of dank earth hit my nostrils and a worm appeared out of the wall. There was no light or warmth. I was given a blanket and a deckchair to sleep in but sleep was impossible. Things improved when narrow wooden bunks were installed.

Dorothy Crofts pictured next to her aunt's Anderson shelter in Burder Road, Hackney.

Brick-built surface shelters in Myrdle Street, Whitechapel.

Residents needed a garden for an Anderson shelter and they were rare in parts of the East End. Alternatively, refuge was sought beneath the kitchen table, under the stairs or in surface shelters built in streets. These shelters were quickly constructed and typically consisted of brick and lime mortar walls with a 9-inch slab of reinforced concrete on top. When the shortage of steel spread to one of cement, some of these shelters were built with no cement in the mortar at all. They were to prove unpopular, liable to collapse, and some gained an unsavoury reputation as raucous venues for drinkers and prostitutes. Other public shelters were opened beneath East End railway arches and in basements and cellars. The stories associated with these shelters, described in the pages that follow, were to pass into Cockney folklore when the bombers came.

While the populace made its shelter arrangements, London itself prepared for the worst. Concern had been growing about the River Thames after calculations estimated that a single bomb penetrating the tunnels between Charing Cross and Waterloo could lead to the flooding of half of London's Underground system. As a result, 25 floodgates were installed, as well as additional safety devices on water mains and sewers.

Around the capital, anti-aircraft guns and searchlights also sprang up and huge silver barrage balloons, or 'blimps', measuring 62 feet in length, soared into the sky. Tethered to steel wires, they rose to 5,000 feet and provided a passive form of defence against enemy aircraft. At that time, low-flying aircraft were the least vulnerable to anti-aircraft fire and defending fighters because there was insufficient time to aim either guns or searchlights before the enemy vanished.

Although the balloons forced the attacking aircraft to fly higher, where they could be dealt with more easily, the blimp wires also proved lethal to RAF aircraft. The blimps were first installed in October 1938 and as many

as 1,000 would float above the capital, creating the most obvious symbol of defence.

One day in Canning Town, five-year-old Doris Capon (née Everest) pointed her podgy finger into the East End sky, causing adults to look upwards. There, amid the clouds, a barrage balloon had become a fireball. She recalls:

This balloon was attached to a lorry which was parked at the end of our road, Clifton Road. It came off the lorry and was floating over the houses before it suddenly erupted into flames. It landed in a garden opposite and the fire was huge. All the neighbours rushed out with buckets of water to put it out. It was so comical at the time and like something out of a Charlie Chaplin movie with all these people rushing madly about. Bits of the old balloon were salvaged and the tough silver material used to black out the windows.

Only 24 enemy aircraft are known to have been brought down by balloons during the the Second World War but they certainly gave a sense of security to the populace and caused inconvenience to the enemy.

Food, as always, was the currency of survival, and rationing began on 8 January 1940, the coldest January for 45 years. Ration books had been issued to everyone at the end of September 1939 and citizens had to register with a retailer of their choice before 23 November 1939. Retailers could then obtain supplies according to the number of customers on their register. When customers presented their ration books, the shopkeeper would cancel the coupons for each portion of food received. Rationing started with butter, bacon and sugar. Meat followed in March and was rationed by price rather than weight, with each person over six years old being entitled to 1s 10d [9.5p] worth per week, which would buy about 3 pounds of beef, pork or mutton. Rationing of tea, margarine and other fats followed in July. Essential foods for each person were thus rationed to a weekly 1s 10d worth of meat, 3 pints of milk, 8 ounces of sugar, 4 ounces of butter or fat, 4 ounces of bacon, 2 ounces of tea, 1 ounce of cheese and one egg. Other foods, such as rice, jam, biscuits, tinned food and dried fruit, were rationed by points and bought using coupons. Butter was always a rare treat, margarine (or 'marge') reigned supreme, and jam or any other spread usually went on dry bread in poorer homes, except perhaps when visitors called. One of the commonest wartime snacks was thick-sliced toast coated with whatever was available. Alternatively, it was dunked in tea.

Wastage of the nation's most precious commodity was a sin, as 11-year-old Maisie Myers (née Gable), living in Old Ford Road, Bethnal Green, discovered:

I once decided to make some cakes while Mum went up to Petticoat Lane. That meant using one of our sacred eggs. I made the cakes and put them in the oven and then the siren sounded and I went to the shelter in a nearby church crypt. When I got home, Mum was relieved to see me but then she saw the black and ruined cakes and changed in an instant. She went mad, shouting about wasted rations and I got a hell of a walloping.

However, one Canning Town lad, Charlie Smith, discovered that some culinary delights remained plentiful:

One food that never seemed to be in short supply in the East End was the Cockney's staple diet, eels, mainly of the jellied variety and usually sold in markets, particularly Petticoat Lane, where Tubby Isaacs did a roaring trade. In Queen's Road Market near to West Ham Football Ground, there was always a thriving fishmonger's stall – Thakes of Barking Road – where I was mesmerized by the three big shiny metal trays, each holding a squirming mass of live eels. Though every creature looked the same, the trays were mysteriously marked 1/0d, 1/6d and 2/6d [5p, 7.5p and 12.5p] per pound. I was even more mystified when I watched eels slither up from one tray and plop into another. Old man Thake never seemed bothered. Once I saw an old man gazing at the trays too. Then he thrust out a lightning arm to grab a large specimen and, in a practised move, stuffed the eel into the low inside pocket of his shabby

Ministry of Food advice on mealtime planning.

(far right) Advice on ensuring Anderson shelter comfort.

raincoat. South of the Market, my family lived near the Tate and Lyle refinery at Silvertown and now and then enjoyed a little bit of sugar smuggled out by a large and mostly unwholesome lady neighbour. This illegal process came to an abrupt end, however, when my mother was told that the woman in question nicked the sugar and brought it out in her extra large bloomers.

Other youngsters, meanwhile, gave careful thought to ration planning. Hackney girl Pat Patmore (née Moore) recalls:

We were allowed 2 ounces of sweets per week. My sister, cousin and I used to receive just 1 ounce and our parents would save the other rationed ounce for us so we could have extra sweets at Christmas. All that saving was well worth it because we could then buy a big box of Cadbury's 'Milk Tray', which was a huge treat. Otherwise I only used to get a pair of slippers at Christmas.

Food rationing was accompanied by encouragement to 'Dig for Victory', a phrase first coined in an *Evening Standard* leader article and officially used in leaflets in November 1939. The campaign urged owners of spare land to place it at their council's disposal and soon great swathes of ground were being cultivated for food production. While householders converted lawns to vegetable patches, those with no garden of their own were busy on the newly available allotments. Even the drained moat around the Tower of London became an allotment for vegetable growing.

Yet, as December 1939 approached, there was still no sign of the bombers after three months of war. That first war winter of 1939/40, was beautiful, too. As a result of petrol rationing and the perils of blackout driving, there were fewer cars on the roads and the air was wonderfully fresh. Londoners suddenly marvelled at the twinkling blanket of stars overhead and, as Christmas approached, the East Enders dropped their guard. Fewer people were carrying gas masks and more chances were being taken. Even the sticky tape used on buses to strengthen windows was absent-mindedly picked off by passengers peering out to see if they had arrived at the correct destination. Cinemas, theatres, sports grounds and meetings reopened in December 1939, when the Government judged their contribution to morale was more important than their vulnerability to attack. For the East End's soccer-mad fans, there was also the welcome news that a special 'War Cup' competition would replace the suspended FA Cup contest in the New Year.

There was not, however, a great deal of money to spend on entertainment. An average man's wage was around £4 a week but working-class living expenses of rents and bills could amount to £3. Nonetheless, dance halls were packed and there were more dance bands playing in the West End than before the war. Museums also reopened (the Imperial War Museum exhibited the Munich Agreement) and libraries enjoyed a boom, with gardening and cookery books in great demand, together with novels and Hitler's prophetic *Mein Kampf*. East End life was almost normal, yet peculiarly abnormal. The Cockneys were at war but it didn't exactly feel like it. Britain experienced a strange, curious lull, which became known as the 'bore war' or by the Americanism, the 'phoney war'.

Then there were the East End children and mothers who had left for a safer life with strangers. Had there been any point in evacuating them? Perhaps it was now safe to have a proper family Christmas and bring them home. It had certainly crossed the minds of James and Sarah Siggins, now settled in their new flat at Searle House in Stepney's Duckett Street. The flat was depressingly quiet without their evacuated children, Eddie and Irene. The children's young brother Leslie had initially left Stepney too, but his stay in Slough was short-lived and he was now back in Duckett Street, where a new baby, Peter, had arrived that summer.

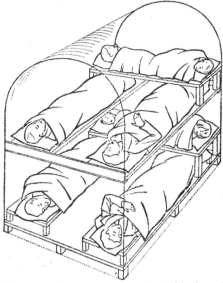

YOUR BED

BY FAR THE BEST bedding for any shelter is a properly made sleeping bag. Nothing else can give so much warmth. Here is a simple way of making a sleeping bag from the blankets you already have, which does not spoil them in any way. Or you can use old woollen skirts, parts of old blankets, and so on.

Take any Army or similar thick blanket about 7 ft. long and 6½ ft. wide (or pieces of old blankets could, of course, be joined together). Line with muslin or cotton material to within a short distance of the top. Sew straight across both blanket and lining horizontally at intervals of about a foot, making pockets which should be well stuffed with folded newspaper. The newspaper stuffing should be changed every month.

Fold the two sides of the blanket towards the centre and sew together to within about 2 ft. of the top. Sew together at the bottom. Sew tapes on the open sides of the bag at the top so that they can be tied together when the person is inside.

James and Sarah Siggins remembered how Eddie and Irene had huddled at Red Coat School in Stepney Green with brown-paper identity labels flapping from their lapels. Sarah had told her children that they were just going on a holiday but her weak smile came close to betraying her churning anxiety. They had kissed and waved at the station and then, with a sudden jolt, the train lurched forwards. It chugged out of Liverpool Street and into the unknown with hundreds of pale, thin arms waving madly from lowered windows.

Chapter three

The banished

STEPPING THROUGH THE HEDGE, Eddie Siggins and his sister Irene found themselves in an enchanted forest. Above, the trees had formed a green canopy, their branches entwined like lace, and sunlight filtered between the broad leaves, casting an eerie green glow. Beneath this leafy ceiling, bright green moss covered the ground and the bases of the tree trunks. Bright red toadstools with white and yellowish spots stood out against this mossy carpet, as did a scattering of long-spiked foxgloves, their bells fully open, revealing their milky mauve-spotted interiors. It was like a dream, and Eddie half expected to wake up and find himself back in Duckett Street, with Mrs Norris wandering by with her wicker basket full of cats' meat, Old Liz bellowing about bagels, and the police in hot pursuit of the Anchor and Hope gamblers. After all the worry about evacuation, they had found themselves in paradise.

In fact, Eddie and Irene were in Higher Denham, in Buckinghamshire, where a pleasant three-bedroomed detached house had become their home. The house was called 'Rutland', after the county where the owners, 'Aunt Maggie' and 'Uncle Harold', were born. They were a childless couple, caring and 'salt of the earth'. It was Uncle Harold, an electrical engineer, who introduced the children to open spaces and the wonders of nature. He even gave Irene a small plot at the side of the house to cultivate and taught them both how to sow seeds and tend the garden. On other occasions, the couple would take them into Uxbridge on the bus to visit Woolworth's before going to the cinema. The day was invariably rounded off slurping ginger beer in the back garden of a High Street pub. Happy days indeed.

Such idyllic surroundings and adventures, seemingly straight from the pages of an Enid Blyton book, were not in store for everyone. Some children ended up in loving homes. Others did not. Some coped well with the transition and were soon scribbling letters to their parents and educating them about hot-water taps, upstairs lavatories, carpets and bed coverings

Mothers behind the barriers at London's Waterloo Station watch their children leave the capital under the evacuation scheme.

called eiderdowns. Others seemed to be utterly traumatised. It was not only the evacuees who were affected. The situation could be equally bewildering, even shocking, for the host families as different lifestyles – and habits – collided. Six-year-old Jewish girl Paula Charig (née Operchinsky) found herself in Henley-on-Thames, a far cry from Shacklewell Lane, near Ridley Market in Dalston.

I stayed with an elderly couple and their garden was so long that a trip to the outside toilet was like going to the next street. It was all very foreign to me. The

East End children keep their gas masks handy as they leave for their evacuation destinations on 2 September 1939.

old man also smelt of dogs, earth and pipe tobacco, and looked and smelled like no other grandpa I had ever seen. He quite scared me at first. I had never actually seen anyone smoke before.

Adults also displayed naivety and ignorance, as Cecil Levart, a 10-year-old Jewish boy, recalls:

I left home in Maplin Street, near Mile End Station, and was dropped off from a lorry with another child of my age, Sidney Hicks, at a farm that had been converted into a pub in Lower Arncott near Bicester, Oxfordshire. The farmer asked what religion I was and I told him. Then he started putting his hands on my head. I asked him what he was doing. He replied in all seriousness: 'You're Jewish so we're looking for horns.' They were actually very nice people but just totally ignorant of Jewish people.

Some 3.5 million children and mothers were evacuated and the experience had a particularly profound effect on youngsters who had left alone. Every life, even a very young one, needs a context – the experience of parental relationships and patterns of activity in relation to environment that we call home. When someone is suddenly removed from this reassuring familiarity and transplanted to a new place, he or she has to reconstruct a new life from scratch.

The destinations of the evacuees were often kept secret and sealed letters were given out to party leaders only at the last moment. Then the great exodus began and the journeys themselves were frequently the start of the youngsters' ordeal, as the following three testimonies reveal. Maisie Myers (née Gable) recalls:

I was living in Old Ford Road, Bethnal Green, and my younger sister Angela and I joined local children and marched down to Cambridge Heath Station and boarded a train. Unfortunately, it had no corridor and we were all stuck in our compartment until Norwich. We were on that train for seven hours. Every child in there wet themselves and we just had to put up with it until we arrived. Terrible, just terrible.

It was no better for young Pat Cook:

I was enjoying our annual hop-picking holiday at Horsmonden in Kent when news came through that we wouldn't be going home to Anne Street in Plaistow. The family would be evacuated from Kent and when the transport arrived I remember my Mum and Nan – and everyone else – fighting to keep their babies and small children with them. Some were arguing that their teenage sons were still too young to be separated from them. We were going to Blackpool and I'll never forget the journey. We stopped on the way and I

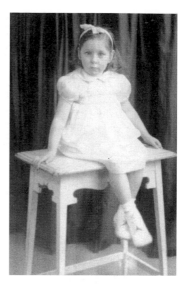

(from left to right):

Young Cyril Levart.

Maisie Myers (née Gable) with her mother, Fay, outside the family shop, the 'Gables', a general store in Old Ford Road, Bethnal Green.

Pat Cook, pictured in Blackpool shortly after the death of her sister Rita.

recall going through huge iron gates of what appeared to be a mansion. I was put on a trolley in there with a couple of cousins and told to sleep. Then Nan asked someone where the nearest fish shop was, only to be told: 'Once you're in you cannot leave – the gates are locked for the night.' She asked why and was told we were staying in a mental asylum in Kirkham, between Preston and Blackpool.

After that, all mums demanded to sleep with their kids and no one slept a wink. We eventually got to Blackpool and Dad later brought up my sick sister Rita. I insisted she sleep with me but she was not very well and was later sent to Victoria Hospital, where she died on her seventh birthday from rheumatic fever.

Gwenn White (née Mazin) would also never forget her evacuation.

I was eight-and-a-half and evacuated with the children of Christian Street School in Whitechapel, opposite the Talmud Torah Synagogue. My Mum and aunt thought it would be okay because the war would only last two weeks. Evacuation morning was horrendous and I can still see all the mums and dads screaming as we all marched off to Shadwell Station. The train pulled off and we were told to sit like good boys and girls and eat our sandwiches. Then I reached for my orange and found it had gone rotten. That was it. For an eight-and-a-half-year-old just parted from her Mum, this was truly the end of the world and I cried and cried until one of the older girls tried to console me. Then one of the older boys decided to lean out of the window and ended up falling out onto the track. The train stopped and he was taken to hospital.

On arriving at their destination, the children were shepherded into a reception area (often a school hall), where they were 'picked' by the foster parents. Here, their anxieties were often compounded by cruel rejection. Many of the foster parents were motivated purely by commercial concerns and the prospect of the weekly Government payment of 10s 6d [52.5p] for the first child taken in and 8s 6d [42.5p] for each additional child. They quickly chose those who appeared to be the least troublesome, while scruffy, less angelic and handicapped youngsters were commonly left milling around at the end with no one to claim them. The final ordeal came when the children entered their new homes, where they had to overcome feelings of despair and fight creeping loneliness. Some also had to confront the additional psychological trauma of neglect, or physical and mental cruelty, as the following memories reveal.

Valerie Merralls (née Spiller) left Dagenham at the age of four and arrived at a farm in Lapworth, Warwickshire, where two of her brothers were already staying.

I would get the buckle end of the belt across the legs just for not eating breakfast and if I dared to sit on Mum's lap when she visited, I was later called a big baby and hit for it. The farmer's wife was the one who dished out the punishment and it took its toll. I regularly wet and soiled the bed, something I had not done since I was a baby. The consequence of this was being made to stand out in the yard in all weathers, washing out my dirty nightclothes in a small tin bath. The couple's son was just as bad and told tales, which resulted in my eldest brother, Ian, getting beaten. Every Sunday afternoon, without fail, the three of us were ordered to leave the house and go for a walk so the family could have peace and quiet in the warmth of their farm kitchen, where they tucked into our sweet ration. It was on one of these walks that I slipped into a canal and was rescued by a passing man. My brothers Neil and Ian ended up getting a real whacking for not looking after me.

(from left to right):

Valerie Merralls (née Spiller) with brothers Mick (left), Ian (behind her) and Neil (right).

Ruth Migdale (née Mazin), aged two, before her evacuation to Cornwall.

Ruth Migdale with her older sister, Barbara, photographed a few months after their return home.

I would also be put in 'The Punishment Room' – a coat cupboard under the stairs. When a teacher unexpectedly popped in one day, I was in the cupboard and the farmer's wife was caught out. But the wife just casually opened the door and said: 'Have you found your boots yet, Valerie?' and got away with it. Teachers used to notice the bruises on my body but I just made up excuses.

Then we escaped. When the wife went shopping she would always push us out of the house, lock up and hide the key. One day we hid and watched where she put the key and as soon as she had gone Ian ran to get it. He collected our pocket money and left a note which read: 'Dear Mrs M. We have gone home. Love Ian'. We made our way to the local train station and were inside the waiting room when the ticket-seller came out onto the platform and called out to a porter: 'Don't let those children go, someone is coming for them.' I ran for it with a brother on either side of me holding my hands. It was 6 miles to the next station and there was snow on the ground and Ian ended up carrying me. We even chanced knocking on a door during the journey and were rewarded with cups of lemonade before we made our excuses and left. We got to the station and caught a train to Barking and then the bus home. We blurted out what had happened to us on the farm and then a policeman knocked on the door. We never heard from the law again and it took Mum ages to get our belongings back from the farm.

Ruth Migdale (née Mazin) also suffered at the hands of her new 'parents':

I was a two-and-a-half-year-old Jewish child and was sent away from Wellclose Square near Cable Street to join my sister Barbara, aged seven, *in Polgooth near St Austell in Cornwall. It was a nightmare. My sister had already been brainwashed by our guardians and told she had better stay with them or be killed when she got back home. That was why she had told our parents it would be fine if I came too. The first thing they did was sit me on a stool in the garden and cut off all my long hair with big shears to make it more manageable. The couple were strict chapel-goers and, although we had a student rabbi who gave us Hebrew lessons, the couple insisted we go to chapel with them too. Once my sister refused and I recall how I hid behind a wall while they beat her with a cane. It was a truly terrifying experience. The couple didn't like Jews at all and I remember how they made fun of my Mum when she visited.*

My parents were oblivious to what was going on and we were too scared to tell them. We were sent food parcels and clothes, but all this was intercepted and given to one of the couple's own daughters instead. We were starving and the man of the house used to give us just the rind off his bacon and the shell of the egg with the inside already eaten. Eventually, the woman's own sister-in-law reported her to the authorities because we were so thin and scabby. Then our school headmaster wrote to our parents and told them we had been badly neglected and felt we should return home. Our parents were shocked by our derelict appearance. We were emaciated, lousy, and had impetigo and scabies. We were taken to a cleansing station, plastered in a lotion and then plunged into a very hot bath. I was badly traumatised by it all and have had food and weight problems ever since. I also hate being away from home to this day – even to go on a luxurious holiday.

The life of nine-year-old Phyl Stableford (née Spackman) was similarly turned upside down when she encountered a new 'Auntie':

Alma (on the left) and Phyl Spackman (now Phyl Stableford) pictured shortly after their arrival in Wivenhoe, Essex

Alma (on the left) and Phyl Spackman pictured in West Ham after the war.

I left Myra Street, West Ham, and went to Wivenhoe in Essex with my eight-year-old sister Alma. We arrived in a hall to be 'picked' by our new parents but no one wanted two little girls. A couple eventually took us in and then a letter arrived to say our Mum had died. Alma didn't understand and asked when Mum was coming. The wife said: 'Your Mum has gone to the angels.' Alma dropped her head straight down into her dinner. I didn't cry and the wife turned to me and said: 'You stony-hearted little bitch', *which totally shocked me.*

We moved soon after and ended up on a smallholding in Letton, Herefordshire, with an elderly couple who had four of their own children. My younger sister Margaret had joined us now and the three of us were segregated from the start. We had to have breakfast first – bread and milk or lumpy porridge – and then we were kicked out to amuse ourselves, regardless of the weather, even in snow. Alma once swallowed a lump of porridge and was sick out of the window. She prayed the lump would not be seen by the couple or they would have thrashed us for wasting food. The birds ate it and Alma was convinced there was a God after all.

We were always hungry and in the night we would creep out of bed and make for a store of apples kept under the roof eaves. Once an apple rolled down the stairs and it woke up 'Auntie'. She immediately got out a thin stick and thrashed us both there and then. The food situation got so bad Alma took to eating swede peelings from pig buckets and we both ate raw sugar beet from the fields. On other occasions, we were beaten for being late back with the bread from the shop, and the woman's son once held Alma upside down over a well and threatened to drop her because she had refused to show him her knickers.

One day we had had enough. We had often sat in a hollow oak tree to discuss escaping and now we did it. We ran off during the day and found our schoolmistress and told her everything. Our absence caused a real stir and our

'escape' was even in the papers. The local vicar got involved and we were moved on. I ended up as a nanny's help to a Lord and Lady Brocket at their mansion, Kinnersley Castle, near Letton. I helped the nanny bring up the Lord and Lady's daughter, Elizabeth, whose godmother was the late Queen Mother. It was a different world and I stayed in the servant's quarters in an annexe. Life was fine and I even went with the family to Scotland where they went hunting. My sisters were placed with other families in the same area of Herefordshire.

Young George Mooney, the lad who experienced the 'Battle of Cable Street' (see page 63), was shocked when he visited his younger brother:

Jimmy had been evacuated to Brighton and my Mum and I went down there to see him. He was staying at a grand place owned by a colonel. Mum asked Jimmy, who was 10, where he had been sleeping in such a magnificent house and he turned and pointed to the stables. That was it. My Mum got hold of a bucket and began filling it with horse dung from Jimmy's stable. Then she marched up to the front door and rang the bell. When the colonel answered, she barged straight past and emptied the bucket on his expensive lounge carpet. She walked back out telling him: 'If you think my son is going to live in it, you can do the same.' We brought him back home to Exmouth Street in Stepney after that.

Life was not much better for June Smith (née Meddeman). She recalls:

I arrived in Cambridge from Bridport Place in Hoxton and was only four. I was with my older brother John and we both knew the score immediately. The woman of the house sat down to a lovely tea with her three children while we

received just bread and jam. Then she took my hand-made clothes and just gave me a simple dress to wear. Next she took a lovely kilt and fur coat, made by my grandma from the rabbits she kept. My double-jointed doll vanished as well. I never found out what happened to these things but the steady pattern of disappearing items left me distraught. We ran back to the reception area, which was a school, and told a WVS woman who was there. We ended up in the house of a piano teacher, a Mrs Sylvester, who was wonderful. She was just like a mother to us and wanted to adopt John and I in the end.

Many tormented parents agonised over whether they had done the right thing in sending their children away. Cyril Demarne, a sub-officer instructing Auxiliary Fire Service personnel at Abbey Road School in West Ham, recalled:

I had studied gases for my work and everyone said Hitler would be using them. That influenced me and I said to my wife, Alice: 'You have got to go with the children.' We talked about it for hours but she wanted to stay with me. Then we were informed that the schools would be evacuated. We lived in Littlemoor Road, Ilford, and I recall seeing our girls, Josephine, seven, and Marjorie, five, ready with their clothes and respirators. We took them to the school and left them there, while we went on to Barking Station to see them off. We gave them a hug and a kiss at the station before they went and our eyes fixed on them until the very last minute. We were all very tearful indeed, and my last memory was looking at the youngest, who staggered back a bit when the train suddenly jolted off. Goodness knows where they were going.

We went back to a silent home and cried and cried. It was very harrowing and we wondered whether we had done the right thing. Three days later, we received a postcard with an address for them in Bradford-on-

(top left) The West Ham Fire Brigade Drill Class in June 1925. Cyril Demarne is in the back row, second from the left; (top right) Tea time for the children of Columbia Market Nursery in Bethnal Green at Alwalton Hall near Peterborough; (above) Young Charlie Smith with cousin Joyce.

Avon in Wiltshire. I was busy enrolling and training hundreds of auxiliary firemen, equipping them and transporting them to their stations throughout West Ham. However, my wife was able to go and see the children. They were in a loving environment, but terribly homesick and kept getting nervous illnesses. My wife asked the billeting officer what would happen to them if we were killed and he said the children would probably be sent to an orphanage. Alice rang to tell me. That was it. Hitler had also claimed he would not be the first to use war gases so I got them home for Christmas and they stayed with us for the rest of the war.

It was not just parents in the East End who were feeling the strain. Evacuated mothers could also feel completely isolated, as Rosie Somers (née Ferman) recalls:

I was 21 with a newborn baby, Harold. We were evacuated to Brettenham in Norfolk, where we stayed with a family. There were lots of other evacuated Jewish mothers in the hamlet and my husband used to travel from our home in Stoke Newington to visit us. When he arrived the scenes were unbelievable. As soon as the other women saw him, they rushed up to him and asked him about their husbands in London. Then, when he was getting in the car to leave, they came up to him and said: 'Don't leave without our letters.' They desperately clung to him and the car. My husband was the only one who came to visit and these other mothers just looked totally abandoned.

The young evacuees' efforts to adapt were constantly tested by overwhelming loneliness, grim surroundings and even exploitative foster parents, as the following extracts show. Charlie Smith (whose description of life in Canning Town appears on page 44) left for Portland in Dorset.

I spent my 10th birthday in Russell Road School evacuation centre in Custom House, being prepared for what I thought was a holiday. To most of us the world only went as far as Southend, Margate or the hop fields of Kent, so travelling in a fleet of buses away from Custom House gave me a feeling of fear and excitement as we reached the London rail terminals. As the train sped along, many of the children, with eyes tightly closed, wanted to feel the rush of fresh air on their faces and stuck their heads out. They soon retreated to the safety of the compartment for a spit wash after they were taunted about their sooty faces. The excitement soon went too, when the rations ran out and we realised we wouldn't be going home for tea. There were lots of tears and I felt very lonely.

At the reception centre, boys were separated from girls regardless of family ties. It was upsetting because Mum had ordered me to stay with my cousin, Joyce Galvin, who lived in the same road. The two groups were then taken off to a collection point outside a bank, where the foster parents arrived and chose who they wanted. One woman arrived and told the billeting officer: 'I will only take two nice, clean girls from nice homes.' She looked down with distain at us boys, some of whom were trying to look angelic. Darkness gathered and I choked back tears as I realised I was the only one left, together with a boy called Andrew Monteith, a fatherless boy who had been in a sanatorium with tuberculosis. A large man, Mr Marsh, then arrived late with a girl who we later learnt was his daughter, Lily, aged 15. He took us but before we left, the billeting officer asked us if we had spare clothes and

a toothbrush and flannel. We said yes to everything but I had never cleaned my teeth before.

Mr Marsh lived in an isolated house with his wife, daughter and two sons. It was like the setting for a Brontë film and seemed to be on the edge of 'nothingness'. In the morning we saw why. The house was next to a massive quarry which went on forever. Andy and I were given a bare, cold attic room with a tiny window over the quarry. Our bed was an antique iron one with a flock-filled mattress which smelled damp. It had belonged to old grandmother Marsh who, the two boys gleefully told us, had died in it. She must have been large and slept in it alone because Andy and I rolled towards each other in the centre. I recall crying one night because I wanted to go home and Mr Marsh's daughter, Lily, came in and comforted me. While Lily was there, Andy wet the bed, which caused Mrs Marsh to demand: 'Do all evacuees leak at both ends?' The other lingering memory was Sunday dinner, which always seemed to be a pig's head (with an apple stuffed in its mouth), which Mrs M would carve and dish out in order of seniority. Andy and I were therefore last and I prayed I would be left out altogether.

At the local school there was plenty of banter between the 'townies' and 'country bumpkins'. They accused us of running scared from the bombers, which riled us. Portland was a wonderful place to explore but I lost my best friend there. Munchie (Maurice) McCall had been playing around the large quarry at the back of the Marsh's house and slipped and fell into the depths, where he was crushed by a dislodged boulder. This finally persuaded my mother to get me home and I left Portland after five weeks. Cousin Joyce followed me back to Canning Town.

Dorothy Crofts similarly struggled to settle in her new surroundings:

I was 11 and evacuated to Northampton with four school friends. We stayed in a pub and shared an upstairs bedroom, which was warm and comfortable. Yet I missed my home in Woodland Street, Hackney, and as soon as I returned home from school each day, I went up to the bedroom to cry in private. The sound of the pips at the beginning of the 6 o'clock wireless news always sent me into floods of tears, as I recalled the chinking of the teacups and my mother setting the table for the evening meal at that time. I couldn't contain myself any longer and I wrote three letters home on one day. As soon as I posted the first I had doubts about the words I used and guilty about the position I'd put my parents in. They couldn't just drop everything and get me, let alone cover the cost of doing so. I wrote a second letter playing down the first letter. Then I sent a third which was based on an evacuation propaganda leaflet I had seen. It contained the words: 'Your courage, your cheerfulness, your resolution will see us through'. I quoted it in my letter, saying it would be my motto from

A fancy-dress party at the Brady Girls' Club in Hanbury Street: Miriam Moses, founder of the club, is sitting in the front row, dressed in black.

Helen Erlick (née Huscovitch) with brothers Dave (centre) and Jack.

Young Northampton evacuee Dorothy Crofts, pictured on 12 September 1939, aged 11.

now on. All three letters arrived on the same day and my brother Bill sent the last one to the magazine Tit Bits and was paid a guinea for it. Soon after I nonetheless returned to London.

Pat Patmore (née Moore) was totally unprepared for the conditions awaiting her:

My sister, cousin and I were evacuated for just 10 days – and that was quite enough. We had ended up with a mining family in Glamorgan in South Wales. She was a tough woman who wouldn't let us send letters home unless she read them first. They had a son of their own who they once beat with a

chair and I never forget it. The three of us evacuees shared a double bed and it was running alive with bugs. We sat up all night crying and watching these horrible creatures. We eventually smuggled out a letter and Mum and her brother came and took us home to Chalgrove Road, Hackney.

Meanwhile, the breaking of one of the countryside's golden rules added to the woes of evacuee Helen Erlick (née Huskovitch):

I recall being nearly seven and standing at Liverpool Street Station clutching the hand of my nine-year-old brother, Dave. All around us were boys and girls I knew from the Robert Montefiore School in Vallance Road, Whitechapel, and the Jewish Brady Clubs for boys and girls, where we enjoyed so many great occasions. I could also see my best friend, Ivan Saffer, with his parents. They lived in Hughes Mansions opposite our school in Vallance Road. When we arrived at Ely station, we went to a school where a family picked Dave and I, together with a boy called Sidney who lived next door. As soon as they got us home, they deloused us in the bath and the three of us were shown the room we would share on their isolated farm.

Next day, disaster. My brother was seen taking an apple from a tree by a farmer and then he left a gate open as he ran off, leaving cows to escape. There was a terrible row about it and the family kicked Dave and I out, leaving Sidney there. A billeting officer then spent four hours driving us around until he could find someone to have us. I went to one family and Dave went to another. I moved to other billets after that and was generally treated well. However, one couple of spinsters used to leave my bread-and-jam tea in the shed because I wasn't allowed in the house until they got home. I would eat it on my own in the garden in all weathers.

One day, Dave and I had had enough and we made our way home, using money we had earned picking fruit in the fields. However, we both ended up being sent back to another Cambridgeshire village, Stretham, and my younger brother Jack stayed with Dave there. In fact, Jack grew up as a country boy and didn't want to leave in the end. He was the last to come home. Jack viewed his foster parents as his real parents and saw us as strangers. He used to go back and see them in his school holidays and they even left him their cottage in their will but he didn't accept it.

In sharp contrast, 10-year-old Ron Warner endured a miserable existence as an unpaid employee of his new 'parents':

My brother and I were evacuated from Powell House, Lower Clapton Road, in Hackney, and we ended up in Sawbridgeworth in Hertfordshire. We were picked by a young couple who had a small dairy business. They had three carts, and a small Ford van which was used to collect milk from farms. The milk was then bottled for delivery. Before long my brother George and I were roped in to help too. We started at 3.00 a.m., when we collected the milk from farms. Then we would drop the bottles off to homes or fill cans and leave them at the side of streets. We were exhausted and fell asleep in school and received absolutely nothing for our trouble. We later discovered money sent to us by Mum never reached us either. My parents came to get George and I after six months and they collected us in the same clothes we wore when we had arrived. They were the only ones we had worn – and we seldom washed either them or ourselves.

The fortunes of evacuees could sometimes dramatically change, however, as Marjie Evans (née Pope) recalls:

I was evacuated from Kingsland Road, Hackney, with two sisters and a brother, to Aberangell in Wales. I remember the four of us sitting on one side of a dinner table and the host family on the other. The man of the house brought pork to the table and it was crawling with maggots. We stood up to say the Lord's Prayer before the husband announced: 'They (the maggots) will not hurt you. They are God's creatures.' He then proceeded to scrape them off with his hand. We said nothing but he angrily ordered us to go away when we wouldn't touch the food. We later crept down to the vegetable patch and ate raw turnip, cabbage and potatoes instead. The man of the house was a champion fisherman and fresh salmon was once put on the table. There was none for us, though. We were given a plate of runner beans, while they tucked in.

Rose Horscroft (née Rands) is pictured on the left, with her sister Brenda on the right and Barbara (the Hackmans' daughter) in the centre. The photograph was taken in Rugby when the Hackmans visited relatives.

We were later evacuated to a Somerset pub where the landlady immediately declared: 'Don't expect butter on your side of the table'. So we had margarine and they had the butter. There were 12 evacuees there and we used to wash each other in the same bath water and fend for ourselves. We were all totally infested with lice. There were hundreds crawling in our hair and we'd shake them out onto newspaper. We eventually smuggled a letter back home and Mum came to see for herself. Mum cuddled us and was so upset and angry because she thought she had let us down.

We planned our getaway straightaway. Mum had to shave our infested hair there and then or the coach-driver would not let us on, and then she hid us under the seats so no one saw us leave. However, there was a huge row just before we left – almost a fight – when the foster parents demanded us back and also money owed to them. We finally ended up in the servant quarters of a mansion near Wisbech. We had a wonderful time there and enjoyed total freedom. Our family was together there too, apart from Dad who was in the Home Guard in Hackney. Local kids blamed us for bringing the bombers to Norfolk – they insisted they were chasing only the Cockneys – and used to wait in gangs of 30 or so and hurl frogs at us. However, back at the mansion lived a son of the landed owners who was a bit of a rebel and he took a shine to us. He treated us to trips out in his Dad's pony and trap, until he was grounded and told not to mess with the evacuees.

Frank Rose and younger brother Cyril photographed in Soham, aged 13½ and 12 respectively.

Sheila Carter also experienced both sides of the evacuation coin:

I was just four when I was evacuated with my Mum and two younger brothers from our house near Bromley-by-Bow gasworks, to Wallingford in Oxfordshire on the River Thames. We lived in a massive country house vacated by the owner, who had gone to live abroad during the war. There were stables, a castle folly in the grounds and vast rooms. It was like being in a palace and we, unbelievably, were living there. One of our neighbours was Agatha Christie. It was wonderful, but later we ended up in Oxford in a place which may well have been a former Victorian workhouse. It was packed with hundreds of people, most of them elderly, and the whole experience was like something out of a Dickens' novel. We slept in a corridor, which was full of people, and we all ate in a hall where we had to stand for prayers before sitting down at long tables. It was terrible.

Many children, like Eddie and Irene Siggins, eagerly embraced their new world, and treasured their memories and adventures all their lives. Rose Horscroft (née Rands) arrived in Acocks Green, Birmingham, with her sister Brenda.

We were living with a couple called Hackman and had a wonderful time. They lived in a lovely big house with a garden, which was a real change from our home in New North Road, Hoxton. At home we lived very poorly with worn clothes, no shoes and no toys and our family shared two rooms at the top of a house and used a communal sink on the stairs. The place in Birmingham was a different world. I had never even seen a garden before at the back of a house – just old yards where the toilets usually were. The Hackmans' garden was big too and I spent many, many hours wandering up and down the paths, which were surrounded by nasturtiums, which remain one of my favourite flowers to this day. We also used to visit their relatives in Rugby. They had a smallholding and those visits were also special experiences.

Back home in Hoxton we never had a sink with running water and we used 'Sunlight' soap on our hands and to scrub the floor with. So at the Hackman's I couldn't resist spending as much time as possible in their indoor bathroom, washing my hands over and over again with their lovely-smelling pink toilet soap. My guardians knew why I kept disappearing up there. They also knew I had only previously bathed in an old tin bath in the living room in front of the fire. Christmas there was amazing too. I'd never seen a Christmas tree before and this one reached the ceiling. Mrs Hackman also made me a settee and two armchairs out of matchboxes and covered them with pretty flowered cotton. We thought we were in heaven and never wanted to return home where it was so miserable.

Bob Humphreys, aged 12, also enjoyed his evacuation:

I was evacuated with Beal School in Ilford, where we were now living. A kind lady picked me and another boy, Bobby Youd. The lady took us home, fed us with jam sandwiches and we then discovered our new home was in Ipswich. We had been billeted with a lovely couple in their fifties, Mr and Mrs Cross, and after the meal they insisted we write home to reassure our parents. Mr Cross used to take us fishing off the end of Felixstowe pier but we couldn't go on the beach because it had been barricaded off with barbed wire and was mined. On all public transport there were posters too: 'Careless Talk Costs Lives' and 'The Enemy is Everywhere'. There were no railway or road signs anywhere.

Everyone carried their gas masks over their shoulder and once we spotted a man with an interesting name written on his box. It was 'IVAN/GER 573298'. We thought he must be a spy. His name was Ivan and he was German, as the label said. We followed him along various roads, hiding behind lamp posts and trees to see if he was going to sabotage anything. Then we came across a policeman and proudly told him we had been shadowing a Nazi. The policeman approached the suspicious character and we waited nearby, expecting a medal. However, both men were smiling. The policeman explained the writing was simply his National Registration number but he praised us for being vigilant.

Nine-year-old Reg Baker also gratefully entered a different world, when he swapped the cramped surroundings of a Globe Road flat in Bethnal Green for the fields of Weston-on-the-Green in Oxfordshire.

A blacksmith and his mother picked me out, with a boy from Paddington called Ronnie Norton. It was a good life and the grandma bought me my first pair of pants and a grey jacket and shorts. It was the space that struck me – and the light. The streets of Bethnal Green were so narrow that there wasn't much sunlight at all, and now in the country it was almost blinding. The only animals I had ever seen had been glimpsed from trains during day trips to Southend and now they were really close up, and it was very strange indeed. We took to chasing them around until a farmer educated us. He said: 'The sheep will give you wool, the cow will give you milk – and the horse will give you a bloody kick if you don't behave.'

Evacuee Frank Rose discovered how caring foster parents could help to calm young fears:

For many of the schools in the East End, the journey to a new world began at Liverpool Street station. Among the schools heading for Ely was my own school, the Jews' Free School (boys and girls) near Bishopsgate, together with the Davenant Foundation School in Whitechapel Road, All Saints School in Shoreditch and the Robert Montefiore Junior Boys School in Underwood Street. My school, the Jews' Free, was in Middlesex Street, known as Petticoat Lane.[1] Most of the pupils were Jewish and from the East End and it was renowned for its charitable gifts of corduroy suits to the boys and free shoes. Poor children were also given breakfast every day and meal tickets.

When war came, the school closed [and bombing in February 1941 ensured that it never re-opened] *and the evacuation brought many pupils to Ely, Littleport and Soham. I had just turned 12 and my parents made a last-minute decision to let my brother Cyril, who was 10, accompany me, issuing constant pleas: 'Whatever you do, don't let him be separated from you.' And so we left our home, which was a flat within the complex of the Great Synagogue, also known as the Cathedral Synagogue, in Duke's Place, where my father was an official. We were going to be sent into something called the 'country', known more from picture books (kindly looking cows, fluffy white clouds, a darling lamb) than from any first-hand contact. It was possible to feel guiltily excited. That morning we marched out of the school gates for the last time and past streets lined with weeping mothers and waving hands. We*

brought the Bishopsgate traffic to a halt. All over the capital similar scenes were being enacted. It was goodbye forever to a world that died that weekend. Our world.

Mr Rose and his brother ended up in Soham's Church Hall, where they were picked by two women:

The elder distinguished-looking lady was Mrs Boyce, our new foster mother, who had two sons of a similar age, and the younger woman was her friend, a nurse named Mary Smith. How kind they were, how transparently good, like characters in an E. M. Forster novel. One thing had to be addressed without delay. My parents, strictly observant Jews, had brought us up to have our heads covered at all times and I asked if we could keep our caps on in the house. I needn't have worried. No fuss was made and we never felt self-conscious. Mrs Boyce's children took us under their wing too and it was wonderfully exciting to hold and stroke the rabbits in their garden. I was an animal-lover deprived of the company of animals. There was also a gentle old dog roaming about with doleful eyes, and plum and greengage trees at the bottom of the garden. There was so much to take in.

Mrs Boyce's husband, a farmer, was a strong reassuring figure who also welcomed us that first day. He needed all his tact and good humour to cope with us as we took our first tea with the family that afternoon, struggling to keep back the tears. Evacuation was a trauma out of proportion to the size of our young, over-protected lives, and the overwhelming nature of the reality of what was happening caught up with us in those minutes. On our best behaviour, trying to be polite, there we sat, my brother and I, to all intents and purposes in the midst of aliens. Nothing was familiar. The butter was deep yellow and tasted salty and for the first time since leaving school I was being addressed as 'Frank' instead of by my surname or the family nickname, 'Chicky'. The friendly aliens were doing their best, but it was patently and pathetically obvious that we were not at home. I had the vague fear that we were lost in the middle of nowhere. How was anyone going to find us?

The couple's two sons, Donald and Tony, took us to 'the field', our future 21-acre playground, which was 10-minutes walk away and bounded by a river. In Petticoat Lane, hens were creatures cooped up in wooden crates or carried squawking and fluttering upside down by their legs. Here they wandered freely around the hen houses and bullocks grazed by the river. The highlight of the experience was watching the pigs being fed, the low point the stinging nettles. This was the country as it really was, not the sanitised edited version fed to town children. We were even told that we could help collect the eggs in the evening if we wished. Things might have been a lot, lot worse. We wrote to our parents without delay, informing them Mr Boyce had over

---

[1] Founded in 1817, the Jews' Free School was reputed to be the largest school in England, with 3,500 pupils in the 1890s.

Sheila Raznick (née Schwalb), aged 8, and her brother Raymond, aged 10, pictured in their hand-knitted swimsuits during the summer of 1938.

Mothers and babies waiting to be evacuated from Victoria Station, London, on 2 September 1939.

1,000 chickens and Mrs Boyce wrote too, promising she would care for us as she did her own two boys. That night, the first ever away from parental care, we were woken by a cracking thunderstorm and she came into our room to allay any fears, asking if we would like Donald to stay with us. It was a time of adaptation and discovery.

Soham at the outbreak of war was a village with a population of 5,000, uncluttered by cars and uncluttered by throngs of people, even in the humming High Street during the busiest hours. With its imposing church tower dominating the village skyline, its quiet lanes, its gas-lit cottages and houses, its windmill, its fields and the surrounding Fens, it was about as far removed from built-up central London as most of us could imagine. And what better time to be there? Day followed day, basked in mellow sunlight, blackberries ripened in the hedges and the countryside was tinged with the colours of early autumn. Donald and Tony taught us how to care for rabbits, how to ease the sting from nettles with a dock leaf, and other bits of wisdom that the experienced impart to the inexperienced. In return, we taught them chess, which Mr Boyce told me he was grateful for during the blackout nights. In some very basic ways we educated each other.

We were lucky, of course, but idyllic, life was not. Homesickness, concern about the war, uncertainty about the future, the need to fit into the ways of two cultures, combined to create a sense of underlying unease seldom far below

the surface. Once Mr Boyce had some business in a neighbouring village and he asked if Cyril and I would like to cycle there with him. It was a glorious day but fell during the Jewish Festival of Succoth (Tabernacles), when many mundane activities, including cycling, were forbidden. Mr Boyce, seeing my indecision, said: 'I'm sure God would never punish a boy for going out on a day like this.' The remark had a ring of such common sense that I have never forgotten it. I went on the ride and, looking back now, I feel neither shame nor pride, only a keener awareness of the inevitability of our confusion, and the way Mr Boyce's remarks so often seemed to point to a refreshing truth. God, so to speak, had other things on his mind. The year was 1939.

It was the ability and willingness of both children and foster parents to adapt that ultimately determined mutual contentment, as Sheila Raznick (née Schwalb) recalls:

I left Stoke Newington and arrived in the village of Barnack, which is near Wittering in Cambridgeshire. The family who cared for me were wonderful but I found it a totally bewildering place. First, I was warned about things called stinging nettles – and then promptly walked through some. Then I saw my first cows (I'd only seen them in books) and, being Jewish, was totally shocked to discover the family killed their own pigs. There was no sanitation

Eddie Siggins's younger brother Leslie in the Duckett Street garden of his 'Nana', Mary Ann.

in the village either. Everyone used a bucket as a toilet and a man with a horse and trap would come and collect them each week. The family bath was also kept up the road and I remember having to carry it down when it was my turn. However, I came to love the countryside and gradually felt more and more at home there. I enjoyed walking and admiring the great scenery, and found the small community atmosphere had great warmth to it. I also learnt to swim in the River Welland and tobogganed in the winter at a place known as the 'Hills and Holes'. Meanwhile my brother Raymond really landed on his feet. He stayed with a major in a mansion and lived like a lord.

As the Christmas of 1939 approached, those children evacuated during the 'phoney war' were sorely missed by their parents. The festivities would not be the same without the youngsters and, since the anticipated bombing had failed to materialise, it seemed safe to bring them back home. Despite its poverty and grime, the East End offered a sense of belonging. Its appeal was magnetic and families and communities spontaneously re-formed, seemingly aware that their collective strength would be the key to future survival. Even by October 1939, 50,000 mothers and children had returned. That number had doubled by November. By January 1940, at least 200,000 children – about half of whom were returning evacuees – were in London requiring education. Yet some two-thirds of the schools had been taken over for the war effort and, by 11 January 1940, only 15 of the London County Council's 900 schools were open. Still the evacuees came. By late spring of 1940, the vast majority of evacuees had returned and there were an estimated 400,000 children in London.

Eddie Siggins and sister Irene had spent Christmas 1939 with 'Aunt Maggie' and 'Uncle Harold', the man who had introduced them to Denham's enchanted wood. The couple had made a great fuss of the children at Christmas and had even put on a party for them and their friends. Yet it

now seemed safe for them to return home to Stepney too. So the children left for Duckett Street where brother Leslie, now almost six, and baby Peter were waiting inside Searle House. Further up the street, the children's Nana – Mary Ann Bowyer – was also excitedly anticipating their return.

Frank Lewey, who had become Stepney's Mayor in November 1939, later offered his own theory for the East End migration home. He wrote:

> *Some were just homesick for the crowded streets and jumbled houses; in the open spaces of the country they grew afraid. Visits from parents unsettled them badly. It sounds callous, but it's undoubtedly the truth, that parental visits brought back hundreds of youngsters to the danger area, and were presently responsible for many deaths that might have been avoided.*

He added:

> *Many parents, too, brought back their children even against the children's will, because they found their homes desolate without them. It was natural; but it was selfish and dangerous, as bombing later showed. Some children, too, could not settle down without cinemas and shops. Most of all, they missed the good old fish and chips. There is something more potent than opium for the adolescent 'slummy' in eating fish and chips and watching the celluloid lovers of the screen. They could not breathe without it; they yearned to go home – and home they went.*

The Government, alarmed by the deluge of returning children and in anticipation of raids, sought to register parents for a new evacuation scheme. Again the uptake was poor and only 800 out of a possible 10,000 were on the new list in East Ham. The trouble was that nothing had actually happened to encourage parents to relinquish their children.

While the lull persisted in Britain, terror reigned in Europe. Poland, like Austria and Czechoslovakia, had been occupied and was being subjected to the brutal regime that was a Nazi trademark in conquered lands. Hans Frank was appointed Governor General of Poland by Hitler and promptly announced that Poles would become 'the slaves of the Greater German Empire'. Hundreds of thousands of Jews were now deported to the East through blizzards and temperatures of minus 40 degrees Centigrade, and a town called Auschwitz, near Cracow, was selected as a suitable site for a new 'quarantine camp'. The eventual discovery that over 1 million inmates of Auschwitz had been put to death sent shockwaves of anger and grief around the world, and Britain's Jewish heart in the East End was broken when news emerged that 6,000 people a day had been gassed in four huge chambers.

As the Cockney evacuees became re-acquainted with the streets and markets of home, Hitler pushed west once more. In April 1940, the Germans invaded Norway and then, a month later, Belgium, Holland and France. Churchill, who succeeded Chamberlain as Prime Minister on 10 May 1940, was dumbfounded by the Nazi progress. On the same day, 23 incendiaries tumbled towards East Stour Farm in Chilham, Kent – the first bombs to fall on England since 1918. Then, just five days into his premiership, Churchill was awoken by a telephone call from Premier Paul Reynaud in Paris, who told him: 'We have been defeated!' When Churchill did not respond immediately, Reynaud said again: 'We are beaten, we have lost the battle.' A massive army of German tanks, of a size and concentration unseen before in war, was pouring unchecked towards the English Channel. The German army groups, supported by the Luftwaffe (German Air Force), stretched back for 100 miles.

Ahead of the tanks, cut off and stranded at the French coast, were the remains of the Belgian Army, nine divisions of the British Expeditionary Force and ten divisions of the French First Army. The German tanks were poised for the kill and the greatest German victory of the campaign. However, 24 May marked one of the war's pivotal moments, when Hitler ordered the tanks to advance no further on the trapped enemy at Dunkirk. Hitler agreed with Field Marshal Rundstedt that more infantry support should be brought up. He also observed that precious armour should be conserved for later operations against the French south of the Somme. The final decision was greatly influenced by Hermann Goering, chief of the Luftwaffe, who offered to finish off the stranded units with his aircraft alone.

The halted German advance provided a brief window of opportunity. The Allies' Operation Dynamo swung into action and ensured that a third of a million men were evacuated from Dunkirk's beaches, right under the noses of the Germans, using an armada of 850 vessels of all shapes and sizes, from destroyers to small sailing boats. An exhausted army returned, and their deliverance was celebrated, but Churchill reminded the nation that 'wars are not won by evacuations'. In fact, Britain's predicament was grim. She had a greatly reduced army and a weakened Royal Air Force (RAF), and the Luftwaffe was now based just across the Channel.

As the Dunkirk drama was unfolding, attention was turned to a perceived internal threat and, on 16 May, 2,000 non-nationals were picked up in London. During the last week of May, 1,600 British citizens were also seized, including Oswald Mosley, who was arrested at his home by Special Branch and imprisoned on 23 May. Seven days later, his British Union of Fascists party was also dissolved and its publications banned. Virtually all Mosley's cohorts were also rounded up and jailed.

The famous 'Barrel Organ King', Albert Faccini, a neighbour of young Eddie Siggins in Stepney, was also interned in 1940. A proud Italian, Faccini had refused to become a British subject, and his imprisonment infuriated the residents of Ernest Street, where his organ business was based on the corner with Duckett Street. They organised a petition demanding his release and, in December 1940, he became a free man again. Gradually, more and more people were released but over 40 remained incarcerated. Mosley remained behind bars, even though his accommodation at Holloway Prison was a modest flat rather than a cell.

Churchill now attempted to galvanise the nation and a mood of defiance swept through the East End after his great House of Commons speech on 4 June, which ranks with the greatest ever made in history:

We shall fight in France, we shall fight on the seas and oceans, we shall fight with growing confidence and growing strength in the air, we shall defend our island, whatever the cost may be, we shall fight on the beaches, we shall fight on the landing grounds, we shall fight in the fields and in the streets, we shall fight in the hills; we shall never surrender…

Four days later, East Enders had a chance to take their minds off the grave world situation when 'The Hammers' played at Wembley again to contest the new Football League 'War Cup' against Blackburn Rovers. Sam Small's 34th-minute goal earned West Ham the trophy before the players split up and returned to their Service units. It was only a temporary diversion for the fans too. Italy declared war on Britain and France two days after the Hammers' victory, prompting chaos in Italian quarters of London, where some restaurant and hotel staff were suddenly sacked and other eateries stoned.

The Swastika flew over Paris on 14 June 1940, and four days later Churchill again delivered a momentous rallying call to his people:

What General Weygand called the Battle of France is over. I expect that the Battle of Britain is about to begin. Upon this battle depends the survival of Christian civilization. Upon it depends our British life and the long continuity of our institutions and our Empire. The whole fury and might of the enemy must very soon be turned on us. Hitler knows that he will have to break us in this island or lose the war. If we can stand up to him, all Europe may be free and the life of the world may move forward into broad, sunlit uplands. But if we fail, then the whole world, including the United States… will sink into the abyss of a new dark age, made more sinister and perhaps more protracted by the lights of perverted science. Let us therefore brace ourselves to our duties, and so bear ourselves that, if the British Empire and its Commonwealth last for a thousand years, men will still say: 'This was their finest hour'.

France surrendered four days later on 22 June 1940 and now, at last, it was Britain's turn.

The first major raid on mainland Britain had occurred on the night of 18/19 June as a reprisal for a RAF bombing raid on the Ruhr in May. A total of 70 Luftwaffe aircraft attacked and, while there were civilian casualties in Cambridge, bombs in the London region fell on arable land at Addington in Surrey. Aerial activity escalated and, on 10 July, the Luftwaffe lost 13 aircraft to the RAF's 6, in a confrontation that the head of Fighter Command, Air Chief Marshal Hugh Dowding, later defined as the opening of the 'Battle of Britain'. History's very first great battle of the air had begun.

Six days later, Hitler issued Directive 16, an historic statement to his inner circle declaring that Britain would be invaded 'if necessary'. This bold initiative was code-named Operation Sealion but the Fuehrer himself realised that a massive land invasion of Britain could only be attempted if the RAF and Royal Navy were somehow neutralised. If the skies and seas could be cleared, six infantry divisions would leave the Pas de Calais in France and hit the beaches between Ramsgate and Bexhill, while four would cross from Le Havre and land between Brighton and the Isle of Wight; further west, three divisions would leave the Cherbourg Peninsula and land at Lyme Bay. It was hoped to land a quarter of a million men within three days.

The man entrusted by Hitler to clear the skies was Hermann Goering, who became Reich Marshal, Hitler's deputy, on 19 July. Thus, Goering and the RAF's Hugh Dowding now held the destiny of the world in their hands. Britain had more than 600 fighter planes to defend itself while the attackers had over 3,000 bombers and fighters.

Goering's long-awaited *Adler Tag* (Eagle Day) offensive began on 13 August, with the aim of smashing the RAF and their bases. It proved a disaster. The RAF, with the crucial advantage of radar, picked off the Germans with ruthless efficiency and the Luftwaffe lost 45 aircraft compared with the RAF's 13. Two days later, 15 August went down in the annals of Luftwaffe history as *Schwarze Donnerstag* (Black Thursday), when the great German losses left Churchill so famously to declare: 'Never in the field of human conflict was so much owed by so many to so few'.

Yet by the end of August, RAF Fighter Command was near breaking point. Worse, five forward fighter fields in the south of England had been extensively damaged and key sector stations so severely bombed that the whole communications system was on the verge of collapse. The RAF had also lost a quarter of its available personnel through death or injury. A few more weeks of this and Britain would have no organised defence of its skies. Britain had only a fragile foot against the front door and one final push would enable Operation Sealion to commence.

Then, quite suddenly, the Luftwaffe shifted the focus of its attack from the

Men of destiny: Hitler's Luftwaffe chief, Hermann Goering and the RAF's Hugh Dowding.

airfields and radar stations, where the RAF was being punished, to British cities. This proved to be another tactical error, just three months after the Dunkirk blunder, and an error that would be of historic significance to world events.

The origins of the tactical switch can be traced to 15 August 1940, the day the Luftwaffe suffered the aerial horror show of Black Thursday. Amid the flaming carnage, German bombers emerged from the evening haze unable to find their target, Kenley. Instead, they hit nearby Croydon airfield, in the London suburbs. Hitler had specified as early as August 1939 that any attacks on London had to be authorised by him. Then came the fatal mistake. On the night of 24/25 August, London itself was hit – apparently unintentionally – due to a navigational error between two aircraft. Looking for the oil tanks at Thameshaven on the estuary, two bombers drifted across central London and, for the first time since the First World War 25 years earlier, blindly dumped bombs across the City and the East End.

Intentional or not, the first bombs on the City struck Fore Street while high explosives fell on Stepney, Walthamstow, Leyton, East and West Ham, Edmonton, Tottenham and Islington at various times between 11.00 p.m. and 1.30 a.m. Then, at around 3.00 a.m., Stepney, Bethnal Green, Hackney and Finsbury were on the receiving end again. In all, nine people were killed in London and over 50 hurt, while 100 Bethnal Greeners were made homeless.

Hitler, assuming that Britain would now retaliate by striking Berlin, was furious and his Reich Marshal threatened to post those responsible to infantry units. Hitler was right and Churchill did retaliate. The night after

Goering (sixth from right) at Cap Griz Nez, savouring the moment when wave upon wave of Luftwaffe bombers flew overhead to London for the start of the Blitz.

the London bombing, the RAF hit Berlin. There was dense cloud cover and strong winds that evening and only 10 of the 50 twin-engined Wellington, Whitley and Hampden bombers found their target. Structural damage was negligible and two people were slightly hurt in the northern district of Rosenthal. Yet the psychological effect on German morale was devastating. Goering had assured Germans that their cities would never be bombed – and they had believed him. Berlin was well defended by two great rings of anti-aircraft guns but the aircraft had attacked for three hours. The RAF had even dropped a few leaflets declaring: 'The war which Hitler started will go on, and it will last as long as Hitler does'.

The next day, Berlin's daily newspapers all carried the same headline: 'COWARDLY BRITISH ATTACK'. Four more RAF raids followed over the next 10 days and panic rose as German editors detailed the activities of the 'British air pirates'. Hitler realised he had to face his people. On 4 September 1940, he told a crowd of social workers and women at the Berlin Sportpalast that the invasion of Britain was coming and added:

If the British Air Force drops two or three or four thousand kilos of bombs, then we will now drop 150,000, 180,000, 230,000, 300,000 or 400,000 kilos or more in one night… If they declare that they will attack our cities on a large scale, we will erase theirs. We will put a stop to the game of these night pirates, as God is our witness.

As the deafening applause eventually subsided, Hitler made up his mind. The destruction of London itself was now viewed as the strategy to destroy the British will to resist invasion. Thus, Hitler's bombing reprieve for the RAF's airfields became an unfolding tragedy for the East End.

On 5 September 1940, Churchill was standing on the roof of the Air Ministry in Whitehall when the clear afternoon sky suddenly filled with waves of enemy bombers. They were high above the Thames and heading for the docks. Shellhaven and Thameshaven were hit and plumes of smoke belched from the 2,000-ton capacity oil tanks. Fireman Cyril Demarne, who had agonised over the evacuation of his two daughters (see page 92) recalled:

I was a sub-officer in charge of the central control room based at Abbey Road School in West Ham. Six pumps from West Ham had joined the Thameshaven operation and they confronted a massive blaze. Relatively few firemen in the country had experience of fighting a major oil fire and it was even more of a challenge when Messerschmitt aircraft machine-gunned the men as they worked. We were fighting that fire for 24 hours before the crews came away. The next day, the 6th, a few isolated bombers also dropped fire and explosive bombs on Silvertown and Custom House, and I was up until 4.00 a.m. on the 7th. I then tried to get some sleep but I was strangely restless. It could have been a premonition, I suppose. We were all tired by lunchtime on 7 September and I tried to get my head down again, but I couldn't rest for some reason, when normally I would have slept like a log. Everyone who could be spared caught up on sleep that afternoon and there was little going on at the Abbey Road School HQ, which was the London Fire Region's J District Control Room.

As these men slept, Hermann Goering stepped from the ornate mahogany-panelled carriage of his personal train. He had arrived at the Pas de Calais on the French coast, from where he swiftly travelled to the observation post of Air Fleet 2 at Cap Gris Nez, near Calais. There Goering watched as the dark Luftwaffe swarm, stretching across a 20-mile front, moved overhead towards the capital of the British Empire. The din was deafening as almost 1,000 German aircraft headed for the English coast between Deal and Margate.

The weather was sweltering on that afternoon of 7 September 1940 and conditions were perfect for the occasion. Indeed, the great bend of the Thames would be clearly visible and its warehouses and port installations surely unmissable. Goering returned to his train to prepare for an address to the German people. He emerged to take a microphone from a radio announcer before broadcasting news of the unfolding assault:

I have heard above me the roaring of the victorious German squadrons which now, for the first time, are driving towards the heart of the enemy in full daylight, accompanied by countless fighter squadrons.

It was, he said, an 'historic hour' and Hitler had ordered a 'mighty blow' against London. He felt sure this single devastating attack could destroy London's morale and make the bombardment of Rotterdam and Warsaw seem pinpricks in comparison.

At 4.00 p.m. on that glorious Saturday, British radar stations picked up small aircraft formations over Calais. Initially, it was thought to be the start of another assault on sector stations and aircraft factories. Then the controllers watched spellbound as the plots revealed something they had never seen before. The most devastating aerial assault on a city the world had ever seen was taking shape before their eyes. The target was London itself, where, by the end of August, 2,500 evacuated children were returning each week, swelling the ranks of some half a million youngsters of school age already in the capital. Twenty RAF squadrons rose to meet Goering's fleet but there were just too many aircraft to repel. The city's air-raid sirens continued their dismal chorus, by which time a huge wave of enemy bombers was sweeping up the Thames estuary.

Ten-year-old Eddie Siggins, home from his evacuation in Buckinghamshire, was playing in Duckett Street outside Searle House. He noticed people staring up at the sky and looked up too. The Stepney sky was full of aircraft. Someone suggested that they must be German. Others laughed and said the RAF would never let them get this far.

Then Black Saturday began.

Chapter four

Streets of fire

AS EDDIE SIGGINS WATCHED the black rash spread across the blue south-eastern sky, a policeman turned into Duckett Street on his bike. A piece of cardboard was hanging around his neck and written on it in chalk were the words: 'AIR RAID TAKE COVER'.

Wide-eyed, the officer was shouting at everyone to get off the street. Then he put a whistle to his mouth and began to blow it hard. Yet Eddie and the residents of Stepney seemed strangely rooted to the spot. They were utterly spellbound as countless German aircraft crowded the skies. 'Up West', oblivious young couples were kissing in St James's Park. Others were queuing for *Gone With The Wind*, starring Clark Gable and Vivien Leigh. Then the drone of engines was heard, faint at first but becoming steadily louder. The heavens were rumbling in the east.

Stan Mayes had chosen to take things easy on the Thames at North Woolwich that afternoon. Sunbathing on the deck of the 300-ton barge *Celtic*, he had been wondering about work. How long would he have to wait before his skipper obtained another order to transport grain, timber or cattlefeed down the Thames and round to Cornwall or the Humber? He had been twiddling his thumbs aboard *Celtic* for two days now, along with Jockie, a lad from Ipswich. A dozen or so other barges were also moored to the aptly named 'starvation buoys'. Stan had worked on the barges for four years and liked the work, even though it was tough and they were only paid for each ton of freight moved. If there was no work, there was no money. He was 19 now, and working on 'London River' (as the barge lads called it) had become a way of life.

As Stan mused, East London smouldered in the summer heat and young children paddled in the thick brown sludge left by the low tide. Suddenly, like Eddie Siggins, he became transfixed, mesmerised by the waves of black shapes that were filling the sky. High above, the bomber squadrons

Young Stan Mayes and the 300-ton barge *Celtic*.

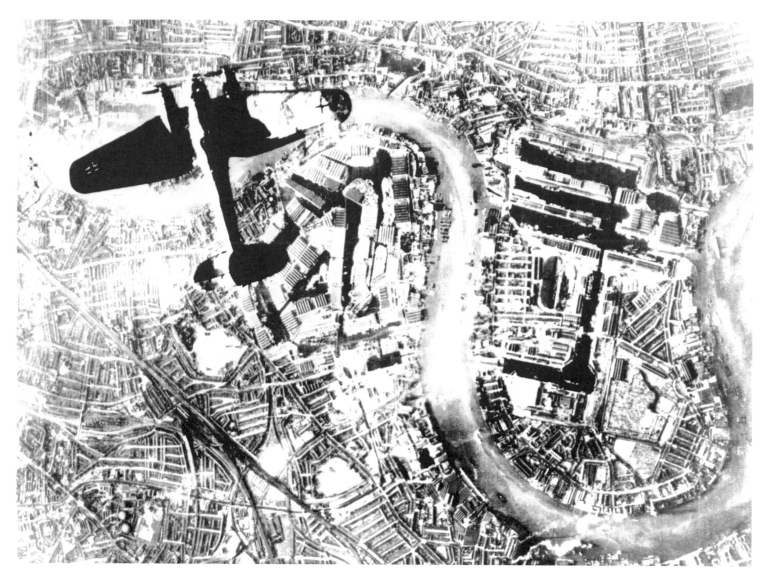

were passing overhead, accompanied by layer upon layer of fighter escorts that glinted as they danced protectively around the enormous air fleet.

At Wapping, the Dockmaster of the London and St Katharine Docks had emerged from his pierhead residence. Other dock officials joined him, intent on enjoying the warmth of another scorching afternoon. Behind them lay nearly 125 acres of docks at the heart of the Port of London. The vast century-old warehouses were packed with imported wool, tea, rubber, spices and canned foods, while the vaults were full of wines, brandy and spirits. The deep murmur of approaching engines had now become a roar and the assembled group watched in stunned silence. The Dockmaster started to count the aircraft but gave up when he reached 140 because so many more were still coming up behind.

In a garden in South Molton Road, Canning Town, Charlie Smith was also gazing heavenwards but was diverted by the sound of a neighbour's

'Black Saturday': a Heinkel III flies over Wapping. Away to the right is the classic U-bend of the Thames containing the Isle of Dogs and the distinctive shapes of the West India Docks at the 'neck' and Millwall Docks further south.

voice. Mr McCall was jumping up and down on his air-raid shelter and waving a clenched fist at the black invaders overhead. 'You bastards! You bastards!' he was screaming at the top of his voice. Charlie knew why. The previous night, a stray bomb had killed his eldest son, Jackie, as he stepped off a bus at the end of the road after work. His other son, Maurice – Charlie's best friend 'Munchie' – had been evacuated to Portland and fallen to his death in a stone quarry (see page 93). Mr McCall was beside himself with grief as he ranted at the Luftwaffe.

The skies then began to crackle into life. Eddie Siggins in Duckett

106

German Dorniers attack Silvertown on 7 September 1940: the distinctive shape of the oval West Ham Stadium (formerly Custom House Sports Ground) in Nottingham Avenue, Canning Town, can be seen between the aircraft. Opened in 1928, the much-loved speedway and dog-racing venue closed in 1972.

Street watched smaller aircraft – he assumed they were RAF fighters – swarm like hornets among the black flies, their machine guns chattering. One plane was on fire, black smoke billowing from its tail. Another seemed to explode in mid-air. Suddenly, there was a big bang off Bale Street and a great cloud of dust rose from the earth. Eddie's trance was broken and he ran into Searle House for shelter.

Aboard the *Celtic*, Stan Mayes flinched as the anti-aircraft guns boomed into action, their sound punctuating the constant thunderous roar of aircraft engines. Puffs of sooty smoke began to smudge the blue canvas where the black shapes, in batches of 40 or 50, moved relentlessly closer to the Royal group of docks.

High above the East End, the bomb doors of 300 bombers opened, marking the beginning of Black Saturday, 7 September 1940. At 4.35 p.m., countless sticks of black high-explosive bombs fell like dominoes through the blue sky, while the incendiaries dropped more gracefully, like silvery fish, through the scattered woolly clouds. The aerial symphony, previously dominated by the sharp crack of the anti-aircraft guns and the clatter of machine guns, was now accompanied by a deafening crescendo of whining screams as the bombs plummeted to earth. Finally, there were the violent thuds of heavy explosions as red-hot metal ripped, shredded and shattered houses, factories, ships and people. The very bowels of the East End, the very streets tramped by Dickens and Dr Barnardo, seemed to groan and spew in protest, rolling, turning and flailing like a great wounded beast. The East End was being disembowelled alive, and with a clinical precision that the elusive Victorian Ripper would have admired. The first bombs fell on the Ford Motor Works at Dagenham. Next to be hit was the Beckton Gas Works, the largest in Europe, which gave off a foul, sulphurous odour and caused many to panic about a German mustard gas attack.

The bombers were now over Woolwich Reach, with Silvertown and the three large Royal Docks just beyond. This was their main target and showers of bombs soon descended upon the Royals, the commercial heart of the docklands. Billowing smoke engulfed the docks' towering cranes and grain elevators, while fire swept through warehouses packed with foodstuffs and essential war materials. The workers' tiny dwellings surrounding West Ham's dockland area were flattened and Queen Mary's Hospital in Romford Road was hit, killing nurses Annie Bond and Agatha Credland and six patients. Harland and Wolff's was on fire; Tate and Lyle's sugar factory was badly damaged; and the Silvertown Rubber Company's warehouse was also ablaze.

Fireman Cyril Demarne, the West Ham sub-officer, had been fighting fires in the County Borough for nearly 14 years but had never seen anything like it. He remembered:

On the 7th, I was in the yard outside West Ham's control room at Abbey Road School in Abbey Road. The booming of the bombs was soon sounding everywhere and the shock was so severe it came right up through the soles of my feet. It was as if someone was under the ground and banging right beneath me. It was like an earthquake and I went back into the dark control room, which had been strengthened by beams and had had all its openings built up by sandbags. Inside the calls were coming in thick and fast from places like Dagenham and Barking.

Then the lights went out and we used our back-up – candles in jam jars. We had six telephonists on duty and they were working flat out answering the phones, writing down the details and placing the written reports in an ever-increasing pile. We called for 500 pumping appliances for West Ham and Silvertown alone.

I recall a tar distillery had been hit in Silvertown and a molten tar slick of fire 18 inches thick ran down North Woolwich Road, cutting off Silvertown and stopping the fire pumps from getting down there. Meanwhile

fire pumps on the River Thames faced blazing barges coming towards them. Some had been set adrift by well-meaning people trying to save them. Crews had to wrap their faces in soaked towels even to get near the burning wharves. In fact, it was so hot that boats on the south side of the River, 300 yards from the Royal Docks, had their paint blistered.

The street mains couldn't cope at all after the bombs fractured them and even those men using Thames water could see their hoses were having no effect. We were overwhelmed within the first few minutes and were well aware of that fact. Yet still the calls kept coming in from Dagenham, Barking, East Ham and West Ham. Nobody in the country had ever experienced anything like it and when I came out and surveyed the bomb craters, the gas mains flaring up, the water shooting out and the tangled, ruined mass of telephone cables, I just shook my head and said: 'We can't possibly stand up to this sort of punishment.' I actually thought London was finished.

The great fireball from the Royal Docks rolled west, consuming the Thames' factories and warehouses from Woolwich Reach to Wapping and Tower Bridge. Sugar refineries, oil depots, chemical works and varnish works were engulfed, the smells of each combining with burning tar and rubber to produce choking, acrid fumes. One detachment of bombers broke off and headed over the river for the Surrey Commercial Docks, to the left of the great Thames U-bend. Here, there were 250 acres of pitch pine and fir wood, kept in stacks 25 feet high. A wall of flame soon leapt hundreds of feet into the air as the wharves, which served Canada and the Baltic ports, burned out of control. Telegraph poles smoked like giant cigarettes, the wooden-block road surface spontaneously ignited and the sodden tunics of firemen steamed in the intense heat. There were four temporary fire stations in the Surrey Commercial Docks, manned mainly by auxiliary crews. It was the first fire many had ever seen – and even the regulars had never seen anything like this. Many, close to being cut off, and with blistered hands and puffy, smarting faces, ran for their lives and straight past their fire stations, which were already ablaze.

Rotherhithe Street, one of the two roads into these docks, was blocked by a wall of flame 130 feet high. The other, Redriff Road, became an escape tunnel through which 1,000 shocked and blackened people were helped through the inferno. The bombers had used magnesium incendiaries, which fell in inaccessible places, and oil bombs that flashed and spread flames quickly.

A brisk southwesterly wind now blew the smoke back over the river and its blazing barges, where huge columns of smoke mingled with the pall rising above St Katharine, Millwall and London Docks. On the Isle of Dogs, the West India Docks were alight from end to end and had become a giant flame-thrower, shooting blazing spirit from warehouse doors. Even the river

Thousands of tons of timber go up in smoke at Surrey Commercial Docks on the night of 7/8 September 1940 in London's biggest blaze since the Great Fire of 1666.

seemed to be alight. One ship was hit by a bomb that smashed through the main deck and the shelter-decks before coming out of the side above the waterline, holing her like an armour-piercing shell.

Stan Mayes, still aboard the *Celtic*, watched dumbfounded as barges were sunk and warehouses destroyed before his eyes. He recalls:

The sky was full of incendiaries and one fell on the deck of our barge. I quickly kicked it over the side. I got ashore with Jockie, the lad from Ipswich, and was directed to a street shelter in Storey Street in North Woolwich, which was only about half a mile away but I'll never forget the journey. The streets were full of flame and wrecked properties. It was total chaos, with people screaming, crying and calling out for children. I saw people being taken from homes on stretchers and it all became a blur as we just focused on running to safety. It was so noisy you couldn't talk to anyone and we were in a state of shock by the time we got into the shelter, which consisted of three bomb-damaged houses in a terrace of 20. We spent a terrible night in there.

Back on the Thames, nurse Freda Moon (née Lovell) was aboard an ambulance ship heading towards East London. She recalls:

I had been relaxing off duty in Southwark Park in Jamaica Road and had made my way to where our ship, the Abercorn, *was moored at Cherry*

Garden Pier, just east of Tower Bridge on the south bank [opposite Wapping Pierhead, where the Dockmaster had watched the start of the raid]. Our crew – two sisters, six nurses, four stretcher-bearers and a doctor – set off and I could already see the billowing smoke coming from the Royal Docks in the distance and waves of bombers overhead. Then the warehouses on the Wapping side – one had skins and furs – suddenly blew out and the whole frontage just collapsed before us and tumbled into the river. On the south side, Dick's the paint works was also engulfed in a wall of flame some quarter of a mile in length. One of our girls was in total shock and just gazed at it, saying: 'I'm terrified of fire.' I thought I was going to die and it felt like we were floating down towards hell.

As Freda Moon sailed past Wapping Pierhead, the Dockmaster and his team began to disperse around the area to assess the damage. They discovered huge warehouses and quay sheds shooting out flames and red-hot debris while black smoke and showers of sparks blotted out the sky. Wapping, one of the most congested areas in the world in 1940, was simply burning like tinder. Its narrow streets and tall warehouses restricted the fire crews but they valiantly pushed forward, many men smouldering in the intense heat. Women, dockers and residents yelled that Wapping mustn't burn and shouted curses to Hitler as they helped the firemen with their hoses.

One bomb had fallen in the road immediately outside St George's-

Police of Thames Division watch Surrey Commercial Docks blaze from the roof of Wapping Police Station.

in-the-East Hospital, exploding in a massive blast and sending lumps of masonry and road surface flying great distances in all directions. The front of the building had been torn apart but, miraculously, the patients and staff were largely unharmed. The fires in Wapping spread rapidly and began to threaten an ammunition magazine next to a blazing warehouse. A nearby block of flats would have been obliterated if the ammunition store had gone up. Port of London Authority officers ran through a curtain of flame to reach the store, only to find the door twisted and jammed by the heat. Officers stripped off their tunics, smashed the door down with a crowbar, and began to carry away the cases of ammunition, avoiding the advancing flames as best they could. A docker's hand-truck was found and loaded precariously with ammunition before being wheeled away through the streets of fire. The police officers who led this operation were later awarded the George Medal, introduced that month by the King, who wished to establish a civilian equivalent to the Victoria Cross.

Yet heroism mingled with horror. A human tragedy was steadily unfolding in the humble streets beyond the Thames docks, where the insular Cockney world, defined by its tightly packed streets, shops, markets and pubs, was being randomly destroyed. Young Eddie Siggins cowered inside Searle House as Stepney, where nearly 200,000 people lived at an average of 12 per dwelling, was being pulverised. It felt as if there was a huge giant outside, repeatedly thumping the ground with a massive club, shaking his Duckett Street flat and making its contents vibrate.

On the other side of Stepney, 16-year-old George Mooney was looking for his Mum. Mr Mooney (whose childhood recollections appear on page 47) remembers:

We were living at 73 Exmouth Street just off Commercial Road. That day all hell broke loose and my widowed Mum, Margaret, started to get really worried. She remembered the Zeppelins of the First World War and suddenly she left the house in a bit of a panic. I went to find her and was met in Jamaica Street by the milkman, Chandler. It was chaos in the street and he said: 'Where are you going, you silly sod?' I left him there and went up to the George pub, where Sutton Street meets Commercial Road. Still no sign of her. My uncle, John Warchen, then appeared and he said Mum had gone into Gran's house – No. 19 Blakesley Street just down the road.

I was on the pavement approaching the front door of No. 19 when the whole place just suddenly disappeared before my eyes. It literally just collapsed in a heap. A bomb had hit and the house had fallen into two cellars beneath. The next thing I knew, a man was putting a cigarette into my mouth and saying: 'This will calm your nerves, son.' I said: 'Don't worry about that – where's my Mum?' I got up and stood among the rubble and noticed a neighbour, Mr Goggins, who said: 'The last time I saw your Mum she was standing at the window in this house with her arms outstretched.'

We carried on searching through the rubble in the knowledge that a big

The ambulance ship *Abercorn*.

Freda Moon (née Lovell) is second from right, looking at Sister Martin (seated with white hat), who was in charge of the *Abercorn* nurses.

party had been held at the house to celebrate my Gran's return from hospital. Then, in the debris, I saw my cousin Jean McNamara, who was 10. She had no legs and said: 'Will I live, George?' I replied: 'You'll be OK, love' and we did what we could for her. Then we found my Gran, Margaret Rockell, and she was dead. Next, I came across the body of her son, Joe, who was 33.

The heavy-rescue people were on the scene by now and we were ushered away. I still didn't know where Mum was and a pal, Billy Clarke, joined me as I walked round all the hospitals – the Children's Hospital in Shadwell Park, the London Hospital in Whitechapel, St George's in Wapping, Bancroft Hospital and the Jewish Free Hospital in Stepney Way. No joy. I went back to Exmouth Street and news came through that Mum had gone to Epping Forest and was safe. The neighbour who thought he saw her at the window had therefore been mistaken. However, a real disaster had unfolded at Gran's place in Blakesley Street. Seven members of the family had been killed. They were Gran, Margaret Ada Rockell, who was 65; my uncle, Tom McNamara, who was 42; my Mum's two sisters, Lillian McNamara, aged 42, and Miss Rosina Rockell, 26; my 9-year-old cousin, Jean McNamara; my uncle, Joseph Rockell, aged 33; and my cousin Joan Collins, aged 27. Both Joan and Rosina had intended to announce their engagements that day.

The church service for the victims was held at Christ Church, Watney Street, by two well-known local vicars, Rev. St John Groser and Rev. Jack Boggis. The deceased were then buried at Bow Road Cemetery in two graves.

I'll never forget the sight of the seven hearses, each containing one coffin. The following month, Mum and I survived when a bomb wrecked our home in Exmouth Street and then we moved to Northolt, near Greenford. Poor old Mum was very badly affected by the family tragedy and found it hard to struggle on.

During the afternoon of Black Saturday, the 'Troxy' cinema in Commercial Road, Stepney, had been packed for *Gaslight*, the tale of a Victorian schizophrenic and his mad wife. Ann Platman (née Jolka) watched excitedly with her Mum as actor Anton Walbrook tormented his spouse (Diana Wynyard) and pushed her into an attic. She recalls:

Then the bombs fell and mayhem started outside. The fall of the incendiaries on the roof seemed to coincide exactly with Walbrook's clomping in the attic on screen. Then, when it got worse outside, everyone started to leave. I noticed my gas mask and ID card were missing and we were the last to leave, after spending time trying to find them. Outside was a huge swarm of bewildered people rushing about in all directions. We ran up Commercial Road and were met by my brother, who had come to meet us. We then went back to our home in Varden Street and used our cellar kitchen as a shelter. A delayed-action bomb suddenly sent choking brick dust pouring into the cellar and a dog my Dad had bought that day at the market was killed in his outhouse. We all

The seventh victim was Joe Rockell, the middle son of Margaret Ada Rockell and also George Mooney's uncle, pictured here with fellow employees from Triplex, the huge glass firm in Hythe Road, Willesden.

Six of the seven victims of the bomb that wrecked 19 Blakesley Street were photographed together in late 1939 at the marriage of Albert Rockell, youngest son of Margaret Ada Rockell, and his fiancée Lillian Carter. They included Margaret Ada Rockell (in black, behind the groom); Tom McNamara (back row, fourth from right); Rosina McNamara (bridesmaid sitting next to bride); Joan Collins (behind Rosina's left shoulder); Lillian McNamara (in the middle, two rows behind the bride) and Jean McNamara (sitting at the very front on the left). Margaret Ada Rockell was the grandmother of contributor George Mooney, who is pictured just peering over her right shoulder while his mother Margaret is just behind him to his left). George's brother Jimmy (whose unfortunate evacuation experience is recounted on page 91) is seated on the floor to the right.

scrambled out and spent the rest of the night going from shelter to shelter. I had rescued a leather chair from our house for Mum to sit on and I carried this with me as we wandered around. We luckily missed out one of the brick shelters on our travels – one which was destroyed by a bomb.

At 6.40 p.m., a steady two-minute blast on the siren signalled the

all clear. The bombers, many of which never saw a RAF fighter the whole afternoon, had left at 6.00 p.m. However, it was obvious to most people that the great blaze would act as a marker for the Luftwaffe that coming night. At 7.30 p.m., a second fleet of 250 bombers resumed the attack and successive waves continued the bombardment until dawn on Sunday 8 September 1940. Heinkels and Dorniers stacked up for their chance to drop bombs and the population in the Tidal Basin area was severely hit. Their homes, constructed in the 1850s for the workers who built the Royal Victoria Dock and the Silvertown factories, were flattened and great gashes appeared in the streets, like odd keys violently prised from a piano.

Bombs fell into the inferno that had been created in the afternoon, and fire crews, reinforced by personnel from Birmingham, Nottingham, Brighton and Swindon, feared for their lives as jets of water turned to steam in the great roaring flames. Still the bombers came, and more damage was caused on both banks of the Thames as Luftwaffe crews attacked and then returned to their bases in France, to refuel and reload for yet another sortie.

In Silvertown, there were 13,000 people crammed into a sliver of land between the Thames and the Royal Docks. Now they were trapped. Those living in the streets adjoining the southern boundary of the King George V Dock were suddenly confronted by towering flames in the docks on one side and a line of huge fires along the length of Factory Road opposite. These frantic families discovered exit after exit blocked by debris or fire. Some managed to reach a public shelter in Oriental Road, only for it to be hit by a random bomb. For the rest, there was only one road out, and that was also blocked. Finally, residents braved a huge wall of fire to reach North Woolwich Pier, where they packed onto small Thames craft to escape.

In Wapping, night-time was like daytime and a blood-red moon hung in a orange sky. It was bright enough to take a photograph. Men on the lookout for bombs falling near St Paul's Cathedral stared across at the East End from Wren's great dome. Finally, one said: 'It looks like the end of the world.' A colleague replied: 'It is the end of the world.'

Six-year-old Audrey True (née Marshall) also surveyed the blazing lunar landscape.

Leslie Norman (nearest the camera) with matron hovering in the background.

We lived on the sixth floor of Peabody Buildings in Glamis Place, Shadwell. The sight was incredible. There was a strange, brilliant red backdrop which glowed and you could see the outline of the buildings against it. Our window faced Stepney Green and it was just a mass of flames in that direction. Flames just filled the panorama from left to right. The river was ablaze too and flowed through it all like a shimmering snake.

Back at ground level, indescribable terror gripped the community. Violet Hattley (née Aslett), then 14, recalls:

Dad was a carpenter and joiner at the Albert Dock and we lived nearby in Garvary Road, Custom House. We were told to leave the house because of a time-bomb and my father, brother, three sisters and I went to a neighbour's house, which was just outside the road barrier sealing off our house. There were many women crowded into a tiny Anderson shelter, while the men – including a soldier who was meant to be manning the barrier – sheltered in the passageways between houses. Bombs were going off everywhere and, inside the Anderson, women were crying, screaming and praying. I just sat there numb.

We had to go outside sometimes just to breathe and I noticed the flames were all around us. The smoke and fumes were stifling and dogfights were raging in the sky as searchlights scanned and criss-crossed the heavens. One plane exploded and I saw it come down. That night seemed never-ending, and eventually Dad came in and said we were returning home, time bomb or not. I just burst out crying at that point and couldn't stop. Dad had to slap my face to snap me out of it. I suppose the terror had made me hysterical.

Others were left with poignant images and profound impressions, as the following two accounts show. Leslie Norman, a 23-year-old male nurse probationer, working at Hackney Hospital, recalls:

That day I had gone down to London Hospital to see if I could help in any

way. The scene there was unbelievable. There were shells of burnt-out trolley buses and huge craters, one with a bus actually inside it. Beyond the Mile End Road, the whole sky in the east was black with smoke and there seemed to be fire engines absolutely everywhere. Hundreds of people and cars seemed to be in a mad, frantic rush to go west. As darkness began to fall, the flames lit the sky in the east. Everything, just everything in that direction seemed to be ablaze. Fire engines continued to tear along as reinforcements arrived, and crowds of people gathered outside Whitechapel Brewery for the shelter.

Making my way back home to Hackney, I looked back from Cambridge Heath Road and the scene reminded me of two pictures I had seen in books. One was the Great Fire of London. The other was the crowd fleeing from the destruction of Sodom and Gomorrah.

Seventeen-year-old Dorothea Johnson (née Henning) adds:

I was living in Hesperus Crescent on the Isle of Dogs and I had gone south of the river to shop in Greenwich with a friend, Pat. We decided to get home during the raid and we picked up my brother Sid, his wife and their new baby, Michael, who lived in Greenwich. We got down to the river and it was chaotic. On the far bank, looking towards the Isle of Dogs, all I could see was a wall of flames and smoke. A rowing boat then appeared and the man in it said he would take us across. As we sailed towards the burning bank, masses of burning wood and debris floated past us. I then distinctly remember looking down at the lovely new baby, Michael, all wrapped up in a blanket. He was so fragile and innocent amid the hell around us. I immediately felt: 'This is a historic moment, something that will be talked about in the decades to come.'

Ron Wood and his wife Joan on their wedding day in April 1941.

Tower Bridge silhouetted by the docks on fire on the night of 7 September 1940,

Meanwhile, Ron Wood, aged 23, was involved in a desperate search in Silvertown:

My girlfriend Joan and I both worked at Tate and Lyle and had gone to Stratford to shop. I had left from my home in Woodford and she had met me there from her place in Bradfield Road, Silvertown. We were in the Roberts Department Store behind Stratford Parish Church when the sirens went and sheltered there in a boiler room. Afterwards we heard that the raid had been aimed at the Royals and Silvertown, where Joan's Mum lived in Bradfield Road. We made our way down there and it was a terrible sight. The heat around the docks was unbelievable and the Rank's Flour Mills were ablaze. We stood and watched men at the windows of the mills completely stranded and unable to get out. They were on fire and just jumped out of the windows and into the water. We got to the house in Bradfield Road and no one was in and we were frantic with worry. But it transpired Joan's Mum and her sister had crossed the River to Woolwich to shop that Saturday and had returned to the north side and been pushed from shelter to shelter. They were both safe.

Fireman Cyril Demarne would never forget the horror he witnessed during the afternoon and evening of Black Saturday:

Bodies littered the streets and roads and were tossed in corners, splayed over walls or just mingled with the dust and the filth. Bits of people were everywhere. There were terrible screams in the street as bodies and limbs were pulled from the wreckage, and it was awful to watch as people dug with their hands for loved ones, only to be completely overwhelmed with grief once they found them. Blankets were used to cover the dead and the bodies were left on

the rubble to await the mortuary van. Meanwhile, the scream of the falling bombs and the thunder of explosions made a brain-numbing din.

The fire service did not have radio for communication in those days, so motorbike dispatch riders were used, many of them women, to relay messages. There were also some very brave teenage boys on bicycles who took messages out to the fire crews. When the call went out in 1939 for these riders, the service was inundated with volunteers. Though the minimum age was 16, many younger lads tried to get in but they eventually had to show a birth certificate as proof. These boys competed with each other for the messenger jobs, even if they had only just got back from an assignment. They faced terrible danger and confronted walls of fire and toppling buildings, but still they worked on. These lads would turn up at the control room covered in muck and cut and bruised, but they just went out again with another message. They were magnificent.

The firemen, of course, were heroes too. We were all frightened out of our lives and were like children in the dark, yet it was a great comfort when a colleague came along to assist you. The men would yell to warn of falling masonry and we all gained strength from the closeness of our colleagues. At about 7.15 p.m. on the evening of Black Saturday, I heard that my pal, Sub-Officer Wally Turley, and two members of his crew had been buried under a bombed building in Abbey Road, which was being used as an ARP cleansing and ambulance station. It was just 200 yards down the road from our control room. Wally had gone into the blazing depot with his mate, Harry Webb, and said: 'You go round the back and I'll do the side.'

Harry ran out with his crew, with the intention of tackling the fire from the rear, and then the whole place caved in on Wally, two other firemen and ten Civil Defence workers. They were all killed. When I got there about an hour later the place was deserted. I looked around and suddenly saw Wally's

Dorothea Johnson (née Henning), on the right, with friend and work colleague Freda Yeoman. Both worked for the Civil Service when the war started.

The late Cyril Demarne, pictured in 2003.

hand sticking out from beneath a slab. I knew it was him because he had a deformed left fingernail and that's what caught my eye. I gently removed his watch off his wrist and took it back to the station and told the Chief Officer. An hour later, Wally's wife came round and asked: 'Where's my Wally?' I said I didn't know because the Chief Officer had told me to say nothing until the body had been officially identified. Then Wally's Dad came down, looked me in the eye and asked where he was. I had to say: 'I'm afraid he's dead.' The old boy broke down and I nearly did too. He said he didn't want the watch and gave it back to me. Wally was a married man with two daughters. He was a man of few words but we were good mates and our families enjoyed days out together. It was a very sad incident.

Just over four hours after the Abbey Road depot was hit, a terrible tragedy unfolded in Bethnal Green. Ellen Ackred (née Neport, whose recollections of her family's 'wardrobe dealings' in the Thirties appear on page 46), remembers:

We'll never forget Black Saturday. I was a young girl of 16 and the eldest daughter of a happy, close family of eight, living in Hassard Street in Bethnal Green. I lived there with Mum, Dad, my older brother Jim, aged 19, two younger sisters Renie and Joyce, aged 15 and 13, and two baby boys, Sammy and Derek, aged five and three. Dad worked on the river unloading timber from barges; my older brother was soon called up and I worked in a ladies' underwear factory in Pollard Row, Bethnal Green. Sister Renie worked in a tailoring firm.

Mum had taken the four youngest children to Yarmouth during the so-called 'phoney war', leaving Dad and I at home. I recall we went to our rooms and cried our eyes out when they left. However, by the time of Black Saturday,

they had returned and our family started to use an underground shelter in an old building called Columbia Market off Hackney Road[1].

Mum and the children had only been going to the shelter for four days prior to the 7th and they slept at the bottom of the Market air shaft, which rose right up to the roof. My Dad and I would pop down and say goodnight to them before returning to our house to sleep. On the evening of the 7th, my boyfriend George and I had gone to the local cinema, the Regal in Mare Street. It was just before midnight when we went to see Mum and the four kids in the Columbia Market shelter, to say goodnight as usual. We met Dad there that night and he told us Mum was at home making sandwiches for the children. He asked George and I to go home and fetch the food and he got up to come with us too. A lady then strongly advised us to stay because the raids were so bad outside, but we carried on.

When we got to the shelter entrance some 50 yards away, we heard deafening screaming and, a few seconds later, a huge explosion. It was a million-to-one chance but a bomb had gone right down the shelter airshaft and exploded at the bottom where the kiddies were sleeping. They caught the full blast from a 50-kilo [110-pound] bomb. We rushed back into the shelter and there was no sign of Renie or the other three children. I just became a raving lunatic and screamed my head off. I was then confronted with the most terrible scenes. I saw one woman with the top of her head split open and the insides piled up on top. She had a dead baby in her arms. All around people were dying and I just lost control.

---

[1] The Columbia Market was a spectacular neo-Gothic creation resembling St Pancras station. Funded by wealthy philanthropist Baroness Burdett-Coutts, it was opened by the Prince of Wales in 1869 but had long been derelict. It was used as an ARP training centre and depot and contained a very large public shelter when war began.

Steel-helmeted members of the London Fire Brigade confront massive warehouse fires at the Surrey Commercial Docks.

Ellen Neport's sister Renie. This photo was taken on the Saturday that she was killed at Columbia Market.

Two weeks before the Columbia Market bombing, victims of the disaster attended the wedding of James Neport to Ellen Bowers. Contributor Ellen Ackred (née Neport), sister of the groom, is pictured third from the right, behind her younger sister Joyce, with her fiancé George to her left. Her sister Renie is pictured far left, next to their father, James. In front of them are her two younger brothers, Samuel, aged five, and Derek, aged three (holding the groom's hand).

Then Dad and my boyfriend started to clear corrugated iron sheets and debris to find my brothers and sisters. Sammy and Derek were killed outright. Renie was very badly injured. She was taken past me on a stretcher and her clothes seemed to be intact. She just looked asleep and I thought: 'Thank God she is all right.' I didn't realise she had bad stomach and head injuries. She was taken to the children's hospital in Hackney Road, where she was bandaged from head to foot. Renie died two days later after singing 'We'll Meet Again' from start to finish and after reciting all our names. Her last words were: 'That 'orrible man Hitler.' My other sister Joyce lost a leg and

died through loss of blood. She had insisted on keeping her legs covered because she didn't want to upset Mummy when she visited.

When Mum was told what had happened she screamed so much you could hear her streets away. Then she never spoke to anyone for weeks. She just sat there with her coat on in a world of her own and never smiled again after that. We later learnt that 57 people were killed in Columbia Market and about 100 injured.

After the incident, Mum and Dad were never the same. Mum just cried all day. One day, later in the war, she went out alone and we didn't know where she was until a lady told us she was over at the local Victoria Park carrying a butcher's knife. Mum wanted to kill the Germans in the prisoner-of-war camp based there. She was stopped but I'm sure she would have tried if she had had the chance. Mum and Dad went to the children's grave at Manor Park Cemetery every week after they were killed until they too passed away, broken-hearted, at the ages of 79 and 92 respectively. I now go to the grave with George – who I married in 1942 – and the memories have never gone. It was like it happened yesterday. One really odd thing about the whole incident was that a Polish woman seemed to have a premonition about the bomb. She had panicked a couple of days earlier and warned it was coming. The lady was calmed down and then two days later it fell.

At 4.30 a.m. on Sunday 8 September 1940, the Black Saturday bombers finally headed for home and dawn tinged the eastern sky 30 minutes later. The Luftwaffe left behind 9 major conflagrations (large areas of fire involving blocks of buildings, spreading and not yet under control), 19 fires each needing 30 pumps and countless 10-pump fires. East Enders emerged to find a rubble-strewn, smoking hell where there was no gas, water or electricity. Civil Defence workers led the homeless – many caked in blood

The wedding of Ellen Neport and George Ackred in December 1942. Ellen's mother is pictured far right.

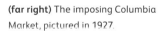

(right) Ellen and George Ackred today.

(far right) The imposing Columbia Market, pictured in 1927.

and plaster, or with shards of glass protruding from them – to rest centres in community halls. Many appeared hopelessly disoriented, as Betty Redwood (née Smith), of Kingsland Road, Plaistow, remembers:

That morning I recall seeing this endless procession of people heading for New City Road School by Tunmarsh Lane. They were carrying children and pushing prams laden with possessions, birdcages, and pets. Some were obviously in a state of shock and didn't know what they were doing or where they were. They were homeless people from the docks area and the school became a rest centre for them. Yet they could have nothing hot to eat when they arrived. There was just one small gas cooker in the place, which teachers used to make a brew in the staff room. Cold food was in short supply too. Nonetheless, a stream of people arrived until it was packed. My Mum, sister and I went down there to help and we buttered bread and made jam sandwiches and tea.

Many Londoners were also searching for loved ones that morning. Dora Kermode (née Rowley) recalls:

I was only 14 and living on the south side of the river at Welling. On the 7th,

my Mum and sister had gone to shop at Green Street Market at Upton Park and were going on to see my aunt in Beckton Road, Plaistow. They didn't come back and I was worried sick all night, particularly as the whole skyline was red over the East End. On the morning of the 8th, my Dad and I got into our Morris Eight and set off. We had to get across the river but the Woolwich ferry was blocked and the Blackwall Tunnel closed. We finally got through the Rotherhithe Tunnel and emerged to find everything shrouded in black smoke. There were wrecked buildings everywhere, firemen's hoses snaked for miles and miles and people trudged along with meagre possessions in prams and carts. I was in a terrible state by now, but found out my mother and sister had been buying dress material in Green Street when the raid started. The Jewish stallholder had been marvellous and barricaded his customers in with rolls of cloth to try and keep them safe. It saved their lives.

During the day and night of Black Saturday, 600 tons of bombs fell on the capital. The raids killed 436 civilians and rescue workers and seriously injured 1,600. Of these, at least 200 were killed in the East End, where 800 were also wounded. The Luftwaffe lost 40 aircraft. However, the East End was already fighting back, as fireman Cyril Demarne recalled:

In a relatively short space of time, the Emergency Damage Repair Squads had done an amazing job. Gas, water, electricity, and telephones were all up and running like a miracle – and it certainly picked me up off the ground. When a telephone cable was severed, over 2,000 wires might need reconnection, but they had improvised and got it together the best way they could. The work these people did was beyond praise. In 12 hours, the phones were working again. You would get the call: 'This is the Post Office engineer testing. What is your number please?' and we were back up.

Then the water was flowing again and it tasted strongly of chlorine, which had been added because of the filth in the water. It acted as a purifier and made a horrible cup of tea. Then the tram wires re-appeared, milkmen too, and off we went again. I remember Queen Mary Hospital in Stratford had been badly hit but, despite the casualties, the staff managed to treat the stream of people going through the door.

What sticks in my mind more than anything was watching people in the first shock of seeing a dead family member. Their grief and hysteria hit me hard. I had to learn not to be moved and cast these things out of my mind or I would have broken down. Some people were not able to do that. I also viewed the fires as living, leaping monsters involved in a strange, deadly battle against the fire crews, who did a magnificent job in taming them. Those of us who worked on Black Saturday were mentally and physically drained and some personnel had had no food or water for the entire 12 hours.

This would be only the start too. The days, weeks and months ahead would be punishing for crews. The men would come back stinking of smoke and saturated with water. A woman working in the control room told me of an occasion when one man leant against the wall, slid down it to the floor and fell straight asleep. He was utterly exhausted. On a personal level, I still recall the uneasy feelings I used to have. When the telephone from Stratford Fire Control rang, it started with air-raid message 'yellow'. This was the earliest warning that enemy aircraft were approaching the coast. Five minutes later came 'purple', indicating they had reached the coast, and then finally there was 'red', which told us they were heading for London. When the 'Moaning Minnie' siren started wailing, gastric acid started to burn in my stomach with the tension of it all and I remember a nurse told me my breath smelt awful as a result. She told me to get some lime and water and I asked a lad to fetch me a 3d [just over 1p] bottle of it. It worked a treat.

I had to get peace within myself because I was responsible for a group of men. They were frightened and looked up to me, and if I had run they would have too. I had to put on a brave face and I found that was my salvation. My only focus was the job of fire fighting and managing the crew, and this prevented my mind from dwelling on my own personal danger. I also became callous as a way of coping with the awful scenes. In normal conditions you would help anybody at any time but I didn't have time to think about everyone now. I couldn't have compassion for everyone so I had compassion for none in the end. That's how I managed to do a professional, effective job.

(far left) Dora Kermode (née Rowley) pictured at Welling.

(left) Oil tanks at Thameshaven still ablaze on 8 September 1940 after being hit the day before.

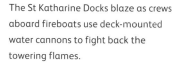

(below) The Rum Quay, West India Docks, on fire on the night of 8/9 September 1940: pounded by scores of high explosive and incendiary bombs, the warehouses were a complete loss and blazing rum poured over the quayside and into the water, turning the dock into a lake of fire.

The St Katharine Docks blaze as crews aboard fireboats use deck-mounted water cannons to fight back the towering flames.

Black Saturday, 7 September 1940, not only signalled the start of what later became known as the 'Blitz', a word snipped from the German word *Blitzkrieg*, or 'lightning war'. Those who witnessed the scenes that day and night believed that it also signalled the start of the invasion of Britain. Large movements of barges had been seen in the Calais area on 7 September 1940, and there were reports of German Army leave being cancelled. There was also a full moon and tide conditions were favourable from 8–10 September.

From the High Command down to the humble East End streets, there was a feeling of uneasy expectation. Indeed, just before Black Saturday began, the Chiefs of Staff had been put on standby. Then, three-and-a-half hours after the bombing started, Brigadier John Swayne, unable to locate his chiefs, issued the code word 'Cromwell', signifying Alert No. 1 to Eastern and Southern Commands. This alert was clear enough: 'Invasion imminent and probably within 12 hours'. The Home Guard stood watch all night for the first invasion in nine centuries, and nervously awaited the appearance of parachutists. Confusion reigned along the entire south coast and rumours began that Germans were already ashore.

After the calamity of Black Saturday, Churchill wanted to be with his battered people and the grim-faced Prime Minister arrived in the East End during the afternoon of Sunday 8 September. He stopped at West Ham and then Stoke Newington, where a public shelter had been hit killing 40 people. Churchill found the site full of people searching for possessions and little

Union flags were fluttering defiantly on the debris. 'We can take it!' someone shouted. 'Give it 'em back!' cried another. Churchill was moved to tears.

While his entourage negotiated the debris-strewn streets, the Luftwaffe was heading back to the East End. A total of 400 aircraft crossed the south coast between Beachy Head and Shoreham and headed for London, the fires of the previous night providing inviting beacons. Bombing started at around 8.00 p.m. and continued until 5.00 a.m.on the 9th. The night raid of the 8th, though small-scale compared to the previous day's activities, caused massive damage to road and rail communications and huge fires erupted across the capital. Once again, West Ham, Stepney and Poplar were engulfed.

During that second night of the Blitz, a Peabody Trust tenement erected in Stepney's Glasshouse Street in the 1880s received a direct hit. Two blocks in the road (re-named John Fisher Street in 1937/8) were involved in the incident, which history would record as one of the East End's worst wartime tragedies. Mary Kavanagh (née Desmond) recalls:

I was 14 and living with my Mum, Ann, in a ground floor flat of B Block of Peabody Buildings. There were nine five-storey blocks altogether and I loved living there. They were very well maintained, and painted and cleaned every spring. It was such a friendly place. My Dad was a docker, working away in Liverpool, and my sister and two brothers had been evacuated to Newton Abbot in Devon. After that first horrendous raid on the 7th, my friend and

I had gone to the laundry room at the top of L Block and looked in awe at the sky. It was a terrible yet beautiful sky of red, rich colours. Our shelter at Peabody's consisted of a converted room next to our flat on the ground floor. It was a large room by the staircase, with boarded windows and sandbags and supporting steel girder pillars in the middle to strengthen the place. The nine children in my block would sleep on one side in a row, while the parents sat opposite on benches trying to get us to sleep.

On the night of 8 September, all the lights were on in our shelter and everyone was chatting. The sirens went and all of a sudden there was a weird rushing sound that got closer and closer. Then there was the most almighty bang, the lights went out and the room was filled with thick, choking dust. At first, the mums thought it was gas and I remember my mother coming over and telling me to get my gas mask on. The air was full but as it settled we realised a bomb had fallen somewhere. There was total confusion because no one knew where the bomb had landed, who was hurt or anything. Lots of people were crying and we couldn't seem to get out of the room for debris. Then ARP men appeared and they were clearing a passage so that we could get out of the shelter and into the open.

Once out, we were told to run to the Brown and Polson factory shelter in John Fisher Street. As we went on our way, I remember being told not to look back at the Peabody Buildings. Of course, I sneaked a quick look and saw that the block opposite ours – all five floors of K Block – was flattened and just a heap. I nearly passed out as I realised they had taken the hit and all the victims must have been in there somewhere. All the debris from the bomb had also been flung at our block. As we ran to the factory for shelter, the anti-aircraft guns were shooting and lumps of hot shrapnel were pinging all around us and rebounding off walls. It was only a short journey, but it was dreadful as we dodged the flying lumps of jagged metal.

The next morning we walked back to Peabody and stood there in a state of shock. K Block had vanished and we later found out D Block had also been damaged and would have to be pulled down. That morning was like a living nightmare. Rescuers were on the rubble looking for people and they would blow a whistle when a body was found. Then men would remove their hats as a sign of respect before the body was covered and taken off to the nearby porter's shed. The whistle never stopped going and I went cold every time it sounded. Everyone from our B Block was just standing there in a huddle, crying. Then relatives of the dead started to come to the porter's shed to try and identify their loved ones. I later heard one neighbour had come to identify what was left of his Mum and two sisters. There was only a hand left of one of the sisters and he recognised the rings on the fingers.

That morning we were told we couldn't go into our flat to collect our things because a small bit of K Block wall was still standing and it was thought it might fall on ours. Mirrors still hung on this part of the wall and they were glinting, so rescuers smashed them because they were worried about light being reflected into the sky. We pointed out we had no clothes or money and were finally let back into our block for an hour. Our door had been blown in and all the windows smashed. We had had a Sunday roast that lunchtime before the raid, and the remains of the joint was still on the table ready for our cold meat supper. It was now covered in a layer of dust and debris 2 inches thick. My Mum packed a trunk with all our things and then realised there was no way of carrying it. So we both left wearing two layers of clothing, so at least we had some fresh clothes with us. A fireman reassured us he would make our front door secure.

Eventually Mum and I managed to get to Paddington Station and we crammed into one carriage on a Servicemen's train to Newton Abbot, where my sister and two brothers were staying. We left Paddington at 12 mid-day and arrived in Devon at midnight. En route, Bristol and Bath were being bombed and the train had to go very slowly. We just prayed we wouldn't be hit again. Our family eventually moved into an old Victorian house in Newton Abbot and Mum returned to Peabody's to get that trunk packed with our stuff. I think she got a cab to transport it this time. The bomb that destroyed K Block had landed on a Sunday night, when many of the residents had relatives and guests staying there. I know the official record says 78 died but I'm certain many more lost their lives – probably over 100. There were no funerals because there was no time. They were simply buried where they were found.

Next, it was Canning Town's turn. A number of Silvertown survivors, many with no possessions other than the clothes they wore, had congregated at a rest centre set up in South Hallsville School in Agate Street. Some were in a terrible state, traumatised and shouting hysterically. Others sat in complete silence, staring in shock. The corridors, halls and classrooms soon became packed. Yet it was hardly a safe location, situated, as it was, near the Royal Victoria Dock.

Coaches had been due to collect the homeless on Sunday 8 September at 3.00 p.m. and take them away from the dock area. However, nothing arrived and it soon transpired why. The organiser dealing with the Agate Street contingent had telephoned a transport firm and ordered coaches to meet at The George pub. Crucially, the firm was not given the full address because The George at Wanstead was so familiar to all East Enders. (In fact, the name appeared on the destination boards of buses crossing London every day and was a favourite watering hole for day-trippers.) As a result, the firm sent the coaches to a different 'George' pub. Despite apologies, the coaches still failed to arrive on the following day, Monday. Tempers and frustrations

Mary Kavanagh (née Desmond) and two friends pictured outside 'B Block' of Peabody Buildings.

Photograph taken after the wreckage of 'K Block', which fronted the road, had been cleared. The windowless 'D Block' behind it was later pulled down. The 'B Block' where Mary lived can just be seen on the other side of the road (far right).

A memorial plaque is today attached to 'L Block' on the Peabody Estate. It was from the laundry room at the top of this block that Mary Kavanagh surveyed the aftermath of Black Saturday.

Erected to the Memory of the Victims of the Air-Raid on Peabody Estate Whitechapel on the 8th September 1940

RESIDENTS

ALGERNON	ARIS	30	EDITH	DRAPER	73	CHARLES	McCARTHY	52
SHEILA	ARIS	3	ELEANOR	DRAPER	44	HONORA	MURPHY	78
VIOLET	ARIS	34	DANIEL	FOLEY	5	JOSEPH	MURPHY	?
ALICE	BAILEY	28	MARY	FOLEY	26	FLORENCE	O'BRIEN	30
JOHN	BAILEY	4	JAMES	FOSKETT	70	ANNIE	RACKHAM	53
PHILIP	BAILEY	29	ELIZA	FREEBODY	65	ALFRED	ROSS	46
JOHN	BLACKEBY	31	MARY	FREEBODY	52	SUSAN	ROSS	40
GEORGE	BLANKING	2	THOMAS	FREEBODY	24	GEORGINA	SHAW	75
MARY	BLANKING	29	DOUGLAS	GROOM	31	THOMAS	SHAW	75
PAULINE	BLANKING	8 MTH	MATILDA	GROOM	32	BLANCHE	SKINGSLEY	58
WILLIAM	BLANKING	32	VERA	GROOM	4	ELIZABETH	SKINGSLEY	56
MARY	BLOWER	63	ALFRED	HARE	6	EMMA	SKINGSLEY	60
ARTHUR	BOWLER	27	HELENA	JARMAN	12	FLORENCE	SKINGSLEY	51
FANNY	BOWLER	27	JOSEPH	JARMAN	9	AUDREY	STANNARD	18 MTH
FRANCES	BOWLER	2	JOSEPH	JARMAN	43	CATHERINE	STANNARD	28
ANN	BROOKS	65	SOPHIA	JARMAN	47	JEAN	STANNARD	2 MTH
ANN	BROOKS	29	ELIZABETH	KEEPING	?	ELLEN	SULLIVAN	55
MARY	BROOKS	34	ALBERT	KREEGER	18	AMELIA	TARGETT	57
JULIA	CLARK	63	ALBERT	LIVERMORE	29	EDWARD	TARGETT	19
LOUISA	CLARK	24	DOROTHY	LIVERMORE	31	PHYLLIS	TURPIN	19
MAUD	CLARK	19				LOUISA	WARD	63
CHARLOTTE	CRONK	75				CHARLES	WHITE	30
WILLIAM	CRONK	73				ELIZABETH	WHITE	31

VISITORS

CHRISTINE	BAILEY	25	66 CALDERON ROAD LEYTONSTONE	ALICE	HARE	29	63 SHERIDAN STREET
JEAN	BAILEY	22 MTH	66 CALDERON ROAD LEYTONSTONE	ANNIE	HARE	20	63 SHERIDAN STREET
ALICE	BLACKEBY	69	222 ROYAL MINT SQUARE	WILLIAM	HARE	24	63 SHERIDAN STREET
JOHN	BLACKEBY	67	222 ROYAL MINT SQUARE	ELIZABETH	KENTER	48	42 HALF MOON PASSAGE
ALICE	CLEWLEY	14	19 AYLWARD STREET	ELLEN	WHITE	18	28 CUTTLE CLOSE
VERNON	ELY	26	28 EASTMINSTER	WILLIAM	WRIGHT	69	63 SHERIDAN STREET

began to boil over and half of the people were transferred to another school in nearby Frederick Street while the remainder continued to wait.

There were still 300 people inside South Hallsville School as darkness fell on Monday, 9 September 1940. Some of the frustrated occupants attempted to keep up their spirits by singing. Others prayed or attempted to rest. Then, again at around 8.00 p.m., the third night of the Blitz began as a Luftwaffe fleet of 170 aircraft approached from between the Isle of Wight and Dungeness and attacked London. The raid steadily intensified and, at 3.45 a.m. on 10 September, a bomb smashed through the reinforced concrete roof of South Hallsville School.

The building was sliced in two and half of it fell into the bomb's crater. The carnage was appalling and the gruesome search for survivors went on for 12 days. Romford Road swimming baths was drained of water and used as a temporary mortuary, as was the municipal pool in Drew Road. At both places, workers were presented with the ghastly puzzle of piecing together the body parts of victims. Meanwhile, the scene of the incident was concreted over, a news blackout was hastily imposed and a security cordon was placed around the school.

The official death toll was put at 73 and whole families – including six Glovers, seven Gunns and six Lees – were completely wiped out. Many

The appalling effects of the bomb that fell on South Hallsville School on 10 September 1940. Many houses in surrounding streets were simply abandoned because they were so damaged in the blast.

(right) A *Daily Express* front page detailing the new anti-aircraft barrage and a daily casualty list posted outside West Ham Town Hall.

maintain to this day that other victims were simply buried where they lay in the crater and that the sealing of the site was to hide the fact that nearer 200, or even more, had perished.

For three nights, the East End had endured an aerial pounding never before witnessed on earth. A total of 842 people were killed in London on 7 and 8 September. A further 370 perished on 9 September. Over 1,200 lost their lives in just three days – and the ordeal had barely begun.

Feelings in the East End were now running high – and the bitterness was not only directed at Hitler and Goering. The Cockneys became increasingly enraged by tales of luxurious shelters beneath the 'posh' hotels and shops 'up West'. The rich seemed to be living as lavishly as ever. Some even had the nerve to conclude their theatre trips with a detour east to see the blitzed lunar landscape for themselves. East Enders were getting the worst of the punishment and, it seemed, the worst assistance.

Had King George VI heard boos when he visited the East End on 9 September – or was he mistaken? It was therefore fortuitous when, a couple of hours before South Hallsville School was struck early on 10 September, a bomb fell on the terrace outside the north wing of Buckingham Palace, blowing in the windows of the King's sitting room.

The King and Queen were staying 20 miles away at Windsor Castle at the time, but when the King went to inspect the Palace damage on 13 September, six more bombs fell on the quadrangle, the chapel and the forecourt. Three staff were injured but His Majesty was unscathed. Queen Elizabeth wrote: 'I'm glad we've been bombed. It makes me feel I can look the East End in the face.' The Palace bombing helped to ease the tension, as did the fact that the Royal family stayed put and shared the ordeal rather than head for the country. Indeed, when the Royal couple later visited the South Hallsville School site, they walked through the rubble even though an air-raid siren was sounding. The Queen put her arm around people covered

in blood and grime, earning the East End's deep affection and respect which endures to this day.

It was also on the 10th, the day the Palace and South Hallsville School were bombed, that one of the worst fires England has ever seen erupted from St Katharine Docks and London Docks. That night, three Thomas Telford warehouses in St Katharine Docks, containing wool, copra, hides, hops and wax, were gutted in a five-hour inferno that ignited its seven floors in minutes.

Constant showers of incendiaries fell and fire crews, ARP workers, police and civilians fought them doggedly with sand and stirrup-pumps. The three warehouses were soon burning beyond control and the fires spread to two great warehouses in the London Docks, with devastating results. Stepney Mayor Frank Lewey described the scene:

Flames leapt hundreds of feet up into the sky, and dense columns of smoke rose like the Tower of Babel. Flying embers and lumps of red-hot material showered continuously like a scarlet blizzard on the firemen, and overhead enemy bombers flew steadily, hour after hour, raining down large high-explosive bombs into the midst of this great conflagration. Electric cables became severed and kept falling like enormous striking snakes into the roadways. Red-hot cranes toppled over and fell on fire-parties or went hissing down into the dock water.

Hundreds of people had to be evacuated and some were killed by bombs as they fled. The surface of the docks became one huge area of flames and the fire-floats themselves became engulfed in fire. The blaze raged into the early hours and fears rose of another Great Fire of London. However, 350 fire appliances and many fire-floats battled on and the nerve, courage and skill of the personnel overcame the inferno. Nonetheless, a terrible price was paid. Firemen died where they stood and some men were blown into the hold of a blazing ship where, according to Mr Lewey, they 'seemed to shrivel up like butterflies'.

On 11 September 1940, the fifth day of the Blitz, the bombers returned but, meanwhile, the city's hitherto ineffective anti-aircraft defence had been improved. After the first three nights of the attack, new guns had

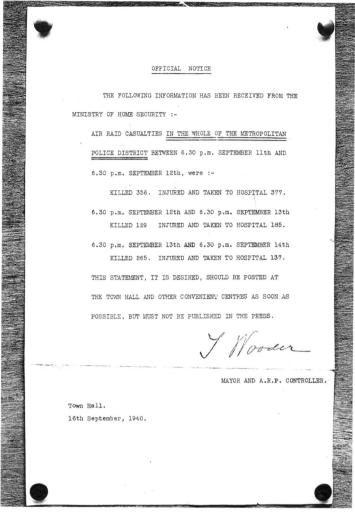

been rushed to the capital from the RAF bases and factories which had previously required them. The number of guns was increased from 92 to 203 and the impact on the 11th was both dramatic and deafening. *The Daily Express* reported:

Chains of shells burst high in the sky, a curtain of steel. The sky must have been full of flying shrapnel. It spattered on the rooftops at times like machine-gun fire…with every minute the barrage increased, the gun flashes making an almost constant glow, the thunder of the guns shaking houses, even drowning the bomb explosions.

However, the guns were incredibly inaccurate. Figures from 1940 reveal that, on average, a single aircraft hit required an expenditure of 2,444 rounds from heavy guns. The lumps of hot, razor-sharp metal and unexploded shells rained down on the streets. Young Bob Humphreys was brought home to Ilford by a schoolmaster after one such incident:

I remember the awful shock of seeing our house in Herent Drive in ruins. The whole of the top floor had been blown apart and rubble was strewn over gardens and mixed with clothes, curtains and furniture. Water was still pouring out of ruptured pipes too. Mum and Dad were safe and we spent a couple of hours trying to salvage items. We then found out the damage had been caused by an anti-aircraft shell that had been fired from Barking Park. The shell had failed to explode in the air and only did so when it hit our house. Dad found the shell nose in the rubble. My parents had been in their Anderson 30 feet from the house and thought the world had ended when the almighty blast came, because everything went so quiet. They hadn't realised that the explosion had made them deaf. They carried on living at the house and simply threw a big tarpaulin over the place to keep the rain out.

The falling shrapnel may well have been eagerly collected by children, but the din of the guns added to the Londoners' sleep problems. An estimated one third of the capital's population did not sleep on the night the barrage began and the situation scarcely improved thereafter. Moreover, the cascades of jagged metal continued to kill and injure more Londoners.

Hitler, still undecided about implementing the invasion of Britain, continued his bombing operation. On Thursday 12 September, a massive 800-pound bomb, over 5 feet long, landed in front of the steps of St Paul's Cathedral. It penetrated to a depth of 15 feet but failed to explode. After a complex three-day digging operation – which saw it slip down a further 12½ feet – the device, nicknamed 'Hermann', was eventually extracted. The bomb was heaved onto a lorry and a route was cleared through the East End to Hackney Marshes, where it was exploded, blasting a crater 100 feet wide and cracking windows half a mile away. The men who saved the cathedral were awarded the new George Cross medal. However, on the next day, 13 September, a West Ham school was not so lucky. Ravenhill School was providing shelter for the homeless and there were 50 casualties.

By now London was in a state of collapse, at least according to the Nazi Party's newspaper, published the following day. Its editorial bragged:

Those parts of London not already deserted have become pick-up places for good-time girls and prostitutes, offering themselves to the playboy plutocrats who have dodged conscription. Meanwhile, the abandoned women and children are left to find what shelter they can in a city largely gutted by fire.

However, Hitler was still unsure about invasion. The Fuehrer should have announced his decision about Operation Sealion on 14 September, but he chose to delay his verdict for three more days. An event then occurred that made up his mind for him. On 15 September, the Luftwaffe decided to carry out a great daylight assault on the burning capital. This was to prove one of the greatest air battles of all time and a decisive battle of the war. For Goering, it was an opportunity to finish off the London job. Around mid-day, a German armada almost 2 miles wide appeared over the Channel and crossed the coast at Dungeness. It was cloudless and clear after the previous week of bad weather. However, RAF Fighter Command had tracked them on radar and 22 squadrons intercepted the invaders as they approached London.

It was a bloody encounter. When the first raiders reached the capital, they were met by, among others, 12 Group's 'Big Wing', a five-squadron formation which was brought into the action at precisely the right moment. It was a terrible sight for the Luftwaffe crews, who had been constantly told there were only 50 Spitfires left. Two hours later, an even stronger German formation formed in three successive waves. The first two were turned away and the third ran into almost 300 RAF fighters, 31 squadrons in all.

It was claimed that 185 enemy planes were shot down compared with the RAF's 31 – although post-war research showed that there were nearer 60

Luftwaffe casualties. Even so, the victory represented Hugh Dowding's finest hour, the 'crux' as Churchill called it, and an historic day that subsequently become known as 'Battle of Britain Day'. Churchill himself had been there to see it all happen, sitting with Dowding's right-hand man, Keith Park, inside 11 Group Headquarters at RAF Uxbridge.

During that day of heroism, other issues were preoccupying East Enders. Disquiet over inadequate East End shelters had encouraged leading Communists Phil Piratin and 'Tubby' Rosen, and about 100 people, to march upon the Savoy Hotel on the Embankment, demanding entry. Ironically, an air-raid siren sounded and they were invited in by the manager to sample the comfort for themselves. He nonetheless called the police. A potentially ugly confrontation was averted and the protesters left, but news of the demonstration reached propaganda maestro Joseph Goebbels in Germany. The story was given suitable spin and the German public were informed that Cockneys had stormed luxury hotels as police shot at them.

The real story that day was rather different. Quite simply, Hitler's British invasion plan was in tatters. Aerial supremacy was a prerequisite of the Sealion offensive and, after the momentous RAF victory of 15 September, that dream was over. Indeed, the Luftwaffe never fully recovered from the savaging it received over Britain that late summer. On 17 September, two days after the aerial massacre, Operation Sealion was postponed indefinitely.

For the first time in the war, Hitler had been stopped and England, the base from which the Allies would attempt the re-conquest of Nazi-occupied Europe, remained safe. The nation did not know it then, but the Battle of Britain had been won. There was, however, a sting in the tail. The success of the RAF injected fresh impetus into a Nazi rocket-research programme, the implications and consequences of which would duly unfold.

In the meantime, a new terror arrived on 16/17 September, and Bethnal Green, Stepney and Dagenham were on the receiving end. Cylinders, 8 feet long and 2 feet in diameter, swung silently down at 40 m.p.h. These parachute mines did not enter the ground on landing and their blast could throw a man a quarter of a mile and hurl a tramcar into the air like a cardboard box. Churchill called them 'an act of terror' and ordered a news blackout, thus ensuring that their existence was not publicly disclosed until 1944.

The Battle of Britain may have been won, and invasion may have been averted, but Goering's Luftwaffe did not stop bombing. The Blitz was to prove to be a war of exhausting attrition, an airborne version of the dreadful trench warfare of the First World War. London was pounded for 57 consecutive nights between 7 September and 13 November 1940. On average, 160 bombers dumped 200 tons of bombs and 180 canisters of incendiaries every night, mostly on the poor.

During those bleak September and October nights, the sky was

Ruth Perham, who died when the baker's shop was hit. Her stepfather also lost his life.

After the Duckett Street bomb: taken in 1941, the photographer would have been standing outside Searle House (to his left) and looking north. On the flattened right-hand side was Betts the baker on the corner Bale Street. The home of Eddie Siggins's 'Nana' Bowyer had been cleared nearby.

clear and the snaking Thames, the city's famous hallmark, reflected the dazzling moon like a mirror. Goering's pilots were nightly presented with an illuminated and inviting target of 700 square miles and the East End alone received 38 major attacks between 7 September and 5 October.

One night that September, Eddie Siggins finally fell asleep inside Searle House in Duckett Street, Stepney. It had proved rather difficult to rest, since all the children in the four-storey building used the Sigginses' ground-floor flat as a shelter. Bedding was laid out along one wall of the living room and the block's youngsters had excitedly discussed the sounds of the bombs and planes before drifting asleep. They had also been giggling at the latest 'Germany Calling' radio announcements made by a strange man, dubbed 'Lord Haw Haw', who taunted Britain from Berlin. No one knew who the English traitor was but his peculiar voice had advised: 'You can come out of your holes now, you rats!' Suddenly the whole bedroom lit up. It was as bright as day and Eddie lay motionless, frozen on his mattress. He remembered:

I saw the door leave its hinges and drift in slow motion in an upwards direction towards the far end of the room, followed by a lightshade and the cord holding it. The curtains did the same thing, leaving just a couple of inches still attached to the window frame. Other pieces of furniture and picture frames also left their places and travelled in the same direction. The air seemed to sparkle and shimmer like crystal as shattered glass from the windows flew slowly through the air too. This all happened at the same time in slow motion and in total silence. As the door reached the far wall, followed by all the other stuff, the sound came back and all hell let loose. It was dark and we were groping for our clothes in the thick dust that seemed to come from nowhere. Mother thrust

an eiderdown at me as I couldn't find my trousers. Then she told me and the rest of the kids to go outside and wait until it got light. We all sat in a huddle on the bottom flight of concrete stairs leading to the floors above.

The bomb had landed in the road outside Searle House and homes were now great heaps of rubble. Fires in the docks and nearby Harford Street gasworks had reflected onto the clouds to create a red backdrop, against which these shattered buildings were now silhouetted. A broken water pipe added to the strange landscape. It was sticking up 10 feet high and curved down to dispatch a weak, steady stream of water. People were frantically trying to get others out of the wreckage and I then noticed Searle House had been badly blasted. In fact, the wall we had been sleeping against had been blown through into the bedroom behind. Sister Irene and my two brothers, Leslie and Peter, were thankfully unhurt and so was everyone else. Mum and Dad then decided to gather a few things together and make our way to Aunt Jess's house in Leytonstone. As we walked, we saw the bomb crater on the corner of Bale Street, which looked big enough to fit a bus in. The two pubs either side of Searle House – the old Anchor and Hope and the Prince of Wales – were both badly damaged and Betts the baker at No. 73 was just a pile of rubble. We later learnt the baker and his 17-year-old step-daughter, Ruth, were killed doing the early morning bake and both were found several days later, holding each other, by the oven.

Then we walked past my Nana's house, Mary Ann's place at 63 Duckett Street. The front door was lying in the road and her bewildered cat was sitting on it. The back of the old house had been completely blown away and was lying in the garden. It was like looking inside a doll's house at the rear, with the three floors completely exposed. Thankfully Nana had left No. 63 for the weekend to stay with her daughter – my Aunt Jess – in Woodhouse

Road in Leytonstone. That's where we were now going. However, a couple of Nana's neighbours, Mr Holmden and his son George, had used her Anderson at No. 63 and were dug out after they were buried in debris.[2]

Mary Ann would never return to Duckett Street, where she had grown up in the days of Jack the Ripper. In fact, none of us would be going back and it was like the end of an era for the family. As we left Duckett Street, my sister Irene picked up Nana's cat, Mini, on the way. It was very sad as we trudged down Duckett Street. Our family in Stepney had been completely uprooted in just a split moment.

Eddie and his family ended up at his Aunt Ada's house in Stratford, but he returned to Duckett Street on a salvage mission. His uncle, John Bowyer (Ada's husband), had been given compassionate leave from the Army and both of them set off to rescue Nana's furniture from the wreckage of No. 63. Uncle hired a costermonger's barrow and pushed it – with Eddie on top – the 3 miles south to Duckett Street. Once there, they piled the barrow high before beginning the gruelling return trip. They made a second trip later that day. Although they managed to collect many of Nana's bits and pieces, there was one defiant old saucepan that refused to be rescued. This was wedged beneath a top-floor window frame which was supporting the remains of Mary Ann's shattered roof. Duckett Street was oddly quiet now: no street traders, no gamblers outside the Anchor and Hope, no hustle and bustle. Nothing. Just cats – deserted by their bombed-out owners – had met them in Nana's old yard, where Eddie and his uncle gave them some milk to nourish their thin bodies.

Soon the Sigginses were on the move again. They had been staying with Nana and Aunt Gladys in a large rented house in Cann Hall Road, Leytonstone. Now the Sigginses moved out and headed for the People's Palace in Mile End Road to await evacuation.

One bomb had changed everything. When that cylinder twisted and turned towards Duckett Street, Nana's old community only had seconds to live.

---

[2] The Holmdens featured on page 69 in connection with a Stepney Housing Trust report on substandard homes.

Chapter five

Subterraneans

A BEAMING VICAR and the ladies of the Women's Institute were there to greet them. Pleasantries were exchanged and, in a trice, the bombed-out family were ushered into a small cottage alongside the White Horse Inn. What a sight met them! A long wooden table, draped in a clean cloth, was groaning beneath the weight of an assortment of laden plates. The kind villagers of Kedington in West Suffolk had all chipped in to make the spread possible. The Rev. John Turnbull, who seemed to have a perpetual dewdrop at the end of his nose, pushed a way through the assembled group so that the visitors could inspect the table. Eddie's Mum was overwhelmed.

It felt good to be away from the East End again, particularly after what had happened in Duckett Street. It felt safe. It also smelled wonderful and it was such a shame that the rest of the family could not be there. Nana remained with Aunt Gladys in Cann Hall Road, Leytonstone, while Dad continued his lorry-driving war job, which kept him away for weeks at a time.

The cream Suffolk cottage was Eddie's new home and warm memories of the enchanted wood at Denham in Buckinghamshire came flooding back. He felt sure it would be special here too. Opposite the cottage was a wheatfield, where the four Siggins children soon joined the local youngsters chasing rabbits, now in great danger of becoming a supplement to the food ration. When Shire horses pulling giant haycarts transported the wheat to the thresher, Eddie, Irene and Leslie rode on the horses' backs as bemused locals smiled at the Cockneys' antics.

The blitzed East End seemed far away and the Siggins family was not alone in finding an escape route. Back along Stepney's Mile End Road, Mayor Frank Lewey emerged from the People's Palace (now the Council HQ and home for the homeless) to see hundreds of prams abandoned by mums as they headed for trains out of the East End. He recalled:

Eddie Siggins's sister Irene, aged 12, pictured in a wheatfield in Kedington, West Suffolk.

The Siggins family in Kedington, Suffolk: Mum Sarah is pictured in the centre with daughter Irene on her immediate right and sons Eddie (on her left, in light clothes) Leslie (on her right, in dark clothes), and Peter (in front).

Young Leslie Siggins, pictured in
Kedington, West Suffolk.

Freddie Le Grand with cocker spaniel
'Topsy'.

*Tragic old prams! There they stood, chipped, dirty, broken, many repaired
with string – they had not been very good ones in the first place, because East
London was so desperately poor – now they were left; the children had fled
away.*

East Enders were enduring a punishing ordeal and the common
portrayal of the resolute Cockney, jesting amid the ruins, is as simplistic as
it is dangerous. Equally, while there was certainly shock, despair, plenty of
anger and overwhelming grief, there was neither true panic nor a potentially
disastrous collapse in morale. Morale did not collapse in the East End for a
number of reasons.

First, those devastated by loss of home, possessions, or family, left
to convalesce with caring relatives if they could. Second, those who simply
could not cope with the present situation, or believed they would have
problems in the future, moved out too. Thousands left during those early
Blitz mornings, pushing prams and carts to places like Reading or Windsor.
Others simply slept in fields outside the capital or went to open spaces such
as Epping Forest, where thousands were accommodated in special camps.
Chislehurst Caves – a vast network of tunnels dating back 8,000 years – was
another option and special trains ran from Cannon Street each evening, to
help some 15,000 people make the 12-mile journey to the chalk labyrinth.

Finally, those who wanted to stay, or who could not move for reasons
of work or duty, adapted to the new life in order to survive. It helped that East
Enders had peered into the abyss and confronted death before. Generations

of Cockneys had been exposed to extreme life-threatening conditions, and
now they faced the ultimate test of survival.

Adaptation to the new threat began with acceptance. Acceptance of
boredom in shelters during raids; of the wasted time spent on long, weary
journeys through the crater-filled streets; of the disruption to washing,
cooking and using the toilet; and, of course, acceptance of the debilitating
effect of continuously broken sleep. Dorothy Crofts, living in Woodland
Street, Hackney recalls:

*It was amazing how, over time, the bombing did become an accepted part of
everyday life. But I stress accepted not acceptable. People began to weigh up
their chances in different situations. Based on experience, you developed an
instinct whether to stay in a particular cinema during a raid, or to leave. We
also got used to spending nights awake and the body adjusted to snatching rest at
other times. My Dad was in both the ARP and Home Guard and Mum and I
would sit on our Anderson bunks waiting for him to return, each of us wearing
one of his tin hats. Mum also held a thick towel round her head to muffle the
sounds outside and there we sat all night. There was also a genuine upsurge in
togetherness, which helped everyone accept a new way of life. People started to
look out for each other and a great grapevine of information would start in the
streets after a raid, so everyone knew what had happened and who needed help.
There was a sort of collective will to survive and it automatically took over.*

East Enders learned to accept the new sights, new sounds and new
smells. Londoners began to look for the 'Bomber's Moon', often in the
middle of the month, which illuminated the night sky and most favoured
the Luftwaffe. They also grew accustomed to the siren alert, a warbling that
rose and fell for two minutes. Next came the wait for the bombers and the
throb of their engines, described by Graham Greene as resembling 'Where
are you? Where are you?' Next the neighbourhood noises: barking dogs,
bombs swishing through the air, dull thuds, clattering incendiaries on roofs,
the roar of flames, the bells of fire engines. The swish of a bomb falling half
a mile away gave you 10 seconds warning, but there was no warning from
the bomb 'with your name on it' because the sound wave arrived at the same
time as the bomb.

As Freddie Le Grand, living in Lillechurch Road, Barking, recalls:

*It was like being on a stormy sea inside the Anderson. The vibration was
transmitted from the ground and right through it. Then the noise of the bombs
was truly frightening. Sometimes they were high-pitched whistles; other times
it sounded like the coal man emptying 5 hundredweight of coal into a bunker.
A crashing, rushing sound that made you shiver. You just had to get used to it.*

Outside, the colours of death could be beautiful when flames reflected from cloud. Writer Evelyn Waugh described the sky over London thus:

Glorious ochre and madder, as though a dozen tropic suns were simultaneously setting round the horizon… everywhere the shells sparkled like Christmas baubles.

Elsewhere, brilliant incendiary showers cast a whitish green glare over the industrial landscape, painting new shadows and new silhouettes. The ever-present smell of bombing also lingered. It was the smell of the dirt itself, of plaster and pulverised brick, and of dust disturbed after many decades in corners and crevices. Now it hung in the air. Above all, there was the smell of the tons of soot that had collected in the houses since the days when they were built. These strange, dark smells emerged from the East End's nineteenth-century fabric. Sucked out and freed by blast, they were the smells that once so offended social commentators like John Hollingshead, a pupil of Dickens, who observed 'every conceivable aspect of filth and wretchedness' during his literary forays into the Victorian gloom.

The stink of gas arose from smashed pipes and combined with the acrid stench of explosive. On 10 September 1940, the Northern Outfall sewer was hit and its foul contents flowed into the River Lea. The following month London's main sewage outfall was destroyed and the smell of excrement became overpowering. To the East Enders, this mixture of smells – pungent, musty, sickly and chemical – was as much a reminder of their living hell as the smashed buildings and covered corpses.

These smells had to be accepted – as did new sights. The weird, the bizarre, the tragic and the contradictory played havoc with normal, rational thought processes. The blast of a bomb, for example, could tear a person to shreds, splattering the body parts against walls and among the debris and covering them with dust before their traumatic discovery. Alternatively, civilians could be killed by the blast and left completely unmarked. Blast, the powerful wind generated by an explosion, could also kill its victims with extreme heat or asphyxiation. Intact bodies discovered in Anderson shelters had commonly met their end in this way. In fact, most Blitz deaths were caused by blast, splinters or fallen masonry, and survivors could spend days trapped next to mutilated corpses.

The fates of homes and buildings also contributed to the mind games. Sections of properties could be bombed with such surgical precision and perfection that it looked like a giant cheese-wire had been at work. Gaping interiors, looking like giant dolls' houses, could be perfectly preserved, with cups, saucers and ornaments remaining intact upon the shelves, but, for some reason, a property next door would be reduced to a heap of collapsed bricks. Likewise,

a whole row of buildings could escape damage except for one in the middle, which would have completely vanished, like a pulled tooth. Other bombs made the ground wriggle in waves, twisting under the soil like giant maggots, creating earth tremors and sparking new gossip about 'secret weapons'.

Once the new world had been accepted, the process of adaptation could begin, as Stepney's Mayor Frank Lewey describes:

We learned what it was like to have raiding at top pitch from about 9 o'clock every night to about 5 the following morning, and then to have three or four biggish daylight raids during the day. One could get two hours' sleep after 5.00 a.m.; then a wash and clean-up and a good breakfast (amazing how food and hot coffee or tea put heart into one); then a day's work till 6 or later; then a hearty night meal, followed by an hour's sleep before the sirens went again.

Life simply went on, as this colourful insight by Mr Lewey reveals:

Stepney? The Prospect of Whitby pub and Paddy's Goose, where the police at one time dared not go; the Mile End Road, crowded with smart little Cockney girls and boys walking, of a Sunday, between the smoking skeletons of houses and over the fallen stonework, but wearing their Sunday best, singing as they strolled arm in arm, just to show whether they were downhearted or not. Stepney? A vista of gashed streets, with the ambulances slowly moving, and ARP men frantically digging like dusty little terriers, and a coloured doctor held by his heels and hanging head-downwards in a bomb crater, giving morphia to a victim pinned below; and the bitter, bitter, smoke of our burning London drifting chokingly over all; and a six-year-old girl, puny and wizened – a shame on the England that bore her – wearing a too-large yellow apron and lustily sweeping up debris with a broom taller than herself, while she sang like a startled canary at the top of her voice.

Mr Lewey also recalled the reaction that followed the goading, English-language broadcasts transmitted from Germany. The well-spoken announcer had been dubbed 'Lord Haw Haw' in the *Daily Express* due to his aristocratic, nasal drawl. Mr Lewey observed:

And then, from some loudspeaker, at a nearby window with jagged bits of glass in it, these words:
'The English music hall, trying frantically to avert all eyes from a victorious Jarmany, is lustily bawling the latest ditty: 'Run Rabbit Run'. I'm afraid the Luftwaffe bombers are now making the running…Hardest of all, the Luftwaffe will smash Stepney. I know the London East End! Those dirty Jews and Cockneys will run like rabbits into their holes.'

As that voice – the voice of Lord Haw Haw – echoed across the ruins, it was answered by a real coster laugh – hoarse, coarse and irresistible. Another and another took the laugh up… it was London's answer, typically London's answer, and if I live to be a hundred I will never forget it.

Adaptation and new routines also resulted in a breakdown of British reserve. Classes mixed as life became more important than money, and the most unexpected conversations occurred between the most unlikely individuals. Standards of dignity, individual privacy and morality also changed. While gangs took full advantage and looted, others convinced themselves that theft from blitzed sites was no worse than taking a fallen apple from beneath a tree.

Similarly, Authority, with its lumbering central and local infrastructure, had to adjust and respond to the demands of a Blitz society and economy. Massive problems were created as thousands of people were made homeless, hospitals were damaged, communications wrecked, drains smashed and light, gas and power paralysed. To compound these problems, nearly a million exhausted people were emerging from the shelters each morning and attempting to do a day's work.

Frank Lewey recalls how the People's Palace was overwhelmed with homeless people demanding money, clothes, transport – and an evacuation destination. Others wanted information about evacuees:

At first we were far too busy to keep records of the evacuees… then of course we began to be besieged by relatives, who had no idea where their dear ones had vanished to, and we could not tell them. We could not even tell them whether they were evacuated or just buried under the local rubble by some bomb explosion.

He recalls dealing with an old Jewish woman, whose only son was sent to Glasgow and was never seen again.

For weeks, the old woman used to come, blinking back her tears and ask: 'Haf you heard of my Solly?' I had to shake my head and swallow the lump that rose in my throat.

A postcard system, whereby evacuees could fill in their destination details and post them back to Mr Lewey at the People's Palace, was then introduced.

While their pre-Black Saturday fears had centred on the numbers of fatalities, the authorities were totally unprepared for the huge number of displaced and homeless people. After six weeks of bombing, at least a quarter of a million people were homeless and one in six Londoners (1.4 million) were without a roof over their head at some point between 7 September 1940 and May 1941. In Stepney alone, four out of ten homes, flimsy and cheaply built, had been destroyed by November 1940. One in seven of London's homeless went to rest centres, often schools that had been hastily taken over and manned by teachers and volunteers. Their facilities were minimal as it was initially envisaged that people would stay only a few hours and then leave.

Dorothy Crofts, then aged 11 and living in Hackney, recalls one raid – and the sobering experience that awaited her afterwards:

I was an avid reader and was always borrowing books from the library in Forest Road, Hackney. One day the librarian had come up to me in the library carrying a book. 'Saved this for you, Crofts', he said and handed me The Wizard of Oz. *The next day I came home from school and found our road, Woodland Street, was closed off. A bomb had fallen on the library, killing the chief librarian and also the young curate from the nearby Holy Trinity Church. The bomb had also blown the fireplace into the living room at our place, and Dad had quickly made it safe. The next morning, a friend called Stanley popped round, looking rather subdued. He blurted out his Dad had been killed after diving under the kitchen table during the raid. The explosion had lifted the table up high into the air and it had crashed down on his Dad, killing him outright.*

After the raid, Mum, Dad and I were looking forward to a cosy reception at the rest centre – a school that had been converted in Eleanor Road. That school will stay in my mind as one of the worst experiences in my life. It was jam-packed with people, either sitting or lying out on the uncarpeted floor. There was a lot of noise, no privacy and no refreshments. We just had to squeeze into a space and try to sleep. Of course, we didn't sleep a wink.

It could have been worse. In one Stepney rest centre, 300 families were sleeping on the floor, surrounded by ten toilet buckets, seven basins, and with no soap or towels. It was only towards the end of the Blitz that the rest centres were transformed, due to the efforts of organised charities and volunteers. In the meantime, many people lived in the centres for weeks on end while their rehousing problems were sorted out. Rehousing was itself a problem because many of the East Enders were reluctant to resettle up West, or even in West Ham, which was seen as a relatively better-off area. Toynbee Hall, which, like the People's Palace, was a great community focal point, now came into its own. It swung open its doors and allowed 200 people to sleep in its cellars. Two ARP wardens ran a clothing depot for several weeks on the theatre stage, and the Jewish costers and small traders of Petticoat Lane supplied free bread, fruit and vegetables. The Hall also housed the East End's largest Citizens' Advice Bureau and , in 1941, the East London Juvenile Court, as well as providing a play centre, clubs, education classes and a restaurant.

Feeding the homeless was another problem, and East Enders were not slow to take matters into their own hands. In Stepney, the Rev. St John Groser of Christ Church in Watney Street (see also page 48) smashed open a local food depot, lit a bonfire outside his church and fed the starving. No one dared to complain. Then Flora Solomon, head of the staff canteens at Marks and Spencer and friend of Food Minister Lord Woolton, stepped in. Simon Marks had given her permission to apply the company's canteen model to the wider community, and empty premises were snapped up and staffed by borrowed Marks and Spencer personnel. Solomon, dubbed 'The Lady with the Ladle', deserves much credit for preparing the early groundwork for mass feeding.

The official response was 'Communal Feeding Centres' and one of the first was opened in Stratford in September 1940. Churchill disliked the title (an 'odious expression, suggestive of Communism and the workhouse') and suggested calling them 'British Restaurants' instead. In West Ham, 11 such feeding stations were in operation by April 1941, plus a dockers' canteen, and they served up to 10,000 meals a day.

By September 1943, there were over 2,000 restaurants, serving half a million meals a day priced at about one shilling (5p) per head. The restaurants gave rise to the 'self-service' principle, and here the poor and homeless dined in rather different circumstances from the wealthy, who continued to enjoy the more refined surroundings of the Fortnum and Mason variety. Yet, as Canning Town lad Charlie Smith was told by his grandmother, Kate Maudesley:

I'd sooner have bread and dripping than horses doovers [hors d'oeuvres] with that bleedin' lot.

While the ability of London's local government apparatus to cope during the Blitz varied from district to district, it was the volunteers who truly shone. These individuals were aptly described as the 'militant citizens' by writer J. B. Priestley and included shelter volunteers, Civil Defence workers, the 1.5 million in the Home Guard, fire service auxiliaries, 250,000 full-or part-time policemen, and the Women's Voluntary Service (WVS).

The Air Raid Precautions (ARP) wardens now emerged as vital community workers. The capital had 10 warden posts per square mile and wardens knew where most of their sector's residents slept. This network of knowledge and information proved invaluable to rescue teams, but relationships between the wardens and the public were mixed. Some wardens – those perceived to have an air of self-importance – were snubbed, but the majority of the public found the sight of the steel ARP helmet reassuring.

The wardens, mostly part-timers, were often the first to arrive at a

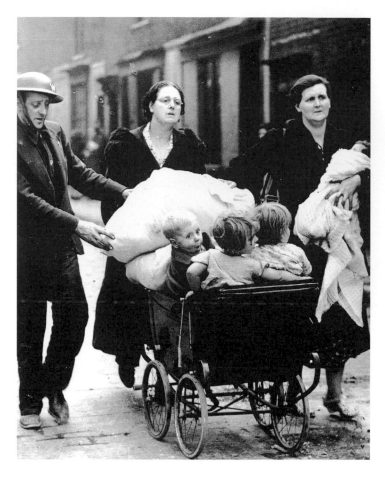

An ARP warden helps homeless mothers and babies move to safety in East London.

bomb scene, with all its ensuing horror. Often, a house had to be completely demolished and made safe before the dead could be retrieved. The wardens would then scour the site, with the task of filling 'the basket of unidentified flesh'. If enough bits were retrieved, they were pieced together at the mortuary. This was a traumatic and deeply upsetting experience for civilians, who found themselves thrust into the front line of war.

James White, a former St John Ambulance worker, was only 18 when he was sent to help at an ARP depot, where he was put in charge of first-aid training. He arrived at Harrow Green depot in Leytonstone:

Up to then, I was only used to 1-inch bandages and inspecting people for cuts. Now I was crawling into bomb debris to inject morphine into patients, while the heavy-rescue teams worked to clear rubble above. A rope was tied round your ankle, which you could yank if you got into trouble, but masonry was falling all the time so fear mingled with intense claustrophobia.

A stretcher party consisted of a requisitioned car occupied by a driver and three first-aiders. We had four blankets, and four stretchers were bolted

Air-raid damage in Southill Street, Poplar. Here a public shelter was hit on 24 September 1940, killing 10 people and injuring 22.

Children in Russia Lane, near Bishop's Way in Bethnal Green, clearing bomb debris to make allotments, which they tended themselves with borrowed tools from fire stations.

The Britannia Empire in Mare Street, Hackney, wrecked after bombing on 23/24 September 1940.

Bomb damage to Spital Street in Spitalfields in 1940.

onto the roof. I had to play God at the bomb scene and decide who needed treatment first, even though there were so many casualties lying around. That meant one had to establish who was bleeding to death – and that wasn't easy, because they were all covered in dust and dirt. Often humour was the only way to break the stressful atmosphere. I recall once how two stretcher-bearers – an unemployed bookie and a bricklayer – were lifting one of the dead too roughly. I told them to slow down and show dignity. Then, as they lifted one, the noise of expelled air came out of the body and one quipped: 'Make your mind up mate – do you want the morgue or hospital?' It was that sort of thing that kept you sane in the midst of awful tragedy. Women ambulance-drivers were the worst hit by it all, but we all were distraught when children were involved.

At Hall Road, near to where I lived, was the mortuary. It was very dark in there and West Ham was using it too, since a bomb had hit their one. When I arrived, I was literally stepping over bodies just dumped inside the door because crews didn't fancy going any further inside. I was bloodied all day, I stank and I was always changing my filthy clothes. We became like sniffer dogs in the end, and could always smell if someone had died at the scene. It was the smell of death, a strange, evil stench like a gas-escape smell. You knew it immediately and it made you feel as cold as ice.

While the volunteers valiantly soldiered on, the authorities were grappling with the acute problem of providing large, permanent public shelters. This was a particularly pressing issue in the East End, where there were few gardens in which to erect Anderson shelters. The Underground stations, which had been used in the First World War, were the obvious choice, but had been rejected because of deep-seated concerns about traumatised people developing a 'shelter mentality' and refusing to come

out again. That left the vast commercial basements and, as contributor John Harrald recalls, the arches of the huge Victorian railway viaducts.

I was seven and lived in Cantrell Road in Bow. Our family decided to use the railway arches which ran along the back of our gardens, and around 40 gathered inside the huge halls before the great wooden doors were closed. I thought as a kid that the atmosphere was brilliant, with all the singsongs and jokes. The camaraderie and togetherness was fantastic. Before that, we used the Anderson, and Dad and Uncle would kneel over my sister and I to protect us from all the muck oozing through the roof joints. Once Dad went out to the loo and the bombing was so bad he was too frightened to get back in. On one other occasion the Bow Cemetery was hit and graves blown up, showering old bones into the street. After that we thought the arches were the best bet.

Young Pat Patmore (née Moore) also headed for the arches, where a family tragedy occurred one night:

Our house in Chalgrove Road, Hackney, backed onto the railway line going east. My grandfather and uncles had their own builder's business and their cars and vans were garaged under the arches. We slept in the cars for a while, and then little wooden shelters with open fronts were built within the arches for our family. The children would put on little concerts at night and my sister, Joan, did a very good Lili Marlene. One night my Grandad went back to the house to get a jug of tea, when an incendiary bomb went off. The shock killed him on the pavement and I remember Mummy crying under the arches 'Oh Daddy, oh Daddy'. She had only ever called him Dad before that.

Trainloads of troops used the line above the arches and they would throw down loose change, some occasionally wrapped in notes saying: 'Tell

(far left) James White (front right) pictured with members of his first stretcher-party squad in October 1939. The photograph was taken at the front of the Harrow Green depot, which was a condemned school.

(left) The Heavy-Rescue squad at Harrow Green depot: their leader, Frank Beard (with white armband and scarf) was awarded the George Medal, the only man at the depot to receive the honour.

Pat Patmore (née Moore), on the left, with her sister Joan outside their grandparents home at 114 Chalgrove Road, Hackney, where the family lived during the war.

Saturday, squeezing into a badly lit, verminous cavern with no ventilation, water or sanitation except a few curtained cubicles. Optician Mickey Davies (1910–1954), a hunchback only 39 inches tall, shared the ordeal that historic Saturday night and later wrote:

After the first few hours, the mingled stench of decaying filth and the body odours of frightened humanity, packed like squashed dates, was such that I'm to this day astounded that children did not suffocate and die in there. The heat of that cellar became literally hardly bearable. A steady stream of semi-conscious or unconscious people was passed towards the doorway, their faces rubbed with wet handkerchiefs, and drops of precious water forced between their lips. As soon as they could stand, they moved back to make room for the next cases. Those lying down stretched head to feet and side to side, just like hard-packed sardines... Those who paced up and down the gangways like caged beasts, their heads turning quickly from side to side, had in very many cases been up day and night for several days. Then, as someone in the dimness turned with a groan on to his side to ease his racked body, into the 6-inch wide opening thus made would dart one of the walkers, with a sound between a claimant snarl and a sob of relief at having found a place to drop down. There would be instant disruption and upheaval and curses.

He goes on:

The ammoniacal fumes of stagnant urine mingled with a sweat of almost putrefying humanity, more than tropic heat, and an occasional tang of carbolic or pine, as some desperate person poured out a bottleful of disinfectant in a pathetic effort to breathe something less than solid poison. The atmosphere was so thick that it seemed that a cup could be stood in it and would not fall to the ground... my first thought was: 'God! This is worse than being out in it!'

Mum I love her' or 'See you all soon'. We would all wave back and shout good luck. At Morning Lane School in Clarence Road, Hackney, we made balaclava helmets, socks and gloves for the troops.

Life could be disturbingly uncivilised elsewhere. The East End's largest shelter, popular during the First World War, was Tilbury Arches, an underground goodsyard on the corner of Commercial Road and Alie Street in Stepney. The plan was to accommodate some 3,000 people in the cellar and vault complex, where margarine was also stored in the 'unofficial' part of the shelter. However, the shelter soon acquired a dreadful reputation as 14,000–16,000 people, a town in itself, crammed in on some nights, and children slept among trodden-in faeces and soiled margarine. The shelter had only two running water taps, for some 8,000 'guests', and 'spivs' and prostitutes joined the motley of races and creeds. Despite the squalor, there were still queues to get in and a mad rush for the best spots – namely those furthest from the stench of the open buckets used as toilets. The shelter became an 'attraction' for West End sightseers and, more importantly, US journalists. With media interest as a catalyst, shelter conditions were much improved, as the King, and Eleanor Roosevelt, wife of the American president, found during a visit in 1942.

The second largest East End shelter was beneath the Fruit Exchange in Spitalfields, which the Minister of Health described as the worst shelter in London. It was grim indeed. The basement had been placed on the list of official public shelters in 1938 and could accommodate 5,164 seated shelterers. However, twice that number entered on the night of Black

Mickey Davies decided to take matters into his own hands and improve the shelter. A Shelter Committee was formed, a Marks and Spencer canteen (serving 'Blitz Broth') was opened, and shelter cleaning was introduced by charging a voluntary weekly levy of 2d [less than 1p] per head. This was followed by the introduction of air ducts, water supplies, waterborne closets, latrines, bunks and lighting, and the opening of a second canteen providing kosher food for the Jews, who represented half of the shelterers. Profits from the canteen enabled all children under 14 and expectant mothers to receive a free half-pint of hot milk each night. The shelter was also painted throughout with cream distemper and the former odour of bodily filth was replaced with a pleasant hospital smell of mild pine disinfectant. The anguished cries of the past were similarly replaced with laughter from the cinema shows and

Rhoda Kohn holding a neighbour's baby in West Tenter Street, close to her Newnham Street home. This Aldgate area, just west of Whitechapel, is located between Mansell Street and Leman Street and just to the northeast of Tower Hill.

dances that were staged. Some people, it was noted, were now living better underground than they ever did above.

Mickey himself became Chief Shelter Warden and was affectionately known as the 'Midget Marshal'. The showplace township that he had created became known as 'Mickey's Shelter', and was a place where 26 different national groups were represented and 14 different languages spoken. When Mickey was replaced by an official shelter marshal, the consequent uproar ensured that he was quickly reinstated.

It was not quite the same story of encouraging improvement elsewhere. While music-hall entertainers such as Nat Travers, 'King of the Comedians', toured the Mile End shelters to bring light relief, other venues were blighted by drunkenness and immorality, and general rowdiness made sleep impossible. There was also a very real fear of disease. As the journalist Ritchie Calder, a Blitz reporter, wrote:

The foetid atmosphere of most of them is like the germ-incubation rooms of a bacteriological laboratory, only the germs were not in sealed flasks but hit you in the face in a mixed barrage.

Lily Towner, (née Barclay), who lived in Dora Street, Limehouse, also recalls:

Our public shelter in Dora House Park, also known as Brickfield Gardens, gave us what we called 'The Itch'. The cement had not dried out and was still wet and the dust which came off gave you a very odd condition. People came out in spots like shingles. It was very itchy – particularly where you sweated – and you couldn't stop scratching yourself.

We were given sulphur to put in the tin bath at home and we smothered

ourselves in 'Licel' cream too. The Itch looked like chickenpox and we had it for months. [Another condition was 'Shelter legs', in which the legs swelled in winter due to sitting night after night on hard chairs or concrete benches.] There were six shelters in the Park with 60 people in each and, apart from The Itch, it wasn't too bad. The very worst thing was when someone had a cough and then my sister and I would be up all night.

Children experienced extremes of emotion in public shelters, as the following two contrasting testimonies demonstrate. Rose Horscroft (née Rands) recalls the good times:

Shelter life could be both exciting and funny. My Dad used to wrap me in a blanket and take me from our home in New North Road, Hoxton, to the public shelter, followed by my Mum and sister. We lived close to the shelter and my Dad managed to make himself a key, which ensured we always managed to get the bunks we needed. We ran down with our own bedding rolled up like a Swiss roll and, by the time the warden arrived, we were tucked in, which always seemed to puzzle him – and amuse us! My sister and I used to lie side by side on the bunk and try and hide our giggles as a fat old lady seated on a chair constantly broke wind all night. Local kids also used to climb up on top of the shelter and pee down the chimney to put the fire out on the stove. The adults used to run out to chase them off and it was like a Benny Hill sketch. It was hilarious.

Others were tormented by nagging family fears, as young Rhoda Kohn (née Rosen) discovered:

We lived in Newnham Street near the City and our family used a public shelter in Alie Street, under the Goldstein Buildings. Other members of the family went beneath the Wiggins Teape paper factory in Mansell Street. It was so hard to do homework, as I had to stand by my bunk and use it as a table. It was impossible, and you could never concentrate with all the comings and goings. My Mum was constantly weeping about the plight of her brother Chiam and his family in Poland too. She also had two sons in the RAF and was often preoccupied about them as well. Even when I told her about my scholarship to attend Central Foundation School in Spital Square off Bishopsgate, she was fairly nonplussed because there were more important things to worry about.

It was a very loving family environment but there was no childhood really. Ever since the age of five, I was aware of this dark cloud hanging over us: what had happened to the family in Poland? Had they survived? My Mum's Dad and most of his children were living in Frankfurt in the Thirties, and so their letters charted the rise of anti-Semitism. These family members had got out of Germany, but our shelter life was dominated by our fears for those still in Poland. We would find out about them in due course.

Pressure mounted to open the tunnels of the Underground system and East Enders refused to take no for an answer, regardless of top-level concerns. They began besieging stations, such as Liverpool Street, buying platform tickets to gain access. Once inside, they stayed inside. At other stations, the gates were closed and soldiers were employed to keep the crowds at bay, as they had done during the pre-Blitz alerts of August 1940. However, the growing demands from the public, the media and key individuals like Stepney Mayor Frank Lewey, won the day. As the crowds piled down the staircases at Liverpool Street, a shelterer shouted: 'It's a victory for the working class'. The right to shelter was one thing, but once inside it was every family for itself and queues formed early for the best pitches. Parents often sent their children to the entrances as early as 10.30 a.m., and dumped prams in line, as the queues grew and grew until the stations allowed access at 3.30 p.m. Within 30 minutes, the stations were packed, but nobody was allowed into the shelter before 4.00 p.m. Between 4.00 p.m. and 7.30 p.m., the shelterers were instructed to keep within a white line drawn 8 feet from the edge of the platform, which left room for train passengers to come and go. From 7.30 p.m. until 10.30 p.m., the shelterers could go as far as a second line 4 feet from the edge. At 10.30 p.m., the trains stopped running, the electric current was switched off and hammocks were slung over the track. Meanwhile, the packed platforms forced many people to sleep on the escalators or on the banisters between them.

The nauseating conditions that had blighted the surface shelters in the early days were now transferred beneath the ground. While the tunnels themselves were slept in at some Underground stations, they became toilets at others. That was bad enough, but those which lay beneath the level of the mains sewerage – and which had no sanitation or washing facilities on the platforms either – suffered the worst stench of all and mosquitoes flourished. At daybreak, the platforms were handed back to the rail staff and commuters, until night descended once more and the nocturnal inhabitants returned with their blankets and folding chairs for another unpleasant ordeal.

The Underground became London's largest public shelter and 15 miles of platforms at all 79 stations were put into use. On average, the nightly attendance was 60,000, including a record 177,000 on 27 September 1940. The deep-shelter mentality failed to materialise and people did come out of the Underground. Only a few hundred people stayed for weeks on end, usually because their homes had been destroyed and they had nowhere else to go. Sanitation arrangements and general comfort also gradually

A group of children bed down for the night at Liverpool Street. This photograph was taken by Bill Brandt (1905–1983) on 12 November 1940 and is one of a series that he was commissioned to take by the Home Office.

Another in Bill Brandt's series of photographs, taken on 6 November 1940, depicts a Sikh family sheltering in an alcove of the crypt at Christ Church, Spitalfields.

Scenes from Bethnal Green Underground station:

(clockwise from above left) three-tiered bunks; the platform hospital; the library; improvised concert hall and stage.

Tube shelter children enjoying a game of draughts.

improved, thanks to the Salvation Army and WVS, who provided food and medical observation to prevent diseases. Three-tier steel bunks were installed in October, and chemical toilets followed, equipped with compressed air systems that forced the waste matter upwards to a level where it could be discharged directly into the sewers. By February 1941, all but three stations had bunks and a system of place reservation, while nightly refreshment trains carrying 11 tons of food had become standard throughout. The Underground may have been crowded and smelly in those early days but at least the bombs seemed physically and psychologically distant. One popular venue was the partly completed Underground station at Bethnal Green, which was awaiting connection to Liverpool Street. This was converted into a deep shelter, along with adjacent sections of tunnel, and opened in October 1940. It could hold 5,000, with extra space for another 5,000 if necessary.

Ten-year-old Alf Morris was one of those who ventured 78 feet below ground, to sleep in a place widely seen as the safest in the Borough of Bethnal Green. He recalls:

Bethnal Green Tube was a very rough affair to start with and it was still being built. There were escalators, but they were not working and we used to carry our big bundles of blankets down there every night. Only one of the tubes was open at first and it was first come, first served. I used to be ordered to go from school and get in line as quickly as possible. ['Spivs' could be paid to reserve spaces.] I would see the superintendent, Mr Hastings, in his office on the way down and then I'd make for our spot. There were various places to pick. No one could sleep on the platform because there was a big canteen erected there,

serving drinks, cakes and sandwiches. So everyone camped down on the track itself and slept either in the 'suicide pit' between the rails, or in the dips either side of it, where the live rail would one day run.

People also went into the tunnel but only into one end, since the other was blocked. The Central Line was still being finished off, so a little way down the open tunnel you would come to all the workers' building gear. It was filthy in that part and there were rats too, which could be seen climbing over people. It was totally disorganised in those early days and that's why we had to get in line so the family could get a good track space outside the tunnel, where it was relatively cleaner.

However, the track was unboarded and so it wasn't very comfortable. I remember lying there looking up at the lights hanging from the domed ceiling. They had long flexes with giant bulbs at the end. I also recall the great atmosphere down there. We'd eat our sandwiches and then the great East End characters would come down after the pubs had shut. All the comedians in the crowd would start the banter and make people laugh. Someone would say: 'Put the cat out, Bertie!' Then someone would reply: 'OK love, and I'll put the bottles out too!' and so it would go on. There were usually singsongs as well and someone would always have an accordion to play.

Gradually the shelter became better organised and it was a bomb up above which helped change things. One night the Falcon pub on the corner of Victoria Park Square was hit. It was right above where we lay and there was total silence when it happened. I was walking along to our pitch with a jug of tea at the time and I concentrated hard so not to spill it. It was a hell of a thud and all the lights were swinging on their flexes. Then we all sat there in silence waiting for the roof to cave in. Thankfully, it didn't.

After that a wall was built right across the platform, halving it, in order to support the bomb-damaged roof. The Tube itself – platform, rails and tunnel – was also closed to the public for a month and a great concert hall with seating, lights and room for 300 was built there instead.

Next a linking tunnel was opened, joining the old Tube to a new, second one running parallel to it, where the public now slept. We slept in the tunnel which would in the future link Bethnal Green to Stratford when it was completed.[1] Concrete slabs were put across the track and three-tier bunks lined the wall inside the tunnel for quite a distance, perhaps a quarter of a mile. The tunnel was also marked into areas – A, B, C, D etc. – and everyone had a bunk number. The tunnel was properly cleaned every day and there was proper lighting too. There was also a hospital on the platform, where a nurse worked, and a branch library with 4,000 books in it.

---

[1] The whole extension from Liverpool Street east to Stratford via Bethnal Green was opened to the public on 4 December 1946.

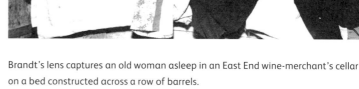

A sleeping family at Liverpool Street Underground station, captured on film by Bill Brandt on 12 November 1940.

Brandt's lens captures an old woman asleep in an East End wine-merchant's cellar on a bed constructed across a row of barrels.

Movement was aided by boarding over the rest of the track to provide a walkway.

There were rules and regulations and, at about 10.30 p.m., the lights went dim and everyone settled down. We rose at about 5.00 a.m., unless there was a raid on, and then leave. All our blankets were dumped at a special shop, the Bundle Shop, which was above ground near the station entrance. We would pay one penny for the service and collect the blankets the next night, rather than take it all home. Further along the road, on the corner, was Jack the potato man, waiting to feed us all with a spud and vinegar. There was usually an organ man there too, trying to cheer the weary.

Fellow subterranean, 14-year-old Peggy Spencer (née Hathaway), adds:

Mum, Dad and I used to catch the No. 8 bus from Bow to get to the tube station. We went there because Mum's nerves were so bad after a bomb had gone off at the corner of our road, Athelstane Grove, and buried residents. Mum firmly believed the next bomb would be ours and she considered the Tube was the best way to avoid it. You could hear nothing down the Tube and it certainly calmed her down. In the early days we slept in the half-made tunnel and kept ourselves to ourselves. We also slept on the stairs going down sometimes. Sleep was always the problem. We were always perpetually tired and my parents would always say 2.00 a.m. was the worst time. When morning came, we'd be up and out and Dad would rush back to wash for work. It was a quick job, mind you. He always called his baths 'Oxford and Cambridge' – in and out like the rowers. It was incredibly smelly down the Tube too. At stations where trains were running, at least there was a gust of air when they came through. However, even those became very musty, stale and suffocating once they stopped at 10.30 p.m. or so. It was not very pleasant at all.

Teenager Ellen Neport, struggling to come to terms with the loss of two brothers and sisters in the Columbia Market tragedy (see page 115), now sought sanctuary below ground too.

I didn't like the Tubes at all but they seemed the safest place to go after what happened at the Market. We used to get on at Liverpool Street and travel down to Bond Street, which we thought wasn't so rough and rowdy. The Tube always stunk of disinfectant and, at 5.00 a.m., we would get a train back to Liverpool Street and go home for a wash and a bit of sleep before going to work. After the Polish woman's premonition about the bomb that fell on Columbia Market, I now seemed to get advance warnings of things as well. For example, my boyfriend George and I were once going to catch a bus to the Tube but I had a bad feeling about it so we walked to Liverpool Street instead. When we arrived, I was shocked to see the same bus we would have caught lying on its end in a crater.

There was another tragedy too. At Bond Street the kids would hop on and off the trains for fun and go on expeditions around the system. They loved playing on the escalators and looking for chocolate machines, while others mucked about on the weighing machines. On one occasion [11 January 1941], a great friend of mine, nine-year-old Ellen Kappes, was travelling around when she got off at Bank. She was blown up outside the entrance and the ticket-collector standing nearby had all his clothes torn from his body in the blast.

The attack at Bank Station – when the roof of the booking hall caved in, killing 56 – followed another appalling bombing incident at Balham in October 1940. Here a roadway collapsed, and ruptured water mains sent gallons of water and sludge down to the station. Some 600 were trapped and 68 killed. Both incidents – and several others – were grim reminders that the Underground did not grant East Enders immunity from the Luftwaffe. However, the popular image of a terrified city living in the Underground system is, in any case, a common Blitz myth. A survey in November 1940 showed that, out of every 100 Londoners living in urban areas, four were in the Underground, five in some other type of public shelter, 27 in domestic shelters, and 64 in their own beds or at work.

Some had no choice but to stay indoors, as this moving account of Lily Ralph (née Leighton) shows:

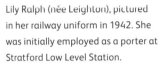

Lily Ralph (née Leighton), pictured in her railway uniform in 1942. She was initially employed as a porter at Stratford Low Level Station.

Lily's father, Frederick Leighton.

My Dad had already lost Mum through peritonitis when I was eight and my brother Harry, 23, was terminally ill with bowel cancer and bedridden. I had to leave work to look after him when he was sent home from hospital to die. We had an Anderson shelter in the garden at our house in Goodall Road, Leyton, but Harry was too poorly to go down there. So to protect him, Dad made a wooden frame covered with roofing felt, which he fitted onto a bay window to stop glass shattering over him as he lay. Dad and I would stay with him too. Harry was very proud of his younger brother George, who was in the Queen's Regiment, and loved seeing him in his uniform. After Harry died in early 1941, George then went missing, which caused even more heartbreak. Eventually a letter came through, telling us he was a prisoner of war in Germany. I don't know how Dad coped with it all. He was always smiling and cheerful. Dad just loved his family – it was as simple as that.

If people were going to leave their homes, they tended to have more faith in the shelters provided by churches and pubs simply because they were more intimate, familiar and comfortable. While Jews were particularly drawn to the vaults beneath Spitalfields Great Synagogue, Renée Rosen (née Saville) recalls shelter life in a pub:

My grandparents ran the Norfolk Arms in Cecilia Road, at the back of the Jewish Ridley Market in Dalston. I was eight and my job was to write down the names of the shelterers who used the cellar. Around 30 pub regulars would arrive and a curtain separated the sleeping area from the toilet buckets. There was one big bed for children and adults used the pub's padded benches. There was a really cosy atmosphere and a piano provided musical entertainment, while adults also played card games. The shelterers became the customers during opening hours and they would bring their own glasses because it was too dangerous to keep lots of glass on the premises. Beer was in short supply too, and so the regulars drank shandy.

However, most people simply stayed put at home, where farcical family situations inevitably arose. Charlie Smith, in Canning Town, recalls:

During one night raid, my Aunt Floss reckoned the bombing would just be a flash in the pan. So Auntie, who weighed 20 stone and was known as Floss due to her love of candy floss, decided not to go to the Anderson. Cousin Joyce and I were playing under the table when there was a large bang and Flossie immediately pushed us into the cupboard under the stairs. Seconds later, we were pulled out again, when Uncle Jack shouted that a gas main had been hit and she realised we had been jammed under the gas meter. Panic over, we started again and headed for the Anderson. Then the woman next door, who had been half-way through preparing the family's evening fry-up, stopped in her tracks as she followed her husband to the shelter. She turned back to the house and yelled back: 'I've forgotten my false teeth!' The husband's unsympathetic retort was: 'They're dropping bombs, not bleedin' steaks, you silly cow!'

Slowly, the East End edged towards a semblance of normality. The cinemas helped. They never shut and customers turned up for every showing. If the sirens sounded before the end of a film, they continued to offer their patrons entertainment as well as shelter. During raids, they usually had standby features to show, while the theatre organist played his heart out and encouraged impromptu song-and-dance routines on the stage. Meanwhile, patrons simply moved back beneath the balcony for safety, leaving courting couples undisturbed in the seats upstairs. By mid-October 1940, cinemas were almost full again as crowds flocked to see Hitchcock's *Rebecca*, starring Laurence Olivier and Joan Fontaine, and *Foreign Correspondent*, which contained a rousing final speech aimed at encouraging America into the war. However, the big film was still *Gone With The Wind*, first premiered in America in 1939, which was destined to become one of the most popular films of all time. As the autumn progressed, theatre also returned to the West End.

Nonetheless, the East End continued to be bombed relentlessly. Between September and November 1940, almost 30,000 bombs were dropped on the capital and the first 30 days of the onslaught claimed almost 6,000 lives. The following two stories give a flavour of shelter life during these weeks.

Hilda Read (née Browning) recalls:

One night my Mum, Dad and sister Dorothy were inside their Anderson shelter at Aldersey Gardens in Barking. I was married with a baby and living 3 miles away at Newbury Park, Ilford. At 9.00 p.m. on 23 September 1940, a large raid took place and there was a great thud near my parents' home. Dad looked out of his shelter and said: 'Some poor devil is unlucky, Mum. We're all right though, nothing broken or damaged.' Then, at 3.00 a.m. on the 24th, that bomb actually went off in the next-door garden and my family – Mum, Dad and sister Dorothy – were buried inside the Anderson. They were dug out but terribly shocked, believing they would be buried alive. Mum appeared to be caked in blood but a vacuum flask containing cocoa had exploded over her.

They went to Swindon the next day, where my brother had been evacuated with his school. Dad died there of tuberculosis, which I feel was a result of the trauma he suffered in the bomb incident. I was left to clear up the mess at the house. The contents were put into storage and the place was unoccupied for 18 months. My clearing-up effort lasted four days and each day I pushed my two-year-old daughter in her pram from our home. It was a 6-mile round trip. Our normal life was turned upside down by that bomb and I took a couple of snaps of the old house with my 1920s' Kodak camera for posterity.

Then Sylvia Woodward (née Templar) lost her brother when he was killed in a shop cellar:

I was born in Roman Road, Bow, in 1930, over a well-known grocer's shop called Sanders Bros, where my Dad, Alexander, was manager. I had been evacuated to Wallingford in Berkshire and one day in October 1940, my foster-mum stopped me and said the pub opposite Sanders Bros had been hit. The grocer's shop was wrecked too and my brother Dennis was dead, together with an ARP man who had been staying there. Mum, Dad and my younger brother Raymond had also been buried in the cellar of the shop, where Dad had made bunks.

I was totally distraught. Dennis had only just had his 18th birthday on 7 October and, as he lay trapped from the waist down, he had called out to my Mum: 'Oh Mum, oh Mum – I can't stand this much longer.' He died soon after. One of my Dad's legs was also badly damaged and he had to wear a calliper after that. Dad was almost killed himself when one of the rescuers, using an axe, almost struck his head by mistake. My younger brother Raymond, just 16, had his nerves completely shattered by the incident and Mum had her shoulder damaged when a beam fell across her.

Large-scale disasters continued to unfold during October 1940. On

(right) Hilda Read (née Browning), photographed in 1933.

Two pictures, taken by Hilda Read with her Kodak camera, of the damage caused when the bomb at Aldersey Gardens, Barking, exploded on 24 September 1940: (below) a close-up of the massive crater; (left) the crater in the neighbour's garden at No. 48. Hilda's parents lived to the right at No. 46.

Sunday 13 October, a bomb hit a block of flats in Coronation Avenue, Stoke Newington, which collapsed, burying some 250 people who were sheltering in a cellar beneath a basement. The bomb penetrated through five floors of flats, leaving the weight of the entire block to press down on the shelter inhabitants. Meanwhile, the ruptured water mains and sewage pipes emptied their contents into the cellar, drowning some of the occupants. Nothing could be done. The rubble was so compacted that it took a week to get the last victims out, by which time rescuers had to wear gas masks to help them remove the decomposed remains. Over 150 died, and today a grave in Abney Park Cemetery records the names of 86 victims who perished in the tragedy. Many of the dead were Jewish and some were never identified.

Two days later, a public shelter at Knotts Green, Leyton, received a direct hit, killing six, while 100 were killed or injured in a trench shelter at Cadogan Terrace in Poplar. That night, with a full moon overhead and parachute mines descending, 200 died in the capital. The casualties increased

the following day, ensuring that over 300 Londoners perished in just 48 hours.

In November, the Luftwaffe changed its tactics. A clue came on 3 November, when the sirens over the beleaguered capital failed to sound. Although the warplanes returned the following night, Hermann Goering was looking to widen the attack and had ordered his bomber crews to begin a blitz of the provinces. Ten days later, during a 10-hour ordeal on 14 November, one third of Coventry's houses were rendered uninhabitable, all railways blocked and 100 acres of the city centre destroyed. Over 550 people were killed and German radio proclaimed that other cities would be similarly 'Coventrated' – physically and psychologically obliterated from the map. The next night bombs poured down on all but one of the London boroughs, killing 142 and damaging such landmarks as Westminster Abbey, the GPO sorting office at Mount Pleasant and the National Portrait Gallery. Then it was back to the provinces and Southampton was attacked.

However, the East End was seldom left out of the Luftwaffe's plans and the provincial blitz timetable could always accommodate a visit to the Cockneys. While Birmingham was next on the list, and duly pounded, Edwina Kerley (née Bond) was contemplating her forthcoming 18th birthday in Gurney Road, Stratford. She recalls:

I was fed up going to our damp Anderson, so I stayed indoors with my widowed Mum when a raid started. It was a rainy night and a road running behind our place was damaged by a land mine and a lot of Gurney Road went too, including our house, which was blasted. The back of the house had fallen down along with a dozen or so others along there. I had to be pulled out and I remember feeling the rain on my face. I immediately thought I was blind in my left eye and a warden took me to a place called the Mechanics Institute, where medical teams were based, near Maryland Point Station.

I was told a piece of bone had been blown out of my forehead just above my eyebrow and the skin had flapped down to cover my eye. I was then taken to Queen Mary Hospital in West Ham Lane, and the stitching was so painful I recall sitting on my badly cut hand because I didn't want them to do that as well. There were two young children in the next bed, crying their eyes out for Mum, who had been lying in the bed on the other side of me. I pointed this out to a nurse. The nurse came close and whispered their Mum had died. My own Mum had been injured and when we later surveyed the rubble we noticed our Anderson was squashed like a sardine tin. We would both have died if we'd gone down there that night.

Meanwhile, Goering's blitz of the provinces was spreading terror across Britain and over 100 were killed in Bristol and over 260 in Liverpool. The bloody month of November concluded with another attack on Southampton, whose commercial and historic heart was ripped out on the night of 30 November/1 December 1940.

A week later, on Sunday 8 December, young Doris Brown (née Exall) was in the front room of the family home in Canton Terrace, just behind the Britannia Theatre in Hoxton:

My grandmother had come down the stairs and the other grown-ups went out to the back yard when a raid started. Grandad came out from his house next door and joined them in the yard too. Then Dad said: 'Get in Pops – it's too dodgy out here.' Everyone came back in and then there was the sound of someone running outside. Dad said: 'That's not running – it's machine guns.' He opened the door and there was a blinding flash, and then deathly silence that seemed to go on and on. The windows and doors seemed to bounce apart and go back together again before collapsing.

We all scrambled out through the choking dust and everyone seemed

Sylvia Woodward (née Templar), with brothers Dennis (with hand in pond) and Raymond, pictured in the garden at the rear of the grocer's shop, Sanders Bros, 233a Roman Road, in Bow.

to be all right, apart from Dad, who had a nail embedded in his head, and Grandma, who had a broken leg. Then we realised Grandad was missing. He was later found dead under the kitchen table, where he must have crawled. That night there had been a party at the back of us in a block of flats in Fanshaw Street. It was a 21st birthday party for twin girls and they held the party in a shelter. A bomb landed, killing them both and other residents too. During this raid, a chemist's wife who lived in Pimlico Walk was also blown into our back yard and killed.

We had to move out afterwards and Mum went to the Anderson to get my school satchel, which contained our house papers. She saw my blazer had been blown perfectly into the roof of the shelter as if it had been ironed into the metal. We went to a flat in Hackney, but after a week that was blasted by a land mine and we were picking the glass out of the walls for ages after that.

Charles Young was also cowering in fear in Hoxton during the same raid on 8 December. He was inside a surface shelter in nearby Britannia Gardens when a land mine fell, destroying four streets:

There was a tremendous gale-force wind and it blew the shelter's two doors in. People were hurt inside, but Dad and I escaped and managed to walk through the streets to Old Street Tube, where the rest of the family was staying. Our feet were very badly cut, which made the experience even worse, and I noticed everything was flattened around our home in Britannia Gardens, which looked completely derelict. We had no clothes – all had been lost in our house – and when we arrived Mum said: 'Couldn't you have had a wash before you came here?' We then explained what had happened.

The next morning, the Queen arrived at St John's Church and she came across to where I stood with my Mum and Dad. It was freezing and I wore a vest with an old coat on top and no shoes. The Queen turned to her group and asked: 'Why haven't these people got clothes?' There was some muffled explanation and she said: 'Well get them something immediately.' The Queen then spoke to my Mum about the incident and soon after we were on a bus with other residents and on our way to a warehouse in Curtain Road. There we were kitted out with clothes and bits of furniture. We then went to Hoxton House School for three weeks, before a place was found for us in Caroline Gardens. The Queen had been visibly shocked to see the state we were in and I'll never forget her kindness that day.

West Ham shared Hoxton's ordeal on 8 December, and fireman Cyril Demarne lost another friend. He recalls:

Routine fire duties had been suspended on Sundays except for operational requirements, and the fire crews had settled down for a leisurely day. At No. 16 Station in Gainsborough Road, West Ham, Officer-in-Charge Fred Dell had told the men to have an early night and by 8.00 p.m. they were asleep. Incidentally, these were the men who had tackled the huge Thameshaven oil depot blaze two days before the Blitz began [see page 102]. At 20 minutes before 10, Stratford Fire Control rang with a yellow warning. Five minutes later came the purple, then the red. The only auxiliary fireman awake went to warn his sleeping colleagues and then the bomb hit, wrecking the dormitory. We heard the explosion of the bomb about half a mile away. Ten men were killed, including Fred. He was quietly spoken, but possessed a devastating wit, and was much admired as a good fireman. The auxiliary man who went to wake the crew, Len Town, luckily survived and recovered after six months in hospital.

Dorothy Brown (née Moss) was also lucky when a bomb fell just before Christmas.

I was 16 and living with Mum and Dad in Grosvenor Buildings in Manisty Street, Poplar, close to Poplar Church. There were four other children in the family but they had been evacuated. Grosvenor Buildings was a six-storey block and we had a two-roomed flat on the top floor, which had marvellous views of St Paul's Cathedral on a fine day. We used to go down to a big surface shelter in the square below and 60 or so people went in there. One night a bomb hit the corner of Grosvenor Buildings and masonry came crashing down

on top of the shelter, blocking the entrance. Mum had had her back to the wall and took the full blast. She looked as if she had died but was in fact alive. However, the entrance was blocked and Dad went down the other end only to find water pouring in. We were soon up to our waists in it and everyone was screaming.

Suddenly the water stopped rising and rescue teams smashed holes in the side to get us out. It took several hours and Dad played his accordion and banjo to help calm everyone. Outside, the strong wind was making our smashed tower block actually sway and I saw that our flat and the ones beneath were completely exposed, as if someone had taken a giant bite out of the corner. I could even see my pale green coat hanging on the back of a bedroom door. My sister was due to get married and had a wedding cake and clothes up there, but no one was allowed into the place. My sister's fiancé did sneak up there, but he could find nothing to salvage for the big day. Meanwhile my Mum went to hospital and pulled through, and the family moved to Slough eventually. When Dad went back to the flats later on, a policeman told him that lots of our belongings must have been stolen. We had nothing left at all.

Through it all children appeared to display both resilience and naïve bravery, as 10-year-old Alfie Brown, living in Shacklewell Lane, Hackney, recalls:

We headed for the surface shelter each night near our flats but, when Mum's back was turned, I'd be out exploring during a raid. I loved wandering about as the searchlights scanned the sky and listening to the terrific din of the big anti-aircraft guns and the falling bombs. I went up to Hackney Downs to watch the action and dodged ARP men and policemen on the way. I never worried about death – even the time a stick of bombs seemed to get louder and louder and be right over me. I was convinced it would never be my turn, but Mum would be frantic wondering where I was. After the raids I went out again, clambering over the bomb sites with my axe, bagging up wood to sell for 2d [about 1p] a bag for firewood.

Bethnal Green youngster June Lewzey (née Guiver) was also alarmingly fearless:

Our family stayed in our flat at Abingdon Buildings in Old Nichol Street at night and, if it was really bad, we just dived under the bed or sat in the passage. One day I bought myself a large Lyon's fruit pie. They were square-shaped and I loved them, even though my mother had forbidden me to buy one with the words: 'You don't know what people put in them in wartime'. On this occasion, a raid had started and I was walking along with the pie. Should I go home with it and be told off, or should I throw it away? No way. I just sat down on the edge of the pavement and ate it, while all hell broke loose around me. But I didn't buy any more pies after that and sweet rationing meant I spent my money on treats like a pennyworth of red cabbage, a penny pickled onion, a penny apple, carrot or a locust bean. The real treat was a drink from Reece's in Virginia Road, where there was a soda fountain machine.

Children presented a massive headache for the authorities. On Black Saturday, there had been over half a million children of school age in the capital and the bombing failed to encourage a mass exodus. In fact, more had left at the outbreak of war and with the anticipation of bombs than when the explosives actually started to fall. The disturbing figures spoke for themselves. In September and October 1940, 35,000 unaccompanied children and about 90,000 mothers with children were evacuated. In November, the figure dropped to 15,000 and, by December, only a few were willing to leave.

It was now Christmas in the wrecked East End and its people were trying to put on a brave face, even though smiles were rather forced. Morale was hardly helped by the fact that the average Londoner's diet was now the poorest of the whole war. Typically, one person's weekly meat ration included a single chop while onions seemed to have vanished (one was displayed on a velvet cushion in a shop window and labelled 'Very Rare Specimen') and oranges and bananas had long gone. Clothing was also hard to find. A 'Make Do and Mend' drive was in full swing and servicemen's suits were unpicked and recycled as skirts or jackets across the capital. In the absence of leather, shoes were also soled and repaired at home with the aid of patented rubber repair kits sold by Woolworth.

The Blitz increasingly became a propaganda war and the cry 'London can take it!' echoed around the city. How many were truly convinced is a matter of conjecture. Businesses also upped the show of defiance. Their slogans, draped over shattered, gaping premises, read: 'More open than usual', 'Broken glass but not broken hearts' or 'Gone with the wind'. People were certainly making an effort for the first Blitz Christmas and the *Evening Standard* attempted to boost morale by claiming that bustling Oxford Street resembled its pre-war atmosphere.

Meanwhile, in Wapping, residents were planning a children's party inside the huge riverside Hermitage Wharf (pictured on page 11), which had become a community shelter. The minutes of the shelter committee reveal Mr Neville Coates was asked to be Father Christmas and 'help run the party from the boys' view of things', while Nurse Edwards would preside over

Grosvenor Buildings in Manisty Street, Poplar: contributor Dorothy Brown (née Moss) was sheltering at the back of her block when it was hit. Her family lived on the top floor, which can be seen exposed, along with the other flats below.

games and entertainment. The party was staged on 28 December and was a great success. By a merciful quirk of fate, the children met Santa the night before another devastating raid on London, during which the Wharf was hit.

Churchill would later call this attack 'an incendiary classic' and the capital would never forget it. Eddie Siggins, a cosy world away in Kedington, West Suffolk, was suddenly jolted from his dream-like existence in the country when news of the raid broke. Taking a cursory glance at an abandoned newspaper, he was left speechless by the headline and haunting front-page photograph.

Chapter six

Heroes and heroines

THE PHOTOGRAPH WAS strangely hypnotic. There was St Paul's Cathedral, Wren's great creation, built between 1675 and 1710, enveloped by billowing smoke and tongues of fire. It was ringed by a sea of flames, but miraculously unscathed. The headline read: 'WAR'S GREATEST PICTURE: ST PAUL'S STANDS UNHARMED IN THE MIDST OF THE BURNING CITY'. Herbert Mason's classic picture, taken from the roof of the *Daily Mail* building, is one of the most famous ever captured by a camera and was destined to become synonymous with British Blitz resilience. Mason later described how the smoke suddenly parted 'like the curtain of a theatre' to present him with his photographic

opportunity. 'It was', he noted, 'obvious that this was going to be the Second Great Fire of London.'

The perfectly timed three-hour raid had started at 6.15 p.m. on 29 December 1940, the first Sunday after Christmas, when 136 bombers dropped large canisters packed with incendiaries and 127 tons of high explosive on London. At the outset, 12 of the largest water mains were smashed by high explosive parachute mines, which immediately compounded the problem of an abnormally low tide on the Thames. Firefighters thus faced a grave battle just to obtain water, let alone extinguish a truly monstrous inferno.

For once, West Ham and the area of the Royal Docks were not the

The most famous photograph of the Blitz: St. Paul's Cathedral stands defiantly amid smoke and flames as the 'Second Great Fire of London' rages.

target. Instead, the incendiary canisters broke open at 1,000 feet above the City of London. The first German crews dumped over 10,000 incendiaries and 54 fires were blazing within 45 minutes. Yet the City, the financial hub of international trade, was largely unscathed. Instead, the rolling flames consumed the historic and religious buildings of old London.

It was both a human and a cultural catastrophe for London. The City, from Moorgate to Aldersgate and from Old Street to Cannon Street, was soon ablaze. Nearly 1,500 fires merged into six giant conflagrations and the streets that had been engulfed by the Great Fire of 1666 were burning again – Creed Lane, Amen Court, Ave-Maria Lane, and all the rest. Yet this disaster, coming 274 years after the first Great Fire, proved different in one key respect. It was on a much greater scale than the one witnessed by King Charles II. Updraughts caused by the 1,000°F blaze created vast walls of hissing, rolling flame that seared most of the ancient Square Mile,

devouring history as it went. Buildings on one side of the wide streets were simply ignited by heat radiated from fires on the opposite side, and eight Wren churches were destroyed or damaged. The fifteenth-century Guildhall – the oldest of its kind in England – was first licked and then swallowed by tongues of flame. Built between 1411 and 1430, and restored partly by Wren after the first Great Fire, it now lost its roof.

Yet, while the 1666 disaster had consumed the old medieval cathedral of St Paul's, this time it was saved, even though many incendiaries hit its mighty 112-foot diameter dome. One incendiary even lodged in the outer shell of the dome and began to melt through it, before tilting sideways and falling harmlessly down to the Stone Gallery. As the flames toyed with St Paul's, Churchill, knowing that its destruction would strike a potentially grievous body blow to the nation's morale, issued instructions that it must be saved at all costs.

(left) The interior splendour of St. Mary-le-Bow: before and after the Luftwaffe had done its worst, with St. Paul's Cathedral suddenly visible across the wasteland beyond.

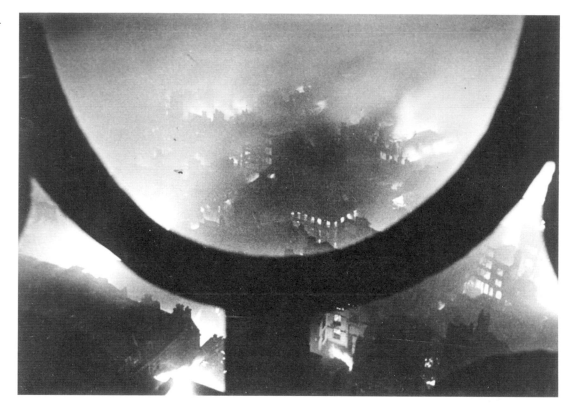

The view from the dome of St. Paul's as the City blazes on 29 December 1940. The view is towards Paternoster Square.

However, Wren's gem, St Mary-le-Bow in Cheapside, was already doomed. The church – special for Cockneys born within the sound of its bells – was gutted. During a raid five months later, its historic bells crashed to the ground in the belfry and smashed. St Mary-le-Bow was not rebuilt for another 15 years. The City was being incinerated and it was feared that the centre of London would become one huge conflagration as 2,000 pumps and some 9,000 firemen battled on. Cyril Demarne, the West Ham fireman, recalled:

The calls poured in and there were great fires in places like Gresham Street, St Martin's-le-Grand, Moorgate and Queen Victoria Street. The London Guildhall and the Wren church of St Lawrence Jewry nearby were well alight and the great maze of buildings around Ludgate Hill, Warwick Lane, Newgate Street and Paternoster Square, the centre of London's book publishing trade, received many fire bombs. We were battling to save the City that night – not just St Paul's – and the men fought for their lives too.

Water was in desperately short supply, thanks to the fractured mains, and relays of firemen heaved and dragged 50-foot lengths of hoses together so the Thames water could be reached. The Thames was at an abnormally low ebb and fireboats edged as close to the banks as possible, before their crews waded ashore through the mud, dragging their hose lines with them which would supply the land pumps with water. The fetching, carrying and laying out of the hoses was *totally exhausting for all concerned – and it was being done in the most trying conditions.*

The official figures at the time estimated that 300 incendiaries fell per minute. This now appears to be an exaggeration but, whatever the figure, they were falling incessantly and were too many to cope with. Although the superhuman efforts of the fire crews prevented the wall of fire from advancing on St Paul's, it was a desperately close-run thing. One crew was ordered to Jewin Street and told to stop the fire from spreading to the cathedral. They found water in the mains and two good working jets, but then the water pressure dropped and they were useless. The fire surged towards the men, who had to squeeze past the fires to escape, only to find that the buildings ahead had fallen, blocking their path. They abandoned their appliance and set off in the opposite direction but that route was blocked when burning oil ignited the road. Their faces were scorched, their hands were burned and the rubber boots they wore caught fire. It was every man for himself, and they ran off, some slipping in oil and incurring fresh burns in the process. One disoriented fireman had a vision of his small son standing in a doorway beckoning him. He went over and found a staircase to a basement and an escape route. He recounted the tale to his wife while his hands were being bandaged in hospital and she recalled: 'There was no flesh on his hands, just bones.'

London was gripped by chaos and pandemonium. The Fire Service had to abandon their control centres as the wall of flame advanced. Guy's Hospital was evacuated and eight other hospitals were damaged. Five railway terminals and 16 Underground stations were closed, adding to the bedlam, and the GPO's Central Telegraph Office in Newgate Street was destroyed, wrecking communications. The Bank of England was perilously close to destruction while, in Middlesex Street, the Hollington's clothing factory was at the centre of a massive inferno that was spreading far and wide. At the inferno's heart – the half a square mile between Moorgate, Aldersgate, Cannon Street and Old Street – a precious part of London was simply wiped off the map. In the meantime, Moorgate Station melted. Aluminium fittings and glass dripped onto the platforms in pools of silver and the railway lines buckled and contorted. Nearby, flames roared from buildings for hundreds of yards along the road, and advancing firemen were forced to retreat when bombs destroyed the mains that were carrying water to the hydrants.

There was also extensive damage to the docks, where the Port of London was temporarily reduced to a quarter of its capacity. In Wapping, the Hermitage Wharf shelter – where the children's party had been held the previous night – was hit by incendiary bombs, high explosives and then a land mine, which smashed a hole in the riverside wall. The water, by now at high tide, poured in. One of the children inside at the time later recalled: 'The water was running in as we were running out.'

No one was hurt and local people were dispersed to the St John, Colonial and Orient shelters – all large warehouses bordering the London Docks. The great Hermitage Wharf would never be used again and its demolition left a site which would attract much controversy in the new Millennium.

Elsewhere in Wapping, rubber, wine and spirit warehouses were ablaze and the flames were flaring hundreds of feet into the air. Bombs rained on Stepney too, where the Rev. H. T. Johnson stood in the middle of Halley Street like a traffic policeman, directing his flock to where the incendiaries lay and barking advice on how to extinguish them. Each one was extinguished and none developed into a fire.

The 'All Clear' sounded before midnight, as fog forced the bombers to curtail their activities. In all, 163 people, including 16 firemen, lost their lives and over 500 were injured. Many of the casualties were in the East End, where homes were damaged along with the Millwall, London and Royal Victoria Docks. As the burnt, cut and blistered fire crews struggled on, the eyes of the East End turned towards the blazing City in a curious reversal of Black Saturday on 7 September 1940, when the west had turned to the fire-ravaged east. Maisie Meadowcroft (née Holmes) recalls:

I was living in Stewart Road, Leyton. We stood in the garden and could see the flames glowing in the distance. The red and orange glow was over a massive area and took up the entire panorama. I stood on the bridge over the railway at Leyton and could see St Paul's between the gap of Draper's Field and Hackney Marshes. There was the magnificent dome and a red glow all around it.

Hoxton youngster Doris Brown (née Exall) went to inspect the City for herself:

Our family was still trying to come to terms with the family tragedy earlier in the month when Grandad was killed [see page 144]. My sister and I were staying with my aunt in Northolt, while Dad, Mum and my younger brother were sheltering at Peabody Buildings in Whitecross Street, off Old Street. That night Dad was called on to help release horses trapped in stables nearby, while the fires raged. He had been an 18-year-old at the Battle of Arras in the First World War and the scenes that night brought back all his bad war memories of the mules at Arras. He said: 'There's nothing worse than hearing horses crying in pain.' Next morning, I went with my aunt to see him and it was terrible. We kept falling over hoses that snaked for miles and the poor firemen were so exhausted they stumbled around like zombies. It was like visiting another planet, because a lot of the recognisable buildings were so badly scorched or burnt out. It was a horrible, alien place to be.

Almost a third of the City of London was reduced to ruins and the crowds of commuters coming over London Bridge in the morning were unprepared for the scenes of devastation that awaited them. They breathed air laden with ashes as they squeezed around smoking rubble and steaming craters, only to find that their offices had vanished. Many were in tears, while others wandered off, unsure what to do next. Some simply offered their lunchtime sandwiches to the fire crews. Signs were hastily erected bearing the names of Watling Street, Bread Street and Friday Street in the great void that now occupied the area between St Paul's Cathedral and St Mary-le-Bow. Young Iris Atkins was with her mother, returning to their Stepney home in Dunelm Street after spending the night in Wood Green:

We got out at Liverpool Street and the scene was unbelievable. Everything was still illuminated red and it was as though your eyes had a red filter over them. We made our way on foot and red embers were cascading down everywhere. My Mum wore a fur coat with a big black collar and it was covered with scorch marks by the time we got home.

Night looks like day as the inferno rages. St. Paul's can be seen to the right.

There was one positive consequence of the disaster. Prior to the Second Great Fire, factories and businesses had been asked to provide their own protection and introduce fire-watching rotas to guard against incendiaries, which proved much more effective at causing structural damage than high explosive. However, the events of 29 December 1940 had convinced the Government that fire-watching should be made compulsory. The case was strengthened by the fact that many shop and office-owners had gone home during the weekend of the Great Fire and taken their keys with them, thus preventing the firemen from getting to the heart of the fires. As a result, the fire crews, with smarting eyes and heat-seared throats, could only watch these premises burn.

On New Year's Eve, Herbert Morrison made a BBC radio broadcast in which he claimed that over half the City's fires that night could have been avoided if there had been fire-watchers on duty. A new Fire Precautions Order was issued but it turned out to be ineffective. It contained so many escape clauses that three-quarters of those who finally registered were exempted from standing watch.

From the roof of the Air Ministry, London's Great Fire had been watched by Air Vice Marshal Arthur Harris, later known as 'Bomber Harris'. Harris later admitted that he had felt vengeful for a moment. With a heavy bombing programme against Germany in mind, he said as he turned away: 'They are sowing the wind.' Indeed, London's Great Fire experience would be totally eclipsed by the devastating firestorms that later engulfed Dresden and Hamburg, courtesy of Allied air strikes.

As the bloody year of 1940 slipped away in swirling plumes of thick, acrid smoke, it was already clear that a diverse group of people had helped to hold the splitting seams of East End society together. This inspired band of civilians, whose activities complemented the sterling work carried out by the emergency, rescue and home defence services, included youngsters.

In Wapping, for example, the 'Dead End Kids' (see overleaf) seemed to epitomise the in-built hardiness and pluckiness of Cockney street children. Stepney's Mayor Frank Lewey wrote about them in 1944:

Come with me to Hermitage Wall, Wapping. Desolate sort of hole, isn't it? Pretty bad before the Blitz and worse now that the hand of the German has passed over it. Not much here except ruins, with the Thames lapping and whispering yonder. Here is a building though: Watson's Shelter. It is closed as a shelter now, because blast has made it unsafe, but we can walk gingerly into it because, inside here, there is a scribbled record of courage that equals the chiselled inscription at the base of any hero's statue. This is no statue; it is a dirty, rubble-strewn, dusty place, very big and very empty and quiet. It sheltered its hundreds, not long ago, from the 'Terror That Flies By Night'. Here is what I wanted to show you: 'DEAD END KIDS' DEPARTMENT', 'RITZ BRISTOL', 'CARLTON TIFFANY'S', 'PARK LANE MARLBOROUGH'... Each cramped cubicle bears the name of some world-famous hotel or restaurant.

Mr Lewey reveals that the Dead End Kids' base, with its humorous hotel

A publicity shot of the famous Dead End Kids HQ inside Watson's Wharf Shelter: (from left to right) Eddie Chusonis; Freddie Pope; Oswald Bath; the gang's leader, Patsie Duggan, with armband; Jackie Duggan, with plaster on face; and Ronnie Eyres.

(right) Graham Bath and Jackie Duggan demonstrate their fire-fighting technique for the press.

(far right) Patsie Duggan mobilizes his team in a mock exercise for the benefit of the media.

(left) Leader Patsie Duggan (with armband) puts the Kids through their paces as they pull a barrow laden with hoses and equipment.

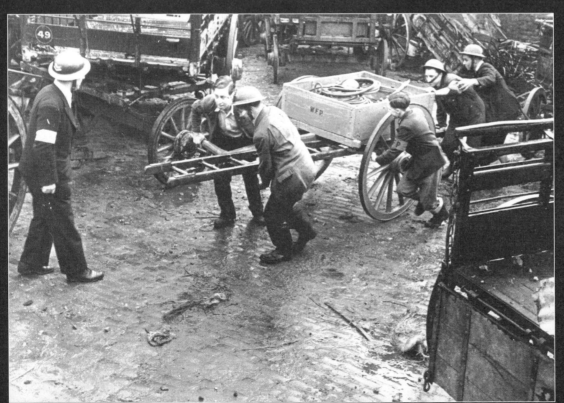

(right) The Kids' HQ, Watson's Wharf. This view of Union Stairs, Standard Wharves and Watson's Wharf was taken in 1937. The causeway at the foot of the Union Stairs enabled passengers to board watermen's skiffs at low tide without getting covered in mud.

signs, contains a story that Stepney 'hides deep down in its heart with a pride that will never forget'.

Patsie Duggan, son of a Stepney dustman and one of 17 children, was the young gang's leader. He was working as a docker when war began but then became a volunteer marshal at Watson's Wharf Shelter, which was situated close to the bombed Hermitage Wharf where the children's party was held. Patsie immediately formed a fire party of his own, which he called the 'Dead End Kids', and roped in members of his family in the process. His gang consisted of his nephews Jackie Duggan and Fred Pope, his 13-year-old sister Maureen Duggan, Ronnie Doyle, Harold Parker, Eddie Chusonis, Joe Storey, Terry Conolly, brothers Graham and Oswald Bath, Ronnie Eyres, Bert Eadon, and George Thorpe, an elderly Wapping Island contact man and honorary member. The Kids were split into four sections, each responsible for a district of Wapping Island, which was then connected to the mainland by two bridges. They had their own hand-trucks, stirrup pumps and other equipment, including steel helmets, rubber boots, gloves, sand-buckets and spades. Mr Lewey wrote:

These Kids did things that were not in the official book of words. For instance, there was an unbreakable law that time-bombs were not to be touched by adult fire-fighters until bomb-disposal personnel from the Royal Engineers could attend them. Two time-bombs came down in the Watson's Wharf area. 'To hell with this!' Patsie Duggan said. 'We'll rope them and get them into the water.' And they did.

One child, sitting on the roof of the HQ to spot bombs descending, would direct a Kids' section to the place where it fell and advise on the equipment required. In one incident, the gang returned with smouldering clothes after leading 30 horses from a blazing building. In another, the gang rescued 230 people from a shelter and led them to safety. Then tragedy occurred in Thomas More Street during the night of the Great Fire. Mr Lewey recalled:

Ronnie's section was running towards some houses on which a load of incendiaries had just fallen when three very heavy bombs came down almost beside them. Ronnie Eyres and Bert Eadon [aged 18 and 16 respectively] were killed almost instantaneously and another boy badly wounded. Patsie Duggan himself was also wounded, but carried on. They carried Ronnie Eyres back to his home and, while his body lay there, his notice to join the RAF arrived. He had been longing for it to come, but when it came he was already called to higher service.

Writing in 1944, Mr Lewey pondered on Patsie Duggan's wish for a posthumous decoration for Ronnie Eyres, which he endorsed, adding 'thousands of people would be glad'.

Patsie Duggan, the gang's inspirational kingpin, died in 1990. His sister Peggy recalls:

Patsie – his real name was Patrick – was quite a leader. When he was very young, he lost an eye after a kid threw a stone at him. He had two false eyes made for him – one was a spare – and they were so perfect I didn't even realise he had lost an eye when I was young. But I wonder now if that gave him an inferiority complex, because he always wanted to prove himself from then on. We lived in Hermitage Street and everyone went to the old Watson's hemp wharf, which was our shelter.

The Dead End Kids probably started out of boredom and just snowballed, and they put all the hotel signs up in there for a bit of a laugh. I met Eddie Chusonis in the Wharf and he became one of the Kids too. We had a shelter romance and eventually married. Strangely, I didn't worry about the Kids and the work they did. Patsie, my Eddie and my sister Maureen were in the gang, and when the raids started they would simply get out of their bunks and get their gear and prepare to go out. It was just accepted and we'd wait for them to come back. In fact, everyone, including my parents, were very proud of them. I remember once my Mum went to the nearby Orient Shelter, and it was late and people told her to be quiet. She replied: 'There are kids out there helping mothers and babies tonight – why don't you go and help too instead of sleeping?'

I used to help make the tea for the Kids at our house. It was made in a huge white enamel watering can and four teenagers would stir it with a broom handle. Eddie died in 1995 and, looking back, he was pretty brave being with me, because my brothers were very protective. He was accepted though, because he was one of them – a Dead End Kid. They all had a very strong bond between them.

The example of the Dead End Kids was mirrored elsewhere. Fifteen-year-old Bert Martin, who was working for a Dalston chemical firm, recalls:

My old school, Thomas Road Central in Poplar, was bombed on 7 September 1940 and I suggested to my brother William that we should do our bit to help. We decided to form our own fire and rescue party and about six of us lads got together. We stole stirrup pumps and sandbags from the ARP and based ourselves in the flats at Kingsmead Estate in Hackney, where we lived. Our gear was kept in the washroom and we would go out to smother incendiaries with sandbags or help dig people out. A bus-driver from Hackney became the

(right) Bert Martin pictured on Hackney Marshes in his Air Training Corp uniform in 1942.

(far right) Bert Martin (top left) with his mother Kate, father Arthur and brother Bill, at their home, 17 Notgrove Street, Limehouse, which was a former pub.

Bert Martin officially joined Civil Defence: this pass, confirming Bert was a member of a voluntary Fire Fighting Party, helped him to gain access to business premises in order to carry out his Blitz work.

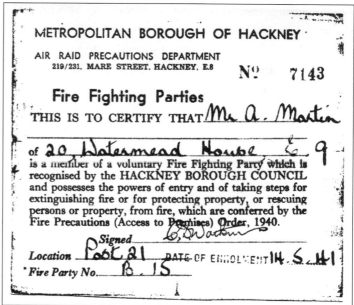

leader of the group. By 1941, the Civil Defence asked us to become part of their official organisation and they gave us some brief, basic training.

I remember feeling real fear on the way to these jobs. Bombs were falling everywhere and there was no running away. It was literally like standing in a forest of fire – which way would you go anyway? People were blown to bits sometimes and it was hard to know what to do first when you got to the incident.

It never got easier. It got harder in fact. You had to make big decisions and they became overbearing. Should you move that person first, help the one screaming over there or what about the noise in the rubble over there? It was like working in hell because bombs were constantly falling out of the sky. I wished sometimes it would end there and then because it was so traumatic. Children were the worst. I remember once seeing a month-old-baby's arm sticking out of the rubble. I touched it to see if it was warm and then held it. It came away and there was no body attached. All the body parts were put in sacks and it all got mixed up in a dreadful mess. I was full of admiration for the fire and rescue parties – they were just fantastic. It never crossed my mind to quit, even though I got low at times. In fact, I became more and more determined as time went on.

The sterling efforts of children were epitomised by the Boy Scouts, who shone through the dark days of the crisis. One lad, 13-year-old John Cox, was a fire-party messenger working at a Stepney church when it was hit and the bells came crashing down. White with fear, young Cox still helped to evacuate people trapped beneath the building and lead them out. A warden at the scene told him off for disregarding his own safety but Cox, who was later awarded the Scouting Silver Cross for gallantry for his actions, simply replied: 'God will take care of me.' His scouting colleagues across the East

End helped rescue Blitz victims, smothered bombs and put out fires. They also put their first-aid training to good use, comforted the dying and even held limbs while doctors amputated them. Fifteen Scouts, just old enough to join the Forces, were awarded the Victoria Cross when they became servicemen during the conflict.

Adults joined the ranks of the unheralded and unsung. Cable Street, scene of the famous battle against Fascism four years earlier, had its own 'angel'. Dr Hannah Billig, who ran a surgery from No. 198, once left a shelter during a ferocious raid and attended casualties in the streets for four hours as bombs fell close by. It was later discovered the doctor herself had been severely wounded. Billig, the daughter of Russian refugees, was awarded the George Medal in June 1941 for her heroism.

Elsewhere, East End communities derived considerable strength from local Missions, where the likes of the remarkable Miss Mabel Knowles, the

(above) Views of bombed South Molton Road in Canning Town, which was hit on the eve of the Blitz. Charlie Smith's family lived in a badly damaged terraced house in this road.

'Rip' was found by ARP Warden Mr E. King and adopted by the Warden's Post in Southill Street, Poplar. 'Rip' helped to find trapped people and was the first dog used in this kind of work. He was awarded the Blue Cross Medal of the Dumb Friends' League for his services.

'Angel of Custom House', and Mrs Strutt helped ease daily burdens. Charlie Smith remembers them fondly and the following recollection is contained in a written family history he compiled:

My family was in a dreadful state in South Molton Road after the street was hit on 6 September 1940, the eve of Black Saturday. The terraced house where we lived – where my grandparents, two uncles and my cousin's family now stayed too – had no frontage. There was just a hastily rigged tarpaulin covering the area damaged by a bomb, while the back windows had all been blasted out and covered with heavyweight blackout material battened to the frames. There was no gas or electricity and smelly oil lamps burned indoors each day, while warmth was provided by the burning of bomb debris on the open grate.

The local Mission Church of St Albans in Butcher's Road became the local focal point for the community, because young and old could mix here at low cost. This was where you could get the 'Bundles for Britain' – the aid from America. The giant bundles from America and Canada would contain all sorts of clothing and footwear. Children would be invited down to the church hall on a certain day and be given the clothes, regardless of age, sex or the season. It was therefore common to see kids at the height of summer wearing clothes designed for harsh North American winters – like heavyweight tartan-check lumberjack coats with deep fur collars and fur hats with headband earmuffs!

The Mission Church was also the place to get a ticket for Mum so she could go to the Monday afternoon jumble sale. This sale had items the rich of the West End had thrown out. However, the ticket was gained by obligatory church attendance every weekday morning at 8.15 a.m., en route to school. Attendance would also ensure a special card was stamped with a star shape, which enabled children to go on the annual church outing to Skreens Park in Ongar in Essex. Around 200 star stamps were needed, reflecting roughly six months' church attendance. Being a Mission Church, we didn't have the services of a resident vicar. Instead there was 'The Angel of Custom House', Miss Knowles, a charming elderly lady from the upper classes, who dedicated her life to helping the community. She was woefully thin and her mainly second-hand clothes from the church jumble sale hung loosely from her tall, stooped frame. Her greying hair was always pulled back into an untidy bun and topped with a woollen or velour hat rescued from handouts. In fact, she was an authoress with the pen name May Wynne, and her most famous book was Whither, a love story centred on hardship and poverty in the docks.

The church scout group – 48th West Ham – became known as 'May Wynne's Own' and she was very proud of it, especially when it won the Scouts Gilt Cross for aiding emergency services in the Blitz. Miss Knowles, a missionary, may have looked like a church mouse but she did so much for Canning Town. She was a saint in our eyes. Through her connections with the rich and privileged, our 'Angel of Custom House' encouraged celebrities to come down to our church to help ease the burden and help people come to terms with their grief.

One such benefactor was the wife of the 3rd Baron Belper who, by her own insistence, wanted to be known simply as 'Mrs Strutt'. A tallish, elegantly dressed woman, the likes of which I had only ever seen in black-and-white films, Mrs Strutt became a regular visitor. She genuinely enjoyed mucking in with the mothers and their children who packed the Mission Hall for Mothers' Meetings or jumble sales. Mrs Strutt would buy Bundles for Britain aid and give it to the poorer mums and she never gave the slightest hint that she was from a different class. It was my mother who was most aware of it, however, when, as tea lady one day, she managed to pour most of the tea into Mrs Strutt's saucer because she was so tongue-tied and nervous. Just as Mother seemed ready to do a royal curtsey, my grandmother glared at her and muttered loud enough for all to hear: 'Gawd blimey Nell, she ain't the bleedin' Queen!' Grandmother then boasted to Mrs Strutt how wonderful my Uncle Frank was at handiwork and, to our amazement, Mrs Strutt said she needed some shelves put up in her West End home. I was invited to go with my uncle, and the excitement of it all filled our house. Mother promised me I could wear long trousers for the first time on my forthcoming 13th birthday, so I would look grown up for the big visit. When the day came, Uncle and I caught the bus from Canning Town to Aldgate and I peered through the anti-blast netting on the windows to see the almost continuous bomb damage along the route.

We eventually arrived at Mrs Strutt's Wigmore Street home, which was a Regency-style terraced mansion. A maid ushered us into a beautiful, tastefully decorated room which looked big enough to accommodate the whole of our house. While I was trying to convince myself it wasn't a dream, Frank was whisked off to work and a large rosy-faced woman with a wrap-around apron came in to look after me. She said: 'My God, lad – you need a jolly good meal. Doesn't your mother feed you?' I felt like an orphan in a Dickens' drama and before I could answer was led by the hand to a large kitchen and sat down. She returned with a big dish of roast chicken and home-baked white bread, with which she made delicious sandwiches. Like most East Enders, I had only ever had chicken on Christmas Day before. Before we left, I noticed a photograph of Mrs Strutt's stepdaughter Lavinia, who was married to the Duke of Norfolk. She had stunning film-star looks. The whole experience was quite surreal but Mrs Strutt was very kind to us.

The East End Mission, with its 'Need Not Creed' motto, was another magnet for traumatised families and the Mission's workers also become local heroes and heroines. Individuals like Miss Lee, Dr Francis Fuller, Dr E. Vincent, Sister Frances Jones, Dr F. E. Robinson, Rev. T. S. Collins, Rev. Harry Lockwood and Dr A. K. Laws are still remembered to this day. Mission staff were at the forefront of relief work and visited shelters, helped to evacuate the homeless and provided accommodation for the Londoners' Meal Service personnel. Mission centres became havens of sanctuary but eight were either destroyed or damaged, including Stepney Central Hall (on the very first Blitz night), the Church of Happy Welcome, Lycett Hall, St George's Hall and the famous Edinburgh Castle, the former gin-palace rescued from iniquity by Dr Barnardo (see page 26).

Other institutions also swung open their doors. Places like the Ratcliff Settlement in Limehouse was 'open house' to those in difficulty and Toynbee Hall was regarded as a refuge for all. In addition to their dedicated service in the East End, Toynbee's staff also opened a rest home in Midhurst, Sussex, where over 400 Stepney people went to recover from their bombing ordeal. There was also SS Mary and Michael's Centre served by convent sisters and directed by Sister Philomena, which opened on 23 December 1940. One of its well-known helpers was Bruna Mentessi, an 18-year-old Italian girl, who had become engaged to Dead End Kid Ronnie Eyres only a few hours before the Great Fire of 29 December. That night, the Mentessi family had been one of the first to seek shelter inside SS Mary and Michael's Centre after their well-known Wapping café was hit. Bruna's fiancé, Ronnie Eyres, had typically stayed out and tried to save the establishment. When Eyres was killed that night in Thomas More Street, a heartbroken Bruna Mentessi decided to join Sister Philomena and devote herself to helping the needy at SS Mary and Michael.

Finally, at the very vanguard of this caring army, were the vicars. The worst raids even became known as 'parson's particulars' in reflection of their invaluable work at times of crisis. Vicars led rescue parties, tended the sick and toured shelters, while some, like Rev. J. Newton Sykes of Stepney's Holy Trinity Church, truly inspired their flocks. Rev. Sykes was a senior fire-watcher for the area and led searches for survivors after homes in Harford Street were destroyed. On another occasion, he had scoured smashed homes in Duckett

Knott Street in Stepney showing large areas of complete devastation in 1941. The photograph was taken from the top of Searle House, where the Siggins family lived before it was bombed out in September 1940. Duckett Street can be seen on the right-hand-side running parallel to Knott Street in the centre of the picture. The roof of St Faith's Church looms in the top right-hand corner while Ocean Street can be seen to the far left.

Street, where Eddie Siggins and his Nana, Mary Ann, had lived before the bombers drove them to Suffolk and Leytonstone respectively. When an oil bomb fell near the Royal pub at the corner of Burdett Road and Mile End Road, Rev. Sykes was in action again. He entered the basement of the pub, believing three people were there, even though it was ablaze. It was empty and the place collapsed just as he left. Then came a terrible incident near Coborn Road Station, where Rev. Sykes arrived to find a wrecked Anderson shelter. He pulled out a badly injured man and the body of his dead wife, before using his bare hands to dig for more victims. He discovered a three-year-old baby, completely buried, and pulled him out alive. The vicar cared for the child at his own home until the father recovered.

The remarkable Rev. Sykes, who also saved the life of a teenager whose leg was blown off at the corner of Grove Road and Ashcroft Road, was in good company. Others who led by example included the Rev. J. S. Birch of Limehouse Rectory, Fathers Cobb and Carter from St Paul's Church in Bow Common Lane and the Rev. Reginald French of St Dunstan's, the Rural Dean of Stepney. The Rev. H. T. Johnson of St John's, Halley Street, the man who had directed the extinguishing of incendiaries during the night of the Great Fire, also made a shelter of his vicarage basement, since less than half of the houses in his area had Andersons. Vicars were simply seen as reassuring figures for many, as Vera Ring (née Morris) recalls:

I was only 11 and our family had been dug out of our Anderson in Bentham Road, Hackney, after being trapped for five hours. Then our new house in Harrowgate Road was wrecked by a land mine and we had nowhere to go. We had no possessions, but felt drawn to the church for help. Our minister, Rev. Middleton, was a wonderful, calm Yorkshire man and we stayed with him at the Bethany Mission in Victoria Park Road. The Mission was used as a sort of hostel, and people just camped down on the bare boards with blankets. Curtains were put up to give some privacy and it was a very comforting and reassuring place to be. We stayed there for two years and we somehow felt protected in the presence of Rev. Middleton. During our stay, he presented the children with New Testaments. Mine read inside: 'In trying circumstances during the London air raids 1940'. On Sundays, us kids used to accompany the vicar to the shelters in Victoria Park, where he played a portable piano. However, we were blown across the road by bomb blast one Sunday night and not allowed to go with him again.

Despite the acute anxiety as 1941 dawned, the days after London's Second Great Fire were relatively quiet. In fact, the relative infrequency of raids – thanks largely to persistent bad weather – only served to heighten the disquiet. What was lurking around the corner? Another 7 September? Another Great Fire? During January 1941, London received only two major raids and just three on a lesser scale. However, one of these, on 4 January, destroyed the famous Great Assembly Hall in Mile End Road. This historic base had been opened in 1886 by temperance preacher Frederick Charrington. From here, he had valiantly crusaded against alcohol and 'the foulest sinks of iniquity', the East End brothels.

There were no mass attacks in February either, due to the appalling weather, although, on 17 January, a bomb hit the archway public shelter in Stainer Street beneath London Bridge Station. A total of 90 bodies was eventually removed from tons of fallen masonry and brickwork.

The majority of Londoners continued to shun public shelters and one in five remained unprotected by any kind of officially provided shelter. Though public shelters were available for 1.4 million and domestic shelters for 4.5 million, the majority of people simply stayed under the stairs or remained in bed. The reluctance of people to leave their homes, coupled with the lack of gardens in the East End for Anderson shelters, led to the introduction of the Morrison shelter in March 1941. Named after Herbert Morrison, who succeeded John Anderson as Home Secretary and Minister for Home Security, this shelter consisted of a steel-topped table with wire mesh sides. It measured 2 feet 9 inches in height by 6 feet 6 inches in length, and could accommodate two adults and two small children lying down beneath the table. Churchill himself tested it at No. 10, before an order for half a million was placed. The shelters were offered free to those earning less than £350 per annum and they proved both practical and popular. Moreover, they were claimed to withstand the weight of a collapsed house. The Morrison's effectiveness would be proved time and time again in the days ahead.

The advent of the Morrison heralded new domestic rituals. Valerie Merralls (née Spiller), from Dagenham (who earlier recalled her harrowing evacuation to a Warwickshire farm, see page 89), remembers:

I was now living with my grandparents in Charlton in a downstairs flat and two elderly ladies lived in the flat above. One of them was very large. The Morrison was in my grandparents' sitting room and served as a table when not in use. When a raid started so did our own military procedure. First Gran, Grandad and I would howl in unison: 'Under the table, Toby!' and the family dog would answer the call and be first under the table. I don't know whether the humans were herded in in order of importance or size, but I followed next. Then it was Gran. While this was going on Grandad would rush up the stairs to get the two old ladies. Then they would all squeeze under too. I have no idea to this day how we all got under there – particularly considering the size of the largest woman. There were times when, after all the shepherding, organising and puffing and panting, the 'All Clear' siren would immediately sound and it had all been a waste of time.

The New Year bombing lull did not last long. On Saturday 8 March 1941, two bombs smashed through the roof of the Rialto cinema in Coventry Street and descended into the famous Café de Paris nightclub in the basement beneath. One of the bombs exploded, killing 34 people and injuring 80. Young servicemen in bloodstained uniforms carried out their dead girlfriends, while looters rifled handbags and took rings off corpses. Many London boroughs were also bombed and Buckingham Palace's North Lodge was damaged by explosive.

Then, on 19 March 1941, came the day the East End would remember as 'The Wednesday'. It was a deeply traumatic day that witnessed the worst loss of life since Black Saturday the previous September. The nightmare began just after 8.00 p.m., when the sirens began to wail and anti-aircraft guns boomed their response. The sky was suddenly lit up by the cold light of magnesium parachute flares, as a massed fleet of aircraft seemed to jockey for position and hover over West Ham. The bombers then appeared to drop their lethal cargoes simultaneously and some 470 tons of high explosive tumbled down, accompanied by 122,000 incendiaries, the largest number yet used against Britain. That night, the Luftwaffe also dropped mines over West Ham, which caused tremendous damage, the first resulting in a massive thunderclap in Richard Street while another, just before midnight, killed several in Rochester Avenue in Upton Park. Early the next day, a land mine in Plaistow Road also hit a fire appliance from Beckenham in Kent, one of a convoy on its way to Silvertown, with the loss of the entire crew.

Poplar and Stepney, together with their adjacent dock facilities and local hospitals, also suffered badly. In Poplar, 44 people were killed in an ARP shelter while, in Stepney, one bomb narrowly missed the SS Mary and Michael Centre before landing just behind it and killing 28 people in Cowley Gardens.

The world of young Ellen Chaplin (née Driscoll) was also shattered. She recalls:

I had been taken by my Mum to stay with friends at their flat in Providence House in Westferry Road, near Limehouse Pier. There were around 70 flats in a five-storey block arranged in a U-shape, and our family lived in one of them too. That night Dad, a 30-year-old casual labourer, was fire-watching close to the flats and was killed trying to put out an incendiary. In those days, people brought their dead home to enable family and friends to pay their last respects. Even so, my uncle thought it would be too traumatic for my Mum to identify Dad formally because his facial injuries were so bad. When the coffin came home the lid remained closed and was not opened as was customary. Consequently, Mum always had doubts about his death and when we were out shopping she would spot people at a distance and think it was Dad. She went up to lots of people just to be sure it wasn't him. She never came to terms

(from left to right)

Two-year-old Ellen Chaplin (née Driscoll) pictured front right with brother Danny, aged six, behind. The two girls beside them are friends Rosie Dent and her younger sister Alice. They are pictured in the Square at the rear of Providence House, in Westferry Road.

Ellen Chaplin's father, Daniel Driscoll.

Ellen Chaplin, aged three, with her mother, Alice. Both in mourning clothes following the death of Ellen's father, Daniel, just four months earlier.

with it. Today, she would have received professional counselling, but of course there was none then.

Meanwhile, at the Beckton Gasworks, which supplied gas to the whole of Central London, two gas-holders were destroyed and others damaged. (In 1986, another bomb from the raid was discovered in water at the bottom of No. 4 gas-holder and three members of a Royal Engineer bomb-disposal team were awarded the Queen's Gallantry Medal for their skill in safely removing it.)

Only on one previous occasion – the land mine attack of 15/16 October 1940 – had London experienced an attack on such a heavy scale. In the East End, 2,000 fires erupted – three of them conflagrations – and hundreds of community volunteers, armed with buckets and stirrup pumps, joined the Fire Service on the streets. There were so many fires and explosions that Luftwaffe crews were unable to make an accurate count of the numbers of incidents. Only one figure really mattered: 631 people perished during the raid of 19/20 March. Around 150 of the victims were killed in West Ham and numerous Civil Defence workers were among them.

When March gave way to April, bad weather ensured another respite from the bombers. However, there was an answer to one puzzle. Since the beginning of the Blitz, German radio in Berlin had been transmitting English-language news broadcasts to Britain. These 'Germany Calling' programmes were fronted by a mysterious, well-spoken announcer, dubbed 'Lord Haw Haw'. On 3 April 1941, the announcer revealed his identity. It was none other than William Joyce, Oswald Mosley's former Blackshirt lieutenant, who had once stood against Frank Lewey in the Stepney borough elections (see page 66). During his heyday, Joyce enjoyed as many listeners as the BBC and his accurate descriptions of future bombing locations made compelling listening.

Yet the Cockney spirit still appeared to be alive and well. Inside the Tilbury Shelter, Yiddish poet Avram Stencl observed the Whitechapel camaraderie between Jews and Gentiles on the first night of Passover, 11 April 1941. He wrote:

They were united in hope and fear which bound them together in life and death. Families sit around on their bunk beds singing the familiar Passover Seder songs – 'Adir Hu', 'El Benah', and finally 'Chad Gadya'. As this ended, a jubilant burst of singing came from our non-Jewish neighbours, and they launched into the ecstasy of their 'Knees up Mother Brown' dance, the singing reaching a crescendo of song. When I heard the singing and saw the dancing, I knew the German bombing would be futile, for a people who could sing like this could not be vanquished.

Their resolve was tested to the full later that month when, on two separate days, London was bludgeoned as never before. The first of the April 1941 attacks occurred on the 16th (also confusingly called 'The Wednesday' by Londoners generally) and was largely confined to the City itself. The second took place three days later, on the 19th ('The Saturday'), when Goering targeted the East End once more. The Luftwaffe bombers killed more than 1,000 people each night and damaged 148,000 houses (compared with an average of 40,000 a week in September and October of 1940).

A response to the RAF bombing of Berlin on 9/10 April, the first raid began just before 9.00 p.m. on the 16th and developed into the heaviest raid on England to date. Nearly 700 bombers were involved and, by 5.00 a.m., 150,000 incendiaries and 900 tons of high explosives had been dropped on London, causing a record 2,250 fires. The bombing was indiscriminate and the rectangle between Hackney, Willesden, Barnes and Lewisham was worst hit. A total of 18 London hospitals, 13 churches and 60 public buildings were either destroyed or damaged. While the docks emerged largely unscathed (as did much of the East End), Oxford Street, Leicester Square, the Law Courts in the Strand, the Houses of Parliament and the Admiralty were damaged. Chelsea and Westminster were ravaged and Broadcasting House, home of the BBC, was bombed. A 250-kilogram (550-pound) bomb also penetrated the roof of the north transept in St Paul's Cathedral and exploded in the crypt, and there was hardly a window left in the Marble Arch area.

The suburbs to the south – Southwark, Bermondsey and Deptford – were also punished, while Bromley suffered grievously. Only 55 bombs fell here during the whole Blitz but 18 fell on 16 April and over 70 people died. In total, the raid killed 1,180 and injured thousands more. One of the fatalities was the popular singer Al Bowlly, who was killed in bed at his home in Duke's Street, Piccadilly. Fear gripped London and, that night, an additional 24,000 were sheltering in the Underground; in Hackney, locals were even clamouring to use the damp, smelly surface shelters that had been deserted for months. There was also renewed talk of compulsory evacuation.

On the night of 19 April 1941, 72 hours later, Geoffrey Maynard went to bed, nervously anticipating his wedding to Ellen the following day. He was in the second year of a six-year career in the RAF and was serving in the Signals Section of Bomber Command at West Raynham in Norfolk. The wedding, at St John's Church in Leytonstone, was to be only a small affair and the newly weds had planned a three-day honeymoon in Morecambe, at a cost of £7. However, the couple's chosen wedding day, the 20th, was also Hitler's 52nd birthday, and the Luftwaffe was busy planning a first – the dropping of 1,000 tons of bombs on a single target during one night. That target was the East End. Mr Maynard recalls:

On the 19th, I came home to Leytonstone, where I lived with my parents in Clarence Road, off Langthorne Road. My fiancée lived in nearby Lascelles Road. That evening the sirens went and we all went to an Anderson shelter down the street, leaving the wedding dress and all the wedding items under the kitchen table for safety. The raid that night was terrible and the whole world seemed to be exploding but we all managed to get a bit of sleep before going to the church. I looked at my brother in the church and there was soot in his hair because his house in Bush Wood, Leytonstone, had collapsed around him that awful night. There were more crashes and bangs during the service, but thankfully that was just a violent thunderstorm.

As the wedding proceeded in Leytonstone, the East End was smouldering after the heaviest attack of the war on a British target. Between 9.15 p.m. and 4.15 a.m. on 19/20 April, a fleet of aircraft dropped 1,026 tons of explosive, plus 153,000 incendiaries for good measure. It was the first

The Maynards' wedding day on 20 April 1941; during the previous evening, the Luftwaffe dropped its heaviest tonnage of bombs to date – some 1,026 tons.

and last time that a raid on such a scale would be conducted. The main target area had been the reach of the Thames, from Tower Bridge downstream to south of Beckton, but the terror also spread west. Despite cloud cover, the raiders came again and again, scattering their payloads indiscriminately because visibility was poor. Many crews made two or even three trips. Over 1,400 fires were started and great blazes engulfed the Royal Victoria Dock, the East and West India Docks and the large granaries in Millwall Docks. The south side of the Thames near Greenwich also blazed. Further west, Chelsea pensioners were killed and a century-old grave in Lambeth exploded, flinging bones over a large distance and throwing one head onto a roof. Many warehouses, timber yards, dock installations, silos, barges, hospitals, churches and museums were either damaged or ruined, while in Nuttall Street, Shoreditch, three blocks of flats and an underground shelter were destroyed, killing at least 46 and leaving an equal number missing. By Bow Bridge, the Fire Service also mourned its greatest-ever loss of personnel. Old Palace School in Bromley-by-Bow was used as a substation and HQ by the local rescue services, and four fire service crews from Beckenham had been directed to report there to provide reinforcements should the docks be struck. Shortly after 2.00 a.m., the school received a direct hit and 34 firemen were killed, including all four Beckenham crews.

The raid of 19 April 1941 left more than 1,200 dead and over 1,000 seriously injured. One per cent of London's population had now been killed or seriously injured in air-raids and Britain's civilian death toll had reached an all-time monthly high in April. Over 6,000 had died.

The plight of Britain – the country that now held out alone – seemed darker and more hopeless than ever. Yet the pendulum of fate was about to swing once more. Hitler was preoccupied with a new adventure. He wanted

(left) Wolverley Street in Bethnal Green was rendered completely uninhabitable after the raid on 19 April 1941.

(right) King George VI and Queen Elizabeth visit Caledon Road in East Ham after the raid of 19 April 1941. Despite the battering, a Union flag can be seen defiantly draped from a window to the right.

(top right) Green Street in West Ham was wrecked during the raid of 19 April 1941.

(below right) The scene in Bethnal Green Road looking west after the raid of 10 May 1941.

to destroy Russia. In March 1941, he had summoned his military chiefs and warned them that a Russian war 'would have to be conducted with unprecedented, unmerciful and unrelenting harshness'. A provisional date for the historic attack was pencilled in: 22 June 1941.

In the meantime, there was still time to hit Britain one more time before the great push east. It would happen exactly two weeks after the famous 'Thousand-Ton Raid' that Goering had delivered for Hitler's birthday. London would be 'Coventrated' on Saturday 10 May 1941 and endure history's most ferocious aerial assault to date.

A beautiful full moon glinted over London on 10 May. The 'Bomber's Moon' also illuminated the Thames, which was again at such low ebb that the river looked more like a village stream. Observers noted there would be great difficulty in sustaining adequate water supplies if the bombers came that night. Little did they know that over 500 aircraft had already begun a shuttle service across the Channel from their bases in northern France, with orders to concentrate on the north side of the Thames downstream from Tower Bridge and encompassing Stepney, West Ham, Bethnal Green and Leyton. The attack began at 11.15 p.m. and West Ham was hit early on. First the Royal Albert Dock went up in flames and a serious blaze began in the Temple Mills sidings at Stratford, then one of the largest railway marshalling complexes in the country. Next, the sheds at King George V Docks erupted. Massive conflagrations also

took hold in Stepney, Whitechapel and Bow and the famous landmark loop of the Thames contained 20 fires. There were even more north of the London Docks area of Wapping and northwest of Hackney Marshes.

It was hell in Stepney, the old stomping ground of Eddie Siggins, which received probably the greatest shower of incendiaries ever dropped on one London borough. Here the railway arch shelter across Chaseley Street collapsed when a parachute mine hit the top of the mid-nineteenth-century viaduct, built by the famous railway contractor, Thomas Brassey. In all, 21 people were killed and rescue workers battled at the site for many hours as bombs seemed to detonate every other second around them. A huge timber dump in Stepney Way was also ablaze, leaving one ARP man to remark:

It was a very cold night but the heat from this timber blaze made me feel as if I was in the tropics for many hours. Steel lamp-posts wilted right over in the heat and paint on the walls of houses ran like water.

Refugees were now streaming to the People's Palace in Mile End Road where, for two weeks, more than 1,000 homeless people a day would be cared for. Meanwhile, Toynbee Hall in Commercial Street, the Palace's great rival, was hit. Although the main building was saved, the Warden's Lodge, the Library and several bedrooms were destroyed. The entire city now seemed

to be under attack as a great carpet of bombs – over 700 tons would fall and 100,000 incendiaries – swept west and across the Thames to the southern boroughs. While the Surrey Commercial Docks and Millwall Docks blazed, the Law Courts, the Tower, the Public Records Office, the Mint, the War Office, and the Mansion House were smashed, and the Salvation Army headquarters in Queen Victoria Street was gutted. A quarter of a million books burnt in the British Museum, a bomb crashed straight through Big Ben, the Elephant and Castle had become Dante's Inferno and whole streets of eighteenth-century mansions in Chelsea and Belgravia crumbled. The churches of St Mary-of-Eton in Hackney, St Mary-le-Bow in Cheapside and St Mary's Church in Bow were also bombed.

The City's infrastructure was wrecked. Six telephone exchanges were knocked out, Beckton Gasworks, the biggest in the world, was blown sky high and every bridge between the Tower and Lambeth was blocked. The main-line railway terminals were also damaged. St Pancras and Cannon Street had been put out of action just after midnight; King's Cross and Euston were evacuated when unexploded bombs were discovered; and Paddington received a direct hit, causing many casualties. Liverpool Street was also blasted, while all three southern terminals – Waterloo, Charing Cross and London Bridge – were out of action. Only Marylebone was still working.

Some 2,000 fires now raged over a vast area from Hammersmith in the west to Dagenham in the east, and one third of the streets of Greater London were impassable. Some 155,000 families were without gas, electricity or water. Large crowds watched the pulsing red glow of London from Cuddesden Hill near Oxford, while German bomber crews could see the inferno as they approached from Rouen in France, 160 miles away.

Still they came. In all, 14 hospitals were hit, including Lambeth, St Luke's, Chelsea and St Thomas's. A bomb also sliced Poplar Hospital in two,

ripping through the ceiling to explode in the ward below. Father George Coupe, who had just held a service there and stayed on because of the raid, was one of the many casualties in the confused darkness. Sheila Barker (née Emerson) was a nurse at Poplar Hospital that night:

Many patients had been evacuated, but that night it was pandemonium. As we tried to get more of them out through Outpatients, there was a stream of people trying to get in. At least three died in the hospital during the raid. A merchant seaman who had been fire-watching on the roof lost his life, as did a patient in an end ward and a sister of Outpatients. We continued to try and get people out to Chase Farm Hospital in North London and we sat in the ambulance for the journeys. There was no light, no equipment and a terrible din outside. The patients were often very traumatised and there was very little

(left top) Buildings at Toynbee Hall were also gutted. The fire spread to the home of Toynbee Warden Dr Mallon, who is pictured in the hat walking past the famous settlement. His Lodge was above the entrance. The main part of the Toynbee Hall complex, formerly hidden from view, survived and could be seen after the raid (right).

(above) The Chamber of the House of Commons: (above) before and (right) after it was destroyed in the raid.

(right) The scene from the Stone Gallery of St. Paul's Cathedral on 11 May 1941, with Ludgate Hill on the left. The area on the right was obliterated during the 'Second Great Fire of London' on 29/30 December 1940.

(left) The post-Blitz scene in Commercial Road/Adler Street on 13 June 1941.

to do or say. Only the desperate cases could be kept in Poplar and as many nurses as possible were moved out. During the raid patients were moved into the nurses home and, when I eventually got up to my room, I found a patient with a terrible disease occupying my bed. It was the final straw. Many of us were then moved out to the London Hospital. If Hitler had seen the East End that night, he would have invaded.

Meanwhile, fire appliances raced towards Birdcage Walk and on to Parliament Square and the Palace of Westminster, where a disaster was unfolding. The roof of Westminster Hall was ablaze and fires had also broken out in the House of Commons Chamber. When the fire crews entered Westminster Abbey, they were confronted with a fireball 150 feet up in the lantern of the roof. Suddenly the lantern came crashing down onto the Abbey floor, landing on the spot where King George VI had stood for his Coronation in 1937. The House of Commons Chamber was destroyed (and would not be restored until 1950) but Westminster Hall was saved, thanks to brave fire crews who took water from craters and sewers because supplies were so pitifully short.

London's ordeal ended shortly after 5.00 a.m., but the last fire pumps did not leave for another 11 days. In this single raid, yet another tragic milestone was reached. A record 1,436 people died, including 35 firemen and the Mayors of Westminster and Bermondsey. It was the highest death toll in a single attack and left over 1,700 Londoners seriously injured.

Evacuee Frank Rose was in Soham in Cambridgeshire when news of

site. The synagogue was never rebuilt after the war because so many Jews had moved out and my parents, who had lost everything, moved away to Kingsbury in northwest London.

The atmosphere at the synagogue will never be forgotten – it was that special. Two cultures dwelled happily side by side there: the passionate Orthodox Jewish practice blended uniquely with British-style formality and authority. The place would gleam with silk hats and candlelight and uniformed beadles would hover like school prefects. The place came alive at weekends and there were huge crowds trying to get in for Friday-night services. These services, with guest preachers and the music of Samuel Alman [one of Anglo-Jewry's greatest composers of liturgical music] became famous. The Synagogue's destruction was also the destruction of my home. I still wonder what would have become of it today. Would it still be a synagogue like the few remaining ones in the East End? Or a museum? Hitler destroyed a very, very special place that day in May, 1941.

While fire claimed the Great Synagogue on Sunday morning, Churchill stalked the ruins of the House of Commons and wept. The Commons' tragedy had once more exposed the woeful frailties of the fire-watching system imposed after the Great Fire. The post-Great Fire regulations had proved difficult to understand and simple to evade and, embarrassingly, even MPs had not organised sufficient volunteers to protect the House of Commons.

A new Fire Guard scheme would now be introduced, making it compulsory for individuals to keep watch in high-risk areas. Three days after the great May raid, the Home Secretary also announced plans for a new National Fire Service. There had been 1,666 local fire authorities before the war, with no standardisation of ranks, words of command or equipment. All the council brigades now became less than 50 fire forces under one unified control, and West Ham fireman Cyril Demarne was appointed Company Officer at Whitechapel by the end of the year, as part of the shake-up.

The raid of Saturday 10 May 1941 also focused media attention on the resolve of Londoners, with one American journalist noting that men now travelled to their offices unshaven. Were they cracking at last? Had it been one raid too many? Mercifully, there would be no follow-up attacks on this scale. After a final raid on Birmingham the following Friday, and an assault on Manchester on 1/2 June, the British Blitz was effectively over. Hitler had a new priority: Russia. Two-thirds of the Luftwaffe had moved to Poland to prepare for Hitler's great attack and the unimaginable horror of the Russian offensive, code-named Operation Barbarossa, would save London and its battered East End. Air raids on Britain would continue for another three years or so, but the heavy and sustained night bombing was over at last.

the great attack filtered through. He recalls:

My Dad was an official, the head beadle, at the Great Synagogue in Duke's Place.[1] The building had actually survived during the night of the raid but, the morning after, flames reached the synagogue from adjacent buildings. Our third-floor flat, which was within the synagogue courtyard complex, caught fire too. The firemen had no water and soon the whole place was well ablaze. Dad ran up to our flat and just managed to salvage some essential papers before the building was engulfed. In those last moments, I understand my Dad also rushed into the synagogue and opened the Ark and rescued the Scrolls of the Law.

The Synagogue, this wonderful place with an unrivalled reputation to create a sense of occasion, was totally destroyed and two years later a temporary synagogue, half the size, was built amid the ruins on the same

---

[1] First established as a place of worship in 1690–1692, the Great Synagogue was rebuilt and enlarged in 1722 before the final synagogue was established and consecrated in 1790. East End Jews commonly referred to the synagogue as 'Duke's Place'.

(far left) Columbia Market was the scene of the appalling Black Saturday tragedy on 7 September 1940, which claimed the lives of at least 57 people, including four children from the Neport family (see page 115). The buildings were further wrecked during the great raid of 10 May 1941.

Firemen at the London Officers' Training School with Cyril Demarne standing in the centre of the back row.

The cold, statistical facts of the Blitz utterly fail to reflect the human tragedy they contain. Between Black Saturday on 7 September 1940 and the end of May 1941, nearly 45,000 civilians in Britain lost their lives and 50,000 were injured. Almost half the deaths occurred in London. In addition, over 1 million homes had been damaged or destroyed in the capital, and one Londoner in six was homeless. Whole communities – their churches, cinemas, theatres, pubs, schools and shops – were blighted.

The punishing Blitz failed to bring London to its knees. Communication damage was always quickly tackled and the City's financial and business circuitry did not fuse. Equally, while industry inevitably suffered severe production setbacks, it never teetered on the brink of collapse and the Port of London continued to function, despite acute damage to warehouses and facilities.

At a human level, the physical health of many of the Blitz children actually improved, since fears of scabies, lice and impetigo led to vaccination against diphtheria, thus cutting disease-related deaths. The wartime public was also swamped with healthy eating advice, which dramatically improved their awareness of good dietary habits. There was also no indication of increases in general neurosis or insanity. The numbers of suicides fell and drunkenness was halved. Even so, the psychological imprint left by the Blitz cannot be underestimated. Those involved in harrowing incidents and grievous loss showed marked and damaging mental symptoms, and the amount of stress-related illness suffered by the Blitzed populace is incalculable.

The exhausted East End Cockneys, conditioned throughout generations in the art of survival, had paid a particularly heavy price to deny Goering his Blitz dream. However, the East End did not collapse and become part of the 'raving bedlam' predicted by Bertrand Russell. The people had displayed resilience rather than rebellion. The East End had stood firm.

Eddie Siggins, bombed out of Searle House in Stepney's Duckett Street soon after the Blitz commenced, had luckily missed the ferocious bombing campaign that subsequently consumed the East End. He was living in a different world, albeit temporarily. Eddie, his Mum, sister and two brothers continued to enjoy their evacuation in Suffolk's Constable country where, it seemed, every effort was made to encourage children to follow in the great artist's footsteps. On most afternoons he would be asked to collect berries, leaves and samples from the hedgerows, which he would then sketch in class. The rest of the time he roamed the Kedington fields, marvelling at creatures he had never seen before, such as stoats, weasels and shrews. He had even caught a bat once. Then there was the ruddy-faced PC Bacon, with an uncanny resemblance to PC Plod in Enid Blyton's 'Noddy' books, who broke the silence, chasing naughty village kids on his bicycle with cries of 'Varmints! Bloody varmints!' Fun indeed.

Yet 11-year-old Eddie often thought about Duckett Street and the night when the Luftwaffe changed his world. He also wondered about his Nana, Mary Ann, who was staying with Aunt Gladys in Leytonstone's Matcham Road. How on earth had she coped with the bombing nightmare? When he

The Wizard of Oz, starring (from left to right) Jack Haley as the Tin Man, Judy Garland as Dorothy and. Ray Bolger as the Scarecrow. Bolger was originally cast as the Tin Man but swapped roles with Buddy Ebsen, who was to have been the Scarecrow. Ebsen then became sick from the metal paint and was replaced by Haley.

Gone with the Wind, starring Vivien Leigh (pictured) and Clark Gable is the only film in history that has been profitably revived every decade since its release in 1939.

visited her, the East End seemed strangely different. Only Nana and Aunt Gladys were the same. Perhaps it was the odd quiet in the street which unnerved him. There were no clanging bells, no ear-splitting explosions and no frantic dashes to shelters. Nana told him it had not always been like this. Leytonstone had shaken and rattled with the rest of the East End during the pulverising raids of 19 April and 10 May 1941. During Eddie's two-week stay, there were no attacks. The threat, the fear that had permeated every brick, street and human fibre, seemed to have lifted, leaving a peculiar indifference and lethargy.

The bombing had dramatically eased because Hitler's troops had poured across the Niemen River and penetrated into the vast Russian hinterland. The assault on Russia, Operation Barbarossa, had been launched on Sunday 22 June 1941, the same day as Hitler's great hero Napoleon had crossed the Niemen in 1812, on his way to Moscow. Goering's Luftwaffe, the London Blitz machines, were now flying deep into Russia instead. At ground level, the Russians were being over-run before they could offer resistance; whole armies had been surrounded and tens of thousands of prisoners taken.

Back in Britain, London suddenly looked scruffier than ever and a depressing air of fatigue circulated the shabby alleys and tenements. When the bombs had fallen, there had been a sense of purpose and an urgency to respond and survive. It had brought out the best in most. Now when the lull came, everyone took a much-earned breather. Sheer and total exhaustion had confined the great city to the armchair where, despite its best efforts, it was easier to slouch and reflect than rise and rebuild. There also seemed less point to the old routines as 1941 progressed. Hence, the number of people sheltering in the Underground was now just 16,000 – a tenth of what it had been at its Blitz peak. The following year it would be just 6,000.

However, there were some encouraging signs that the city was waking from its weary slumber. Libraries noted brisk business, with West Hammers demanding Trollope, Bethnal Greeners in search of Dickens, and everyone in search of contemporary favourites, such as Margaret Mitchell's 1,037-page epic *Gone With The Wind*. Strained, drawn faces would brighten with the sound of Tommy Handley and his 'ITMA' (*It's That Man Again*) radio programme. It had returned to the airwaves in June 1941 and become essential entertainment for 16 million listeners. Handley's bizarre characters became cultural icons, their absurd antics adored from Buckingham Palace to the slums, and their catch phrases destined for a special place in the nation's vocabulary. Mrs Mopp ('Can I do you now, Sir?'), Colonel Chinstrap and Mona Lott ('It's being so cheerful as keeps me going') shone daily light into East End homes. The gloom was further illuminated by London's own programme, *In Town Tonight,* which offered interviews with local people, while the incredibly successful *Brains Trust* cleverly combined humour with discreet education.

At the cinemas, classics of the future were giving *Gone With The Wind* – the undisputed wartime cinema champion – a run for its money. The *Wizard of Oz* made a star of Judy Garland as 'Dorothy', even though makers MGM had originally planned to lure Shirley Temple from Twentieth Century Fox. Cary Grant also starred in a rousing period adventure on the northwest frontier, *Gunga Din*, while *Goodbye Mr Chips*, a sentimental romance in MGM's best traditions, also helped transport East Enders to a world without blackout and starvation. *Casablanca,* a superb studio-bound Hollywood melodrama, and *The Grapes of Wrath*, with its unforgettable portrayal of Oklahoma farmers escaping the dust-bowl disaster of the Thirties, also became big hits. A number of war films followed, which included the archetypal British flag-waver *In Which We Serve* (1942) and *Mrs Miniver*, a Hollywood stab at the British Blitz experience which, despite its questionable sentiments, proved a great morale raiser.

Attempts to shake off the general malaise were not helped by the introduction of clothes rationing in June 1941. Purchase of shop items now

Four women from Dora Street, Limehouse, featured in *Home Chat* magazine in a bid to urge Britons to salvage metal. Second from right is Beattie Barclay, mother of contributor Lily Towner (née Barclay). Beattie is joined by relatives for the photo-shoot. The accompanying article by Walter Whitman urged: *Get the offensive spirit and give our fighting men the materials for those tools they want to finish the war… There's many persons too old to fight, or unable, for other reasons, to get at the Huns but who would like to strike at least one direct blow? Well, a single saucepan provides enough metal for a soldier's bayonet.* And 11 pounds per head of metal would *'provide 27 new ships capable of carrying 5,000 tons of cargo each'.*

required both cash and coupons and women's magazines preached the gospel of 'make do and mend' like never before. Old mackintoshes could become bibs for baby; a father's plus fours made into a suit for his son; and the children's own garments could be unpicked and undergo all kinds of strange transformations.

Londoners now felt oddly detached from the war. By the end of July 1941, only a handful of enemy aircraft were operating over Britain, and just a small group of provincial towns and cities appeared to be reserved for the Luftwaffe's attention. There was, however, a sudden and unwelcome reminder in the East End, as the late Bill Peet recalled:

I was born in Poplar in 1934, into a family which seemed beset by tragedy. My twin Frederick died in 1937 of pneumonia and I also had two sisters, one of whom, Elizabeth, died aged 15 of tuberculosis just before the Blitz. This left my mother, father, sister, grandfather and myself, all living in Broomfield Street. During the Blitz, my Mum, sister and I stayed with an aunt in Shropshire, but we came home after the climax of the Blitz in May 1941, believing everything would be all right and we could get on with our lives. How wrong we were.

On 27/28 July 1941 – my parents' 16th wedding anniversary – we were in the community air-raid shelter at the end of Broomfield Street, which also incorporated a social club and was part of the Coop Spice Factory. A parachute mine drifted down and landed right on it, killing my Mum, Elizabeth, aged 35; Dad, William, aged 39; Grandad, George, aged 75;

Auntie Lillian; and a 12-year-old cousin. A total of 45 people were killed in the incident and some apparently choked to death on pepper and spices from the factory. I have absolutely no memory of the bombing at all – only waking up in hospital. My sister Rosie, aged 13, had survived too, but had been badly injured in the back. A family friend told me what had happened, but it didn't sink in with a seven-year-old child. I was in hospital a long time and I couldn't remember my whole life before that blast. It still is a blur and I only have a few childhood memories before the bomb. However, I do get occasional flashbacks and I have the scars caused that day all over me.

My family was buried in a mass war grave in Tower Hamlets Cemetery, and my sister and I received just £46 insurance between us for the deaths of our parents. We went to stay with an aunt in Enfield and her tiny place ended up packed. Rosie and five grown-up girls shared two double beds upstairs, I was in the back room with three other boys and Uncle and Auntie were in the front room. Then another uncle turned up and squeezed in to make it 13. It was rather tight to say the least.

The return of the Cockney children contributed to the big squeeze in the post-Blitz East End. By the end of 1941, 8,000 former evacuees were pouring back into the capital each month and it was a nearly impossible task to educate them, with too few teachers, books and suitable buildings which had escaped damage. Absenteeism and illiteracy rose as children stayed at home to help with chores, while the post-Blitz environment provided endless

Bill Peet, aged 10.

Bill's father, William Peet, with daughter Elizabeth just before she died of tuberculosis, aged 15.

Bill's mother, Elizabeth Peet, at her daughter's bedside.

Elizabeth Peet holding twin sons Bill (left) and Frederick, who died of pneumonia in 1937. Their grandfather, George, can just be seen in the doorway of the family home in Broomfield Street. Both Elizabeth and George died when Broomfield Street was bombed in July 1941.

People were so conditioned to queue during the Blitz that it became ridiculous. Indeed, queues for London buses, now multi-coloured and supplied from all over the country, could typically stretch 100 yards. If you saw more than a couple of people standing outside a shop, you automatically assumed there was something worth having and you would join them. Us kids liked to deliberately start a mock queue outside a sweet shop and within minutes lots of people would join it without thinking what they were waiting for. It would grow to a point where we would slink away leaving the rest of them to it. We would have a good laugh as some of our more gullible schoolmates slowly realised they were waiting for nothing.

The children had an exciting new world to explore too. Bethnal Green youngster June Lewzey (née Guiver) recalls:

My sister and I had a great time on the exposed bombsite which was left outside our home in Old Nichol Street, Bethnal Green. Our flats faced on to Boundary Street and opposite was a huge space where a large old building had been. It gave a new view through to Shoreditch High Road. Beyond the High Road was another massive gap where buildings had once been, so we were left with a new open park in front of us. You could see for miles and we roamed around the new area and explored the deep chasms that went underground into cellars.

Many sites became covered with flowers and shrubs and it was like being in the country in some areas.[2] We called one site 'Paradise' because it was completely covered with pretty Willow Herb flowers. That became our garden and old bricks were laid out in squares to make the 'rooms' of a house. Next, we would collect the glass fragments and use that for money or diamonds during our games. We would often hear neighbours shout out 'You will kill yourself' as they saw us clambering about, but we always returned, even after being chased off by policemen. Often, low pieces of wall would be left standing on the bombsites and we would tap-dance on the top if we felt brave enough. Then there were the inevitable stone fights with other kids when the sites literally became a battle site. I'm amazed now to think my parents let me explore these places but there wasn't a great deal left for youngsters to do.

Others roamed with a more practical purpose. Six-year-old John Parsons recalls:

Mum and Dad would send me out to return to our old bombed-out house in Wellington Road, Forest Gate. They wanted me to scrape away all the

temptations for East End youngsters to enjoy themselves – and get up to mischief. Queuing had become a national pastime and young Charlie Smith took full advantage in Canning Town. He recalls:

---

[2] Flowers, birds and wildlife – some not seen for decades – returned; most common of all was Buddleia and Rosebay Willow Herb.

Young Londoners collect wood from damaged houses and shops, 5 December 1940.

(below left) John Parsons, held by his mother Evelyn, with sister Margaret at Wellington Road, Forest Gate.

(below right) Young John Parsons with sister Margaret and their parents, Evelyn and Bob.

rubble and try and find the old coal shed. I did find it one day and remember being as proud as punch as I carried my full bucket back to our new place in Norwich Road. It was ironic too that I had to salvage for coal, since I had only just returned from County Durham where I was evacuated. There was loads of the stuff up there.

Children continued to hoard the relics of war, as they had done since the first day of the Blitz. They could spot the difference between anti-aircraft metal and bomb splinters and identify shell nose caps from tail fins. There was nothing quite like the thrill of grabbing a tea towel and racing to a bombsite to pick up the red-hot spoils, or searching for the two-tone blue silk parachute cord from airborne land mines.

Children were supposed to hand in their metal oddments as salvage and deposit their finds in tins or zinc baths positioned outside wardens' offices on street corners. Instead, they were kept as treasured possessions and avidly swapped, as Edward Tilbury, living in Appleby Street, Shoreditch, recalls:

I once returned to the house from our Anderson to find a complete nose cone from an anti-aircraft shell had gone through the roof and landed on my sister Florence's pillow. Luckily, she was in the shelter at the time with me, but what a find that was and everyone wanted to see it. We scoured the sites for

this sort of stuff. Once I went with a mate called Charlie Pilbeam, who was more daring than me, to explore the top of a bombed-out building in Appleby Street. Four of us were up there and we were all egging each other on. We stood looking out of a hole, which was once the window, at the devastation below and suddenly Charlie just went for it. Charlie, who was a little lad, launched himself in the direction of a shed below. He landed on target, flattening the shed in the process in a cloud of dust. Then he howled in pain because a large nail was sticking out of his bottom.

Eight-year-old John Harrald, living in Cantrell Road, Bow, was also a serious Blitz collector:

Aircraft Perspex was the big thing. If you had some of that you could swap it for anything. If we were not collecting, we would be playing soldiers on the sites, or chalking out aircraft on the roads and sitting in them as if we were flying. The boys would throw stones at each other from their 'cockpits' to replicate the firing of guns. Parents could also buy replica military uniforms for their children. That was quite something to have too.

Children would never forget the smell of the blitzed East End streets. The cordite, chemicals, plaster and wet sand mingled into an intoxicating scent as they played. While some merely boasted about the number of fires they had put out the previous night, others ensured they were ready for action. Even very young children took a leaf out of the Dead End Kids' book. They constructed their own fire engines out of soapboxes and old perambulator wheels and their shaky contraptions carried buckets of spilling water through the streets. When incendiaries fell – there could be as many as 72 in an average 'basket' – hunting for one became a sport. There would be competitions to put them out with dustbin lids, which the kids called 'bagging'. They quickly learnt how to grab an incendiary by the fin and hit it on the kerb, which caused the burning part to fall off, leaving the rest as a souvenir.

There could be unpleasant surprises, however. When a bomb fell in a school playground off the Mile End Road, a 12-foot layer of human bones erupted from the earth, belonging to the Great Plague victims of 1665. Similarly, when children might return excitedly from a plane crash site with a pair of flying boots, their faces would pale if they found a severed foot nestling in one of them. There were other dangers too, as Audrey True (née Marshall) recalls:

Dotted around the place were vast, rectangular, brick-built water tanks to help put out fires. They were around 6 feet tall and the size of swimming pools. [Each was designed to hold 10,000 gallons.] There was a big one near us in Brodlove Lane, off Cable Street. They were huge and the kids would run around the edge for fun. Some inevitably fell in and I was aware of at least two children from my school, Broad Street, who fell in and drowned.

In the adult world, women's magazines gave an insight into the strain put on marriages, with husbands serving overseas and lonely wives left at home. Most wives were viewed as loyal and true by nature. *Women's Weekly* therefore published a blunt response to a letter received from a wife, in which she had announced her love for another man. She was curtly reminded that her husband was fighting abroad for her and issued with this reprimand:

Do you think you are worth it? Cut out this affair, give up seeing this man; avoid him as you would the plague and you will soon get over it..

Unwanted pregnancy was the big fear in an age when there was no contraceptive pill and abortion was strictly illegal. Giving up a child for adoption also required the consent of the husband – whether or not he was the father. Freer sexual behaviour saw the venereal disease rate increase between September 1934 and mid-1941 by 70 per cent, and the arrival of American troops the following year sent the figure spiralling upwards. While traditional values were undoubtedly shaken, the majority struggled on faithfully and nervously awaited news of loved ones.

Even marriage itself was not without its delicate pitfalls. Doris Bailey (née Carr), who earlier described her Bethnal Green childhood in the 1920s (see page 36) recalls:

At the age of 23, I married my fiancé, Eric, who was four years older. We were terribly naïve, like a lot of young people. I didn't really have a clue where babies came from and I was obviously a virgin when I married. Like my friends, I was petrified about getting pregnant but then, when I did want children, we didn't know what to do. On our honeymoon, on the Isle of Wight, I asked Eric to buy some condoms but he was shy and kept making excuses. So I went into Boots and a rather snooty assistant said: 'I'm afraid we don't sell things like that. Try Timothy Whites.' I went there and made the purchase, but even then we didn't know how to use them!

The trials and tribulations of domestic life were suddenly and dramatically eclipsed by a radio broadcast during the first week of December 1941. The announcer revealed that an American fleet had been attacked by Japanese warplanes in the Pacific, at a base called Pearl Harbour. That momentous incident on Sunday 7 December saw the USA declare war on Japan the next day. Further, Hitler had made a secret – and thoroughly reckless – promise to the Japanese: Germany would support them in a war against the USA. Hitler was caught out completely by Pearl Harbour and now fulfilled his pledge by declaring war on the USA on Thursday 11 December 1941, ignoring the potential strength of America. This grave miscalculation carbon-copied Wilhelm II's blunder in the First World War. By the beginning of 1942, Germany, who six months earlier had faced just beleaguered Britain, was now allied with Italy and Japan against the might of both the USA and Russia, where Hitler's frost-bitten troops were now retreating in atrocious winter conditions.

Back in London, East Enders settled into a long, dreary, hungry war as 1942 dawned. London was snow-bound in February, and eerily quiet until a major incident occurred just a few streets from where Eddie Siggins's Nana, Mary Ann Bowyer, was staying in Matcham Road, Leytonstone. At 9.30 p.m. on 10 February, a Wellington bomber on a training flight in deteriorating conditions, crashed onto the Harrow Green ARP depot, which was a school in Trinity Street. The plane fell in the playground, one wing hitting the school buildings, the other the caretaker's house. The crew of six, all sergeants under training, were killed, as were five Civil Defence workers.

James White, aged 22, was in charge of the casualty department at the depot, one of three in the area. He recalls:

I was on the top floor of the building that night, in a toilet being used as an office. The tiles on the roof suddenly clattered and I went downstairs to a depot room where men had been rehearsing for a concert. I dashed in and saw three terrified men standing on the fringe of a wall of fire with their backs alight. It was a terrible sight. They had ears, noses and hair missing. They were in a dreadful state and I had no idea then what had happened to them. Once I pulled them out, I had to get urgent treatment for them. I put open gauzes impregnated with 'Vaseline' on their wounds, wrapped them in blankets and helped them to my staff car, so I could drive to Whipps Cross Hospital.

It later transpired a RAF Wellington with a Canadian crew had come down, and the plane had hit the side of the depot and caught alight. I had heard no explosion and no noise. Nothing, just the flapping of the tiles. When I returned from the hospital to see if I could help, I saw some very badly burnt bodies at the scene. In fact, they could only be removed with shovels. One was just an 18-year-old kid and another had only just lost his wife and child a month earlier in a bombing raid.

Ten years later, I met one of the three men I had taken to hospital. He said: 'You're the sod that saved my life and I wished you hadn't.' He meant it too, and he was very angry. He said: 'Look at me. I've had to live with this.' His ears were shrivelled, he had an artificial nose, not much hair and chin grafts. His hands had only minute flesh on them and were very red.

Large crowds lined the streets when four of the Civil Defence workers killed in the incident were taken from the depot to Manor Park Cemetery, where they were buried in the same grave. Hundreds more were present at the cemetery, where a guard of honour of Civil Defence men and women awaited the arrival of the cortège. A private service was held for the fifth civilian at Chingford Mount Cemetery. Today the Cathall housing estate south of Cathall Road has swallowed the Trinity Street site where the tragedy occurred.

When 1942 slipped away and a new year dawned, crisis was enveloping the Third Reich. On the military front, the British Eighth Army, under

James White (centre) pictured with fellow Harrow Green ARP depot workers, his first squad.

James White (left) pictured with colleagues in 1939.

Bernard Law Montgomery, had pushed back the German-Italian armies some 700 miles from El Alamein in North Africa. Anglo-American forces under General Eisenhower had meanwhile landed on the beaches of Morocco and Algeria. Also, the bid to take Stalingrad had failed and 91,000 captured Germans were now hobbling frostbitten and half-clothed to Siberian camps in temperatures of minus 24 degrees Centigrade. On the domestic front, 'total war' had also been unleashed on Germany by the RAF, with a series of air strikes, including the first 1,000-bomber raid in history on Cologne, where over 470 inhabitants perished.

Meanwhile, in an altogether different world, a large empty lorry had pulled up in the village of Kedington in West Suffolk. Curtains twitched and

Huge crowds line the streets as the funeral cortège makes its way from the Harrow Green ARP depot to Manor Park Cemetery. The four Civil Defence workers buried there were: Henry Edwards of High Road, Leytonstone; Joseph Smith of Avenue Road, Leytonstone; Walter Black of Nutfield Road, Leytonstone; and James Gorham of Beachcroft Road, Leytonstone. The fifth man, Albert Stanlon, of Addison Road, Wanstead, was interred at Chingford Mount Cemetery.

out stepped the father of Eddie Siggins, ready to take his family back home to London. The days of playing with his country chums were over for young Eddie. There would be no more punch-ups with the yokels, no more creepy nights listening to Valentine Dyall, *The Man in Black*, on the radio – and certainly no more looking up Miss Hallam's dress in class and sniggering at the sight of her bloomers. It was a sad day. By now, his family – Mum, sister Irene and brothers Leslie and Peter – felt part of the village. There was also a new member of the family – little Betty Anne, who had been born in the country in February 1942.

So the Siggins family returned to the East End and a new home at 3 Downsell Road in Leyton, not far from Matcham Road, where Eddie's Nana, Mary Ann, lived with his Aunt Gladys. Eddie's heart sank as he stood in the kitchen surveying the rubbish dump that the previous tenants had created out of the tiny garden. No more fields and open spaces. Welcome back to drab, grey pavements and crowded terraced houses. Mum soon decided that the family could not stay in Downsell Road. Eddie and brother Leslie were dispatched to hire costermonger barrows and then the family's worldly goods were wheeled down the street to a new abode.

The barrows came to a stop in Crownfield Road, outside the front door of No. 107.

Chapter seven

Nineteen steps

THE SIGGINSES' NEW HOUSE in Crownfield Road was halfway down the street and faced a large bombsite where the homes had been pulverized by a land mine. The cellars had been strangely exposed amid the rubble, and some were now water tanks used by the Auxiliary Fire Service. It was fine at No. 107 which, following the birth of baby Jimmy in October 1943, contained six Siggins children. The family had a three-up, three-down property in a terrace that stretched the entire length of the road. At the rear of their house was an Anderson shelter and their plot backed onto the rear garden of Eddie's Aunt Rose and Uncle Fred Parr. In fact, the boundary line that separated Leyton from West Ham ran between the two gardens. Conversation between Eddie and his cousins – Doreen, Freddie and Ivy Parr – flowed constantly over the fence and laughter floated from one borough to the other.

Crownfield Road was not without action either. Half a mile away was Wanstead Flats, where the 'whoosh, whoosh' of anti-aircraft rockets signalled that it was a good idea to take shelter. On one occasion, Eddie's Dad had been giving one of his famous air-raid commentaries from outside the Anderson as the family huddled inside: 'He's diving, they've lost 'im, he's twisting in the sky… BLOODY 'ELL!' – at which point a lump of shrapnel had torn his jacket as he dived headfirst into the makeshift corrugated home. In another incident, a bomb had landed in Major Road at the top of Crownfield Road, killing a number of people, and once an Army lorry carrying a mounted Bofors gun stopped outside No. 107. When the gun started pounding, the house shook like jelly and Eddie was grateful that the glass in the window frames had long been replaced with roofing felt.

However, the boom of the Bofors gun was nothing compared to the deafening sound of a new anti-aircraft defence installed three miles to the southwest in Bethnal Green's Victoria Park. Here the crew of a Z-rocket battery fired salvos of over 100 rockets at a time, which accelerated to 1,000 m.p.h. in 1.5 seconds before exploding simultaneously in a thunderous roar.

The entrance to the Bethnal Green Underground shelter.

These guns were to play a crucial role in Britain's worst civilian wartime disaster at Bethnal Green Underground Station. The station's half-finished extension of the Central Line had opened as a deep shelter in October 1940 and, at the peak of the Blitz, some 7,000 had used the station and bedded down 78 feet beneath the ground. However, by early 1943, there was just a band of hardy regulars numbering a few hundred.

During the wet, dreary evening of Wednesday 3 March 1943, 13-year-old Alf Morris and his Aunt Lillian approached the Underground's single entrance – and its only exit – as they had done for two years. Mr Morris recalls:

That day the radio went dead, which was a sure sign an attack was coming. My Dad told me and my aunt (my Mum's sister, Lillian Hall), to leave our home in Old Ford Road and go to the Bethnal Green Underground shelter, and he would follow after he had locked up. He was going to bring Mum and the latest addition to the family, my two-week-old sister, Joyce.

As we walked, the air-raid siren sounded soon after 8.00 p.m. and then the searchlight suddenly came on in Bethnal Green Gardens as we approached Victoria Park Square. This searchlight was radar-sensitive and it picked up a plane. Other lights then fixed on it too. We both hurried towards the Tube, expecting bombs to come any moment. Auntie and I were soon at the Tube entrance, which consisted of wooden gates that opened inwards and gave access to an enclosed staircase going down.

We started to go down the long flight of steps before us, which consisted of 19 steps in all. At the bottom was a small landing, which measured 15 feet by 10 feet, and a facing wall, which forced people to then turn right and descend a shorter second flight of six steps before you reached the entrance hall and the booking office. Then you could go through and down to the Tube itself, via a couple of stationary escalators. There were lots of people going down the first staircase that night and Auntie and I were carried along in the mass. Those 19 steps were only about 10 feet wide between the walls and were not even properly made up. In fact, they were rough concrete with square wooden insertions on the edge of the tread, and these bits were worn. There was no central handrail like there is today either – just one on either side of the walls. It was pretty dark down there too, because only one bulb illuminated the way forward. [This was a dim 25-watt bulb in the ceiling and even that shone weakly from beneath a regulation blackout slit.] I recall many people were clutching blankets and bundles of clothes, and visibility was very poor.

I was about five steps from the bottom, almost onto the landing in front, when there was an almighty din up above. We didn't know it at the time, but the new anti-aircraft guns in Victoria Park had opened up about a third of a mile away. The noise was deafening – a tremendous 'whooshing' sound. No one had heard anything like it before and assumed we were being attacked and bombs were falling. People were shouting: 'It's bombs! It's bombs! Get down the shelter! Quick! Quick!' We all shoved and jostled our way forward but it was getting increasingly difficult to move, and I remember Auntie shouting: 'Come on Alfie! Come on Alfie!' Meanwhile, it wasn't just the regulars who were trying to get down the first staircase of 19 steps. A lot of people were getting off buses at the top and were heading down too, because they feared an attack.

Auntie and I were soon stuck near the bottom of the staircase. I was in front of her and both of us had been edged against the wall on the left-hand side going down. People in front of me had tripped and fallen over and were on top of each other, and I was beginning to sway and bend forward on top of them too. I was very scared, roasting hot and shouting for help, because I was completely jammed in from the waist down and the pressure was building behind my back with all the pushing. I tried desperately to stay upright.

Then a lady called Mrs Chumbley, a big 6-foot air-raid warden, saved me. Mrs Chumbley, a Great War nurse, was standing on the landing in front of the scrum along with other wardens, and looking up at us all. The wardens were telling us to move back out, but there was no way we could go backwards. Mrs Chumbley then grabbed my hair, said 'Gotcha' and pulled. She put her arms under my armpits and lifted me out so that I was standing with her on the landing.

Mrs Chumbley then barked in her sergeant-major voice: 'Get down to the Tube and tell nothing of what's happened here, nothing at all.' She

(far left) Inside the Bethnal Green shelter show the sleeping arrangements on the track.

(left) Looking down the first flight of 19 steps at Bethnal Green Underground station. Contributor Alf Morris stands in the position where he found himself stuck in a mass of bodies that tragic day in March 1943.

(right) A flashback to 1943 taken from the same position at the top of the steps looking down. Here workmen are repairing and improving the infamous staircase after the disaster.

(centre) Mrs Chumbley, the warden who pulled Alf out of the crush and **(right)** the young Alf Morris.

(below) Looking up the first flight of 19 steps from the small landing at the bottom; here workmen are securing new handrails after the disaster.

meanwhile tried to calm those in the scrum and get others out, while wardens brought big water containers and started spraying people to keep them alive.

I was crying and did as I was told and went down the second flight of stairs and past the booking office. I didn't say anything to anyone when I got to my bunk. Everyone kept saying: 'What's the matter, Alfie?' but I said nothing.

Fifteen minutes later, my aunt came down. She had had the buttons of her astrakhan coat undone and then been pulled out with so much force that her shoes were left behind as she came free. That's how tight it was. Auntie had been wedged against the wall, which was jagged and made of rough concrete. She was black and blue with bruising but at least we were free. Neither of us said a word. We were both in complete shock and were not aware at that stage that people had died. I would later learn that 173 had lost their lives.

By now, my Mum, baby sister and our lodger, Harry, had left our house in Old Ford Road to join us in the shelter, unaware of what had happened. However, my Mum, sister and Harry were diverted to a shelter beneath a church in Old Ford Road. By the time my Dad had locked up and got to Bethnal Green Underground and saw the bodies being brought out, he thought he had lost all his family down there.

It had taken a matter of seconds for that first staircase of 19 steps to become packed solid with 300 people, and those at the bottom were now pressed against the facing wall or crushed on the small landing in front of it. Adults had fallen helplessly on top of children. There were terrible screams, then groans, and then nothing. Piled up to 10 deep, people simply ran out of breath, and arms that were thrown around little babies to protect them squeezed the life out of them in the crush.

Several steps behind Alf Morris on the staircase was terrified Peter Perryment, aged 12. Minutes earlier, Peter had set off from his Morpeth

The Perryment children - Iris, Peter
(centre) and Alfie (right) - pictured
at Meath Gardens, off Roman Road,
Bethnal Green where Peter was born.

Peter's sister, Iris Perryment, pictured
two weeks before the disaster. She is
wearing the coat she wore that day,
which her mother kept until her own
death in 1983.

Peter's cousin, Barbara Land (seated),
who also died that tragic day.
She is pictured with her younger sister,
Joan.

Peter Perryment (front left) and sister
Iris (far right) pictured with four friends.

Street home and headed for the shelter with his mother, Aunt May, sister
Iris, 17, and cousin Barbara Land, 7. When the gun salvo erupted in Victoria
Park, his mother had told the three youngsters to run on and take shelter in
the Underground.

Now, over halfway down and in the middle of the staircase, the
children were wedged in. Peter managed to curl up into a protective ball
and, glancing up, noticed that his sister and cousin were still standing just in
front of him, to his left. He recalls:

*After a long time, I felt people were being moved behind me. I realise now they
were dead people. Then a policeman took me outside and there were all these
bodies laid out along the pavement. He took me to the shelter under the nearby
railway arch next to Salmon and Ball pub and told me to stay there until the
'All Clear'. So that's what I did and when I walked home, I met my brother,
Alfie, who was 18 and about to join the army. He said: 'Mum is looking for
you, Iris and Barbara'. The next day my family toured the hospitals looking
for Iris and Barbara but had no luck. Then my Dad came home from work at
mid-day and he eventually found Iris among the dead at a makeshift church
mortuary near the London Chest Hospital. He came home and said to Mum:
'She's gone, girl'. My aunt was now desperate to find Barbara herself but Dad
told my brother to do it instead. Alfie was walking along a line of bodies when
he noticed Barbara's little black shoes. Alfie asked an attendant there to turn*

over the body and it was her. Iris and Barbara were buried together.

*I was very close to both of them. My sister was a lovely person and
helped the war effort by making uniforms for soldiers; and the day before she
died, I took cousin Barbara to see a Lancaster bomber on display in Trafalgar
Square.*

*I lost classmates like Jimmy Taylor on that staircase too. Another, Alfie
Hoye, survived by crouching down on his hands and knees, just like me, but
he lost his mother and three sisters down there.*

*Our family was never the same after Iris and Barbara were killed.
Every Sunday without fail, we went to their graves and my parents were
devastated by their loss. My Mum died in 1983 and hanging in her wardrobe
was Iris's biscuit-coloured coat she had been wearing when she died. Mum
had kept it hanging there for 40 years, until her dying day.*

Likewise, the Brind family, who lived in Globe Road, cherished the
wooden Tommy Gun belonging to two-year-old Barry, who died in the
arms of his aunt, Ivy Brind (née Seabrook), that night. Ivy, then 25, suffered
permanent injuries from the crush, including a partially paralysed face, and
the sights and sounds of that night and the death of little nephew Barry
troubled her for the rest of her life.

She had been caring for Barry while her sister-in-law, Rose, went into
labour. Ivy rarely went to the Underground shelter herself but sister May

insisted they go if a raid began, saying she would kill herself if anything happened to Barry. Consequently, Ivy, with Barry in her arms, headed for the Tube on that fateful evening but became separated from May and their mother, Sarah Seabrook, who were walking ahead. Ivy recalled hearing a terrific bang when she reached the shelter entrance and tried to turn back. However, the rush of people coming towards her prevented escape and she was pushed down the steps. Ivy was forced onto her back in the surging crowd, holding the baby in her arms but unable to protect him from the pressing weight of people falling on top of them.

She was trapped for three hours, clutching the terrified boy, who said 'Aunt Fivy', the name he always called her, and then fell silent. Ivy thought that fear had frightened him into silence but, when she was pulled out, Barry was dead in her arms and taken from her. Ivy was laid down on the wet pavement, still unaware of what had happened to sister May and their mother, Sarah.

May had been pulled out alive from the staircase. She had been trapped close enough to her mother to hear her call out: 'They're walking on me, they're killing me'. Although May was now back home, there was no sign of her mother or Barry. The next morning Ivy found the little boy in a mortuary, his body unmarked 'as if I'd just bathed him'. After walking up and down the rows of bodies, Ivy couldn't find her mother and was about to leave when an attendant advised her to look again. This time she recognised her: her mother's black hair had turned white.

Ivy, who died in 1994, tormented herself that she could have done more but also thought of Bethnal Green boxer Dick Corbett, a British and Commonwealth bantamweight champion, who also died in the disaster. As Ivy reflected in later life:

He was killed down there and even he couldn't save himself. That Tube, my mother, the baby… even now if I sat around this flat thinking about it, I'd be in the mad house.

Ivy's daughter, Sandra Scotting, adds:

It took 50 years for Mum to say anything about it. Even then she wouldn't open up and would say something like 'We all loved our Barry' in such a way that it was clear she didn't wish to discuss it any further. Mum did not sleep very well and every night of her life when she lay down in bed, she said she could hear the screams and cries.

She once took my son to his playgroup and insisted that she stay there with him. She explained that it was the anniversary of the death of her nephew and she didn't want to lose her grandson as well. I just didn't realise

Ivy Brind.   Barry Seabrook with his Tommy Gun.

the horror she had gone through. My Mum kept Barry's Tommy Gun safe in a cloth bag. After she died, I took possession of it and gave it to Barry's sister, Joan. He loved that gun. The picture of him holding it must have been taken just before that terrible day at the Tube station.

Rescue teams, who arrived around 9.00 p.m., would also be emotionally scarred for life and find it difficult to discuss that night in subsequent years. Six light-rescue and two heavy-rescue squads worked in relays at the scene, but they could not make real progress until the 'All Clear' sounded at 9.43 p.m.

Among the rescuers was James Hunt, a 15-year-old messenger boy who had already lost three brothers, who were serving in the forces, the previous year. Keen to join his older friends as a messenger, James had lied about his age and was attached to the ARP post in Digby Street. He remembers:

We used to cycle around delivering messages and being only a tiny lad of 5 foot, I had to stand on a box to get on my bike. On 3 March 1943, I remember talking and laughing with friends at the entrance to the Bethnal Green Tube before I cycled the five-minute ride back to the Digby Street post with my friend, Tubby Aimes. When we got there, we heard and saw the rockets going up from the guns in Victoria Park. I too had never heard anything like it and almost fell off my bike in shock. I was used to hearing the large boom that came from the big mobile gun attached to the railway truck on top of the arches by the Salmon and Ball pub, but this noise was something else. It sounded deafening, like the shells fired from a battleship. A message then came through

Young rescuer James Hunt.

about an accident at the Tube station and Tubby and I were sent to help out. I ended up going down the staircase many times, where I was handed eight or nine little ones to take back out. These babies and small children were dead and mauve in colour and I laid them on the pavement outside before they were loaded onto lorries. There was no time to think about it and I just blocked the whole thing out of my mind. I never spoke about it for many, many years.

What struck me was how the whole community rallied around afterwards to support families. Bethnal Greeners were close before the war because everyone knew everyone else and everyone worked very hard to make ends meet. That same togetherness was then transferred below ground when the Bethnal Green Tube became a shelter. No one could split those people up and, if they were close before, they became even closer after the disaster.

I still use that staircase at the Tube station and always think about that night as I go down the steps. Even now, I can clearly see the little children I picked up all those years ago.

There were soon frantic calls for more vehicles to transport casualties to hospital, and lorries, cars and handcarts, even a bus, were requisitioned for the purpose. Thirty-one ambulances also whisked away the injured, but the last casualty was not removed from the stairway until 11.40 p.m. Survivors, suffering from bruising, shock and minor cuts, were mostly found at the very bottom of the stairway, where they had been kept alive by tiny pockets of air. Sixty-two were injured and detained in hospital.

Dr Joan Martin MBE was working at the Queen Elizabeth Hospital for Children in Hackney Road as a junior casualty officer that night. She recalls:

It was my first job, I was inexperienced and I had certainly not been in a position of responsibility before.

The hospital had an arrangement with the local ARP that it could be used for casualties if there was a local incident and a phone call came at about 8.45 p.m. We were told to prepare for 30 patients from the Bethnal Green Tube shelter. We had to take the cots down, stack them and then put up the adult beds. My immediate reaction was that it was an exercise to see how quickly we could prepare for casualties in an emergency situation.

I had two male students from the London Hospital working with me and they were very helpful, particularly in helping move the furniture. We had hardly completed the task when one dead person after another arrived on stretchers. The faces of the casualties were mauve in colour and wet from the water thrown to revive them.

It was sometime before a small boy with a broken arm gave us some idea what had happened on the station staircase. I remember the ambulance men were extremely upset as their own families were in the shelter and they demanded the stretchers and blankets back immediately.

We had about 30 bodies there and a Senior Casualty Officer had hysterics. She was angry with us because we were taking bodies off stretchers and rolling them into rooms, which she felt was sacrilegious. We were just being practical but it was all too much for her and she went off duty. I suggested we open one of the consulting rooms and put the bodies in there because we didn't know how many more were coming and had to maximise space.

There was no counselling and I was back at work the next day. That morning we were told not to discuss what had happened and to this day I can't think how we were silenced. We just obeyed and I didn't even tell my mother the details when I phoned to reassure her. I just said I was perfectly alright but something dreadful had happened. It played on my mind afterwards that we had been sworn to secrecy and that was hurtful. In those days you didn't question officialdom whereas today people would have simply gone to the newspapers. I didn't say anything for 50 years and when I did it was a great release.

I have tried to suppress the ghastly memories of that night. At times I still have nightmares of people being trampled, but not like I used to. I still tend to get in a panic if I am involved in a crowd at a Tube station.

The entire East End was in shock after the incident, which claimed 173 lives, one-third of Bethnal Green's total wartime dead, in mere seconds. Alf Morris again recalls:

Everyone knew someone who had died and there were 10 funerals a day. It was dreadful and the East End had never seen anything like it. I think Auntie and I were the last ones pulled clear from the bottom, and I would have been killed if I had been going down the stairs a few moments later. I was plucked

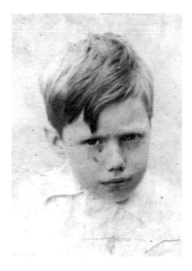

Young Reg Baker who luckily escaped the disaster, thanks to his father.

were unmarked but others were distressingly difficult to identify because of severe bruising, crushing, or the imprints of boots or heels, which had distorted their faces. Items of individual clothing or jewellery were the only means of identifying these casualties and one daughter only managed to recognise her father by his belt and a button that was missing on his jacket.

Fate, however, intervened to save others. Young Reg Baker, aged 13 at the time, recalls:

When the sirens went, I was at home in Gretton House, Globe Road. Then, as Dad and I walked to the Bethnal Green Tube, a huge din started, which we also believed were bombs but later transpired to be the new guns in Victoria Park. Everyone was running to the Tube by now and the noise was so scary we both lay down in Roman Road at one point. When we got to the Tube entrance, I was just about to follow a large man down and Dad suddenly did something which saved my life. He gripped my shoulder and said we should go to the arches behind the Salmon and Ball pub instead. In that split second our lives were saved. My sister Dolly arrived later at the Tube and she went down. Luckily, she was pulled out from on top of the bodies but she recalled how soft it felt walking down the stairs. She didn't know at the time that she was treading on dead people.

Some young children did not discover their tragic loss until they were adults. Margaret McKay was 20 when she learned that she was the youngest survivor – and that her mother had perished in the disaster. She recalls:

My father, George, never mentioned anything to me about the Bethnal Green Tube accident and I didn't know [that] my real Mum, Ellen 'Nell' Ridgway (nee Edwards), died down there and I was carried out. I was just a baby of six months and afterwards my grandparents looked after me until my Dad came back out of the army. He then remarried and I grew up believing his wife was my real Mum. One day, when I was 10, I was playing in the street and one of the boys, Jimmy Thomas, came up and said 'You have a step-mother.' I was upset and went home for an explanation and my 'Mum' said 'Don't be stupid' and that was that. I accepted her answer but it niggled in my mind. Then, when I was 20, I was going to leave England for Australia to take advantage of a scheme to encourage young people to work there. My friend and her family were going and I also wanted a fresh start. However, my Dad had to sign the papers for me to go and then said there was a trust fund for me but I couldn't have it until I was 21. I naturally wondered: why would I have a trust fund?

The truth came out about my real mother as we travelled to Bethnal Green Town Hall on the Tube to deal with the paperwork which would give me access to the £160 fund before I went abroad. I was devastated and

out just as more and more were falling at the front, and the mound of stuck people on top of them was getting bigger and bigger. By the way, we only got a small sum in compensation from the authorities and the next day we were approached by newspapermen offering all sorts of money for our stories.

One story will always live with me and concerns a mum and her daughter who lived in Morpeth Street. The girl, Vera Trotter, was seven and she went down the Tube that day with her mum, Lilian. A few days earlier, Vera had told my Dad she had a nail in her shoe and he had prised it out for her. When my Dad went to St James the Less makeshift mortuary opposite the Chest Hospital after the disaster, he tried to find the two of them, but the bodies were so marked it was impossible to identify anyone. Then he spotted Vera's shoe – and that was the only way he knew it was her. Vera's mum, who was 36, was dead too and Dad was very upset. The disaster at the Tube was caused, in my view, by a tragic chain reaction which began when the searchlight suddenly came on. That in turn led to the guns in Victoria Park firing for the first time and no one had heard that incredible noise before. That in turn led to fear of falling bombs and panic on the staircase. Once that huge crowd was pushing down the steps, disaster was inevitable and a woman with a child was the first to trip near the bottom. [A Daily Telegraph journalist reported the woman's husband had forced his way through the scrum to reach his wife. The woman survived but the child was dead.] I believe all the victims would still be alive today if that searchlight had not come on and started the chain reaction.

The list of 173 victims revealed 62 children and 84 women had died, and that whole families had been devastated. These included: six Meads from Peary Place, four Ellams from Wessex Street, four Roches from Canrobert Street and the four Hoyes from Roman Road. Many of the retrieved bodies

(from left to right):

Ellen Ridgway.

George Ridgway.

Ellen Ridgway with baby daughter, Margaret.

disappointed Dad hadn't told me earlier. I adored my Dad but why hadn't he told me? At the Town Hall, a little old man said: 'You're the last of the children to collect the money.' Apparently, six babies had grown up without a mum or a dad and been entitled to the fund and I was the last to collect it. He also said: 'I'm so glad for this to all be over'.

Further details came out as the years passed. I discovered I had been pulled out of the crush on the stairs that day by an off-duty policeman, Thomas Penn. He had been scrambling over the crowd trying to help people and said to my Mum: 'If you are going to die lady, pass me your baby'. Then she handed me over. According to Thomas's son, his dad never spoke about the disaster but did say: 'I wonder what happened to that baby?'

I have been told my Mum was a very nice woman who would have loved my children. I get very emotional to think about that because I've been robbed of growing up with her. I have never been able to trace members of her family and have also been unable to find her grave in Manor Park where she was buried.

It was very strange when I obtained a picture of her. I just couldn't stop looking at it. A picture of Mum holding me has pride of place on my wall and a picture of Mum at school stays in my handbag. She is with me wherever I go.

Two days after the disaster, on 5 March, the Ministry of Home Security issued a statement to the press, divulging limited details of what had happened. It revealed that 'a serious accident' had taken place near the entrance of a London Underground station on Wednesday evening and incorrectly stated that 178 people had been suffocated to death. Furthermore, according to a large number of 'eye-witnesses and members of the police and Civil Defence Services', there had been 'no sign of panic' and 'no bombs fell anywhere in this district during the evening'. The tragedy, the statement added, had been caused by a 'middle-aged woman burdened with a bundle and baby', who tripped near the bottom of the stairs. Her fall tripped an

elderly man behind her and, within a few seconds, a large number of people were lying on the lower steps.

The London press duly reported the disaster as an accident and there was no mention of panic. However, the *Daily Mail* cited the 'gun flashes from Wednesday's terrific barrage' as the immediate cause.

On 10 March, Home Secretary Herbert Morrison informed the House of Commons that he had appointed Laurence Dunne, one of the Metropolitan Magistrates, to conduct an inquiry into the disaster. However, he also told the House:

As many aspects of the incident concern Civil Defence arrangements related to acts of war, on which it is undesirable that information should be given to the enemy, the Government have decided in the national interest that the inquiry should be held in private; but the conclusion will, subject to security considerations, be published.

In a parallel development, an inquest was held at which Coroner W. R. H. Heddy heard evidence from 18 witnesses before addressing the jury with his closing statements. He made a point of noting that there was 'nothing to suggest any stampede or panic' and, on 20 March, the jury returned a verdict that all victims had died from asphyxia due to suffocation and the cause was accidental. This was the only inquiry held in public.

Meanwhile, the private Laurence Dunne inquiry began on 11 March and concluded on 17 March. Dunne's resulting report highlighted 'the state of mind of the people' as an important factor in the unfolding tragedy. More specifically, he noted the public's 'strong apprehension' of reprisal bombing raids. When the newspapers of 16 January 1943 reported a British attack on Berlin, a 'fair number of people' had headed for the Bethnal Green Underground shelter on following nights, 'particularly during the light German reprisal raid on 17th

January'. Then, on Tuesday 2 March, the day after the RAF struck Berlin again, over 850 people used the Bethnal Green Tube compared with 587 on 1 March and just 500 on 28 February. The general expectation, however, was that a German reprisal raid was 'far more likely to be launched on the 3rd', said Dunne.

When the sirens sounded at 8.17p.m. on Wednesday 3 March, many believed another night of severe Luftwaffe punishment was about to begin. Dunne stated that 500–600 people were already inside the shelter and the wailing of the siren saw more heading for the Underground. In addition, at least two cinemas and three omnibuses emptied their customers nearby too.

During the 10 minutes following the siren warning, some 1,500 entered the shelter. Then, at 8.27p.m., the new Victoria Park guns sounded a third of a mile away which, said Dunne, caused 'a great deal of alarm' and a surge towards the Underground entrance.

Dunne's report revealed that no enemy bombs dropped within 'a radius of some miles of the shelter'. Nonetheless, there was a 'severe and sudden pressure upon the backs of those already descending the nearly dark stairway' and a woman, either holding or leading a child, fell on the third step from the bottom. His report noted:

This was observed both by a witness on the landing below and by at least two people in the crowd on the stairs behind her.

Dunne reported that a man then fell on her left and:

So great was the pressure from behind that those impeded by the bodies were forced down on top of them with their heads outwards and towards the landing. In a matter of seconds there was built an immovable and interlaced mass of bodies five or six or more deep, against which the people above and on the stairs continued to be forced by the pressure from behind.

Dunne wrote that the stairway was 'converted from a corridor to a charnel house in from ten to fifteen seconds' and observed:

I have not been able to establish definitely whether the woman's fall was fortuitous or caused by pressure. I think there is little doubt that it was the latter. One woman, and one woman only, escaped from the mass trapped on the stairs and she seems to have been forced along the extreme left. After a few seconds, the jam was completely across the full width of the stairway.

Meanwhile, another 150–200 people were 'violently anxious' to get in, believing they were being prevented from entering.

Dunne's description of the death scene conjured more disturbing images:

When those capable of moving and most easily moved had been got out from above, it was found that the pressure, and possibly the pitch of the stairs, had produced a strange and terrible result. The bodies of the few still alive and the dead were pressed together into a tangled mass of such complexity that the work of extrication was interminably slow and laborious.

Only 51 of the victims were registered for bunks and were regular users of the shelter. The majority of the dead were casual users or newcomers, while the large number of children involved was put down to the influx of evacuees following the end of the Blitz. Their presence was also believed to have slowed the progress of people down the 19 steps. Up above, Dunne noted that it was 'unfortunate' that no police constable arrived at the shelter entrance until some 10 minutes after the alert.

He then dealt with 'two specific allegations which have received some publicity'. Firstly, Dunne dismissed as an 'absurdity' suggestions that a panic had been induced by Fascists or criminals. Secondly, malicious claims that Jews had allowed fear to turn to panic were also 'demonstrably false' since their numbers in the shelter were 'so small as to constitute a hardly calculable percentage'.

Next, the magistrate turned his attention to the contributory causes of the accident which he separated into two main groups – 'psychological' and 'physical'. In the first category, Dunne said apprehension of reprisal raids was fostered by newspaper reports of the effects of new types of bombs, and a realization that new bombing tactics would allow less time to get under cover. Among the physical causes, he highlighted the absence of a crush barrier as the main structural defect because it allowed 'a straight line of pressure from the crowd seeking entrance to the people on the stairs'. Dunne also highlighted the single entrance as 'an exceptional feature' and noted that the Underground station had not been specially designed as a shelter. He wrote:

For myself, I confess surprise that the accident has not happened before and no one, I think, can exclude the possibility of it happening elsewhere.

Dunne's report then revealed that the town clerk of Bethnal Green Borough Council had written to the HQ of the London Civil Defence Region two years earlier, asking for permission to replace the wooden hoarding at the Tube entrance with a more permanent brick wall. The Borough Council had anticipated new raids and feared the wooden structure would collapse in the event of larger crowds seeking shelter. The request to spend an estimated £89 to complete the work was turned down and, instead, the Borough Council was advised to strengthen the entrance with salvaged timber.

Dunne said this matter had no relevance to the accident itself. However, he pointed out the Bethnal Green authorities had clearly anticipated the renewal

SITE OF THE WORST CIVILIAN DISASTER
OF THE SECOND WORLD WAR
IN MEMORY OF
173 MEN, WOMEN AND CHILDREN
WHO LOST THEIR LIVES ON THE
EVENING OF WEDNESDAY 3RD MARCH 1943
DESCENDING THESE STEPS TO BETHNAL GREEN
UNDERGROUND AIR RAID SHELTER

NOT FORGOTTEN

Today, the memorial plaque is screwed above the staircase which claimed 173 lives at Bethnal Green Underground station.

of enemy activity and was 'entrusted by statute and moral duty' with the task of protecting local people with the resources available to them.

He also criticised the London Civil Defence Region for treating the correspondence with Bethnal Green as nothing more than 'a routine application for the expenditure of public funds'. Dunne ended up accusing both parties of failing to ensure a raised issue of great importance was properly understood and considered by their technical officers. Despite these failings, Dunne stressed 'it by no means' followed that any steps that might have been taken would have been adequate to prevent the accident.

After the disaster, the entrance to the shelter was altered to include a covered way leading to the stairs. Dunne also reported that the stairs had been divided into three lanes by two sets of handrails and 'direct pressure into the covered way' was 'controlled and prevented by a crush barrier'.

The magistrate concluded that the 'main and approximate cause' of the accident was 'a sudden rush for the entrance by probably 350-400 people'. His report ended with two 'short propositions':

(a) This disaster was caused by a number of people losing their self-control at a particularly unfortunate place and time.
(b) No forethought in the matter of structural design or practicable police supervision can be any real safeguard against the effects of a loss of self-control by a crowd.

On 3 April 1943, the Home Secretary presented the War Cabinet with a memorandum which summarised Dunne's findings. It stated that the main cause of the disaster was a sudden surge by people who had been 'considerably

alarmed by the discharge of a salvo of anti-aircraft rockets'. The War Cabinet, including the Prime Minister, believed any such suggestion of a psychological cause posed a national security risk since its revelation 'might encourage the enemy to make further nuisance raids'.

It was therefore decided to keep the crucial role of the anti-aircraft salvo in Victoria Park secret. The Home Secretary instead told the House of Commons on 8 April that it was impossible to present a fair summary of Dunne's report, or even his conclusion, 'without conveying information valuable to the enemy'. He did, however, reassure the House that modifications had been made to all shelters as a result of the magistrate's inquiry.

In the absence of a public airing of Dunne's conclusions, Bethnal Green Borough Council felt it would be unjustly blamed for the disaster. Moreover, the Official Secrets Act prevented councillors from making any public clarification themselves in a bid to temper local criticism. The Home Office simply reminded the Borough Council that the Home Secretary's Common's address on 8 April had also included the comment that 'acts of culpable negligence are not properly to be included amongst causes'.

Nonetheless, in July 1944, Bethnal Green widow Mrs Annie Baker, after losing her husband George and 14-year-old daughter Minnie in the disaster, sued the Borough Council for negligence. Justice Singleton accepted the evidence of witnesses that there had been previous complaints about the poor condition of the shelter's steps and lighting.

He awarded Mrs Baker £1,200 for her husband and £250 for her daughter, plus costs. The Ministry of Pensions awarded widows and children a pension of 50 shillings a week after the ruling.

By the time Dunne's full report was finally made public, six months later, events had overtaken the magistrate's essential finding that the anti-aircraft salvo had induced a 'loss of self-control by a crowd'; by then the Annie Baker court ruling had established that the Bethnal Green authorities were negligent. This had far-reaching consequences and, over the next six years, nearly £70,000 was paid in compensation.

Today, the memories of 3 March 1943 continue to have a profound impact on the Bethnal Green community. The annual memorial service at the Church of St John on Bethnal Green is always well attended by survivors, who confide that the passage of time has failed to dull memories or make acceptance any easier. Opposite the church, the railings near the 19 steps are often adorned with floral tributes, touching messages and poignant photographs. However, today's commuters, anxious to enter London's cavernous underbelly, hurry past with barely a glance. Then they are gone, descending the same stairway, which, apart from the addition of handrails at the centre and a small black memorial plaque above, has changed little since that tragic day in 1943.

The V2 long-range guided missile lifting off from its launch-pad.

Hitler's 'revenge weapon' – the V1 flying bomb.

The East End hardly had time to absorb the magnitude of the Underground horror when another location on the Central Line became a scene of carnage just nine days later. A top-secret Plessey factory – employing 2,000 at its peak – had been established at Ilford, inside the tunnels of the Central Line loop from Leytonstone to Gants Hill. Plessey also had a factory complex on the surface and it was attacked on 12 March. Thirty-one people were killed in the streets to the south of the plant as bombs from low-flying aircraft landed horizontally and skidded along the roads and pavements, before hitting houses at ground level.

Fifteen days after the Plessey bombing, microphones picked up a conversation between two German generals in their bugged cell at Latimer Park, in Buckinghamshire. They were heard to mention the 'rocket business' and 'huge things' that 'would go 15 kilometres into the stratosphere'. For months, various reports from underground units in occupied Europe and agents in Germany had claimed that a long-range rocket – together with a pilotless, jet-propelled flying bomb – were being developed among the thickly growing trees of Peenemunde, a small German fishing village 110 miles north of Berlin, where the River Peene flows into the Baltic Sea. RAF photo-reconnaissance planes had also returned with images of odd components lying on road vehicles, which suggested that jet-propelled aircraft were being developed as well as rockets.

In fact, German scientists had been perfecting these two new weapons since 1930. The new, pilotless flying bomb was to be known as the V1, the 'V' being derived from the German word *vergeltungswaffe*, or 'revenge

weapon'. The first efforts frequently crashed, but steady progress was made after a woman test pilot volunteered to lie on the V1 fuselage floor during a flight to monitor its progress and spot design faults. While the Luftwaffe tested the V1's potential, the German Army pursued the second weapon project at Peenemunde – a long-range guided rocket known initially as the A4 and later as the V2. Walter Dornberger was director of the rocket programme and worked on the project with his young whizz-kid assistant, Werner von Braun. In July 1943, Adolf Hitler was ushered into a small cinema where Dornberger and von Braun presented footage of the A4 rocket blasting off at a speed faster than sound. When the two scientists left, Hitler told Albert Speer, his Armaments Minister:

The A4 is a measure that can decide the war. And what encouragement to the home front when we attack the English with it! This is the decisive weapon of the war and, what is more, it can be produced with relatively small resources. Speer, you must push the A4 as hard as you can.

Mass-production of the new rocket began. The weapon was 46 feet long and weighed nearly 13 tons, and Hitler wanted 900 produced monthly. This proved impossible due to technical problems, and then RAF Bomber Command attacked Peenemunde. Forty-one aircraft were lost during the attack and casualties at the base included 600 Polish labourers and Russian prisoners of war, many of whom had been barred from taking shelter. Hitler's rocket director, Dornberger, survived but 130 scientists were killed and mass production of the rocket was further hit. Test firing was then moved to Poland and mass production to underground caves near Nordhausen, southwest of Berlin. In a lonely valley in the Harz Mountains, a complex system of caves had been established before the war for the storage of vital military chemicals. Now the tunnels were enlarged by a vast slave army of 15,000, which toiled 24 hours a day in perpetual darkness without proper sanitation or drinking water. When rocket production started in January 1944, a workforce of 32,000 was housed within the Dora concentration camp nearby. Tens of thousands would die, either building the plant or working within its noisy, dusty and freezing interior.

Hitler also demanded progress with the pilotless V1 flying bomb and preparations were made in France to build concrete bunkers and launch ramps. Over 50 V1 sites were then built facing the Straits of Dover. Meanwhile, back in Britain, RAF officers were poring over thousands of aerial photographs. These covered the whole of northwestern France within 150 miles of London and, by 22 November 1943, over 90 suspicious sites had been identified. Some were occupied by peculiar flat-roofed, windowless buildings, some 260 feet long and just 10 feet wide, dubbed 'ski sites' because of their shape. It was obvious that these sites had something to do with Hitler's secret weapons, but what was their purpose? Then Flight Officer Constance Babington-Smith, working at the RAF's photographic interpretation unit at Medmenham, Buckinghamshire, recalled a series of photos taken the previous June. She retrieved them from the unit's library and carefully looked at them again using, ironically, a German-made lens. The flight officer suddenly spotted a tiny midget aircraft, like a minute crucifix, on what appeared to be a ramp. It was banked up with earth, with supporting rails that inclined upwards, ready for a catapult launching. She was looking at a V1 flying bomb

Rough calculations predicted that the sites so far identified could be capable of launching 2,000 bombs each day. Heavy RAF bombing began in earnest but, by the end of December 1943, only seven sites had been destroyed and more basic launch areas were coming on-stream that involved minimal construction. Consisting of just a ramp, concrete roads and a few buildings, a site could take just six days to construct and simply be abandoned if discovered.

While the London public remained blissfully unaware of the potential nightmare posed by V1 flying bombs and V2 rockets, other stresses and strains were presenting themselves. Food shortages were biting hard, while soap rationing threw routines out of the window in the East End, where the Monday wash was a weekly ritual. There was growing working-class resentment and a familiar figure from the past became a target for their anger – Oswald Mosley. When Mosley was released from prison in November 1943, it was immediately alleged that his freedom had been bought through his connections with the rich and famous. In fact, five doctors had advised the Home Secretary, Herbert Morrison, that Mosley's release was essential to give him any reasonable prospect of recovery from thrombo-phlebitis. Mosley was allowed to return to his Oxfordshire residence, but was banned from travelling further than 1 mile from his home. There was uproar. In Hackney, Morrison's constituency, 8,000 people signed a petition of protest and a further 100 protesters – chanting 'Mosley In, Morrison Out!' – tried to force their way into Parliament. The fury refused to subside, even when Morrison tried to explain himself in the House of Commons. He told the House he was unwilling to let anyone die in detention unnecessarily:

This policy is not based on the inexpediency of making martyrs of persons who do not deserve the honour, but on the general principle that those extraordinary powers of detention without trial must not be used except in so far as they are essential for national security.

On top of this, in the New Year, the bombing of London was suddenly resumed. On the night of 21/22 January 1944, a period of short, sharp, concentrated raids began, which Hitler called Operation Steinbock and which Londoners dubbed the 'Baby Blitz'. Most of the damage was south of the Thames and, over the next four months, London was the target on some 15 occasions. On the night of 29/30 January, Poplar blazed once more and the railway station at Leytonstone was hit, killing 11 people. Then, during February, seven major raids on London left nearly 1,000 dead. On the night of 18/19 April, in what was to be the last major raid on London, 39 were killed as Leyton, Walthamstow and Ilford were hit by bigger, more destructive bombs. The Luftwaffe then turned its attention to other ports and shipping, in an effort to delay a possible Allied invasion of occupied Europe.

Meanwhile, the East End was changing. There were new sights, new sounds and new accents. American troops, who had begun to arrive in Britain in January 1942, were now flooding in and, by that summer, had become a common sight in the capital. The visitors had been advised about respecting British sensibilities and customs, and warned that the tables would be bare and the cellars empty. They were told to react with courtesy and understanding – and to show the utmost respect to the Royal Family. The accents of the US east coast, west coast, mid-west and south were soon heard across London, and the American Red Cross Club on the corner of Shaftesbury Avenue and Denman Street ('Rainbow Corner') became a famous entertainment venue. The Americans quickly declared British beer disgusting, the films old-fashioned and the dance halls inferior. There was, however, no shortage of pleasing attention from the opposite sex. Girls found them excitingly different – and relatively wealthy. Yet for every American propositioned, another, more gullible, was fleeced of his cash, while the *New York Times* was soon describing the area around Leicester Square as a 'veritable open market', capable of shocking the most sophisticated of New Yorkers. Prostitutes targeted the streets outside the Red Cross Club, Lyons Corner House and the entrances to Underground stations, while more gathered around Piccadilly Circus, which Americans called 'London's Times Square'.

Some, naturally, resented the new visitors. The old taunt – 'over-paid,

The busy quayside at North Side, King George V Dock, during the Second World War. Despite heavy bombing, the Port of London remained open for 'business as usual'.

over-sexed and over here' – was thrown in one direction, while the retort 'under-paid, under-sexed and under Eisenhower' was thrown back. However, most Londoners welcomed the Americans, and their generosity to the city's children became legendary. In Eddie Siggins's old haunt of Duckett Street in Stepney, US jeeps and trucks arrived to take children to a party at the American Embassy, and all returned home laden with carrier bags containing sweets, toys and pens. It was a gesture repeated across the metropolis. London had aged and gone grey during the Blitz years and the Americans gave the place a long-overdue boost. It was as if the grimy, shambling old capital had been given a massive injection of vitamin pills.

There was, as Doreen Dennis (née Cook) recalls, a new zest for life:

The Americans had a fabulous image which had been secured by the pictures. British films were quite patriotic and the very Englishness of them amused us, whereas the American films were so sophisticated. The West End had the films first, so we would get a 6d [2.5p] ride to Piccadilly from Clapton Park. The place was full of Americans and Canadians and they had great charm and lovely clothes. It really was as though the film stars had come alive.

There was a huge influx of Americans over the Whit Weekend of May 1944 as the build-up to D-Day – the Allied invasion of Nazi-occupied

Europe – intensified. That weekend, troops were moved from Scotland and the North and billeted in West Ham's football ground, resulting in a famous security scare. The troops had studied maps showing where they would be landing in Normandy when the operation began, and had also been issued with French money. However, beer – or rather the lack of it – was their main concern and what there was had soon run out. The soldiers, aware that it was Whit Weekend and the NAAFI depots were closed, took matters into their own hands. Scores of briefed D-Day soldiers slipped out past sentries, crawled beneath barbed wire and soon filled the East End pubs. The soldiers were rounded up and returned to their billet, but a couple of East End publicans were kept in custody until the invasion was underway because the soldiers had told them details of the D-Day operation.

While specific details could be kept secret, it was impossible to disguise the relentless build-up to the invasion operation. As the East London dock complexes became besieged with endless movements of troops, equipment and supplies, the question was no longer what was happening but when it was going to happen.

London was to be one of the principle D-Day springboards and Montgomery, the hero of El Alamein, had already been to the docks in March 1944 to give 16,000 port workers a pep-talk. Meanwhile, guards were posted on the dock gates while large prisoner-of-war cages sprang up on

Wanstead Flats. The roads leading to the dock complexes were now choked for hours on end, both day and night, with convoys of troops, tanks, artillery and stores of all sizes, shapes and descriptions. The lorries rumbled on and on. Some bore the telltale slogans of the mission that lay ahead: 'Look out Hitler, Here we come', or 'Berlin or Bust'. Children were showered with gum as the endless convoys trundled along Commercial Road while, beyond the great highway, bomb sites were being used for D-Day training.

Thousands of troops passed through the capital on their way to the south-coast ports, and many were temporarily housed in makeshift camps erected in the blitzed wilderness of Silvertown and Canning Town. In West Ham, residents presented large quantities of cake, fruit and sandwiches to the columns of soldiers as they snaked through the bomb sites, some daubed with the slogan 'Pay them back for this'. At night, the din of lorries was matched by the drone of aircraft roaring towards northern France, to bomb fortifications and bridges, while the following morning children watched in awe as the huge waves of bombers returned from their sorties.

There was activity of a more mysterious nature in the docks. The entrances of two of the port's wet docks, the East India Import Dock and the South Dock of the Surrey Commercial Docks, were dammed and the water pumped out. A bed of rubble, obtained from blitzed sites, was then spread over the bottoms, on which strange concrete towers were erected by labourers working around the clock. These giant structures were called 'Phoenix caissons' and were part of the top-secret 'Mulberry Harbour' project. This was one of history's greatest feats of unorthodox warfare and involved the construction, in sections, of two vast portable harbours, which the invasion armada would take across the Channel and assemble off the landing beaches of Normandy. The two structures, each the size of Dover Harbour, would swiftly transfer tanks, jeeps, trucks and the bulky paraphernalia of war from the rough seas off Normandy to *terra firma*. Only the hulls of the caissons could be built inside the dammed dry docks, so they were cautiously towed by Thames watermen to the port's wet docks for completion. Two-thirds of Mulberry's eventual 8½ miles of harbour were built in the port.

The D-Day invasion plan also involved the laying of a petrol pipeline along the seabed from Britain to France, enabling a million gallons of petrol a day to be pumped to the war zone. The project was code-named PLUTO (Pipe Line Under The Ocean) and six huge drums, each wound with 70 miles of steel piping, were built and launched at Tilbury for this purpose.

D-Day was close. The clubs, pubs and restaurants of London gradually emptied of troops as the big day dawned and those still in the capital were confined to barracks, awaiting orders. Posters everywhere warned 'Dangerous Talk Costs Lives' while dock workers were banned from going home in case they divulged any secret information. Their letters were also censored.

However, 16-year-old Dorothy Crofts recalls:

The whole thing was hardly a secret. My brother Bill came home saying he had to go away and we saw him off at Waterloo Station. The place was jam-packed with soldiers. Suddenly one lad from a bashful group of boys came over and kissed me. Then all of his mates did the same. It was odd because it was as if they knew they wouldn't be coming home again. They had that look in their eyes – they seemed to know, and I did too. Then, as we left the station, I vividly recall seeing a woman who was absolutely distraught. She had obviously said goodbye to someone she loved very much indeed. That day it felt like something really momentous was about to happen. A day when the world was about to change.

On the other side of London, a headmaster stood solemnly before his pupils in Leyton. 'Let us pray' he said to the children, who duly shuffled to their feet, clasped their hands together and closed their eyes. What Mr Lester next said excited them all, as Eddie Siggins established when he opened one eye and looked around the assembly hall at Goodall Road School. Their Headmaster had asked them to pray for the brave soldiers and sailors who, that day, had begun an invasion of Nazi-occupied Europe by landing in France. It was 6 June 1944.

By the afternoon, the Americans had a toehold on two beaches and the British had penetrated inland for a distance of between 2 and 6 miles. Over 155,000 troops reached France by the end of that first day and the great push to Germany had begun.

When Eddie Siggins returned home from school, massive convoys of fresh troops were snaking along the bottom of Crownfield Road, where women and young girls gave them tea and cigarettes. He recalled:

At the end of our road was the junction with High Road, Leytonstone, and an enormous amount of hardware was pouring out of East Anglia and heading for the docks. All the kids were excited about it and we went down to have a good look at the spectacle. Dispatch riders on motorbikes had taken up positions at the road junctions and seemed to be directing traffic. They had Sten guns slung across their backs and wore long leather khaki overcoats. The incessant stream of lorries and armoured vehicles was non-stop. There were lorries with trailers loaded with equipment of all sorts, sturdy-looking trucks pulling big field guns and howitzers behind them. Tanks on low-loaders and other tracked vehicles also added to the constant stream. Then there were the endless columns of trucks packed with soldiers. It seemed to go on like this for days and the pavements were packed with people watching. You had to be quick crossing the road or be flattened.

(above) General Montgomery arrives at London Docks to address the Port's workers on 3 March 1944.

(above right) A Mulberry Harbour unit at the East India Docks in 1944. Mowlem was the principle contractor.

(left) The unmistakeable figure of Winston Churchill on an inspection tour of Mulberry Harbour construction work in the East India Docks, 1944.

(right) The last 'Phoenix' unit to leave the Port of London is towed out of the King George V Entrance Lock in 1944.

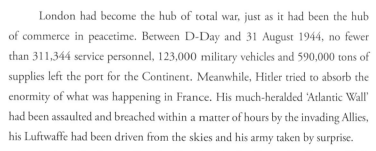

London had become the hub of total war, just as it had been the hub of commerce in peacetime. Between D-Day and 31 August 1944, no fewer than 311,344 service personnel, 123,000 military vehicles and 590,000 tons of supplies left the port for the Continent. Meanwhile, Hitler tried to absorb the enormity of what was happening in France. His much-heralded 'Atlantic Wall' had been assaulted and breached within a matter of hours by the invading Allies, his Luftwaffe had been driven from the skies and his army taken by surprise.

Only a few hours after the first D-Day landings, the German High Command gave orders for an immediate attack on London. It was time to take the covers off the V1 'revenge weapon' developed in Peenemunde. The small plywood and sheet-steel pilotless monoplane contained a ton of high explosive, bolted to its 150-gallon petrol tank, and could cover 130 miles if necessary. While a pre-set compass controlled the V1's course, fuel starvation cut the engine, sending the bomb plummeting earthbound at 200 m.p.h. The age of missile warfare was about to begin.

However, after the Normandy landings, the French coast was in disarray and only 18 of a possible 64 V1 launch sites were operational. Hitler had ordered an attack on London on 10 June but it was another three days before 10 of the new flying bombs were at last hauled onto their ramps. At 3.30 a.m. on 13 June 1944, the battery commanders were ordered to begin their attack, but they did not enjoy the best of starts. Five of the V1s crashed immediately and then one plunged into the Channel.

They had better luck with the remaining four V1s. At 4.08 a.m., two members of the Royal Observer Corps, a builder and a grocer in peacetime, were watching from the top of the Martello tower at Dymchurch on Romney Marsh when the first one streaked across the pre-dawn sky. The Observer Corps, together with the police and ARP, had been given notice of a possible new German weapon in April. Now, it seemed, it was on its way. Reaching for the telephone, the men repeated the words they had been practising for so long: 'Mike Two… Diver! Diver! Diver!' Alarm bells jangled across the

The first V1 flying bomb to hit the East End struck the railway bridge over Grove Road on 13 June 1944. This photograph of the aftermath was taken looking south along Grove Road. The side road to the left is Antill Road and the wrecked building on the corner was an off-licence. The owner was on fire-fighting duty at Shadforth's the chemist, on the other side of Grove Road, that morning. He was killed as he headed back to the off-licence to check that his wife was safe.

country and sentries at a US camp started shooting wildly at the incoming bomb and ended up wounding a comrade.

The first of the four V1s headed for Gravesend, where it fell and exploded on open farmland at Swanscombe at 4.13 a.m. Seven minutes later, the second landed in a field at Cuckfield in Sussex. The third headed towards the East End. Like a flaming meteor, it soared over the Kent hayfields and cherry orchards, while policemen at Maidstone, believing it was an enemy aircraft on fire, cheered like excited schoolboys. Fourteen-year-old Freddie Le Grand was standing at his bedroom window in Rusper Road, Barking, when a peculiar object with a blazing tail rushed past, sounding like a roaring motorbike without a silencer. His sister Enid joined him at the rattling, vibrating window and exclaimed: 'Look – there's a plane on fire'.

At 4.25 a.m., the V1 hit the railway bridge over Grove Road in Bethnal Green, which carried the main line from Liverpool Street to the northeast via Chelmsford. The bridge, a stout Victorian structure, stood up quite well to the 1 ton of high explosive but two tracks were ripped up, the parapet partially collapsed and nearby homes severely blasted, leaving 200 homeless. Six were killed, including a 19-year-old mother and her eight-month-old baby boy. Thirty were also injured and extensive damage caused, as Ken Snow, then 12, recalls:

I was inside our Anderson in Haverfield Road, just off Grove Road, with

A blue English Heritage plaque on the bridge commemorates the drama of 13 June 1944.

Looking north along Grove Road today from Mile End Road.

my Mum and Dad, four sisters and a brother. When the bomb landed, it made a deafening explosion and the whole place vibrated and shook. Local shopkeepers, who used to take it in turns to carry out ARP duties, were soon swarming about looking for victims. I went round the corner too and there was complete devastation around the bridge area and the homes near it. I remember everyone was saying a plane had crashed and all the talk was about the whereabouts of the pilot. Where was the body? Was he alive? There was lots of screaming piercing the air and it reminded me of the sort of reaction that used to come from homes when the telegram boy dropped messages off with bad news from overseas. A terrible wailing would come from beyond the front door if the telegram revealed a loved-one was lost. It was the same in Grove Road that morning. I helped sift through the rubble and what struck me was the way everyone helped each other. We were all in the same boat with absolutely nothing to our names and that bred this great camaraderie. Everyone was in Grove Road working frantically to help their neighbours or comfort those in distress.

The fourth V1, which landed harmlessly at 5.06 p.m. at Platt near Sevenoaks, Kent, concluded the first barrage. It was hardly the 'thunderclap at night' that Field Marshal Keitel, Chief of the German High Command, had promised. Yet, during the 24 hours following mid-day on Thursday 15 June, more than 120 V1s were reported and 60 got through to London. Billy Tomlinson, then living in Hackney Road, Shoreditch, recalls:

Friday 16 June was my 14th birthday and I was doing my paper round as usual. I suddenly noticed strange noises coming through the clouds. Rumours had been going round for a couple of days that a new weapon was coming over and everyone was puzzled by the whereabouts of the pilots. Of course, we later realized they were pilotless. On my birthday, I was amazed to hear these strange, spluttering sounds and there was a terrific blast when they landed. The doors and the letterboxes would rattle furiously with the impact and shake my hand as I tried to push my papers through.

On both 16 and 17 June, considerable damage was caused in Lewisham, Westminster, Croydon, Wandsworth and Battersea. The King George V Dock fared little better and the wild rumours that began to circulate around the capital had to be addressed. Thus, on 16 June, Herbert Morrison was forced to announce to the House of Commons:

It has been known for some time that the enemy was making preparations for the use of pilotless aircraft against this country. He has now started to use this much-vaunted new weapon.

Londoners were shown the full destructive power of the 'revenge weapon' two days later. On 18 June, a bright Sunday morning, another V1 was fired at the capital and the bomb hit the Guards' Chapel attached to Wellington Barracks in Birdcage Walk, the home of the Brigade of Guards. A morning service was in progress when the building folded into a mass of sloping, impenetrable slabs. Beneath the collapsed grey walls and roof, 121 died, including many distinguished officers present for the service. It was the first major tragedy associated with the V1 in London and would be the worst in the whole nine-month V1 campaign. Newspapers were requested not to publish the obituaries all at once in order to minimize the effect on national morale.

V1s now began crossing the Channel at the rate of about 100 a day. Shortly after midnight on 21 June 1944, 17 people were killed in West Ham and 31 seriously injured when a V1 brought horror to the Barking Road and Beckton Road area. Fireman Cyril Demarne, who had been made a Divisional Officer in 1943, recalled West Ham's worst V1 incident:

One man was standing outside his home, which had been completely demolished. He was an auxiliary fireman who I had trained, and was a key worker at Tate and Lyle's. He had gone to work that night and then received the dreaded message to go home. He stood outside, while workers looked for his family by wriggling into tunnels bored into the debris. They brought out one of his children and he went over and identified him. Then another dead child was brought out. Then his dead wife was discovered. He identified them all without any sort of emotion, and just stood there rolling and smoking cigarettes. I was looking at him and thinking 'poor bugger', and after a while his fourth child was brought out dead. Then, once they were all out, he suddenly collapsed and broke down and was led away. Next door, an entire family of six had been wiped out and there were more dead in the other houses.

The horror continued and a catalogue of appalling incidents blighted the month. On 24 June, a V1 shot down by a fighter hit the Newlands Military Camp at Charing, Kent, killing 47. Two days later, tragedy once again beset 33-year-old East Ender Joan Young. Her husband, RAF Sergeant Albert, had already been killed two years earlier when a bomb hit a pub in Fakenham, Norfolk. Mrs Young had been pregnant at the time and Albert never knew his daughter Barbara Ann, who was born in 1942. Then, on 26 June 1944, a V1 landed in the garden of 33 Oakleafe Gardens in Barkingside, Ilford, where Mrs Young lived with her mother Grace, and the baby. Grace received horrific injuries from flying glass and had to have both eyes removed in hospital, while 21-month-old Barbara Ann died the next day in Ilford's King George Hospital.

The damage caused in Upton Avenue, West Ham, by a V1 on 16 June 1944.

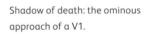

Shadow of death: the ominous approach of a V1.

On 30 June, a further 48 people died when a V1 fell at The Aldwych as office girls sunbathed on the roof of the Air Ministry Building, Adastral House, and lunchtime shoppers thronged the streets below. On the same day, 22 children, evacuated from a London nursery, died when a V1 hit an isolated school, Weald House, in the Kentish village of Crockham Hill, near Chartwell. Even before that incident, more than 200 boys and girls under the age of 16 had been killed by V1s.

Within just one week of the new Battle of Britain, a total of 756 civilians had been killed and over 2,500 injured, while 12 hospitals, 12 schools and 4 churches were already destroyed or damaged. Within two weeks, 1,600 people across the southeast were dead and 4,500 badly injured, particularly by flying glass. At this rate, the V1 would create as much damage in two months as the entire 1940/41 Blitz had caused in nine months.

Hitler's V1s were a huge blow to morale that June, a month when hopes had been raised by the momentous D-Day landings and the fall of Rome two days earlier. Moreover, talk of Nazi 'secret weapons' had long been dismissed as German propaganda, so the deadly reality brought the nation out in a collective cold sweat. 'It was as impersonal as a plague', wrote Evelyn Waugh, and 'as though the city were infested with enormous venomous insects'.

The immediate response was public defiance, before despondency crept in during late June and early July. Once again, however, Londoners dug deep into their reserves of resilience and East Enders drew on their survival experience. The mood lifted and the city once again adapted to the new danger and adopted appropriate new routines. Londoners soon became attuned to the note of the V1 exhaust, and those with the sharpest hearing were quick to yell the increasingly common cry: 'There's one coming!' The new weapons were initially referred to in the newspapers as 'pilotless aeroplanes' or 'P-Planes', but were nicknamed 'doodlebugs' (because they sounded like cheap cars) 'bumble bombs', 'buzz bombs' or 'robot bombs' by the general public. Typical East End gallows humour added another name: 'Bob Hopes' – 'Bob down and Hope for the best'.

The sheer number of V1s soon resulted in the almost continuous sounding of the air-raid sirens, which began to disrupt factory production and cripple the war effort. As a result, a new system was introduced, using local spotters, who sounded klaxon horns to warn factory workers to take cover.

Above all, people had to come to terms with the defining feature of the V1, which introduced a new, psychological dimension to the description 'terror from the skies'. This was the 12-second silence that occurred when the V1 engine, starved of fuel, cut out before falling to earth. This dramatic pause, when life seemed to be suspended, is recalled by Dorothy Crofts, then aged 11 and living in Woodland Street, Hackney:

I will never forget the sheer fear of those few seconds it took for the V1 to fall to the ground. It was a terrible silence once the engine cut out. Once I persuaded my Mum to let me go upstairs to the comfort of my bed rather than the garden dugout. I was luxuriating in the pleasure of stretching out my limbs in a warm, comfortable bed when I heard a V1 droning right over the house. Then the engine stopped. This was my first taste of real terror. There was no use diving beneath the bedclothes so, stupidly, I found myself sitting bolt upright in bed, every muscle in my body taut, willing with all my might that it would come down somewhere else. The wait went on and on and on. When it suddenly exploded nearby, I heard Mum calling from the dugout. I went downstairs crying and promised never to stay in again. Soon after that incident, my Dad, an ARP warden, came into the dugout and was very upset indeed. He had just tended a policeman writhing in agony in the middle of the street with a lump of shrapnel in his stomach, after another V1 attack.

The impersonal nature of the attacks created new fears and a new type of nervous strain, as young June Smith (née Meddeman) recalls:

I had returned from evacuation in Cambridge to a new home in Seven Kings, Ilford, and remember how the V1 brought a terrible new sense of vulnerability. I hated school for one reason and one reason only: I dreaded coming out to find my home and parents gone and no one to look after me. My fear had not been helped by the fact a buzz bomb once blew down an internal wall in our house,

showering two sisters and I as we cowered inside a Morrison shelter. All the window glass blew in and embedded everywhere. Strangely, my brother John was sleeping in a bed in the front parlour and that was the only place which did not receive a single shard.

The unpredictable behaviour of the V1 added to the general unease, as Stanley Bartels remembers only too well:

I was working at an engineering firm in Great Eastern Road, Stratford, when a V1 appeared. The factory girls headed for the dugout but us lads just watched. The V1 went past once and the girls came out. But then the same bomb appeared again and the girls went for cover once more. We carried on watching and, in all, the V1 circled us three times before it cut out and crashed nearby. Another time I was at the barbers in Sebert Road, Forest Gate, when the barber and I went out to watch a V1. I still had the towel around my neck. The V1 was heading straight towards the barber's shop and we were staring straight at the cone. There was nowhere to run and we just stood there dumbstruck and frozen to the spot. At the very last moment it veered off – yet we still stood there speechless with fear, unable to move through shock. It landed 300–400 yards away in Field Road, Forest Gate.

Yet life had to go on and a general, albeit wary, acceptance of the new threat slowly settled. Milk-delivery boy Tom Evans remembers:

My father owned J. J. Evans and Sons, a dairy business in Royal Mint Street. He used to supply the London docks and the Royal Mint and I had a permit to visit these areas to deliver milk, a job I would fit in before school. I was very struck by how people learnt to take the new bombs in their stride. They were basically as cheerful as ever after a while. Around 60 of us local kids occupied Raine's Grammar School, which had been evacuated. The top two floors had been blitzed and I recall six of us doing our chemistry exams in the old basement gym when a V1 landed on the police station in Arbour Square. It was a huge blast but we just carried on with our exam. We later learnt policemen were killed there. On another occasion, I was leaving the Troxy cinema in Commercial Road when three V1s flew overhead in formation. That was odd enough, but I once saw a V1 with a roaring engine crash into Lloyds Bank in the Minories. The engine had not cut out at all.

Eddie Siggins also had a close encounter with a V1. He recalled:

I must have seen one or two V1s each night, coming over towards Leytonstone. They always looked to me like small blowlamps scudding across the sky,

Tom Evans (seated third from the left with his back to the wall) pictured with classmates from Swan Street School in Whitechapel. Swan Street is now Portsoken Street.

until suddenly the light went out and it was time to get under cover. The most frightening experience I had was late one sunny afternoon, when I was helping my brothers and sisters into our Anderson shelter in the garden at 107 Crownfield Road. My Mum, who was at my side with baby Jimmy in her arms, suddenly said: 'Look!' I looked up and saw a V1 coming silently towards us. It was just like an owl gliding towards its prey, wings outstretched, body straight and silent. We both stood on the spot and stared at it, totally paralysed. It seemed to be at the bottom of Crownfield Road and about to glide along it towards us. Suddenly it dipped down and there was an enormous explosion, which shocked us out of our trance. We rushed out into the street and looked towards the Thatched House pub. As we looked I saw the baker's shop, Barton's, collapse in a pall of reddish smoke, as did the properties around it. The V1 had come down in Borthwick Road and a number of people had been killed.

As always, the strength of the family unit was of fundamental importance. Leonard Rose, living in St Mary's Road, Plaistow, notes:

Most of the family lived in our road. Next door to us was my great grandmother, then my great aunt Harriet, then Aunt Win, then Uncle Dave – and many, many more, right up the street in a row of at least six houses. At the back was a corresponding long row of Andersons belonging to our family. Dad was the clan's figurehead and he helped erect all the shelters, where the adults, and at least nine Rose children, took cover. In July 1944, a V1 hit the Russell Road Technical College and the blast rolled over all our Andersons and smashed our houses behind. The whole row was destroyed. Then the family network went

into overdrive. My Dad's brother lived in East Ham and Mum, my sister and I went there. Dad went to live with his grandma in Clova Road, Forest Gate, and all the other family members were quickly absorbed too. It was amazing how family and friends just automatically opened their doors and the whole family in St Mary's Road was efficiently swallowed up elsewhere.

Families also learnt that self-help was often the best policy. Young Iris Atkins recalls:

Our house in Dunelm Street, near Arbour Square, was damaged by a V1 and a tarpaulin was put over the roof. We couldn't use upstairs, but at least we could stay in the house during the day and sleep in the Aldwych Tube at night. Then, two weeks later, there was a terrible storm and a river of water poured down the stairs and flooded us. We had been waiting for permission to occupy a vacant house in Senrab Street and now we couldn't wait any longer. We piled all our possessions into a barrow and literally broke into the new property. We informed the authorities the next day. They didn't try to remove us.

Few fires were started by V1s but their blast effect was severe. In fact, when the V1 threat emerged, National Fire Service personnel were given special training in rescue work. Even so, all emergency workers suffered chronic physical and mental fatigue when dealing with the menace. The following two snapshots help give further impressions of life in the shadow of the new 'revenge weapons'.

Fourteen-year-old Ron Warner, of Pedro Street, Lower Clapton, Hackney, recalls the aftermath of a V1 attack:

Grandad was part of a heavy-rescue team and my brother and I would take them tea and sandwiches to keep them going. They could be on a site for days, digging people out. It was frightening, but at the same time exhilarating for us. One morning a V1 landed in Elderfield Road and Dad, brother George and I rushed to help. We were pulling rubble away and looking for people. The thing I remember was the effect of the flying glass. Great shards of it were sticking in people like swords. Everywhere was covered in dust too and the blood oozed through and discoloured it. Us kids were ushered away in the end by the wardens. On a lighter note, I recall the US troops who were based for a while in Kenninghall Road in Hackney. They were lounging about on the pavement, looking smooth and trying to impress the passers-by. Then some V1s came over. They dived over the nearest wall for cover while us kids just laughed at them and stood there watching the bombs. We were pretty fearless by then.

Walter Dornberger (in uniform) and Werner von Braun at a dinner to celebrate the first successful test launch of the A4 rocket, later known as the V2.

Contributor Ron Warner's grandad, Sam Warner (second from the left), pictured with ARP Heavy Rescue colleagues at Mandeville Street School in Clapton.

Cyril Demarne, the Fire Service divisional officer, never forgot one particular V1 bomb scene:

I attended a flying bomb incident in Dagenham which has stayed with me ever since. It was around breakfast time when I got there and it was my practice to stop the car on the outskirts of a bomb incident and then run towards the centre. As I ran that day, a demented man ran past me, clutching a baby to his chest. I don't know whether the child was alive or dead, but the man was in despair and the little baby's fat legs were bumping up and down as he ran. The poor man was beside himself with grief and I shed tears that day. In fact, everyone – even the toughest firemen – cried if a child was among the casualties. We would remain haunted by those sorts of incidents.

I also remember going to an incident in Blake Hall Crescent, Wanstead, and women and children were being removed from the debris. As we worked, several V1s roared across the sky and there came a chorus of 'Sieg Heil, Sieg Heil' from hundreds of German throats in the POW camp along the road. How I prayed for one of those bombs to come down smack in the centre of that camp, but the bombs flew on to crash in Poplar or Stepney. The camp was nearly hit soon after, when a V1 crashed on the anti-aircraft rocket installation on the opposite side of Woodford Road, killing gunners and ATS girls in a slit trench.

Londoners' Blitz experience helped them to cope. They instinctively headed for the Underground stations once again and, by mid-July 1944, more than 70,000 were living there, many staying all day. Demand also grew for the opening-up of deep shelters, which had been completed too late for the 1940/41 Blitz. The first opened at Stockwell, but none of the eight that were finally completed was located in the East End, which raised eyebrows considering the area's track record.

On 1 July, London County Council began to register mothers with young children who wished to be sent away. Two days later, the first evacuees left and northbound trains packed tight with women and children set off every five minutes from Euston and Kings Cross. On 7 July, 15,000 left on special trains for East Anglia and it suddenly felt like 1939 all over again. Without the young faces and laughter, there was the same apprehension and the same deserted streets. By the end of July, some 170,000 official and 530 'private' evacuees had already left the capital, a number that grew to 2 million as the V1 campaign progressed. The evacuees headed for the Midlands, the North (Blackpool was a big favourite), Scotland, South Wales and the West Country.

Fireman Cyril Demarne also managed to get away – but only for a week – after being granted leave. He recalled:

My wife and I decided to go to Cambridge and just get away from the V1 nightmare for a few days. It was a terribly stressful time and there was so much nervous tension. As we left Liverpool Street Station, a V1 dived in the vicinity of Mile End Road. Immediately my mind conjured up the scene while I sat there in the railway carriage. The choking dust and the smell of freshly spilled

In July 1944, a Hackney bakery hit the previous night by a V1 proudly opened for business the following morning; the bread was baked by a competitor and supplied under the Bakers' Mutual Assistance Pact.

After the same Hackney V1 incident, a housewife returns to her demolished home to gather together some personal belongings.

blood; the shocked, dazed people; and the shattered buildings and the frenzied rush to help. All the sights, sounds and smells came to me in an instant. As the train moved on, we passed the legacy of the V1: great gaps in the streets of small houses bordering the railway line and demolished factories with tarpaulin pulled over the roofs. When we arrived in Cambridge, the sun was beating down and the streets there were reminiscent of the pre-war East End. It was all so peaceful. American servicemen strolled around with smiling girls in summer dresses and they didn't have a care in the world, in sharp contrast to the shocked, drawn Londoners I had left behind. We had been transferred to a different world and it was very odd indeed. My wife and I were the only ones who instinctively ducked when the sound of aircraft filled our ears. They turned out to be a formation of US Mustangs, roaring low over the station, and our actions caused great amusement to onlookers.

Cyril Demarne was back in London in time for a chilling July, the worst month for V1s, when 1,106 fell on the London Civil Defence region and 20,000 houses were damaged each day. The month began with devastation in Croydon, which became the area worst hit by the V1. Then, on 3 July, 64 were killed when the US Army billets in Sloane Court, Chelsea, were struck. It was the second-worst V1 incident after the carnage at the Guards' Chapel in June. Three days later, on 6 July, Churchill addressed the House of Commons in the wake of growing concern and disquiet in London. He

stated that, up to 6.00 a.m. that day, 2,752 people had been killed by Hitler's new bombs. He revealed:

This invisible battle has now flashed into the open...between 100 and 150 flying bombs, each weighing about 1 ton, are being discharged daily, and have been so discharged for the last fortnight or so... A very high proportion of these casualties... have fallen upon London, which presents to the enemy...a target 18 miles wide by, I believe, over 20 miles deep... It is, therefore, the unique target of the world for the use of a weapon of such gross inaccuracy. The flying bomb... is a weapon literally and essentially indiscriminate in its nature, purpose and effect... The House will ask: 'What of the future?' Is this attack going to get worse?... Will the rocket bomb come? Will improved explosions come? Will greater ranges, faster speeds and larger warheads come upon us? I can give no guarantee that any of these evils will be entirely prevented before the time comes, as come it will, when the soil from which these attacks are launched will be finally liberated from the enemy's grip... I must, however, make it perfectly plain – I do not want there to be any misunderstanding on this point... We shall not allow the battle operations in Normandy, or the attacks we are making against special targets in Germany, to suffer. They come first, and we must fit in our own domestic arrangements in the general scheme of war operations... There can be no question of allowing the slightest weakening of the battle ... It may be a comfort to some to feel that they are

sharing in no small degree the perils of our soldiers overseas… I am sure of one thing, that London will never be conquered and will never fail…

The next day, 7 July 1944, 16-year-old Doris Mathis (née Cundale) sprinted home to Richmond Road, Dalston, when the siren sounded once more. She remembers:

I had been out at work all day and had just put the key in the front door lock when the whole house came down. A V1 had landed at the back somewhere. I recall the never-ending cascade of bricks as the house fell on top of me. When I came to, I dragged myself out of the debris and noticed the front door had been blown across the road. Then I recall being in the ambulance with my brother Stanley, who was 18, and my Dad, George. Stanley had been out in the garden with his binoculars to see what was going on and said he had felt the heat of the bomb as it had flown over. He was lying flat on his back in the garden, peering through the binoculars, when they were suddenly blown from his hands. Dad was alone in the house and had been standing at a bay

window, ordering Stanley to get back in. When the bomb went off, all the glass hit his face. He looked terrible in the ambulance and that was the last time I saw him. He died the next morning at the German Hospital in Dalston.

After the incident, there was no counselling and I went to stay with the family of a work friend in Hackney, while brother Stanley went to Sandhurst. I remained traumatized and my doctor advised me to join clubs to get over it. He also wrote a letter of recommendation, which enabled me to get a job at the American Red Cross Club in Piccadilly as a hostess, where I served coffee and doughnuts and danced with the troops. I met a man there, an Air Force sergeant, who was later to become my husband.

The Dalston incident was followed by further V1 tragedies during the second week of July. Eighteen died in Norlington Road/Claude Road in Leyton, and ARP Rescue Service and Home Guard personnel were killed when their base at Hermitage Wall School in Wapping was hit. One of the five victims was Home Guard member Fred Eastland, aged 37, whose evacuated wife Anna and six-year-old son Freddie received the devastating news in Burton. Mr Eastland, who lived at the family home in Jubilee Buildings in Wapping High Street, was killed outside the school and his grieving wife went grey overnight. Then it was the turn once more of Grove Road in Bethnal Green, the scene of the East End's first V1. Fourteen lost their lives on this occasion.

That July a camera lens captured poignant imagery of the aftermath of a V1 explosion. One of the most famous photographs of the war showed a fireman carrying an 11-year-old girl from the ruins of her home in Arundel Road, Leyton. That girl was Eileen Clements (now Alexander) who recalls:

I was playing ball in the street on my own during the evening of Monday 24 July. My parents were at the pictures and my sister Lily, 18, was indoors. The siren sounded and I ran through the house and got to the steps of our Anderson shelter where I saw the V1 coming over. The engine cut and then I was suddenly blown from one end of the shelter to the other. It went pitch black and I recall hearing my neighbour saying: 'Are you all right?' I could have got out of the shelter myself but I was shaking and crying and wouldn't move until a fireman came along. When one arrived he reassured me but I said: 'I'm not walking outside in case there are dead bodies on the ground'. He replied: 'Okay – I'll carry you then'. I then noticed our house had gone – in fact the whole row had disintegrated. I was wondering what had happened to sister Lily and at this point my photo must have been taken, but I was unaware of it.

I was taken up the road where there were hundreds of sightseers. My parents, who had been at the Academy in Leytonstone Road watching a Tessie

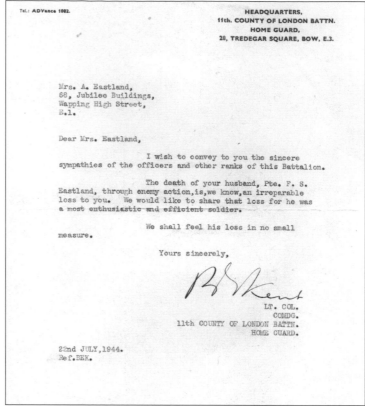

O'Shea film, met me there and I couldn't stop crying. I told one of the ARP wardens that Lily was missing and we had to endure a terrible wait to see if they could find her. Lily was eventually found about 30 minutes later, unhurt beneath a wardrobe. She had luckily been combing her hair, using the wardrobe mirror, when the V1 fell. The wardrobe had fallen over Lily and protected her from the masonry. I was black and blue and didn't learn that my collarbone had been broken until later in life, when I was pregnant and a routine inspection showed it up. I was evacuated to Norwich after the bombing, which killed several people.

The photo that made me famous was taken by a fireman who sent it to the Daily Mirror. *They used it on their centre pages, and so did all the other papers but I was never identified. The picture was then published by a magazine in 1972 and I wrote in and finally revealed who the little girl was for the first time. Following a television appearance in 1985, the wife of the fireman who carried me also made contact. Unfortunately, her husband, Bill Sayers, had died a couple of years earlier. The incident had a profound impact on my life. To this day I cannot stand the sound of aircraft, I never fly and always look up to see that an aircraft has actually passed overhead and hasn't come down.*

Three days after Eileen Clement's ordeal in Leyton, appalling scenes were witnessed in a road nearby. The firewoman who drove Cyril Demarne to Dames Road shortly after 6.00 p.m. on 27 July was so sickened by the sight that she asked not to accompany him to the centre of future incidents. In Dames Road, close to the Holly Tree pub, a trolleybus crammed with workers had received the full blast from a V1. The roof and upper deck had been sliced off and dismembered bodies littered the roadway. Standing passengers on the lower deck had been flung out and splattered over the brickwork of houses on the other side of the road, while those left on the lower deck were sitting in their seats, as if waiting to pay their fares, without their heads.

Bob Somerville, aged 14, witnessed the incident unfolding as he stood waiting to catch a bus home.

I had been working at the nearby Oliver's factory and was keen to get home to Katherine Road in East Ham. I was with a colleague who suddenly said: 'Christ – look at this!' Then a V1 appeared and I actually saw the front and curvature in a split second. When it landed, the blast caught a bus that had arrived opposite us near the Holly Tree pub. In a fraction of a second I left the real world. As the debris fell down, I found myself in someone's gateway, where I must have been blasted. My immediate thought was I must have gone to Heaven because I was so disorientated. My colleague and I then noticed a woman who also worked at Oliver's, whose legs were badly cut. We helped her across to the Holly Tree, where the bus was completely stripped down to its platform and people were still in it. My mate said: 'Come on, let's go –there's nothing we can do' and off we walked. I recall seeing a bicycle standing by the kerb with no paint left on it at all. I was in a state of shock. I had pains in my chest, my eyes were bloodshot and my hair was in tight ringlets and totally black with dirt.

James White, an ARP Supervising Officer of First Aid based at the Harrow Green depot in Leytonstone, turned round the corner with his crew the moment the V1 landed. Mr White (who earlier described the day a Wellington bomber crashed on his depot in 1942, see page 173) recalls:

(left) Fred Eastland's marriage to Anna in 1936 and (right) the letter of condolence sent from Home Guard HQ to his widow.

(above) Eileen Alexander today.

(right) Young Eileen Clements (now Alexander) became famous when she was carried from the wreckage of Arundel Road by fireman Bill Sayers. The picture became one of the most well known of the entire war.

We had a roof-spotter at the depot and so had a pretty good idea of where the V1s were going to land. Dames Road happened right in front of us. Once the black smoke had lifted, I remember a passer-by handing me a baby who was alive. I passed the child onto an auxiliary nurse and said: 'I've got no time for children – people need help here'. The scene was awful and nothing was recognizable at all. Everything – the bus and the people – were ripped to shreds and it was hard to make out anything. There had been around 60 people, either on the bus or passing by – at least that was the total I helped lay out in the forecourt of the Holly Tree pub. I know the official death toll is put at around 30, but there were a lot more than that lying there that day. It was a shocking affair and I still have nightmares about it to this day. Certainly the worst incident I ever attended. It is impossible to even begin to describe the scene.

The next day, 28 July 1944, southeast London's worst V1 incident occurred when a bomb landed in front of the clock tower in Lewisham High Street. It was just before 10.00 a.m. Blast tore through the market stalls lined up outside Marks and Spencer, Woolworth and Sainsbury, and 51 shoppers and traders were killed.

So, what of London's defences? Allied daylight raids on V1 launch sites in France had put only four out of action by mid-July. This left the city with three lines of defence. The first was a layer, 31 miles long and 11 miles deep, of some 1,750 balloons, tethered by steel cables, which floated over the North Downs and covered air space from Redhill to Chatham. The second was a belt of anti-aircraft guns on the seaward side of the Downs, while fighters took to the skies to complete the third line of defence. The latter included deployment of the 400 m.p.h. Tempest V, the only aircraft capable of consistently intercepting the V1. They led the battle in the skies against the V1 until the new Spitfire X1V, fitted with the powerful Griffon engine, joined the fray. One pilot, Australian Flying Officer Ken Collier, discovered a novel method of halting the V1's journey. He used his wing tip to flip the V1 onto its back, which sent it falling to earth out of control. This entailed flying at 330 m.p.h. alongside a ton of explosive, yet soon many pilots were using the technique.

Nonetheless, it was difficult to coordinate the three lines of defence, and planes from Fighter Command were at risk of being fired on by their own anti-aircraft defences, while anti-aircraft batteries competed with Balloon Command for sites. In practice, the use of anti-aircraft guns in London proved a major problem, since they merely brought the bombs crashing down somewhere else, thus inadvertently diverting the misery to new locations.

By 17 July, all 400 heavy guns on the North Downs were re-sited between Beachy Head and Dover, where they could fire unhindered out at sea as the V1s approached the English coast. Over 500 light guns joined them two days later and gunners now enjoyed the benefits of improved gun accuracy, better shells and a new US radar tracking system. It was a massive success and the switch of location saved countless lives. The success rate in June 1944 had been very low, with between 9 and 13 per cent of incoming V1s repelled. Yet, by August, half of the flying bombs were being destroyed before they could reach London, culminating on 28 August with what Churchill hailed as 'a record bag'. Of 95 that approached Britain that day, all but four were destroyed.

However, spasmodic attacks saw 395 killed in London within the first week of August. In one incident a V1 ploughed into a restaurant in Beckenham Road, Beckenham, killing 44. That month, 17 also died in the area of High Street and Hoe Street in Walthamstow and fireman Cyril Demarne lost two colleagues at the Abbey Road School HQ in West Ham, where he had witnessed Black Saturday unfolding four years earlier.

Charles Young will never forget that month either. He recalls:

On 6 August, I was enjoying a drink in the Basin pub in Kingsland Road, Hoxton, with my parents and two friends from the Navy. A V1 suddenly exploded at the back of Old Street and plaster fell from the pub ceiling into our drinks. We got out in one piece and my two mates and I planned to go back to my parents' house in Caroline Gardens, for tea. Then a telegram came through telling me to go to Liverpool for a medical. I left Euston at 3.00 p.m. and my two mates came to see me off. Two hours later a V1 hit my parents' house and the first I knew was when a Navy Commander asked to talk to me the next day. He told me to sit down and he read a telegram, which revealed my Mum was missing and presumed dead. I went back home and discovered Dad had been in a surface shelter at the time, but Mum had popped into the house to make tea. Mum was dead and Dad was a complete mess afterwards. He had been trapped in the shelter and his nerves had gone. Poor Dad just couldn't cope any more. A friend of mine had volunteered to be a mortuary attendant, but he was badly mentally affected after seeing the state of my Mum. He said he didn't want me to see her body and he gave up his job after that.

Beyond the shattered East End, Hitler's world continued to collapse. On 25 July, the Americans broke out from the west of France and began to sweep through the country, while, to the east, the Russians were within walking distance of Warsaw in Poland by 1 August. On 25 August, the Tricolour once more flew above Paris after the Germans surrendered the city to the Allies. Four days later, Montgomery began an offensive that took the British Second Army from the River Seine to Antwerp in five days. On their way, troops over-ran abandoned V1 launch sites. There were no Germans to be seen. They had evacuated and retreated east with their equipment into Holland, leaving London practically out of range.

The main V1 attack had lasted just 10 weeks, from 13 June until 1 September. London's Civil Defence region had received the greatest number of Hitler's 'revenge weapons', followed by the counties in so-called 'Doodlebug Alley' – Kent and Sussex. Tower Bridge had seemed to be the aiming target and one V1 even passed through the central arch and sank the Tower Bridge tug on the other side.

British Intelligence had played a part in skewing German calculations so that the city could be spared. Intelligence had attempted to deceive the Germans into aiming short or wide of the city by feeding false information about the timing and location of their hits in the centre. Most V1s landed south of the River Thames, where some areas were pulverised. Croydon, in particular, lay in the path of the majority of V1s and scarcely a road escaped damage as 141 landed. It was the V1's greatest killing ground; nearly 59,000 houses were damaged and over 200 people killed. Those bombs that missed flew on to Mitcham, Streatham, Wandsworth or Penge. In the East End, West Ham received most by September (58), followed by Poplar (39), Barking (37), East Ham and Hackney (36), Ilford (34), Stepney (30), Dagenham (28) and Leyton (24).

Nonetheless, September witnessed a new optimism in London, and for good reason. First, the attacks had tailed off. Second, Germany was in desperate trouble. By the end of August 1944, German armies in the west had lost half a million men and almost all their tanks, artillery and trucks. On 5 September, the day after Montgomery entered Antwerp, there was even a rumour that the war had ended and people left work early and began to fill the streets in anticipation of a Churchill broadcast at 6.00 p.m. Bunting appeared and preparations were made for one almighty East End celebration. Two days later, on 7 September, Churchill's son-in-law, Duncan Sandys, leading Britain's hunt for Hitler's secret weapons, even told a press conference that the 'Battle of London' was over 'except possibly for a few last shots'. He added that the 80-day V1 bombardment had seen Hitler launch over 8,000 flying bombs at Britain, of which some 2,300 had got through to the London region.

Sandys' optimism proved premature. The 'few last shots' continued for another six months as V1s were fired from planes and from Holland, even though most were brought down and only 79 reached London between September and March 1945. They nonetheless added to final statistics, which revealed that a total of 2,419 V1s hit London between 13 June 1944

Charles Young (centre) with friends Billy Rose (left) and Charlie Farrell (right). Charles had a narrow escape in December 1940 when his home in Britannia Gardens, Hoxton, was bombed. (See page 144)

Charles Young's mother, Jane Young, pictured in 1937.

and 29 March 1945. They killed 6,184 in Britain, including 486 in the two Civil Defence areas covering the East End.

Sandys had also spoken too soon in predicting the end of the 'Battle of London'. The V1 menace may well have dwindled after September 1944, but the German Army was about to demonstrate how technology could be more ably harnessed to terror. It was time for the V1's big brother – the V2 rocket.

The day after Sandys' reassuring press conference, Hitler decided to launch the ballistic missile age. Allied troops were now advancing swiftly across northern France and swarming throughout Belgium but there was just time to throw a spanner in the works. Hitler chose to derail Allied progress by directing the first V2 at Paris, which the Allies had liberated the previous month. The Paris missile, painted in conventional grey-green, was fired at 7.40 a.m. on Friday 8 September from the little hamlet of Rouges Fosses, near Gouvy, in Belgium. Five minutes later, six people were killed without warning when the rocket ploughed into the Parisian suburb of Maisons Alfort. That morning, the newspapers that Londoners read over breakfast contained the reassuring, up-beat Sandys' speech beneath the headline: 'The Battle of London Is Over'. Ironically, V2s would be heading for the capital by teatime.

Even so, it was touch and go for the Germans. After the Paris launch, technicians had been forced to flee Belgium as the Americans advanced, but a safe launch area had already been established on the far side of the Rhine in Holland, just within range of London.

At 6.43 p.m. on 8 September, a V2 fell to earth in the west London suburb of Chiswick, claiming Britain's first three rocket victims. Throughout the capital, people heard a double thunderclap after the impact, and those in the British scientific community immediately recognized its significance. The first bang was the explosion of the V2 warhead, which was followed by a roaring whistle as the sound of the V2's descent caught up with it. Moments later, there was a second bang as the supersonic boom, caused by the sound

barrier being broken somewhere in the stratosphere, finally arrived. As the dust settled, a crater 30 feet wide appeared in Stavely Road.

Some 16 seconds after the Chiswick missile, another V2 headed towards London and came down at Parndon Wood in Epping. Both had been aimed at a point just south of Southwark Bridge and now they started arriving thick and fast. Between 10 and 12 September, two rockets landed near Southend, one crashed to the south of Swanley in Kent and others hit Kew Gardens, Dagenham, Biggin Hill and Magdalen Laver near Harlow. On 14 September, the tenth rocket became the East End's first, when it landed in Walthamstow, flattening the southern end of Farnan Avenue, demolishing 24 houses and killing six people. On 16 September, Barking was hit, followed the next day by Green Street in Upton Park, where seven were killed.

Hitler's last throw of the dice would ensure that London became the first city in the world to come under sustained long-distance rocket attack. With the Allied armies advancing upon Germany, Hitler was convinced that victory could still be snatched from the jaws of defeat and London obliterated with the new weapons, now being mass-produced.

In Britain, the weapon was officially referred to as a long-range rocket, abbreviated to LRR, but the code name 'Big Ben' was introduced to help security, just as 'Diver' was used with V1. Its very existence was unconfirmed for two months, despite the growing incidents. It was simply felt that ignorance was bliss. This, after all, was a weapon which could travel at around 3,500 m.p.h. and arrive without warning via the stratosphere; it took just five minutes from launch to deadly impact; and it could fly at an altitude of 50–60 miles for a maximum distance of 225 miles, before landing almost vertically at over 2,000 m.p.h.

Most disturbing of all, V2s could not be evaded and its victims never knew what had hit them. The missile's rapid descent from 20,000 feet lasted only four seconds, leaving a vapour trail for only 30 seconds. Developments

Eddie Siggins's fighting cousins: (left) Freddie Parr and (above) Stanley Bowyer.

in radar technology helped to improve the warning times, but the V2 was simply too fast and travelled too high to be tracked down. The rocket's size alone hinted at its destructive capabilities. Its 13 ton cylindrical body, equipped with four stabilizing fins, towered 46 feet into the air on its launch pad, and the 1-ton warhead was situated on top of 9 tons of fuel.

It was superior to the V1 overall, even though 48 doodlebugs could be built for the cost of one rocket and their relative blast effects were more or less comparable. However, the V2 created utter devastation at the point of impact, although much of its energy was absorbed by the ground that it penetrated. Critically, its speed, stealth and undetectability induced deep psychological fears in the city's inhabitants. The only available defence, indeed the nation's only hope, was to destroy the V2s at their launch sites or storage sites.

As more of the rockets were prepared for firing, the evacuees who had fled the V1 menace were now flooding back to London at a rate of 10,000 per week. By 18 September 1944, half of the official evacuees were back in London. They would now share the city's final ordeal, as, from September 1944 to March 1945, decreasing numbers of V1s and increasing numbers of its formidable big brother were fired continuously at the capital.

That September, Eddie Siggins found himself in reflective mood as he sat astride a roof ridge, surveying the splendours of Leyton. Eddie, now a 'carpenter's assistant', had been mending the roof of Leyton's former Mayoress, Mrs Burrell, and was deep in thought. After the arrival of the V1s in London, Mum had taken the family away once more. They had gone to Leeds, where their stay was as brief as it was unhappy. So back to Leyton and Crownfield Road they had trooped, and Eddie had joined a local building

firm. He was a trainee and his contribution to the family business was fixing roof rafters damaged by bombs. There was certainly no shortage of work since Leyton had seen its fair share of war action. There had been the buzz bomb he had watched land in Borthwick Road, and the dreadful incident involving the trolley bus in Dames Road had occurred just up the street.

At least his family was safe. Nana, Mary Ann, was well and lived just a stone's throw away in Matcham Road with her daughter Gladys while Mum was pregnant again. Eddie, his brothers Peter, Leslie and baby Jimmy, and his sisters Irene and Betty Anne, could expect an addition at Christmas. Another baby would add to the fun in a house where the din of childhood spilled out to the garden and was amplified by the chattering of cousins Ivy and Doreen Parr on the other side of the garden fence.

Two of Eddie's other cousins were abroad, serving their King and country. Freddie Parr had gone off to war in Burma and a lot of drink had been consumed at The Castle in Stratford when he left. As Freddie turned the corner of the street, his mum, Eddie's Aunt Rose, had a strong premonition she would never see her son again. It was a disturbing prophecy for young Eddie to hear, since Mum's side of the family seemed to have psychic powers. Time would tell. Meanwhile, Eddie's cousin Stanley Bowyer was serving in Holland. He had joined the Essex Regiment, whose distinguished ranks had once included his own grandfather, Nana's husband Alfred (who died at Cambrai during the First World War). It was, Eddie thought, a strange coincidence. Nana was so proud that two of her grandchildren had followed in the footsteps of her beloved Alfred, but the whole family could only pray that they would not meet the same fate as their grandfather.

Eddie's reminiscences were rudely interrupted. A large bang shook his perch and a column of black smoke poured from the earth. At the same time, he felt strangely breathless, as if the air had been sucked out of his lungs. This was followed by a second boom, high in the heavens. Tyndall Road had been hit – and Huxley Road – and people were no doubt dead. It could only be one of the mysterious new rockets that were the talk of Leyton. Eddie had seen two explode in the sky before, and now he watched the coiling black smudge streak the blueness. Sirens were sounding and people were running towards Tyndall Road.

Eddie's mind raced back four years to 1940 and the Duckett Street bomb, when Searle House was blasted and the baker's shop opposite was hit. He vividly recalled the state of the blasted Anchor and Hope pub and Nana's home, No. 63 Duckett Street, with its rear surgically sliced away. It somehow wouldn't be right for his family to suffer any more.

Eddie Siggins noticed the sky had suddenly darkened over the rooftops.

Chapter eight

Mary Ann's heartbreak

THE SIGGINS FAMILY stared at the clock. 'It's a bad sign. I don't like it', said Eddie's Mum after a lengthy pause. 'It could be some sort of warning.' The domestic drama, if it could be described as such, had begun during an early-morning flying-bomb attack. It was 3.00 a.m. and the family was sitting in the kitchen at Crownfield Road, huddled around the dying embers of the coal fire. Mum had suddenly pointed at the clock on the mantelpiece. 'Look', she said. 'The clock has stopped at a quarter to twelve again. It's been doing that for a number of days now.' She then explained how the clock had stopped at exactly that time each night. Always at the same time and always accompanied by the howling of a dog at the back. 'If there was something wrong with the clock it would stop at quarter to twelve during the day as well. But it doesn't. Can anyone explain that?' No one could and Mum proffered dark theories about bad luck and omens. Eddie remembered the noise of the dog. It was the most awful mournful howling – really blood-curdling.

These were strange times for many in the East End. First, after D-Day in June 1944, there had been a tantalizing glimpse of the war's finishing post, but the V1s had dampened the euphoria. Then, after the V1 bombardment petered out and the Allies surged towards Germany, a new weapon – the V2 – began pounding London.

The public knew something odd was happening, even if the Government chose to refer to the booms as 'gas-main explosions.' The sudden and shattering explosions made people all over London jump. The new weapons even made holes in the clouds, leaving gigantic ringed doughnuts in the sky. Tiles would crack before your eyes, even if the explosion was miles away. Then, of course, there was the bizarre boom that followed the initial explosion.

The public was not fooled. The V2 was the least secret of the secret weapons and everyone commonly discussed the new rocket that had succeeded the V1. The only area of speculation concerned what it looked like

A photograph released by the Air Ministry showing the long and complex preparations required for a V2 launch. The rocket is undergoing final fuelling and adjustments of the control apparatus.

The day after Churchill's public confirmation of the V2 threat, the front page of the *Daily Herald* announced the big story of the day. 'It is a sinister, eerie form of war', wrote the newspaper's reporter.

and what size it was. Rumours began to circulate that the Germans had made a gigantic missile weighing 80 tons with a 10-ton warhead that could flatten 50 acres of London in seconds. With tongues firmly in cheeks, Londoners began calling the new projectiles 'flying gas mains', in a less than subtle dig at the authorities, but all acknowledged that the V2 was no laughing matter. As Doreen Dennis (née Cook), living in Chatsworth Road, Clapton, recalls:

The V1 had a bit of a comical image with its peculiar 'phut phut' noise and lots of silly names were given to it. The V2, however, was just called the V2. It was simply feared, very scary and there was nothing even faintly amusing about it. There was no sheltering or warning now. No strange engine sound to give you a chance. You just had to carry on with life and hope you would survive the day. We were determined not to be beaten now, after all that had happened.

Defiance once again combined with East End pride, as June Lewzey (née Guiver) remembers:

Despite the new fear, appearances were important. When a rocket fell near our home in Abingdon Buildings, Old Nichol Street, in Bethnal Green, our sitting-room window was blasted and the curtains blown down. I'll never forget my Mum. She loved her shiny windows and immaculate curtains, so she was furious. She said: 'Look what that bloody Hitler's done now. He's spoilt my lovely window and curtains and I only did them this morning.' People still kept things up together and everything was swept clean and polished. The range was black-leaded every day and the hearth whitened. The guard in front had a brass top and you would never see a finger print on it.

On 17 September 1944, three days after the East End's first V2 landed in Farnan Avenue, Walthamstow, British airborne forces began landing at Arnhem in a bid to capture the Rhine bridges. The operation suddenly threatened Hitler's rocket units, which were now quickly withdrawn from the suburbs of The Hague to a thickly wooded hamlet in the Gaasterland district of southwest Friesland, in Holland, from where only Ipswich and Norwich could be reached.

Yet the East End remained vulnerable. The V2 may have been out of range, but more German aircraft were now capable of launching the V1 and they now flew across the Thames Estuary. Billy Tomlinson, then 14, recalls:

On 23 September, a V1 fell in Bethnal Green Gardens, at the library entrance in Cambridge Heath Road, about 50 yards from the Bethnal Green Underground station. The blast damaged shops and the living quarters above them from Birkbeck Street to Witan Street, and many people were buried alive. St Patrick's Girls and Infants, the first Catholic school in Bethnal Green, had been prepared for Mass and had suffered much blast. I went inside the school soon after and it was so strange. Everything had been laid out for Mass and many statues were smashed. Yet other statues were completely unmarked amid it all. The altar was also intact. The school had to be demolished in the end and a temporary home found at Stewart Headlam School in Brady Street.

The V2 reprieve did not last long either. Two rocket batteries were returned to The Hague to resume the British attack, and East London and Essex were back within range in October. Wanstead, Walthamstow, Ilford, and West Ham were hit on numerous occasions, and one V2 smashed Hermitage Wharf in Wapping, where the children's party had been held on the eve of London's Second Great Fire (see page 146) It was time to come clean about the V2 in Britain. Once the German Home Service had announced that rockets were hitting London, Churchill finally admitted that Britain had been under attack since September by the new, long-range V2s. On 10 November 1944, he informed the House of Commons that 100 had fallen since the first at Chiswick (the figure was in fact over 160), before adding the sentence which sent a shudder throughout the capital:

Because of its high speed, no reliable or sufficient public warning can, in present circumstances, be given.

Shortly after the speech – and as if to illustrate its gravity – the 164th V2 brought death to the area around Middlesex Street (Petticoat Lane). The rocket landed on Brunswick Buildings in Goulston Street and the resulting fire swept through the Norwegian Navy Stores, killing 19 and seriously injuring almost 100. While propaganda continued to report limited damage and presented V2s as a nuisance rather than anything more serious, there could be no disguising its grave psychological impact. The attacks were sickeningly unpredictable and often in daylight. Furthermore, it seemed as if the worst had been saved up for the very end after five years of terrible war.

The death toll mounted in November and, on the 21st, tragedy came again to Walthamstow. Leslie Huxtable remembers:

It was noon and a V2 fell in the gardens between Trevose Road and Longacre Road. I was only 15 and working as a van boy for Holdstock and Son, a baker's and confectioner's. When we arrived in Trevose Road with our bread delivery, the road was sealed off and I could see our customers' houses on the left-hand side were reduced to rubble. Ted, the van driver, said: 'We won't need to call there any more' and drew two lines down the list of customers. It was a devastating moment and we were both very upset about it. Those customers of ours were such lovely people.

Twelve houses were destroyed, 8 people killed and 50 injured in the incident.

The next day, 25 died in Totty Street, Bethnal Green, and a further 18 perished in McCullum Road, Poplar, on 24/25 November. Then came Britain's worst V2 incident of all – and one of the most tragic of the whole war. At 12.26 p.m. on 25 November 1944, the 255th rocket fell to the rear of Woolworth in New Cross Road, Deptford, when the store was full of women and children. The shop collapsed inwards and the Co-op next door crumbled too. Passers-by were thrown like bundles of rags over great distances and a bus was sent spinning like a top. Lorries burst into flames, office workers were killed at their desks and people over 400 yards away were pushed backwards by the force of the blast. It took three days to remove

Young Ernie Merritt (second from right) with sisters Sylvia (at the back) and Doreen (in front) and cousin Lenny (right).

the bodies and the official death toll of 160 seemed woefully conservative. Some 120 were seriously injured and 11 people were missing, including two women who went to Woolworth for tea, with their babies in prams. They were never seen again.

In the East End, November's incidents gave weight to the theory that places hit by one rocket were highly likely to receive another. For example, two more hit Barking, ten hit Ilford and West Ham, three hit Poplar, two hit East Ham and Dagenham, and treble strikes were recorded in Walthamstow, Stratford, Hackney, Bethnal Green, Silvertown, Waltham Cross, Wanstead, Stepney and Leytonstone.

Terrible scenes unfolded in these streets. Ernie Merritt, then aged 15 and living in Barrett Road, Walthamstow, recalls one appalling local incident:

I had forged my age so that I could get into the ARP a year early. I became a messenger and was based at the warden's post at Barrett Road School, where my job was to go out and pass messages between posts about fallen telephone lines. When a V2 fell in Shernhall Street, I came across a woman standing at her door in a total trance. She held a baby which was covered in blood and I saw that one of the baby's ears was missing. I immediately got first-aid help and then noticed that parts of bodies were stuck in the trees. By the end of the war, there was hardly a road in the Shernall Street and Barrett Road area that was untouched by bombing and death.

By late November 1944, six V2s a day were being fired at London and, as winter approached, acute hardship faced the capital. Evacuee children had

returned in such large numbers that the housing crisis worsened by the day; some foods, particularly potatoes and vegetables, were in desperately short supply, and the homeless faced the harshest, coldest winter for 50 years. Broken windows, cracked walls and missing roof tiles combined with a shortage of fuel to make a Christmas and New Year of utter misery for many. The usual East End destinations also received a Christmas visit from the V2s. They landed in Leyton, Walthamstow, Dagenham, Hackney (where 22 died on the 7th), Barking, Ilford and in Prince Regent Lane in West Ham.

At least there was something to celebrate in the Sigginses' Leyton household that grim Yuletide. On Christmas Day, Sarah Siggins gave birth to her eighth child, Stanley. Hitler spared the area further V2 misery on the big day, but a huge blast at Wanstead on Christmas Eve was rather too close for comfort. The new baby joined brothers Eddie, Leslie, Peter and Jimmy, and sisters Irene and Betty Anne, at the family home in Crownfield Road, Leyton. Nana, Mary Ann, was overjoyed and toasted the good news with daughter Gladys at the home they shared in nearby Matcham Road.

By the New Year, the V2s were averaging 10 hits a day and 1945 was barely four days old when the East End's mother church was hit. St Dunstan's, to the south of the Siggins's old home in Duckett Street, Stepney, was badly damaged by Britain's 450th rocket, which hit the northwest corner of the churchyard. However, it was the human cost that made the month tragically memorable. At Ilford on 12 January 1944, 14 died when a V2 landed on houses between the Hippodrome and Pioneer Market. Inside the theatre, the cut and bruised orchestra musicians played on amid swirling dust, while the shaken audience cheered them on. Outside, pubs in the High Road and Ilford Lane had been flattened and there were scenes of sickening carnage.

The New Year also had a double blow in store for West Ham, where 20 died after Plaistow Road was hit on 4 January, and a further 15 died in Freemasons Road, Custom House, on Saturday 13 January. Johnny Ringwood, then eight, recalls:

There was a bombsite area where the New Gog pub now stands in Freemasons Road and one of those silent beasts, a V2, suddenly landed, killing my young mates, Jimmy and David Lee, who lived in Devonshire Road, Custom House. They were aged 10 and 6 respectively and had been playing with me and a boy known as 'Sparrow' on a patch of wasteland which we called 'Debris.' It was a very popular play area, where we made battle zones and camps and dug trenches. I had to leave to get in my Mum's washing and then I felt the blast of the huge explosion, which blew me through the front door of our house in Jersey Road. I was relieved that I had left in time but absolutely shattered to learn what happened to my three pals. I think the lads were still playing at 'Debris' when they copped it.

Charlie Smith adds:

The Freemasons V2 dropped around noon near 'The Gog' pub. I was on my way home from my Saturday morning work as a 14-year-old apprentice at the local electricity generating station. I was about half a mile away from the scene when I saw a blinding flash and was almost bowled over by the blast. I ran to the scene, forgetting my Mum would be worried if I was late home. I wish I hadn't gone to see the site. It was unreal. A once-red trolleybus had been stripped of its aluminium body metal by the blast and its smashed windows revealed seated bodies burnt black or mutilated beyond recognition. Two young boys thought they had found a tailor's dummy outside Lipman's gents outfitters until they realized they were playing with a badly burnt adult body. My Mum didn't know whether to hug me or hit me when I got home.

(opposite, from left to right):

Young Johnny Ringwood with his parents, John and Winifred.

Pat Skeats (née Shread), aged eight.

Kay, Pat's sister, aged six.

Tom Keyworth, a Civil Defence messenger boy.

The meal she prepared was wasted because I just couldn't get those sickening scenes out of my head.

The following day, 14 January, was Barking's turn, as Pat Skeats (née Shread) recalls:

On that Sunday, the nineteenth-century church in the road next to ours, St Paul's in Ripple Road, got a direct hit. The place was full of people, including many children at Morning Prayer. Eight were killed and over 200 injured. I was just six years old and playing with my young sister Kay outside our house in St Margaret's Road, just before the rocket fell. After the explosion, a lump of wood hit my head and I grabbed my sister and carried her to the shelter in our back garden. Our worried parents thought we had taken shelter in an old shed at the top of the road, which had disintegrated, and were very relieved when we turned up. My Dad, an ARP warden, then went out to help others. He found a neighbour showered with glass and my Dad had to coax her into allowing him to remove a piece lodged in her breast.

That night we moved to my Nan's house in George Street. During the evening, the Central Hall in East Street, Barking, was hit and 14 more were killed. On that occasion we were all sitting in the middle room at Nan's, when the front door was blown straight through the house until it hit the kitchen at the back.

A few days later a few of us kids went to the Central Hall and climbed up the steps. The place was ruined and there were no walls standing. We discovered a huge Bible and it took the combined strength of all of us to lift it and take it away with us. We got the Bible back to Nana's after a huge struggle. She went mad and we then had to struggle back with it to the Hall.

Towards the end of January 1945, as the Russian Red Army moved to within 165 miles of Berlin, West Ham suffered another double blow. First, 28 were killed in Upton Park's Grosvenor Road, and then 16 died nearby when a V2 fell alongside West Ham's football ground in the Priory and Boleyn Roads area. Inside the stadium, a dozen buses and coaches were destroyed, their bonnets ripped off and hurled in all directions. Outside, a soldier raked through the rubble of his home to confirm the worst: six of his family had been killed.

There was no let-up for West Ham in February, when the highest death toll in the borough was recorded during the early hours of the first day. When the 645th V2 fell on Barnby Street off West Ham Lane at 3.00 a.m., 30 people lost their lives.

Tom Keyworth, an 18-year-old Civil Defence messenger boy, recalls:

We lived in a small house in Paul Street. My younger brother John and I had to share the same bed and we had had a bit of a barney, so he had pushed me onto my side of the bed and I had shoved him over to the other. It was just as well. In the early hours, a V2 landed in the middle of Barnby Street [at the rear of the Town Hall, not far from Stratford Market] and a massive lump of clay and rock was blasted out of the road and straight through our roof. It smashed between the two of us, breaking our bed in half. The house was wrecked and the roof came down over my sister Violet, trapping her. Luckily the roof section caught the corner of her cast-iron bed frame and we were able to tunnel into the debris and get her out pretty easily. Mum and Dad were okay too and we managed to get out of the wrecked house. It took three or four rescue workers to lift that huge lump that had crashed on the bed, so it was lucky we had had the row or it would have killed us both.

I recall a couple of vivid images from that awful incident. I remember looking at the massive crater in the road and I noticed seeing someone there looking around with a lamp. I was immediately reminded of those images of Jesus with a lantern looking for his flock. It was incredibly eerie. Then my brother and I noticed a bundle of rags up where the roof once was. We looked closer and realized it was one of the neighbours who had been blown up to the chimneys. He was still alive but later learnt he had lost his wife.

Our family then went down Romford Road to visit a house that was being used by the WVS to hand out clothes. We hardly had anything to wear and I remember going down the road in odd shoes with plaster in my hair. The taste of the plaster in my mouth was foul and it never seemed to go away for ages. We got to the house and there was already a queue. We were late because Dad was a fire warden and I was a messenger and we had stayed around at the site to help out. To make matters worse, many of those queuing in front of us hadn't even been involved in the incident – they were just there

Young Joe Marks.

feeling. I told her I hurt badly. My ear had been hanging off, there was now a metal plate in my head and my nails and teeth had gone. Bits of glass and concrete kept working their way out of my skin and little bits still come out of my head to this day. My right ear still burns to this day too, due to the after-effects of blast, and I get bad headaches. I was moved to St Margaret's Hospital in Epping after the incident and I just couldn't stop crying. I was once walloped by a doctor for it, who said: 'What are you crying for son?' Then I was told a friend and next-door neighbour, Dennis Brown, was dead, which upset me further. In fact, at least 16 people were killed that morning. It was just will-power in the end that pulled me through, but I was told I would never be all right because I had caught the full blast. While Mum and Dad had survived the incident, Dad was affected mentally.

Some time later, the actor Howard Keel was in Drury Lane, starring in Oklahoma!, *and I went backstage to see him with my bandaged head and I told him what had happened to me. Years later, when I was Assistant Director of the 1962 film* Day of the Triffids, *I met him again, but he didn't remember me. I suppose it was ironic that in 1965 I was Second Unit Director on the film* Operation Crossbow, *which told the story of the Allied efforts to halt the V-weapons. It starred Sophia Loren and George Peppard and I recall complaining about the silver flying bombs on the set. I insisted they should have been painted black and I nearly lost my job over it. After what happened to me in February 1945, I think I was entitled to voice an opinion.*

Finally, to complete the family's misery, we discovered that our relatives were victims of the Holocaust. Mum had received a telegram from the British Red Cross in 1942, which was signed by my uncle who lived near Lublin in Poland, to say he was all right. However, she felt instinctively that he had been forced to sign it and that that was the last thing the Germans did before they killed you. Mum made three visits to Israel after the war and she established the truth. Ten of our relatives – including my uncle – had been killed at the Treblinka concentration camp.

for a handout. My mother pointed this out and the WVS woman got annoyed with her and said everyone was equally entitled to help. My Mum responded by lifting her skirt and saying: 'Yes, but I bet they're not walking around with no drawers on!' We were given a clothes voucher after that and then went to West Ham Baths for a wash. We were later rehoused in Folkestone Road.

Four hours after the V2 landed in Barnby Street, a 14-year-old Jewish boy, Joe Marks, sat down to breakfast in Whitehall Gardens in Chingford, close to Epping Forest. He remembers:

Mum was in the kitchen and I suddenly had a distinct feeling of unease. I don't know why but I sat away from the French windows for some reason.

Dad was upstairs shaving and the next thing I knew everything went black and there was a smell of gas and burning. I later learnt a V2 had hit a gas pipe. I cried 'Mum!' and then everything seemed to be on top of us, with a blue flame of gas hovering in the air above.

I kept calling out, but there was no response and I thought I was finished. Then I remember someone with a torch and the words: 'There's someone down here – he's a gonner.' I was pulled out, however, and it was like being pulled out of a nightmare. My head was hanging off at the neck and I had actually lost part of it. I remember being put in a van and someone saying: 'Don't worry, he won't make it. Hold out your arm and count to ten.' Then the morphine went in and the next thing I recall was days later when I woke up in Whipps Cross Hospital and saw strange shapes going before my eyes – people, white coats and the like. Again people were saying: 'He's dead' and one said: 'Bury him now.' I had no idea who they were talking about but, of course, It was me.

My Mum came to see me in a wheelchair and she asked how I was

In the February of 1945, further harrowing incidents were witnessed in the East End, and East Ham, West Ham, Bethnal Green, Ilford, Dagenham, Hackney and Poplar were again in the V2 firing line. Walthamstow also figured again, as Freddie Le Grand recalls:

I was in the dining room of my grammar school, Sir George Monoux in Chingford Road, Walthamstow, and had just finished lunch. I was pencilling my initials on a table tennis ball for something to do and then I heard this incredible rushing sound, which I now know was the air being displaced by an approaching rocket. There was a vivid flash and a tremendous suction and pushing sensation. The windows very slowly bowed inwards and I put my face

(from left to right):

Connie Cause (née Brown).

Connie's friend, Grace Thompson, who lost her parents, brother and sister in the Queen Street V2 attack in Stratford.

Eddie Siggins.

on the table and covered my head with my arms. The next moment I had been hit on the back of the head and passed out. I woke up a minute later and the school prefect Doug Insole was helping me out.[1] The ceiling and part of the roof had come down but something had fallen across my back, which protected me. Doug took me down to the cloakroom, where he bathed my wounds. He later recalled that I was covered in semolina pudding when he reached me. I must have fallen into the bowl in front of me.

On 13 February 1945, the day three Anglo-American air assaults began on Dresden, Connie Cause (née Brown) had gone to the pictures in Stratford:

I was living in Gordon Road and had gone to see Spencer Tracy in Thirty Seconds Over Tokyo *with a friend, Grace Thompson. Grace and her family lived in the railway flats at 16d Queen Street, Stratford, and her Dad worked on the railway. As we were walking back to her home, we heard an enormous bang. We were just minutes from the Thompson home and, as we got nearer, discovered that the flats had been hit by a V2. It was devastating. My friend Grace had lost her mother, father, her sister Joan, who was 15, brother James, aged 17, and the family dog. I remained in deep shock for a long time after that – and have no recollection of the end of war celebrations.*

Three days after the Queen Street attack, which left 28 dead, Eddie Siggins caught the trolleybus home to Crownfield Road in Leyton after another busy day mending roofs as a carpenter's assistant. He peered through the frosted window and shivered at the thought of another bitter night. Eddie

couldn't wait to get in and resume work on the wooden toys he was making with brothers Leslie and Peter for the younger members of the family – Betty Anne and babies Jimmy and Stanley. Eddie, then 15, recalled:

I remember getting in that day, Friday 16 February. Our house in Crownfield Road was in a terrace and had at one time been used as two flats, each with its own kitchen. We had the use of the upstairs kitchen as a workshop, where there was a sink and water supply, and a gas stove, which was handy for heating up the glue pot for our woodwork projects. We had already made a model of a steam train from wood, with a cotton reel for a chimney, and it was painted dark green and red, the only paint we had. It looked quite good and we were soon onto something else and having a great time in our makeshift carpenter's shop. As long as we never made too much noise and cleared up the mess afterwards, Mother didn't mind and it was only for two or three hours each evening. We eventually got the call to get ready for bed and cleared up, taking care to hang up our prized possession, a new hacksaw bought from Woolies during our brief stay in Leeds for 5 shillings and 6 pence [27.5p], which was two weeks' pocket money.

It was a pretty scary time with the V1s and V2s and only a few days before I had been working in Lemna Road on houses wrecked by a rocket. On a couple of occasions, silence was called for as dead people were carried by on a stretcher and the men around me took their caps off. It was a terrible atmosphere and I never forgot the ruined homes, with people's possessions open to the elements and the curtains clinging to the outside walls through shattered windows, as they always did. There were collapsed roofs and people tried to drag tarpaulins over them, while my little gang attempted to tack roofing felt over the empty window frames. We left the scene in silence and trudged back with our barrow with all our gear in.

---

[1] Doug Insole later became an England cricket star and was made President of the Marylebone Cricket Club in 2006.

 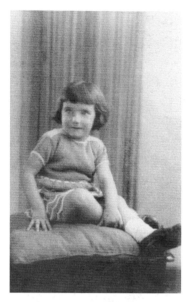

Eddie Siggins's cousins, who lost their lives in the Crownfield Road V2 disaster: **(left)** Ivy Parr and **(right)** Doreen Parr.

Back to the 16th: We had all gone to bed pretty late, I think it was around 11 o'clock. Leslie, Peter and I slept in a double bed on the ground floor, sister Irene had a bedroom upstairs and Mum slept in the front bedroom downstairs with the three youngest members of the family – Betty Anne, aged three years, and Stanley and Jimmy in cots. At around 11.30 p.m., I heard Dad come home from a business trip. He shouted: 'I'm home!' and he asked Mum, who had just gone to bed, if she wanted a cup of tea as he was going to make one for himself. He then walked to the back of the house.

The next thing I recall was waking up and finding I couldn't move. I thought I must still be asleep and thought if I shouted I would wake myself up. So I tried to shout and as soon as I opened my mouth, it filled up with dust and grit and I started to cough and spit it out. Still unable to move, I had the feeling that my head was pointing down, with my feet upwards. It had been silent up to then, but now I started to hear people crying and felt what could only have been Peter and Leslie lying across my legs. My feet seemed to be wedged against one of them. They were struggling and crying and it slowly dawned on me that we were all trapped beneath rubble of some kind. I could feel Peter and Leslie really struggling now and crying too. I started to talk to them and told them not to cry as someone would find us and get us out. They still cried and I tried to comfort them.

I must have been in an air pocket because I could breathe but the dirt still came into my mouth when I opened it. I continued to talk to my brothers but, after a while, I could feel their struggles getting weaker until they ceased

altogether. I felt numb by now and I couldn't feel anything, but remember it was also very hot down there. Every now and then I called out to the boys, but there was just silence. I remember feeling that perhaps they were dead and, if so, it would be my turn next. I remember being curious about this and wondered what it would be like. Strangely, I was not afraid, just curious.

Then I recall seeing a face staring at me. It was an old, pallid face with greyish hair but the eyes I stared into were extra large, wrinkled and empty. There was no expression in them at all. I was looking into an empty void but I was not afraid. I can only put down this experience to a crack on the head or a vivid imagination, but at the time it was very real. After a while I heard muffled voices from up above and pressure on my body as if someone was walking over me. I called out and then the voices came nearer. Then I heard a voice say: 'Here's one' followed by a short silence and then: 'He's gone' and then: 'Here's another' and then: 'He's gone.' Suddenly, I felt the bricks and rubble being pulled away from my head and saw the dark night sky.

I remember thinking how bright the stars were. As I took in great gulps of cold, sweet, fresh air, I heard a voice say: 'Give him a shot of morphine' and I was lifted out and put on a stretcher. I was feeling a bit drowsy but opened my eyes and saw the house was now a big pile of grey, dusty rubble. There were people in dark boiler suits and tin hats moving about the debris, and searchlights and spotlights pierced the darkness. I closed my eyes and felt myself being loaded into something that then sped away from the scene. Next, I recall opening my eyes at some stage and seeing a clock on a hospital wall [he had been taken to Whipps Cross] *which gave the time as 3.30 a.m. I was given some very sweet tea, which made me violently sick and I brought up something like mud into a kidney bowl.*

I had some cuts to the head and a few stitches but no broken bones. I was very fortunate to get away so lightly. It must have been the bedclothes and blankets that protected me when the house collapsed. My Uncle Jim Banham was the first one to visit me and each time he told me Mum and Irene were okay and doing well but never mentioned the others. I knew Leslie and Peter had died and came to the conclusion that the same fate had probably overtaken the others, otherwise he would have spoken about them. So it came as no great shock when he finally did tell me they were all dead. I already knew by instinct.

Sister Irene, aged 16, told me later that all she could remember was waking up to find that she was lying on top of the slated roof of the house and looking towards the sky at the stars. The roof, it appears, was lying on top of the rubble of the house and she had no memory of how she got there. She told me she remembered getting up and walking across the rubble and debris into the road and she was found walking down the middle of Crownfield Road staring straight ahead of her, dressed in her nightgown. She was found by

After the disaster, the Siggins family moved to Whipps Cross Road, Leytonstone, where a Nissen hut village awaited the homeless. Eddie's mother, wearing a light double-breasted coat, is standing second from the right. Looking over her shoulder is Eddie, with his sister Irene to his right. The village residents are enjoying a street party to celebrate the end of the war with Japan.

rescue workers who placed a blanket around her. Irene was unable to utter a single word for almost two days afterwards.

My brothers Peter and Leslie, aged 6 and 11 respectively, had – as feared – died. My Dad, James, who was 40, had died too and so had the three latest additions to the family: little sister Betty Anne, who had just had her third birthday, Jimmy, who was 16 months old, and 7-week-old Stanley, who had been born on Christmas Day. The two babies had been clutched by my Mum, Sarah, who had survived. Mum had fallen through to the cellar and soldiers from the camp opposite had saved her. One had dug a tunnel to reach her and was held by the ankles and lowered into the hole. He was in great danger of collapsing masonry but refused to give up. He took the babies from Mum's arms and pulled her clear. The family found him a few days later and gave him a gift of money they had collected. He was a bit embarrassed and reluctant to take it but was eventually persuaded to do so.

My four young brothers, my little sister and my dear Dad were not the only family members to die. The rocket had landed at the back of the house, close to where my cousins lived over the garden fence in Colegrave Road. My cousins, Doreen Parr, aged 9, and Ivy Parr, aged 20, were also killed, bringing the total number of family fatalities to eight. A total of 25 died altogether in the incident, which was Leyton's worst wartime disaster.

By the way, the rocket [the 784th fired at Britain] came down on the Crownfield Road/Edith Road boundary at precisely 11.45 p.m. that night. That was exactly the time the old clock on the kitchen mantelpiece had been stopping all those nights before and which always caused a neighbour's dog to howl. Was it a coincidence or was my Mum right to have had an odd feeling about it?

After about a week, I was transferred to Chase Farm Hospital at Enfield, from where my uncle, Jim Banham, came to collect me. He brought a new suit and shoes and other items of clothing, supplied by the Government, as all I had to my name was the shirt I had been pulled out of the debris in, and which had been cut off me in hospital. He took me to see my Mum in another hospital. When I saw her, we both burst into tears. I was so relieved to see her. She had an enormous bump on her forehead that looked like the size of an egg.

By the time Mum and I had been released from hospital, the family had been buried in Manor Park Cemetery in Sebert Road, where a service was held in wooden huts because the church had already been bombed. My family was laid to rest in a mass grave which also contained two teenage brothers, Eric and Alan Bunt, who died in the terrible Dames Road trolleybus disaster [see page 198] and four RAF men who died when their Wellington bomber crashed [see page 173]. Unfortunately, the grave fell into dreadful *disrepair and there was confusion over who was responsible for its upkeep. However, Waltham Forest Council put the matter right and a service to re-dedicate a brand new granite memorial was held at the cemetery in 1997.*

After the tragedy, there was only my Mum, sister Irene and myself left, and we went to stay on forest land in Whipps Cross Road, where new converted Nissen huts were erected to house war survivors. The huts were designed to stand for two years and we stayed in the Nissen Village until 1947. My Nana, Mary Ann, was devastated by the whole affair and the subject was never discussed between my sister Irene and I. It was strictly taboo, and has only now been told for the first time.

The Crownfield Road disaster was followed three days later by Walthamstow's worst V2 incident. Several months before the 822nd missile landed, Ivor Morgan recalled hearing the Nazi propaganda broadcaster William Joyce ('Lord Haw Haw') on the radio:

Joyce said: 'We have our eye on a factory in Blackhorse Lane, Walthamstow, and be sure we intend to make it a target.' He was absolutely specific on certain occasions and my brother and I found it pretty exciting at the time listening to him. I worked at one factory in the Lane myself. It was called Bawns, where naval equipment was made, and it transpired that this was the place Joyce had referred to. I had luckily left two weeks before it was hit.

When the V2 landed shortly after 2.00 p.m. on 19 February, 20 were killed and 200 injured. Nine of the victims were women working in the Bawns welding department and one was a 14-year-old lad on his first day at work. He had been on the premises barely an hour. Dorothy Greenwood, (née Huxtable), sister of Leslie who witnessed the Trevose Road disaster three months earlier (see page 205) recalls:

I was 22 and working within the factory complex at a place called Mills Equipment, which was next to Bawns. There were several factories in the complex and we were all involved in making army equipment. I was a weaver and used a loom. The missile fell on the west side of the road, just outside Bawns factory and the office block was demolished. All but one of the Bawns office staff died – including two directors. Hundreds of homes were damaged too.

That afternoon, I had gone to use the toilet and had just come out of the cubicle when there was a great flash of bright light. A friend was with me and she said: 'Cover your eyes.' Then the massive explosion came and I went deaf for a fortnight. Other women were still sitting on the toilets and all the glass came in from the windows, cutting them terribly. My hair was covered in glass while outside passers-by were buried and never found. My supervisor

then came to help and she led us out of the remains of the building. I had only been married three months and I was worried about was my wedding photos, which I'd taken in to show the girls. I managed to grab them before I got out.

Rockets continued to plummet without warning at the end of February. During the last eight days of the month, four landed in Ilford while others fell on Poplar, East Ham, Dagenham, West Ham, and Leyton once more. However, by March 1945, Hitler's Third Reich entered its final death throes. British and American troops had reached the Rhine and the destruction of the Ruhr industrial area, and loss of the Rumanian and Hungarian oil fields, was rendering the German military apparatus impotent.

Nonetheless, the major part of western Holland was still in German hands, and rockets continued to roar away from their Hague launch pads. The last phase of the V1 offensive also began on 3 March 1945, when doodlebugs were fired from ground ramps at three Dutch sites. The deadly combined assault on the capital caused 169 casualties in the first week of March alone. While new radar techniques helped to pick up many of the flying bombs, little could be done about the V2 rockets. It was now simply a race against time to topple the Third Reich before any more damage could be done.

While the net closed, the mayhem continued and one V2 incident was reported every day as March progressed. At 3.00 a.m. on 6 March, Upperton Road in West Ham was hit, killing 31, and 25 died when Ida Street in Poplar was struck the following day. The Poplar V2 fell at the junction of Cotton Street, Bazely Street and East India Dock Road, just before mid-day, and the *East London Advertiser* reported:

It completely wrecked The Eagle public house (in East India Dock Road) and the Home of the Nursing Sisters of the Order of St John the Divine (in Bazely Street). Two rescue parties arrived at the incident within five minutes and immediately went to work on the public house, where most of the casualties were expected. This assumption later proved to be correct.

Among the casualties was Mrs Mary Story, the licensee of The Eagle. Three cranes were brought in to assist the rescue and the workers toiled for 36 hours. Twenty-five hours after the rocket fell, a woman was brought out of the debris alive, but she died after reaching hospital.

Then on Thursday 8 March, traders and customers were queuing patiently for their meat ration at Smithfield Market on the corner of Farringdon Road and Charterhouse Street. At 11.10 a.m., a V2 hit the building and went through the floor, before exploding in the underground railway network beneath. Market shops and buildings on Farringdon Road

Horror at Smithfield: a policeman, civilian and two rescue workers carry a a badly injured woman on a stretcher away from the scene.

were levelled, while many simply tumbled into the gigantic crater as the floor of Smithfield gave way. Freddie Le Grand remembers:

I was working as a copy boy at Reuters in Fleet Street when the V2 landed. The blast was deafening, and afterwards I remember seeing all the paper, tickets and dockets floating past the windows. It was like ticker-tape.

Divisional Officer Cyril Demarne never forgot that day either:

I was based at Clerkenwell Fire Station and my job entailed visiting stations in the City. A little time before the incident I had set out from Clerkenwell, after a good breakfast, and was being driven around in a car, wrapped in an overcoat in the back. As I passed Smithfield that day in February, there was a long queue of people huddled together waiting for food. It was a bitterly cold day and drifts of snow were blowing. I felt really guilty watching the housewives from the warmth of the car. The mood passed, however, and March arrived with a spell of fine weather. Then, at 11.00 a.m. on 8 March, I was having my hair cut at the barbers in Kingsland Road. I was just paying when I heard the explosion of a V2 about a mile away.

I got over there in five minutes and saw a huge crater, the biggest I had ever seen, at the Market. My mind went back immediately to those ladies I had seen queuing the previous month. How many of them were down there

in that hole now? There were bodies everywhere and one man was opened up right down the front. His chest was so open you could see his heart in there. It was strange – I just thought: 'Blimey, that's his heart I can see in there.' I had become immune to the horror and had learnt to move on and think no more about it. All the market buildings had collapsed into the crater and the shops fronting Farringdon Road were reduced to rubble. Apart from those buried on the Farringdon side, the rest seemed to be actually inside the crater.

The official death toll was put at 110 but many believe the figure was considerably higher. The same day Ilford and West Ham were hit again as V2s continued to shake East London. West Ham suffered again on 11 March, and Ilford and Epping on the day after. Then, on 16 March, a V2 landed in Albert Road in Leyton, leaving 23 dead. Two-and-a-half hours later, shortly before 9.00 a.m., it was East Ham's turn.

Mollie Beer (née Lyden) was at work at the Air Ministry that day:

My home was at 2 Lichfield Road, where I lived with my Mum, my second eldest brother, Eddie, who had been invalided out of the Services, and his wife Anne. My Dad had died of a heart attack in the previous year. That day Mum had made them breakfast and was bringing it into the dining room on a tray. In the room sat Anne, on a stool by the fireplace, while her husband was washing his hands at the sink. Then a V2 landed in Lichfield Road, in a garden adjacent to ours, and it destroyed shops in Boundary Road. The glass cabinet in our house fell on my brother Eddie, scarring him but also protecting him from the tons of rubble that fell as the house collapsed. It took the rescuers and their dogs six hours to get him out alive, but Mum and Anne were found dead.

I was contacted at work and told to go home and I was just in a state of complete shock when I saw the place. I then went with my uncle to the mortuary to identify my Mum and sister-in-law. Half of Anne's face was missing and I could only identify Mum by her legs. She suffered badly from varicose veins and that was the only way I could tell it was her. I now had nowhere to go and a friend put me up for a while. I walked around in a daze for six months and really needed some sort of counselling. Just a month after the incident, I remember my doctor shouting at me: 'Come on – pull yourself together', which wasn't much help. I remember salvaging bits of clothing from the debris for the rag- and-bone man, for which he gave me 15 shillings [75p]. The authorities also gave me an extra £10 to help me on my way.

Incidentally, a lady in an off-licence on the corner of Boundary and Lichfield Road, had a premonition about the incident. She kept seeing glasses and bottles falling down in the shop. We thought she was having a nervous breakdown, but she insisted the images were vivid and really upsetting her. When the V2 landed, she died too, along with her small son who was just four. A lady next door at No. 4 also had a premonition that morning and rushed under the stairs for shelter. She was killed as well.

Yet the terror was coming to an end and, a week after the Lichfield Road V2, the Allies crossed the Rhine. The V2 rocket troops were now almost cornered in The Hague. It was time to leave – but not before six more rockets were fired on Tuesday 27 March 1945. The first four landed between 12.22 a.m. and 4.00 a.m. at Edmonton in North London, at Cheshunt, west of Epping, and at Ilford and Hutton Park in Essex respectively. Just over three hours later, the fifth rocket headed for Hughes Mansions in Vallance Road, Bethnal Green.

The Mansions, completed in 1929 and named after their benefactor Mary Hughes, consisted of three parallel blocks, each containing 40 flats. The generous philanthropist was fortunately spared the appalling tragedy about to unfold. From her home at the Dewdrop Inn, opposite the Mansions, she had carried on her tireless work with the poor and needy during the Blitz. However, on 31 March 1941, she was moved to St Peter's Hospital in the same street, where she died soon afterwards. Now, four years on, a V2 was hurtling towards the homes that bore her name. As the rocket approached, the Mansions' families, many of whom were Jewish, were having breakfast, getting ready for work or preparing for Passover.

Suddenly, at 7.21 a.m. on 27 March, the 1,114th V2 ploughed into the middle block, forcing the walls apart and sending its occupants and their possessions plummeting to the ground. The scene was deeply shocking for all those who converged upon it, looking for loved ones. One blood-splattered man was seen running down the street carrying the remains of his baby and screaming for his wife. A soldier just home from Burma clambered over the wreckage and discovered his wife and six children had died.

Fireman Cyril Demarne was there within 20 minutes and recalled:

The rocket had buried itself in the bottom of the foundations of the centre block and there were great heaps of debris, over which people were clambering. There were so many people on the site that we thought it was adding to the weight of the rubble and would make it even worse for those underneath. We started shouting: 'Get back please! GET OFF!' One woman screamed back at me: 'Don't you realise my family is down there?' I politely told her everyone had to get off so we could do our job, but there were a lot of highly traumatised and hysterical people around. We had put rope barriers up as usual, and then actually pulled people off the rubble so we could work. It was a terrible job and the standing flats in the block nearest the road had to be searched too. When bodies were found, we just found a sheet or some sort of covering and placed it on them. I had two children of my own, which made the sight of dead youngsters even more harrowing.

Rose Gowler (née Wiggins) was also there that day, her eyes frantically scanning the debris for her mother and sister:

I was married, with two children, and I spent my time divided between the home of my in-laws in Southwark and my family home in East London – No. 31 Hughes Mansions. The family had moved there in 1932 from Myrdle Street in Whitechapel [see page 35]. There were three council blocks – one lining Vallance Road, a second built parallel behind it, where we lived on the second floor, and a third block behind us. I used to push my pram containing my two babies all the way from Southwark to the Mansions, so I could spend some time with my family. I went one weekend and my mother was dozing in the armchair by the fire, my baby David was crying in the pram and my daughter Susan was playing on the floor. My mother suddenly woke up with a start and said: 'I'm fed up with all this racket. Take your kids home and give your mother-in-law a basinful of this noise instead.'

I was really upset and plonked the children in the pram and made a quick exit. My sister Lilian, who was 22, said: 'I'll come with you, I can't understand Mum going on like that.' I replied: 'Well, why don't you come and stay with me for the night?' She said she couldn't because Dad, a warden, was on duty at the first-aid post and she didn't want to leave Mum there alone. So Lilian stayed and I went off to Southwark.

GROUP REF.	DATE	TIME	LOCAL AUTHORITY	LOCATION	GRID REF.	CASUALTIES			
						K	S	I	TOTAL
					B.P.	391	1213	3054	4658
129	10/2/45	08.25	Leyton	Kirkdale Road/Lemna Road.	838065	5	25	30	60
130	"	11.00	West Ham	Bascule Bridge, K.G. V Dock near Harland & Woolf's.	881991	3	6	47	56
131	11/2/45	12.29	West Ham	Glico Pacific Wharf - Crows Road.	833019	-	-	6	6
132	"	14.53	Walthamstow	150 yds. S. of L.N.E.R. bridge near bank River Lee	796063	-	-	-	-
133	"	16.10	Dagenham	Gravel Pits - Salinas Lane.	927063	-	1	9	10
134	"	18.20	East Ham	Central Park - High Street South.	869022	-	3	23	26
135	12/2/45	20.30	Walthamstow	Council Yard, Billet Road, next to Roger Ascham School.	812097	10	37	71	118
136	13/2/45	18.50	West Ham	Queen Street opp. Warden's Post 3 A.	831041	31	37	96	164
137	"	23.00	Ilford	High Road - Goodmayes - Airburst.	-	-	-	-	-
138	16/2/45	23.47	Leyton	Crownfield Road/Edith Road - boundary incident W.Ham.	831045	25	15	37	77
139	17/2/45	05.30	Ilford	Grounds of Claybury Mental Hospital.	881104	-	-	-	-
140	18/2/45	00.55	Chingford	The Avenue.	820125	-	1	4	5
141	"	04.34	Ilford	Ley Street/Brisbane Road.	868059	4	19	25	48
142	19/2/45	00.45	Ilford	Green Lane, near Highbury Gardens and New Road.	896958	3	18	36	57
143	"	07.25	Wanstead & W.	Lakehouse Road, off Blakehall Crescent.	846057	-	4	36	40
144	"	07.22	Waltham H.X.	Fairmead Bottom - Nr. Palmers Bridge.	853150	-	-	-	-
145	"	14.20	Walthamstow	Blackhorse Lane.	802092	20	81	120	221
146	20/2/45	11.42	Ilford	Roden Street/Uphall Road.	979050	3	39	45	87
147	"	13.39	Waltham H.X.	Broomstickhall Road area.	839202	-	-	5	5
148	"	23.30	Barking	Mayesbrook Park/Westrow Drive.	907037	-	6	33	39
149	21/2/45	12.53	Ilford	Belgrave Road.	871061	1	16	33	50
150	"	22.20	Ilford	Ley Street/Cranley Road.	888068	7	31	6	44
151	23/2/45	00.05	East Ham	Between Locks - Basin Royal Albert Dock	885994	-	-	-	-
152	"	01.04	Waltham H.X.	In field - Lower Lodge Farm.	874214	-	-	-	-
153	"	07.48	East Ham	Airburst. Large parts fell in Dagenham.	-	-	-	-	-
154	"	09.10	Walthamstow	Airburst. Venturi fell Chigwell Rise/Brook Way - Chigwell.	-	-	-	-	-
155	24/2/45	07.42	Dagenham	Chequers Lane - Briggs Bodies.	934022	-	-	-	-
					C.F.	503	1552	3716	5771

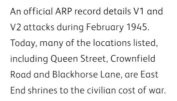

An official ARP record details V1 and V2 attacks during February 1945. Today, many of the locations listed, including Queen Street, Crownfield Road and Blackhorse Lane, are East End shrines to the civilian cost of war.

The propulsion unit of a V2 is inspected at Limehouse. The rocket fell in March 1945 and the damage behind is plain to see.

(left) Dramatic aftermath of a V2 explosion at Forest Gate: the missile fell on Earlham Grove on 6 March 1945 killing 15 people. Over 100 houses were damaged or destroyed.

(above) Mollie Beer's mother, Dorothy Lyden (née Summers), photographed at the age of 21, and (right) Mollie Beer's father, Thomas Lyden.

Dorothy Lyden (left) and daughter-in-law Anne. They both died in the Lichfield Road tragedy.

The following Tuesday I heard a rocket land some distance away and I recall saying: 'Someone's got one!' Then, I was putting the pram outside the door and tucking one of the babies in when a taxi came down the road with a girl leaning out of the window. The girl worked with my sister and she had been sent by her boss to tell me that Hughes Mansions had been hit that morning. He had sent the taxi to help get me there. When I arrived, there was a big crowd and I wormed my way to the front. I couldn't believe my eyes. The middle block, where we lived, had vanished. Simply gone. The other two blocks were severely damaged as well.

I then saw that Dad was digging on the rubble and he came over. He said: 'Your mother is in hospital but I am sorry, Lily is dead.' I was in deep shock and Dad told me to go back to our old road in Myrdle Street and see if any of

Contributor Rose Gowler.

Rose's father, Charles Wiggins, who searched the rubble after the attack and informed Rose that her sister Lilian was dead.

Eleven-year-old Ivan Purssord was also among the crowd outside the Mansions, craning his neck for a view of the scene:

I had heard the blast and immediately thought of my two sisters working near Whitechapel Station, who were due to start work at the time of the explosion. But they were okay and had burst through the door of the family home in Weaver House, Pedley Street, to tell us Hughes Mansions was hit. I then made my way down there to have a look, and it only took a few minutes because the area was so flattened by years of bombing, and I knew all the short-cuts. I was dumb-founded when I saw the missing block in the middle. What struck me was the front of the block on Vallance Road was perfect, but its back was damaged, while the one behind had just disappeared into thin air. People were running around everywhere and I was so shocked I went home. At school, All Saints School in Buxton Street, the Deputy Headmistress stood up in assembly and said one of the lads, Ivor Suffolk, had passed his exams with distinction, but sadly had died in the Mansions. Ivor had only just joined the school and was a nice chap. He was slightly older than me and as bright as a button and I often wonder what he would have achieved if he had lived.

our old neighbours could help me there. When the rocket hit, Lily had been sleeping alongside my mother's bed, where I normally slept when I visited there. The bedroom door next to my Mum's bed had stopped the blast from hitting my Mum, but the blast and debris had gone over her and killed Lily lying alongside. I could easily have been there in that room with my two kids as well.

Lilian was buried in Bow Cemetery. She was going out with a Yank before her death and Mum believed she would be going to America and never be seen again. After she [Lilian] died, my distraught Mum said: 'At least I know where she is now. I can go and visit her and put a few flowers on her grave. I just never imagined she would die before I did.'

Meanwhile, when news of the disaster broke, Basil Shoop immediately thought of the young girl he had met the previous night:

My twin brother Stanley and I were members of the Brady Boys' Club in Durward Street. It was a great club, where you could play games like table tennis and enjoy talks and debates. The girls had their equivalent meeting

(far left) The V2 destroyed the middle of the three blocks. The rear of the block on the left, which fronts Vallance Road, was also extensively damaged, as can be clearly seen.

(left) V2 horror: a close-up of the central block at Hughes Mansions with the block fronting Vallance Road almost out of shot to the left.

(above) Panorama of the Hughes Mansions site: the central block has largely vanished and the blocks each side are extensively damaged.

(right) Contributor Rose Gowler (née Wiggins) submitted this photograph, which was taken in the courtyard of the Mansions' flats in June 1942 on the occasion of her wedding to George Gowler. The central block, which was hit by the V2, is behind the group. Rose is in the centre of the picture, holding her husband's arm, with her sister Lilian, who died in the rocket attack, to her right, clutching a handbag. Her brother Harry is in the foreground and their mother can just be seen behind Harry and to his right.

place in Hanbury Street.[2] *One night, after the clubs had shut, my brother and I took two girls for a walk and we went down Whitechapel Road. I was arm-in-arm with a girl called Lily Harris and my brother was with her friend. Both girls lived in Hughes Mansions and we said goodbye to them in Vallance Road. The next morning we heard an enormous bang and we went over to see what had been hit. It was the Mansions, and we later heard that many members of the Brady Club had lost their lives in there. Lily had been killed, but the other girl survived but was injured. We were deeply shocked.*

Helen Erlick (née Huskovitch) saw the Mansions' V2 go over:

I was 12 and living in Blackwood House, Collingwood Street, near Brady Street. It was a council flat and I recall the 'whoosh' outside the kitchen window, where I was standing with my mother that morning. Then something flashed by. I thought it would hit the flats opposite in Brady Street but it went over the roofs. When it landed, our kitchen windows immediately smashed and showered us with glass, and my brother Dave was blown off his feet on his way to work at a Whitechapel tailoring business. I still left that morning for the Central Foundation Girls School in Spitalfields.

My normal route took me past the Mansions, and on the way I was stopped by the Head of the Brady Club, Miss Miriam Moses [pictured on page 94]. She was in tears outside the wrecked flats and collecting belongings together. She said there would be no school that day for local children because lots had been killed or hurt. Among the dead was Ivan Saffer, aged 12, a dear pal who I had been evacuated to Ely with [see page 94]. His parents also died and his sister Betty was badly hurt. So many Jewish children from the Brady Club and the school opposite the Mansions lived in those flats.

---

[2] The Brady Girls' Club was founded in 1927 by social reformer Miriam Moses who, in 1931, became the first woman Mayor of Stepney and the first Jewish woman Mayor in the country.

Hughes Mansions today.

that Lilian's mum Sarah, her mum's sister and the sister's baby had also died in the Mansions. It was all completely mind-numbing because they were such close friends of the family. Now news reached us about the Nazi death camps and the fate of my Mum's brother, Chiam, and his children in Poland. Two of the children had died at Auschwitz, while Chiam, his wife and the rest of the six children had been forced to dig their own graves in the village where they lived in the Galicia region of Poland. They were then murdered and thrown in. At least my own two brothers returned home safe from Egypt and India.

On 4 May 1945, the *East London Advertiser* published a report detailing the Hughes Mansions tragedy:

The crash came at half past seven in the morning and, in a second, what had been happily occupied homes of many people became two vast piles of debris. The search for the missing went on for three days and nights. Mobile cranes were brought to remove the huge pieces of brickwork, whilst the rescue parties dug down to individual victims. Many of the 90 injured were quickly recovered and taken to the London Hospital… many people who had not been injured were accommodated in the Deal Street Rest Centre, a short distance away, and there was continual coming and going over the short distance between the Centre and the space before the Mansions by relatives of people trapped in the huge mound of debris. Many spent days of anguish as they enquired again and again if any news had been heard of their loved ones.

Twenty-two members of the Brady Boys' and Girls' Clubs were found dead among the debris, and the Girls' Club became the HQ for the heavy-rescue squad digging for survivors at the Mansions. While preparations were being made upstairs for the first night of Passover, the canteen downstairs was used to make tea and sandwiches for the exhausted rescue workers. Young Rhoda Kohn (née Rosen), whose family had been worried about the fate of its members in Poland (see page 136), recalls:

My Dad Noah had gone to Hughes Mansions to collect a weekly sub for the synagogue in Alie Street, and also donations for the Burial Society. There were many, many Jewish families living in the Mansions and it was opposite the big Jewish school, the Robert Montefiore School. That morning, he came back to our house in Newnham Street as white as a sheet. He told us what had happened and added: 'There are a lot of funerals that I will be going to.' Dad had lost his brother-in-law, Joe Isebrook, in there and a school friend of mine, Lilian Nadolnick, had died too. She was just 17 and we later learnt

Family tragedies abounded. Mr Davis Wingrad at No. 81 lost his wife Bessie and two children; Ernest Beckett at No. 40 lost his wife, son, daughter, two grandchildren and daughter-in-law; and John Colverson at No. 44 lost three daughters. His wife Mary also died of her injuries the next day in London Hospital. Three aldermen of Stepney Borough Council died too, including Alderman J. Pritchard, who was Mayor of Stepney in 1941–1942. His wife died with him.

The disaster at Hughes Mansions claimed 134 lives and was the second-biggest British tragedy of the whole V2 weapon campaign after the Woolworth's catastrophe in New Cross, Deptford, in the previous November. The Mansions bombing also resulted in one of the worst losses of life ever seen in the East End.

Shortly before 5.00 p.m. on 27 March, 10 hours after the flats were hit, the final V2 rocket landed in Britain at Orpington, Kent, where Mrs Ivy Millichamp, aged 34, became the last civilian to be killed by enemy action. The next day two flying bombs landed at Chislehurst and Waltham Holy Cross, before two final doodlebugs hit Datchworth in Hertfordshire and Iwade in Kent, concluding the V1 and V2 'revenge weapon' campaign.

Hitler's rocket assault had been mercifully short but, nonetheless, it left a bloody legacy. Some 517 V2s fell on the London region, out of 1,115 fired at the nation as a whole. They claimed 2,754 lives in Britain and almost half of these fatalities were in the two Civil Defence areas covering the East End. As with the V1s, British Intelligence had tried to deceive the Germans into aiming short in order to protect the city. The flow of misinformation filtering back to Germany steadily pushed the point of impact eastwards, perhaps at the rate of 2 miles a week in early 1945. It is no surprise, therefore, that Ilford had the distinction of being the worst-hit London area (35 landed), followed by West Ham, Barking, Dagenham and Walthamstow.

The end of the war was now in sight, but further shockwaves rolled through the Jewish East End during April when British troops entered two German camps called Belsen and Buchenwald. At the end of the month, a film of the death camps was shown in London's cinemas. The crowds queued for hours to get in and then watched in stunned silence. Outside, London's barrage balloons were now being hauled down and the inhabitants of public shelters were asked to leave – much to the anger of those who had no homes to go to. Then, on Monday 30 April 1945, the lights came back on in London, ending the blackout.

Grieving Eddie Siggins in Leyton was meant to be celebrating his 15th birthday on the 30th too. That afternoon, in a Berlin bunker, the man responsible for the death of his father, his four brothers, a little sister and two cousins put a revolver in his mouth as the Russians approached. Adolf Hitler, aged 56, then squeezed the trigger and ended his life. Meanwhile, a man despised in the East End, William Joyce, made his last broadcast from Germany. Drunk at the microphone, 'Lord Haw Haw' said: 'You may not hear from me again for a few months.' His last words were: 'Heil Hitler. And farewell!'

On 4 May, German forces in northwestern Europe surrendered at Montgomery's headquarters on Luneburg Heath and three days later the German Supreme Command surrendered at Rheims, ending the war in Europe. It was left for London to explode into life on Victory in Europe (VE) Day, 8 May, even though many people were preoccupied with thoughts of relatives and friends involved in the Japanese war, which would drag on until an atomic bomb landed on Hiroshima on 6 August.

The war had been full of strange coincidences and uncanny premonitions and VE Day was no exception. In the last hours of peace, early in the morning of 3 September 1939, London had experienced a spectacular storm. On the morning of VE Day, another massive thunderstorm occurred, the worst since 1939. During the day of celebration, Union flags fluttered from East End homes, St Paul's Cathedral was packed with worshippers, and the heroine of the *Daily Mirror* comic strip 'Jane' appeared naked for the very first time. Great crowds filled the London streets but they fell totally silent to hear Churchill's rousing broadcast at 3.00 p.m. from Downing Street which concluded with:

Advance Britannia! Long live the cause of freedom! God Save the King!

Churchill once again ignited the city's touch-paper and a heartfelt rendition of the National Anthem resounded across the metropolis at the end of his speech.

Cockneys flocked 'up West', where vast crowds decked in red, white and blue surged to and fro, like a human tide. American sailors with girls on their arms formed a conga line down the middle of Piccadilly, and friends and strangers alike linked arms to dance the 'Lambeth Walk.' The drink flowed, kisses were planted on familiar – and unfamiliar – faces and the brave and foolhardy shinned up lamp-posts for panoramic views of the capital's party. The approach to Buckingham Palace was packed and the decibel level peaked on each of the eight occasions when the Royal Family appeared. The old warrior himself, Winston Churchill, stood with them on one occasion, before appearing in front of a sea of faces in Whitehall. He waved his hat and conducted 'Land of Hope and Glory' before telling the vast hordes: 'God Bless you all, this is your victory… In all our long history we have never seen a greater day than this.' The tumultuous reception shook the very foundations of the battered capital.

When night fell, London's statues and public buildings were floodlit and searchlights pierced the heavens, one beam picking out the magnificent, triumphant dome of St Paul's. Children wandered open-mouthed through a spectacular illuminated fairyland, while ships in the docks fired rockets and beamed Churchill's famous 'Victory V' salute into the sky. Even the Princesses, Elizabeth and Margaret, mingled with the crowds near the Palace while the rest of central London became a jam-packed, heaving mass of high spirits. Inhibitions were lost as the singing, dancing and drinking slowly dulled the senses. By 8.00 p.m., pubs across London were running out of beer.

The following snapshots help to capture the mood in both the East and West Ends.

Stanley Bartels, then aged 11 and living in Forest Gate, remembers:

The parties went on for days and we trawled around from one to another. There was a massive party on Corporation Street, Plaistow, where a stage had been built outside someone's house. An Army band of four was playing. The atmosphere was terrific and the piano man was thumping the thing so hard the stage was gradually moving forwards. The whole street was going wild. We also went up to Wanstead Flats for wood and a big bonfire was lit in Godwin Road.

VE Day: a street party in Havering Street, Stepney.

The Queen visits Searle House in Duckett Street after the war. The Siggins family had been bombed out of the flats in September 1940 (see page 125) and had eventually settled at 107 Crownfield Road, where six members of the family died when a V2 struck in February 1945. Two of Eddie Siggins's cousins were also killed in the incident.

Fireman Cyril Demarne surveyed incredible scenes from the roof of Cannon Street Fire Station:

I was there with my family and the panorama was like a night of the Blitz. The sky was pink and golden sparks flew everywhere from the thousands of bonfires across London. It proved to be one of the Fire Service's busiest nights. The crews actually came in for some pretty tough handling and verbal abuse when they tried to put some of the dangerous ones out. And these were the heroes of the Blitz! We had driven up Ludgate Hill towards St Paul's and a wonderful sight met us. The floodlights had thrown the shadow of the Cathedral's Golden Cross onto the clouds. A giant black cross was imprinted on the clouds like an emblem of peace.

Maisie Meadowcroft (née Holmes) headed 'up West':

I was living in Osborne Road in Forest Gate. A friend and I used to go dancing at the Lyceum up West, so on VE Day we headed for the city. Four of us went to Plaistow Station and took the train to Trafalgar Square, where we just had enough money for egg-on-toast and one gin-and-orange each at Lyons' Corner House on Coventry Street. The square was packed and all sorts of music bombarded the ears from all directions. We danced with one group and then with another as we made our way down the Mall to Buckingham Palace. I got really close to the railings and the roar was terrific when the Royals appeared. After that, great big circles formed and everyone was dancing. Thousands upon thousands. We made our way back down to Trafalgar Square and people were in the fountains kicking water over everyone. Everybody was in good spirits and I can't recall anyone being rude or offensive. We walked home to Plaistow in the end and there were flags and banners draped from so many East End homes with the word 'Victory' written on them. On the way

we stopped at as many street parties as possible and there were huge ones in Commercial Road and East India Dock Road.

Pat Cook, then aged eight, savoured joyous scenes in the East End:

Anne Street in Plaistow was packed with 300 people and my Nan's piano was at one end and another piano blocked off the other. In between were all the tables and the children were racing round the block, skipping and playing games. Nan and Auntie had Union Jack pinafores and all the houses were draped in red, white and blue flags tied to string, which I had helped to make. There were wonderful, wonderful sights and sounds, and sheer relief we had survived.

The day after VE Day, the Royal Family toured the East End and visited scenes of tragedy in Stepney and Poplar. In Vallance Road, a large crowd awaited their arrival at Hughes Mansions. The *East London Advertiser* reported:

A large square site made by the destruction of the centre block was left clear. Around three sides a large number of people were gathered. Some of them tried to make a grandstand of the balconies of the heavily damaged remaining block but were asked to come down by the police. As soon as their Majesties made their appearance, the crowd began spontaneously to sing the National Anthem. Waving flags the crowd surrounded Their Majesties, singing 'There'll Always Be An England.' The King and Queen talked to members of the crowd, who surrounded them and moved with them as they walked across the site. There was terrific cheering as they left.

Basil Shoop, the lad who walked a Jewish girl home to the Mansions the night before the disaster claimed her life, recalls:

I managed to get really close to the Royal party and could almost touch the car. There was a lot of cheering and I remember looking in the car and seeing the Princesses Elizabeth and Margaret, and thinking how beautiful they looked. The visit was a real tonic for the East End after all the people had been through.

Meanwhile, the end of the war saw the reunion of strangers. The conflict had not only disrupted and fractured the physical landscape but also changed people's expectations and their perceptions of each other. Everyone had become someone else. Women had become accustomed to managing without their husbands and had a new spirit of confidence, fostered by their war work. The mobilisation of women — and the absence of many from their homes for long hours of work — was one of the most radical social consequences of the war. Their returning men, changed by the experiences of battle, were greeted by a shabby East End and more independent wives, which some found hard to accept. So, while the war brought an increase in the number of marriages, it was an even more powerful stimulus to divorce. The number of divorce petitions filed in England and Wales rose from 9,970 in 1938 to 24,857 in 1945, and soared to a post-war peak of 47,041 in 1947. Whereas, before the war, more than half the divorce petitions had been filed by wives, in 1945, 58 per cent came from husbands. Yet perhaps even more remarkable than the family dislocation was the opposite effect wartime had on the great majority of households. Most not only remained remarkably stable but also appeared to grow closer and stronger.

As Britain readjusted to peace, its post-war citizens rejected the nation's conquering hero. Just two months after the war was won, Churchill was on his way out of office as the promises of the Labour Party echoed around a victorious nation. The country needed to rebuild and reinvent itself and the electorate deemed that a fresh approach and a fresh start required a Labour Britain, not a Conservative, Churchillian Britain. Five years earlier, Churchill had toured the East End and cried 'Are we downhearted?' The East Enders had typically responded with a thunderous 'NO!' and cries of 'Good Old Winnie!' Now, during his election tour, they booed Churchill for minutes on end. He angrily decried the 'socialist woolgatherers' and lambasted their 'philosophical dreaming of utopian worlds which will never be seen except with improvements in the human heart and head.' Churchill sat down flushed with rage — and still they booed. East End families were determined to bring back to their districts an improved model of a familiar way of life. Many were socially conservative in their habits and conservative socialist in their politics.

In July, Labour won a resounding victory, with 11.9 million votes to the Conservatives' 9.9 million, and Clement Attlee, the MP for Limehouse, became Prime Minister with an overall majority of 146 seats. The swing

to the socialists had been 18 per cent in London and two-thirds of East Enders followed a campaign poster invitation and 'looked to the future with Labour.' Yet Churchill did not feel the victim of ingratitude. 'Oh no', he responded in his familiar grunt when the question was posed. 'I wouldn't call it that. They have had a very hard time.'

Indeed they had. Eddie Siggins, living in a Nissen hut in Whipps Cross after the family disaster in Crownfield Road, Leyton, was not alone in discovering that the brave new world was also a desperately cold one. The East End had survived but at a dreadful personal cost to thousands. The Crownfield Road disaster was joined in infamy by the tragedies at Columbia Market and the Underground Station in Bethnal Green, South Hallsville School in Canning Town and Barnby Street in West Ham, Dames Road in Forest Gate and Hughes Mansions in Stepney, and many, many more.

The Blitz – which began on 7 September 1940 and climaxed with the great raid on London on 10–11 May 1941 – claimed the lives of almost 45,000 civilians in Britain and, as previously stated, almost half the deaths occurred in London. During the four years of war that followed, the national death toll climbed to 60,595, with the V1 and V2 'revenge weapons' adding almost 9,000 additional lives to the final total. The final breakdown reveals Londoners accounted for 49 per cent of Britain's civilian deaths and close to 2,000 had died in Bethnal Green, Poplar and Stepney alone. The final national toll also includes over 1,000 firemen and women.

Looked at another way, London was threatened once every 36 hours for over five years and was hit by 41 per cent of the V1s and 49 per cent of the V2s. One third of the City of London was razed, the St Paul's area was completely gutted and none of Wren's masterpieces emerged unscathed. In the east, Stepney, Poplar and Bethnal Green lost one fifth of their built-up areas.

Yet London had survived and Eddie Siggins, his mum Sarah and sister Irene were three of the East End survivors. Eddie's Nana, Mary Ann, born in Victorian Stepney in 1877, had also come through another tumultuous episode of East End life. However, the grand old lady, who lost her childhood home in Duckett Street thanks to the Luftwaffe, was now broken-hearted inside her home in Matcham Road, Leytonstone. Prior to the Crownfield Road V2 disaster, she had already learnt that the two grandchildren who had joined the Services would not be coming home. One, Private Stanley Bowyer, had followed in the footsteps of her beloved husband Alfred and joined the Essex Regiment. Whereas Alfred had died at Cambrai during the First World War, Stanley had been killed by a mortar shell in Holland, aged just 19. Her second grandchild, 21-year-old Rifleman Freddie Parr, had been killed in Burma fighting the Japanese – just as his mother had predicted when she waved him off (see page 202). The loss of two grandchildren was hard enough to bear. Then the V2 tragedy at 107 Crownfield Road in February

1945 added the names of seven more: the little Sigginses, Leslie, Peter, Betty Anne, Jimmy and Stanley, and the two Parr children over the garden fence, Doreen and Ivy. Mary Ann had also lost her son-in-law, Eddie's dad, James. Over the course of two world wars, Mary Ann Bowyer had therefore lost a husband, a son-in-law, and nine grandchildren.

The guilty were taken to Nuremberg, where the verdict 'death by hanging' was passed on Herman Goering, whose Luftwaffe had failed to defeat the East End. On the eve of Goering's execution, guards were watching him through a cell spy-hole in order to prevent any attempt to escape the gallows. Yet he still managed to slip a cyanide capsule into his mouth and bite down on it while wiping his face. Meanwhile, the traitor William Joyce was captured, tried for treason and sentenced to death. Joyce, who had not yet reached 40, was buried in an unmarked grave in the grounds of Wandsworth Prison. His former leader, Oswald Mosley, attempted a political comeback after the war. However, it failed and Mosley lived in exile in Paris, where he advocated European unity until his death in 1980 at the age of 84.

Meanwhile, Hitler's 'rocket men', including Walter Dornberger and Werner von Braun, were destined for great things. They were not tried for war crimes and about 500 of the former Peenemunde team were offered contracts to go to the USA to help with the space programme. Most went. In 1960, two years after NASA formed, von Braun was Director of the Marshall Space Flight Center in Huntsville, Alabama, where he was entrusted with the development of the *Saturn* space-rocket programme. Nine years later, in 1969, came von Braun's finest hour when he found himself in the impressive surroundings of Mission Control in Houston, Texas. A giant *Saturn* V rocket, developed at von Braun's Flight Center in Alabama, had blasted the crew of *Apollo* 11 to the moon and, on Sunday 20 July 1969, he anxiously waited with the world for the mission's historic climax. Then came the voice of Commander Neil Armstrong from the moon's surface: 'Houston, Tranquility Base here. The Eagle has landed.' Von Braun joined

'Nana': Mary Ann Bowyer, 1877–1970.

Mission Control's wild celebrations and, four days later, was carried aloft on the shoulders of Huntsville City officials. In the space of 24 years, von Braun had left Hitler's warped world of 'revenge weapons' and helped mastermind the first prestigious moon landing for President Nixon and the USA.

Meanwhile Eddie Siggins's Nana, Mary Ann, was confined to her bed in Leytonstone. The little Duckett Street girl, who remembered kindly Dr Barnardo and Jack the Ripper in a previous century, was 93 and not well. Eight months after the moon landing, Mary Ann joined her husband Alfred and nine grandchildren in a better world.

Postscript

EDDIE SIGGINS PEERED through the car windscreen as the greenery of Essex surrendered to the spectrum of greys that so generously dapple the East End. He had been in two minds about going back to Stepney. Over the years, Eddie had returned just once. That was in 1990, two years after the death of his mother, and he had found the visit strangely unsettling. His current home was beyond the roaring M25, that great ring of tarmac which seemed to contain his family's traumatic past. Yet he cut across it once more and headed for London's heart, past weathered street names that triggered long-buried memories. Dames Road and The Holly Tree pub flashed by before he stopped in Leyton's Crownfield Road. Here, he got out, slamming the car door shut, and the keen June sun began to tease the first beads of perspiration from his forehead.

A brief stroll down the road brought him to a sunken manhole cover in the pavement. As a lad, he had stepped on it many times as he dashed out of the front door of No. 107. Now, in this new millennium, a row of post-war housing, set slightly back from the original properties either side, lined this stretch of Crownfield Road. The subtly recessed terrace marked the place where the V2 rocket fell in 1945, claiming the lives of Eddie's father, sister, four brothers and two cousins.

Returning to the car, Eddie then drove south along dreary highways to Stepney and Duckett Street. On his last visit, over a decade earlier, he had discovered the towering, high-rise blocks of the Ocean Estate looming over the street, which had once contained Queenie's cats'-meat shop at No. 88, Betts the baker at No. 73 and Emma Goody's at No. 72, where the poor could buy a single dollop of jam.

Now Duckett Street held further surprises.

The Anchor and Hope pub, where old ladies once sat with a glass of beer and prepared their vegetables for the Sunday roast, was now a 'Cash and Carry' shop. Flats built from yellow brick had replaced Eddie's old home,

Scene of tragedy: Eddie Siggins in Crownfield Road, Leyton. He is sitting where the front door of his family's house, number 107, would once have opened onto the street.

Eddie Siggins contemplates the past in Crownfield Road, scene of the V2 tragedy.

Searle House, and a smart terrace now occupied the long-blitzed plot at No. 63, where his Nana, Mary Ann Bowyer, had grown up in Victorian days.

The sounds of regeneration assailed Eddie's ears – the clatter of pneumatic drills and the rumble of bulldozers – relieved only by the laughter of playing children. Passing builders clutching plans to further re-shape the

area, Eddie headed for the junction of Duckett Street and Bohn Road, or Bale Street as it was known in his childhood. Here he paused, gazing down at the road. Somewhere deep beneath its surface were the fragments of the bomb that fell in 1940, wrecking his Nana's home, blasting Searle House and killing the baker and his step-daughter. While modern-day life bustled by, Eddie, in his mind's eye, could still see that September night when frantic neighbours dug away at the rubble to find their loved ones (see page 125).

Just before the War, the old Duckett Street estate, founded by philanthropist Barber Beaumont in the nineteenth century, had been sold to the London County Council (LCC) for slum clearance. In 1945, after the Luftwaffe had done its worst, the LCC bought more land in order to build the Ocean Estate, named after Ocean Street where Eddie once lived. By 1957, there were 50 blocks, mostly named after seas, and further sprawl would ensure that it became the second largest council estate in the borough of Tower Hamlets. The Ocean Estate, once branded as the cheapest place in Europe to buy heroin, is still undergoing urban renewal: blocks are being pulled down, new homes built and over 1,000 flats refurbished. Eddie was not alone in being mesmerised by the changes. For the Blitz generation, a stretch of road, a derelict site or a dilapidated building can be full of meaning and memory. The past is always with them, which may help to explain why so many of them find the scale and pace of post-war renaissance so overwhelming. Indeed, few could have anticipated the two great forces that were to so dramatically transform this part of the capital.

The first of these great driving forces was economic change.

Where the bombers failed in wartime, a simple metal box ensured the demise of the old docks in the 1960s. The shipping container, with its standard dimensions of 8 × 8 × 12 feet (2.4 × 2.4 × 12 metres), could be lifted straight from the hold of a large ship, lowered onto a lorry and driven to a local distribution depot complete with customs facilities. Where it once took dockers 10–14 days to 'strip and stuff' an average ship, a container ship could be turned around in 2 days.

Only Tilbury, 25 miles down the Thames Estuary, survived the container revolution, while the London and Royal Docks went out of business. The closure of London's dock systems began in 1967 with the East India Dock and ended in 1981 with the Royal Docks. In south London, the story was the same: the Surrey Docks, scene of the huge fire on Black Saturday in 1940, closed in 1970 and the Thames riverside wharves went the same way. Whole communities were devastated. For every docker made redundant, three workers in dock-related industries lost their jobs and the abandoned dock complex became one of the largest areas of urban desolation in Europe.

However, during the 1980s, the 8½ square miles of the former Port (far left) Eddie Siggins returns to Duckett Street, Stepney, and stands on the spot where Betts the baker once stood on the corner of Bale Street (now Bohn Road). The white van behind Eddie is parked close to where No. 63 once stood, the home of his 'Nana', Mary Ann Bowyer.

(left) The same scene in 1941 after the street was bombed in September 1940.

(below left) Stepney's Bale Street in 1939, leading to Duckett Street in the distance. The white building, in the centre, located on the corner of Bale Street and Duckett Street, is Betts the bakery.

(above right) The reshaping of Duckett Street, Stepney in 1999. Duckett Street can be seen to the left with derelict, white balconied, Searle House next to Kate Hodder's pub. Searle House was demolished shortly after this photograph was taken. Bengal House, the white building, is earmarked for demolition.

The old dwarfed by the new: the corner of Ocean Street and Master Street, Stepney in 1953. The high-rise façade of the Ocean Estate dominates the area.

of London Authority dockland received a makeover so groundbreaking that, in effect, a third city was created to join its distinguished neighbours, the City of London and the City of Westminster. Indeed, where great fires engulfed the West India Docks during the blitz, a new East End has triumphantly arisen.

Erupting from the 97-acre Canary Wharf estate, home to the world's top blue-chip companies, is Britain's first and tallest skyscraper: One Canada Square. Completed in 1991, this is a classic example of urban acupuncture – a point of intensity intended to radiate positive energy to its surroundings. Designed by Cesar Pelli, it is the landmark by which the whole of Docklands is recognised and marketed, the East End's rival to Big Ben, the Monument, and the City's great landmark: St Paul's Cathedral.

Similarly, there has been a dramatic urban rebirth further east where, in 1965, East Ham and West Ham were merged to create the borough of Newham. The closure of Newham's docks – the Royals – in 1981 was hardly mentioned by the national press. Yet these were the largest of the docks and their demise was another savage blow to East End life. However, Newham has since undergone an extraordinary economic rejuvenation. The East End has always been a place of international arrivals and departures and so an important continuity was maintained when the London City Airport opened in 1987, sandwiched on the strip of land between the King George V and Royal Albert Docks. Thirteen years later, the vast bulk of ExCeL, the UK's biggest exhibition centre under one roof, was unveiled on the north side

(right) Aerial view of London and St. Katharine Docks in 1960, looking westwards. Only a few years later, this dock system was closed after a history of over 150 years of cargo handling.

(left) The building continues; the Canary Wharf development pictured from the Thames in 2003 looking east.

(centre) Aerial view of London Docks in the early 1980's with the Western Dock filled in and the News International complex under construction on the site of the North West warehouses.

(below) The same view in July 1989 showing the complete redevelopment of the area for new housing and businesses.

of the Royal Victoria Dock as a vital catalyst in the generation of inward investment for the benefit of Canning Town and Custom House.

However, it was the bestowal of the 30th Olympiad upon London – with Stratford at the heart of the world's greatest sporting spectacle – that has set the East End on a potential fast track to economic regeneration. In Singapore, where the announcement was made on 6 July 2005, the Mayor of London, an emotional Ken Livingstone, choked:

This is the poorest part of Britain. We seize the chance of the Olympic Games to transform the chances of the children of the East End to break the circle of poverty in our time.

While Londoners await the Olympic's legacy, bulldozers plough on with another project: the £9 billion Thames Gateway Scheme. Stretching about 40 miles along the Thames Estuary, from London's Docklands to Southend in Essex and Sheerness in Kent, this is the largest building programme undertaken in Britain in 50 years. With Tower Hamlets and Newham now exerting an economic gravitational pull away from the City, the future of London is now inextricably linked to the future of the East End.

However, the Royals' proud history has not been forgotten. A bronze statue of three 1950s' dock workers moving goods into a barrow with a hoist was unveiled outside the entrance to ExCeL in August 2009. One of the workers is Johnny Ringwood (who lost three friends when a V2 landed in Freemasons Road, Custom House in January 1945; see page 206). The statue was Mr Ringwood's idea and a nine-year fundraising campaign collected £230,000 – including a donation from the late Queen Mother – which ensured that his dream became a reality.

(top) Aerial view of the King George V Dock, 'Centre Road', and the Royal Albert Dock taken in March 1946, looking west. The crowded docks are a clear indication that trade is getting back to normal after the war. Today, 'Centre Road' is the site of the runway for London City Airport.

The giant passenger liner *Dominion Monarch* under repair in the King George V Dry Dock in 1950, towering above the houses in Saville Row, Silvertown.

(top right) Johnny Ringwood with the statue commemorating the Royals dock workers.

The second great force for post-war change was the movement of people.

The Second World War caused unparalleled social dislocation. There were 60 million changes of address in Britain during 1939–1945, among a civilian population of 38 million. Stepney lost half of its population in this massive dispersal of people, while Hitler's Heinkels and Dorniers ensured that there was precious little to return to.

Many people insist that post-war town-planners were as effective as the bombers in isolating people from their cherished roots. Professor Patrick Abercrombie, renowned architect and town-planner, had already produced a plan for the reconstruction and development of London. Central to this was the provision of more open space, the easing of traffic congestion and overcrowding, and the establishment of a series of satellite towns. This required the relocation of 600,000 citizens, including half the population of Stepney, Bethnal Green and Shoreditch, and about 380,000 were expected to move to the new satellite towns. This would also allow areas within the East End to be redeveloped. Abercrombie's plan also required some people to adopt a different lifestyle: in order to make room for the new open spaces, it would be necessary to build high-rise flats, more suitable for single people and childless couples, as well as terraced family homes.

After the war, the immediate problem was housing the servicemen and evacuees who had flocked back to the capital. A baby boom increased the demand for housing, but even in 1950, whole areas were still largely bombsites. A temporary housing programme was authorised, and the aluminium-framed 'prefabs' (cheap but well-designed, mass-produced dwellings) and Nissen huts – like the Sigginses' family abode at Whipps Cross – were still in use more than 20 years later. It was a desperate situation and, in 1951, only a third of the County of London's households had exclusive use of a fitted bath, toilet, kitchen sink or cooker.

The Abercrombie plan was quickly implemented and an ambitious home-building programme began. People were moved out to the new peripheral LCC estates or to the new satellite towns, such as Harlow, Ongar, Stevenage and Stapleford. In the vacated East End, builders, aided by generous government subsidies, delivered the high-rise options that would fulfil Abercrombie's population density and open-space requirements.

Between 1931 and 1955, thousands of Bethnal Greeners moved to the new LCC estates, and the human consequences were investigated by

Bethnal Green in 1963 with the nine blocks of the high-rise Minerva Estate in the middle. The estate is bounded to the north by Hackney Road, to the south by Old Bethnal Green Road and, running north-south to the right, Cambridge Heath Road. The Regent's Canal snakes around the four gasholders north of Hackney Road. To the left of the Minerva Estate is the Grade II listed tower block Keeling House, designed by Denys Lasdun as a 'city in the sky,' and completed in 1960.

(below) The Dorset Estate takes shape in Bethnal Green, 1955. This is Arline Street with Columbia Market, scene of the wartime tragedy fifteen years earlier, visible in the background .

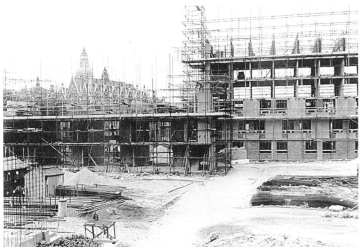

order to gain open space. In addition, street and kinship groupings should have been transplanted as a whole, thus preserving the social cohesion of the community. Town planners, they accused, had put their faith in buildings, believing that neighbourhood units and community centres would be sufficient to give rise to neighbourliness and community spirit.

Young and Willmott noted:

If this were so, then there would be no harm in shifting people about the country, for what is lost could soon be regained by skilful architecture and design. But there is surely more to a community than that. The sense of loyalty to each other amongst inhabitants of a place like Bethnal Green is not due to buildings. It is due far more to ties of kinship and friendship, which connect the people of one household to the people of another. In such a district, community spirit does not have to be fostered, it is already there. If the authorities regard that spirit as a social asset worth preserving, they will not uproot more people, but build the new houses around the social groups to which they already belong.

sociologists Michael Young and Peter Willmott. Their resulting book, *Family and Kinship in East London*, published in 1957, analysed the effect of movement from Bethnal Green to Debden in Essex, which they did not identify and called 'Greenleigh'. These researchers, although criticised for presenting a sentimentalised and romanticised view of traditional East End life, concluded that the dilapidated houses in Bethnal Green should have been refurbished with modern amenities, rather than being pulled down in

By then it was too late. One married woman, who once lived with all her family in Denby Street, told the researchers that she seldom saw her relatives any more. She found her new neighbours 'snobbish' and 'spiteful', and took a part-time job rather than sitting around the house all day, waiting for her husband and children to return. The loneliness resulted in her 'watching the television most nights', and she predicted that the quietness would, in time, 'send people off their heads'. She described her new home thus: 'It's like being in a box to die out here'.

Nonetheless, Essex became the new Cockney homeland, and the streets of the old East End became gradually quieter. Whole families from Bethnal Green, Shadwell, Stepney and Hackney moved to Woodford, Debden and Dagenham. Bethnal Green's pre-war population of 90,130 had shrunk to 53,860 by 1955 and even further, to 30,000, by 1981, but at least its residents had a materially better life. Some 95 per cent now had baths of their own compared with just 21 per cent in 1951.

Meanwhile, new towering East End estates broke the skyline by 1962, affording views, a sense of space, and modern conveniences. However, for many of their inhabitants, they were a world of loneliness, broken lifts, vandals and creeping isolation. About 125 of the high-rise blocks were in Newham and more than a quarter of London's blocks went up in West Ham and East Ham. The old East End had largely vanished. John Blake, born at the turn of the twentieth century, remembered a very different Poplar when he wrote this in 1977.

When I was a boy, Poplar was a thriving place. There were a hundred or more shops in St Leonard's Road and a like amount in the old Chrisp Street Market. Nearly all of those shops, which played such a vital part in the life of old Poplar, have gone, and what a sad thing it was that the old friendship which existed between shopkeeper and customer has been swept away. Nearly all the old pubs have gone, where the older population of Poplar spent so many convivial hours with a cheap glass of beer and enjoyed the company of the 'regulars'. The old cinemas, The Grand Palace, Poplar Pavilion, The Gaiety, The Empire, The Star, have all closed. The only two music halls, The Poplar Hippodrome and The Queens, have disappeared. The Poplar Hospital, after years of healing, is closed, the nurses in Bow Lane have gone. The churches of St Frideswide's, St Michael and All Angels, St Saviours Bromley and St Leonard's have gone, or shut down, and all services are now held in St Matthias and Poplar Church. The North London Railway, and all the goods and freight depots operating in the Poplar area, which once had connections to any part of England, have gone. Whole rows of houses and streets have gone to give place to modern planning. Many industries have moved away to other areas, and so have many people who lived and worked in old Poplar.

The Jewish community also continued its exodus, dispersing to Stamford Hill, Hendon, Gant's Hill and Golder's Green. The Brady Clubs moved too, from their original homes in the East End to purpose-built premises in Edgware. Similarly, the Jewish Museum is today found in Finchley in North London, where at least it has an appropriate address: East End Road. Even Blooms in Whitechapel High Street, London's oldest and most celebrated kosher restaurant, was forced to close its doors in February 1996, after 76 years in business.

Others, though, were arriving in the East End. The transformation of the decaying riverside into a financial and business centre encouraged the City's business class to move into and refurbish the dilapidated and dingy houses. Local bitterness surfaced when properties became unaffordable, and some people felt that the East End's soul was being stolen. The trend was seen across Tower Hamlets and particularly in Wapping and Bethnal Green. Even in Whitechapel's Myrdle Street, former slums became listed buildings, highly desirable and commanding six-figure sums, much to the bewilderment of former residents like Rose Gowler, who recalled a rather different world (see page 34). Even Tower House, a century-old former doss-house at the end of Myrdle Street, was converted into 'loft-style' apartments. This brooding 700-room building in Fieldgate Street was once described by Jack London in his sobering *The People of the Abyss* (1903) as the 'Monster Doss House' and a haven for 'life that is degrading and unwholesome'.

In the early post-war period, colonial immigrants, mainly from West Africa, also arrived, albeit it in tiny numbers. Then, between 1955 and 1957, the number of immigrants, mainly Indians and Pakistanis, surpassed the number of Jews who had arrived in the four decades between 1870 and 1914. Most came from Bengal and the Punjab, the two provinces of British India whose populations had been most uprooted by the India-Pakistan partition of 1947. They settled mainly in Spitalfields, Whitechapel and neighbouring wards, close to their port of disembarkation, like the Huguenots and East European Jews before them. The new arrivals, like their predecessors over the centuries, seized the opportunities available to them. They took over the cheap clothing businesses in Commercial Street and Brick Lane, where the Jewish community had greatly expanded employment in tailoring. These new East Enders also occupied the oldest, barely habitable homes that had been abandoned by their predecessors. The 1990s saw new arrivals from Bengal, Somalia and Eastern Europe who, like others before them, were seeking a better life.

Today, one street in Whitechapel – Fieldgate Street – symbolically reflects the cultural changes in the East End. Here, a tiny East End synagogue sits almost apologetically in the shadow of the imposing East London Mosque, which was built in 1985 and is one of the largest in Britain. The

The Queen in Newham during her successful Jubilee tour; crowds await Her Majesty; Pearlies and dancers join in the fun.

Fieldgate Street Great Synagogue is also dwarfed by the London Muslim Centre next door, yet it defiantly clings to its 111-year heritage. It is one of only four remaining East End synagogues. There were more than 150 before the Second World War but today the Jewish East End population stands at just 2,000.

When Queen Elizabeth II and the Duke of Edinburgh visited the East End in May 2002, the year of her Golden Jubilee, a kaleidoscopic ethnic wonderland awaited. In Newham, home to Britain's first majority non-white population, she was met by an electrically powered elephant on wheels, which, as members of the Hindu community explained, was the Runga Rung elephant, a centrepiece of celebrations for Divali, their annual Festival of Lights. Thousands of well-wishers in turbans, saris and burkas waved Union flags and the royal couple were showered with rose petals by an Asian dancer as their Rolls Royce edged into the East End. Then, in a moment that spanned the area's history, they were greeted by Cockneys of

the Blitz generation, Pearly Kings and Queens, Newham's ceremonial Mayor resplendent in his turban and 30 Sikh drummers.

Economic and social change has completely reconfigured the East End and made it unrecognisable to many of the Blitz generation. Of course, it is easy to be carried away with nostalgia and sentimentalism. Members of the wartime generation, comfortable in their warm, modern homes, would not want to return to the cold, overcrowded, insanitary slums of the past, with their memories of hunger, poverty and disease. Similarly, not all of them find high-rise environments to be unfriendly and soulless, or lacking the neighbourliness of the old terraced housing. Not all, by any means, feel bitter or somehow redundant in the Internet age; neither do they regret taking holidays abroad rather than hop-picking in Kent or spending a hard-earned week in Clacton or Broadstairs. They accept that there must be change and welcome the fact that their grandchildren will not have to sweat and toil in the docks as they used to do.

Far beyond the cranes, the bulldozers and the fashionable wharf conversions of Docklands, many of this book's contributors have also adopted Essex as their home and no longer miss the terraced streets they have left behind.

However, other contributors lament what has happened to the East End. They wish that they could somehow have bottled the old street camaraderie, family support and chats on the doorstep. Then they could have released the magic vapours along the corridors of the concrete blocks or through the letterboxes on their suburban estates. Too many claim that neighbourhood warmth has become Neighbourhood Watch, while the

Christ Church, Spitalfields, built in 1711-29 to the design of Nicholas Hawksmoor.

(centre above) The disc memorial in St Paul's Church Yard is dedicated to Londoner's who died during the Second World War.

There is no national civilian war memorial in this country. There is, at least, a fitting tribute to the nation's firemen and women who sacrificed their lives. Originally unveiled in Old Change Court, the memorial is now located just south of St. Paul's Cathedral.

Blitz fireman Cyril Demarne meets the Queen Mother, when she unveiled the Fireman's Memorial in 1991.

laughter and conversation that once filled the streets has been replaced by the sound of bolts being drawn behind closed, graffiti-sprayed doors. Even shopping, once an opportunity for a chat in the corner shop or in the market, has become mundane and impersonal, thanks to the advent of the supermarket. Instead, television has become a substitute for human contact, with BBC 1's soap opera *EastEnders* offering a curious, dramatized interpretation of 'community togetherness'.

Some buildings still offer a reassuring physical link with the past. While the Isle of Dogs basks in the glory of its guardian angel, One Canada Square, old pubs still stand on the corners of building sites, while council blocks of the Thirties rub shoulders with estates of the Seventies. Lovingly restored eighteenth-century weavers' homes can still be seen in Spitalfields; fine Victorian and Georgian properties can be admired in Bow, Bethnal Green and Mile End; and a seventeenth-century Queen Anne house can be viewed at 37 Stepney Green. Elsewhere, the three glorious eighteenth-

century churches of Wren's protégé, Nicholas Hawksmoor – Christ Church in Spitalfields, St George's-in-the-East on The Highway and the exquisite St Anne's at Limehouse – still pierce the skyline and keep a watchful eye over current proceedings. Ancient pubs like the Prospect of Whitby, built in 1520, can also transport today's customers to the days when it was frequented by smugglers and criminals, as well as by artists and writers such as Charles Dickens, Samuel Pepys and Joseph Turner.

Memorials – ranging from small plaques to large monuments and gardens of contemplation – also help to connect the wartime past to the hectic present.

One of the most important in the capital consists of a simple, raised disc of polished Irish limestone outside St Paul's Cathedral, dedicated to Londoners who perished during the Second World War. A short walk south

of St Paul's leads to a fitting memorial to the men and women of Britain's Fire Service, including those who sacrificed their lives in the conflict. It features a bronze statue sculpted by John W. Mills, son-in-law of Blitz fireman Cyril Demarne, and was unveiled by the late Queen Mother on 4 May 1991.

Mr Demarne was at the ceremony and 14 years later, at the age of 100, also attended the unveiling of a plaque on the railings outside the former Abbey Road Depot in Abbey Road, Newham. The plaque commemorates the death of 13 ARP workers and auxiliary firemen on Black Saturday in 1940, when the blazing depot collapsed on them. Among them was Mr Demarne's friend, Wally Turley (see page 114).

Another plaque, behind Hughes Mansions in Vallance Road, Bethnal Green, is, however, hard to find and difficult to read. This small brass rectangle, a reminder of the V2 attack that killed 134 people, is sadly tarnished and hidden near the ground in a grassy area to the rear of the remaining block.

Further south, in Wapping, is the Hermitage Riverside Memorial Garden. Its centrepiece, a dramatic dove sculpture designed by Wendy Taylor, commemorates the wartime sacrifice of the civilians of East London.

Here, old Wapping dramatically confronted new Wapping when the last warehouses on the Hermitage Wharf site were demolished in the Seventies. The flattened site, with its spectacular views of Tower Bridge, was a developer's dream but a group of Wapping residents had other plans. The residents wanted the 2-acre site to accommodate a fitting national memorial to honour the civilians killed during the Second World War. The site of the former Hermitage Wharf, one of the last pieces of open land on the Thames riverside, was seen as ideal for several reasons. The old Wharf had been a popular air-raid shelter and had staged a children's Christmas party the night before it was bombed in the Blitz (see page 150). In addition, it once stood

opposite Hermitage Wall School, which was hit by a V1 flying bomb in July 1944, killing members of the ARP Rescue Service and Home Guard (see page 197). The site was also close to Watson's Wharf, where the legendary Dead End Kids were once based (see page 151).

In 1993, the London Docklands Development Corporation (LDDC), which already owned a portion of the plot, obtained the rest from Tower Hamlets Council, so the site could then be sold on to developers keen to build luxury apartments. The residents went into battle. In 1995, Marianne Fredericks, Meryl Thomas and Maureen Davies, together with a number of like-minded East Enders, including Peggy Duggan (sister of Dead End Kid leader Patsie), formed 'Civilians Remembered' to challenge the LDDC and fight for a national civilian memorial. A formidable alliance of protesters saw

(far left) The sadly tarnished memorial to the victims of the V2 tragedy at Hughes Mansions in Bethnal Green in 1945.

Actress Barbara Windsor lays flowers at the top of the 19 steps at Bethnal Green Underground Station following the annual Service of Remembrance in 2010.

The Hermitage Riverside Memorial Garden in Wapping.

(below) The Pavilion of Remembrance inside Thames Barrier Park, Newham.

local people standing shoulder to shoulder with politicians, trade unionists, religious leaders and environmental groups.

Many years and a public inquiry later, luxury apartments now overlook the River Thames from the old Wharf site and the Hermitage Riverside Memorial Garden itself occupies only a sliver of the remaining plot. Many of the original campaigners are disappointed, claiming it falls far short of the national memorial that they had so tirelessly worked for.

Further down the Thames, around the famous U-bend to Silvertown, is the 22-acre Thames Barrier Park. Here, south of the Royal Victoria Dock, a soaring Pavilion of Remembrance, designed by architect Andrew Taylor, commemorates the civilians of Newham who died in the Second World War. Inspired by a traditional Mogul garden, this striking structure has a 26-foot high roof supported by random groups of slender poles.

Finally, the East End is still waiting for a fitting memorial to commemorate the worst civilian wartime tragedy – the horror at Bethnal Green Underground station in 1943. The 'Stairway to Heaven Memorial Trust' is raising money to erect a massive upside-down bronze staircase of 19 steps alongside the station entrance, where currently a simple memorial plaque is screwed to the wall. Planning permission has been granted for the memorial, which will be illuminated with 173 small beams of light to represent each of the victims. The memorial will also vividly tell the story of the disaster and provide shelter.

While urban landmarks provide physical links with the past, the Blitz East Enders themselves remain the guardians of the East End's wartime heritage and the keepers of its tragic secrets. Interestingly, the few pockets of London where older East Enders live continue to exude a certain strength and stability. Here, the heart of the old community still beats in time with that of the new. The pulse may be weaker than it once was, but it is still there.

The Blitz generation continued the tradition of East End survival. When the Blitz and 'total war' came to the East End, its people were already endurance specialists. Their particular way of life had bred an attitude of mind far different from that found in more stable societies. As one contributor put it:

The bombs just became something else to contend with. We had nothing to destroy anyway and members of the family were always dying from some sort of illness or another. We just got on with it. It was no big deal.

These were the people whose ancestors had clamoured at the dock gates to catch the master's eye and obtain work. They were the 'mudlarks', the children who waded in the River Thames for items to sell right up to the 1920s, while others crawled through sewerage pipes looking for jewellery. They were the nineteenth-century street urchins, accustomed to surviving through their own abilities as entertainers, chalk artists, model-makers, musicians, and freak-show assistants. They were also the people who had given away their children so that they might have a better life. When little Alice Marshall was sent from the family home to Canada, never to be seen again (see page 40), it was done in the interests of family survival. A generation whose forebears had already suffered the cruelty of the hated workhouse were indeed prepared for almost anything.

Their survival skills and powerful independence also merged to create an indomitable community spirit, captured by the oft-used phrase: 'We was all one'. In this way, a mutual bonding – amply demonstrated by the Jews and Anglo-Irish – was born from shared experience of hardship.

By the time the war with Hitler began, past hardships had bred a community self-assurance and closeness bordering on invulnerability, summed up by the saying: 'We've got nothing but you're welcome to half of it'. Furthermore, as the Blitz unfolded, a direct parallel emerged between the children who climbed over the bomb debris searching for scraps during the blackout and Victorian street urchins scavenging in dark alleys for food. In the intervening time, a razor-sharp instinct had developed to seize any advantage, any chance of a break, any glimmer of hope.

All this is not to suggest that the pain and suffering of war was any less real, any more palatable or any more acceptable. Of course it wasn't. It is merely to suggest that the East Enders, for generations, had been conditioned psychologically and emotionally to cope with desperate situations. They were born survivors.

The 'Blitz Spirit', with its connotations of chirpy Cockneys gallantly smiling through disaster, has been extensively analysed. Angus Calder, in his book *Myth of the Blitz*, suggests that the Blitz spirit was developed either deliberately or unwittingly, encouraged by propaganda, and then accepted by people as the way to behave. It could be equally argued that this spirit already existed and required little external coaxing. Cockneys possessed innate, instinctive, ever-present strengths that simply came into their own during wartime. Despite the natural responses of shock, panic and hysteria, the social order of the East End did not collapse and create a chain reaction throughout London. Instead, the vast majority faced their ordeal with courage, dignity and humour.

Today, there is pride in the way that the war was confronted and rebuffed. Contributor Dorothea Johnson puts it this way:

I feel so proud of our generation in the East End. We were ready. We were gutsy. We survived. We beat Hitler. I actually believe we were history's heroes who saved the world. Forget the politicians. It was us in our little houses.

Meanwhile, contributor Charlie Smith states simply:

In place of money, the East Enders had tremendous loyalty, trust and friendships. It made the community indomitable. Nothing could ever break it. They could have bombed us for a century and nothing could have broken the spirit that had evolved over generations.

Perhaps Stepney's wartime Mayor, Frank Lewey, expressed it best of all: 'Battering only makes Cockneys close up tighter, shoulder to shoulder'.

What Hitler's 'Black Saturday' bomber crews unknowingly faced when they arrived on that fateful day in September 1940 was a vibrant, stoic, resolute society capable of extreme survival even before the bomb doors opened. The Cockneys rose to the occasion and some even became heroes. Hitler had picked on the wrong people. For countless East Enders, the war proved to be the ultimate test of survival, and their bravery and their determination provided the definitive example of civilian courage.

The East End survival challenge is not over.

Poverty is still a constant, niggling and apparently incurable affliction. East End communities consistently feature among the most underprivileged in surveys of Britain. Indeed, a 2005 regeneration study of the Ocean Estate, which sprawls over the streets where Eddie Siggins once played, revealed the area to be among the 10 per cent most deprived in the country. The scourges of the nineteenth century – disease, pestilence and slum life – have been replaced by unemployment, drug abuse, traffic congestion and crime.

Today, the Welfare State pulls most back from the abyss: state benefit agencies subsidise the needy, social services have replaced the workhouse and the National Health Service provides universal medical care. These post-war safety nets prompted 1950s' commentators to claim that the missions and settlements of Victorian times are no longer necessary. They were wrong. The work of Barnardo continues, even if memories of his great deeds have faded with time, and his initiatives still stretch right across London.

In the early years of the new millennium, when Eddie Siggins made his emotional return to his old Stepney haunts, hungry children were once more gathered outside Barnardo's old Hope Place premises, formerly home to the good doctor's Juvenile Mission. The historic building, now a discount fish bazaar, was shuttered and the youngsters were queuing for fish and chips at the shop next door. In nearby Duckett Street, other excited children played on the spot where the bomb had fallen in 1940, killing the much-loved local baker and his teenage step-daughter, while Eddie cowered in Searle House opposite.

Nearby, a man with a clipboard was inspecting a rubble-strewn plot as he sipped hot coffee. Puffs of steam rose from his cardboard cup as Eddie gave him a potted history of Duckett Street. With jabbing finger, Eddie pointed out the location of shops and buildings, long lost in time, and clipboard-man's head twisted this way and that.

The council employee was transported to another world as Eddie breathed new life into the ghosts of the past. Eddie's Nana, Mary Ann, was back in Duckett Street, raising her brood behind the door of No. 63, Mosley and his Blackshirts were marching past and, in the clear blue sky above, the Black Saturday bombers had returned once more.

Select bibliography

Ackroyd, Peter. *London, The Biography.* Chatto and Windus, 2000.

Bailey, Doris M. *Children of the Green.* Stepney Books, 1981.

Bailey, Paul. *The Oxford Book of London.* Oxford,1995.

Barnardo, Thomas. *Three Tracts.* Dr. Barnardo's, 1888.

Benewick, R. *The Fascist Movement in Britain.* Allen Lane, 1972.

Bentley, James. *East of the City: The London Docklands Story.* Pavilion, 1997.

Besant, Walter. *All Sorts and Conditions of Men (1882).* Oxford University Press, 1997.

Binder, Pearl. *The Pearlies.* Jupiter Books, 1975.

Blake, John. *Memories of Old Poplar.* Stepney Books, 1977.

Booth, Charles. *Condition and Occupations of the People of the Tower Hamlets, 1886–87.* Edward Stanford, London, 1887.

Booth, Charles. *Life and Labour of the People of London,* MacMillan, 1892–1897.

Booth, Charles. The inhabitants of Tower Hamlets (School Board Division): their condition and occupations. In: *Journal of the Royal Statistical Society,* volume 50, 1887: 326–340.

Booth, William, *In Darkest England.* International Headquarters of the Salvation Army, 1890.

Bragg, Melvyn, *The Adventure of English: The Biography of a Language.* Hodder and Stoughton, 2003.

Briggs, Asa, and Macartney, Anne. *Toynbee Hall, The First Hundred Years.* Routledge and Kegan Paul plc, 1984.

Brown, Malcolm. *Spitfire Summer.* Carlton Books, 2000.

Calder, Angus. *The People's War.* Jonathan Cape, London, 1969.

Calder, Angus. *Myth of the Blitz.* Jonathan Cape, London, 1991.

Calder, Ritchie. *Carry on London.* English Universities Press, 1941.

Churchill, Winston S. *The Second World War,* volumes 1–6. Cassell, 1948–1954. [Particularly volume 2, *Their Finest Hour,* 1950 edition.]

Churchill, Winston S. *War Speeches,* volume 1. Edited by Charles Eade. Cassell, 1951.

Collier, Richard. *Eagle Day.* Cassell Military Paperbacks, 1999.

Cox, Jane, *London's East End Life and Traditions.* Weidenfeld and Nicolson, London, 1994.

Demarne, Cyril. *A Fireman's Tale.* Battle of Britain Prints International Ltd, 1991.

Dettman, Sean, *The Bethnal Green Tube Disaster of 1943: A Stairway to Heaven.* The East End History Society, 2010.

Farson, Negley. *Bombers Moon.* Gollancz, 1941.

Fishman, William J. (with Nicholas Breach). *The Streets of East London.* Duckworth, 1979.

Fishman, William J. *East End Jewish Radicals.* Duckworth, 1975.

Fishman, William J. *East End 1888.* Duckworth, 1988. Republished by Hanbury, 2001.

Fitzgibbon, Constantine. *The Blitz.* Wingate, 1975.

Hammerton, Sir John. *World War 1914–18: A Pictured History,* volumes 1–2. Amalgamated Press Ltd, London, n.d.

Hey, David. *How Our Ancestors Lived.* Public Records Office, 2002.

Hobsbawm, E.J. *Industry and Empire.* Weidenfeld & Nicolson, 1968.

Idle, Doreen. *War Over West Ham.* Faber, 1943.

Inwood, Stephen. *A History of London.* MacMillan, 1998.

Keegan, John. *The Second World War.* Century Hutchinson, London, 1989.

Kops, Bernard. *The World Is A Wedding.* MacGibbon and Kee, 1963.

Law, John (pseudonym of Margaret Harkness). *In Darkest London.* William Reeves, 1889.

Lazarus, Michael. *A Club Called Brady.* New Cavendish Books, 1996.

Lewey, Frank. *Cockney Campaign.* Stanley Paul & Co. Ltd, 1944.

London, Jack. *The People of the Abyss.* MacMillan, 1903.

Mayhew, Henry. *London Labour and the London Poor.* Penguin Classics, 1986.

Morrison, Arthur. *A Child of the Jago.* Charles E. Tuttle Co., Inc. 1996.

Murray, Venetia. *Echos of the East End.* Viking Penguin, 1989.

Murrow, Ed. *This Is London*. Cassell, 1941.

Nicolson, Harold, *Diaries and Letters, 1939–45*. Collins, 1967.

Ogley, Bob. *Doodlebugs and Rockets*. Froglets Publications, 1992.

O'Neill, Gilda. *My East End*. Penguin, 1999.

Preston, William C. *The Bitter Cry of Outcast London*. London, 1883.

Ramsey, Winston G. (editor) *The Blitz Then and Now*, volumes 1–3. Battle of Britain Prints International Ltd, 1987–1990.

Ramsey, Winston G. *The East End Then and Now*. Battle of Britain Prints International Ltd, 1997.

Rumbelow, Donald. *The Complete Jack the Ripper*. W. H. Allen, 1975.

Sansom, William. *Westminster at War*. Faber, 1943.

Severs, Dennis. *18 Folgate Street: The Tale of a House in Spitalfields*. Chatto & Windus, 2001.

Shirer, William. *The Rise and Fall of the Third Reich*. Secker & Warburg Ltd, 1960.

Speer, Albert. *Inside the Third Reich*. Sphere, 1971.

Sokoloff, Bertha, *Edith and Stepney: The Life of Edith Ramsay*. Stepney Books, 1987.

Taylor, Rosemary. *Walks Through History: Exploring the East End*. Taylor Breedon Books Publishing Co., 2001.

Stow, John. *A Survey of London: Reprinted from the Text of 1603,* volumes 1–2. Edited by Charles Lethbridge Kingsford. Clarendon Press, Oxford, 1908. Reprinted by Oxford University Press, 1971.

Tillett, Ben. *Memoirs and Reflections*. London, 1931.

Whiting, Charles. *Britain Under Fire: The Bombing of British Cities 1940–45*. Century Hutchinson, 1986.

Wicks, Ben. *Waiting for the All Clear*. Bloomsbury Publishing Ltd, 1990.

Williams, A.E. *Barnardo of Stepney*. Allen & Unwin, 1943.

Williamson, Elizabeth, and Pevsner, Nikolaus. *London Docklands: An Architectural Guide*. Penguin, 1998.

Wilson, Colin, and Odell, Robin. *Jack The Ripper*. Bantam Press, 1987.

Woolmar, Christian. *The Subterranean Railway*. Atlantic Books, 2004.

Woon, Basil. *Hell Came To London*. Cassell, 1941.

Young, Michael, and Willmott, Peter. *Family and Kinship in East London*. Routledge and Kegan Paul Ltd, 1957. Reprinted with new introduction in 1986 by Routledge and Kegan Paul plc, 1986.

Zangwill, Israel. *Children of the Ghetto*. Heinemann, 1892.

Zeigler, Philip. *London at War, 1939–45*. Sinclair-Stevenson, 1995.

Index